Praise for
Teaching **Gifted Children** in Today's **Preschool** and **Primary Classrooms**

"A wonderful new book that contains a vast amount of helpful, practical information for anyone interested in gifted education. It will serve as a great resource for teachers, administrators, counselors, and parents of young gifted students who want to learn new and innovative ways to spark imagination and learning."

— Patricia Hollingsworth, Ed.D., director,
University School at the University of Tulsa

"A 'must have' for every early childhood and primary teacher's educational library. Through their collective wisdom and clear understanding of the needs of the *whole* gifted child, the authors provide a plethora of strategies . . . that any primary teacher could use the next day with his/her gifted and talented students."

— Julie A. Brua, Ed.D., assistant superintendent,
Curriculum and Instruction; director of the Gifted and Talented
Education Program for Aptakisic-Tripp School District No. 102, Illinois

"I enthusiastically applaud this update of the already impressive original version. Teachers will find this book both a classic and an inspiration toward teaching with creativity and innovation in today's classroom."

— Dina Brulles, Ph.D., director of Gifted Education,
Paradise Valley Unified School District, Arizona

"This engaging and informative book is filled with current information on meeting the needs of young children with gifts and talents. Practical strategies and examples are given for implementing the ideas . . . a must-have resource for educators and families."

— Mary Ruth Coleman, Ph.D., senior scientist,
Frank Porter Graham Child Development Institute,
University of North Carolina, Chapel Hill

TEACHING
Gifted
Children
IN TODAY'S
Preschool AND
Primary
Classrooms

Identifying, Nurturing,
and Challenging
Children Ages 4–9

Joan Franklin Smutny, M.A.
Sally Yahnke Walker, Ph.D.
Ellen I. Honeck, Ph.D.

free spirit
PUBLISHING®

Library of Congress Cataloging-in-Publication Data
Smutny, Joan F. author.
    [Teaching young gifted children in the regular classroom.]
    Teaching gifted children in today's preschool and primary classrooms : identifying, nurturing, and challenging children ages 4–9 / by Joan Franklin Smutny, Sally Yahnke Walker, and Ellen I. Honeck.
        pages cm
    Revised edition of : Teaching young gifted children in the regular classroom. 1997.
    Includes bibliographical references and index.
    ISBN 978-1-63198-023-7 (soft cover)
 1. Gifted children—Education (Preschool)—United States. 2. Gifted children—Education (Primary)—United States. 3. Gifted children—Education—Curricula—United States. 4. Gifted children—United States—Identification. 5. Early childhood education—Parent participation—United States. 6. Classroom management—United States. I. Walker, Sally Yahnke, 1942– author. II. Honeck, Ellen I., author. III. Title.
    LC3993.218.S68 2016
    371.95—dc23
                                                                                        2015025978

Free Spirit Publishing does not have control over or assume responsibility for author or third-party websites and their content. At the time of this book's publication, all facts and figures cited within are the most current available. All telephone numbers, addresses, and website URLs are accurate and active; all publications, organizations, websites, and other resources exist as described in this book; and all have been verified as of July 2015. If you find an error or believe that a resource listed here is not as described, please contact Free Spirit Publishing. Parents, teachers, and other adults: We strongly urge you to monitor children's use of the Internet.

Edited by Christine Zuchora-Walske, Marjorie Lisovskis, and Pamela Espeland

Cover illustrations by Jackie Stafford; Cover design by Michelle Lee Lagerroos; Interior design by Colleen Rollins; Interior production by Emily Dyer

Photo Credits: page 6, © Monkey Business Images | Dreamstime.com; page 25, © Monkey Business Images | Dreamstime.com; page 41, © Robert Kneschke | Dreamstime.com; page 57, © Monkey Business Images | Dreamstime.com; page 80, © Monkey Business Images | Dreamstime.com; page 96, Anna Baburkina | Dreamstime.com; page 113, © Monkey Business Images | Dreamstime.com; page 133, © Petro | Dreamstime.com; page 142, © Monkey Business Images | Dreamstime.com; page 154, © Andres Rodriguez | Dreamstime.com; page 173, © Monkey Business Images | Dreamstime.com

10 9 8 7 6 5 4 3 2 1
Printed in the United States of America

Free Spirit Publishing Inc.
6325 Sandburg Road, Suite 100
Golden Valley, MN 55427-3629
(612) 338-2068
help4kids@freespirit.com
www.freespirit.com

Free Spirit offers competitive pricing.
Contact edsales@freespirit.com for pricing information on multiple quantity purchases.

Dedication

To all the teachers and families who shared their lives so generously with us and inspired this revision. And to all the young gifted children in our classrooms and homes who hunger for new discovery and creative challenge.

Acknowledgments

We would like to acknowledge the extraordinary support and expertise shown by Margie Lisovskis, Christine Zuchora-Walske, and many others on the editorial and production staff at Free Spirit Publishing. Their careful guidance and meticulous attention to detail were critically important in the process of revising this book. For their many kindnesses, we cannot thank them enough.

We also wish to thank Sarah von Fremd for her invaluable assistance in the evolution of this new edition.

Contents

List of Tables and Figures viii

List of Reproducible Pages. viii

Introduction. 1
Creativity and a Sense of Wonder 1
Teaching Young Gifted Children in a
Standards-Driven Era 2
About This Book 3

Chapter 1
Identifying the Young Gifted Child **6**
On Being a Pioneer Teacher 6
Getting to Know Your Students 9
Enlisting Parents as Colleagues 14
What About Testing? 15
Questions and Answers. 16
Conclusion 17

Chapter 2
Creating the Learning Environment **25**
Why Is the Environment Important? 25
The Challenge of Designing Your Classroom 25
Responding to Children's Needs. 29
Making Every Child Feel Welcome and Valued. 32
Questions and Answers. 38
Conclusion 39

Chapter 3
Planning Curriculum and
Extending Learning **41**
Time and the Gifted Child: A Banking Metaphor. 41
Extending Curriculum for Young Children
Working in Groups 43
Extending Curriculum for Young Children
Working Independently. 45
Documenting Mastery and Planning Extensions 47
Questions and Answers. 48
Conclusion 48

Chapter 4
Promoting Creativity, Discovery,
and Critical Thinking in the
Social Studies Curriculum **57**
Creative Learning and Critical Thinking 57
A Map of Creative Activities. .59
Questions and Answers. 75
Conclusion 76

Chapter 5
Promoting Imagination in the
Language Arts Curriculum **80**
Creative Learning as a Link to
Imaginative Thinking 80
A Map of Imaginative Activities. 83
Sharing Creativity with Others. 94
Questions and Answers. 94
Conclusion 95

Chapter 6
Promoting Discovery and Higher-Level
Thinking in Math and Science **96**
Creative Learning as a Link to
Higher-Level Conceptual Thinking. 97
Discovering Properties 98
Discovering Processes 105
Questions and Answers. 111
Conclusion 112

Chapter 7
Assessing and Documenting
Development **113**
The Assessment Conundrum. 113
IQ Testing 116
Using Portfolios to Document and
Evaluate Progress 120
Documenting Development Through Observations . .122
Questions and Answers. 123
Conclusion 123

Chapter 8
Flexible Grouping to Help All
Children Learn **133**
Grouping for Learning. 133
Drawbacks of Traditional Cooperative Learning. 134
Response to Intervention (RTI) 134
Cluster Grouping: A Flexible Alternative 135
Guidelines for Grouping Young Children. 137
Questions and Answers. 140
Conclusion 141

Chapter 9
Building Partnerships with Parents **142**
What It's Like for Parents 142
Examining Your Own Feelings. 144
You Can't Overcommunicate 144
Questions and Answers. 147
Conclusion 147

Chapter 10
Understanding and Meeting
Children's Social and Emotional Needs **154**
Meeting Children's Many Needs 154
Social and Emotional Issues in Young
Gifted Children's Lives 156
Helping All Children Appreciate Differences 166
Considering Early Entrance and Acceleration 167
Questions and Answers 170
Conclusion 170

Chapter 11
Meeting the Needs of Children
from Diverse Populations **173**
A Variety of Needs Considered 174
Questions and Answers 188
Conclusion 188

References and Resources **189**

Bibliography **210**

Appendix A: Tests for Identifying
Young Gifted Children **215**

Appendix B:
More Resources for Teachers **217**

Appendix C:
Sources for Gifted Education Materials **227**

Index **229**

About the Authors **239**

List of Tables and Figures

Characteristics of Giftedness: Potential
Benefits and Challenges 10
Sample Tic-Tac-Toe Menu: *Blueberries for Sal*
and *Goldilocks and the Three Bears* 44
Sample Resident Expert Contract for Older Child 47
Sample Resident Expert Contract for Younger Child . . . 47
Taxonomy of Creative Thinking 59

Taxonomy of Imaginative Thinking 82
Moving Toward Open-Ended Evaluation 115
Response to Intervention 134
RTI and Differentiation 135
Common Traits of Extroverts and Introverts 163

List of Reproducible Pages

Chapter 1
Your Child's Pictures 18
Information, Please 19
About My Child 20–21
Checklist of My Child's Strengths 22–23
Your Child's Personal Exhibit 24

Chapter 2
Help Me Help You 40

Chapter 3
What I Like 49–50
Tic-Tac-Toe Menu 51
My Plan to Become an Expert 52
Resident Expert Contract for Younger Child 53
Resident Expert Contract for Older Child 54
Plan for Compacting and Extending the Curriculum . . . 55
I Thought You'd Like to Know 56

Chapter 4
Your Child's Cultural Heritage 77
Me in a Different Culture 78
Custom Observation Form 79

Chapter 7
Student Observation Form I 124–126
Student Observation Form II 127
Student Observation Form III 128–129
Student Observation Form IV 130
What I Learned 131–132

Chapter 9
Can You Help? 148
Can You Share? 149
Questions for Your Child's
Parent-Teacher Conference 150
Books for Parents of Young Gifted Children 151–152
Organizations and Online Resources for
Parents of Young Gifted Children 153

Chapter 10
My Problem-Solving Plan 171–172

The reproducible forms can also be downloaded or printed out at **www.freespirit.com/TGC-forms**. Use password **gifted7**.

Introduction

"A beetle has a real short life, but that's okay. After it's born, it mates and lays eggs, and the rest is free time."

"I feel microscopic in the crowded hallways."

"I wasn't playing on the roof—I was seriously on the roof."

Sound familiar? Who hasn't delighted in hearing the wisdom of bright, creative young children like the six-year-olds who made these statements? Often, the choice of words, ideas, images, and phrases we hear from these gifted children are what we might more commonly associate with fourth, fifth, or sixth graders. Sometimes we can't imagine how such sophisticated thoughts and vocabulary can come from children so young.

Some people may ask, "Can you really tell that a preschool- or primary-age child is gifted?" This question likely comes from past experiences. When programs for gifted learners were more prevalent than they are today, most schools did not assess students for special services until third or fourth grade. Some schools began to identify and address the abilities of highly able children as late as middle school or junior high. However, as teachers of young children, we know that the signs of giftedness can appear much earlier. Many of us have watched our students express their talents and abilities in ways that surprise and delight. A question about a rare mammal in Australia ignites a whole room of eager learners. An attempt to dramatize the movement of the planets amazes us.

Every September, we look at our new classes of young students and notice characteristics and behaviors that make some children stand out. The fact that we notice these girls and boys is important. What we do about them—and with them—is equally important. If we listen to them, we hear that their unique words, questions, observations, and interpretations continue to percolate. Every day, we observe their hunger to know more. And we are impelled to ask, as we do for every student, "What can I do for them?" Working with young gifted learners brings its share of challenges, but it also brings adventure to the classroom.

Creativity and a Sense of Wonder

What inspires many of us to teach young learners is the open curiosity and delight they bring to our classrooms. Young children look upon the world with fresh eyes. Rachel Carson, marine biologist and founder of the American environmental movement, called this "the sense of wonder."[1] She valued it above knowledge or skill as an inner force guiding the discoveries and awakening the passions of children in their earliest years of life. Without the sense of wonder, Carson claimed, the seeds of learning cannot flourish, and imagination and curiosity—once felt as a vital link to what children see, smell, hear, and touch—diminish. We educators can preserve children's sense of wonder in our classrooms by using creativity to encourage children to look above, beyond, around, and into the fields they're learning.

But few of us have time to think about the sense of wonder in our classrooms. We are consumed with the pressure to meet higher standards for more students and with concerns about how our districts measure their learning. Today's preprimary and primary educators live in a different world from the one that existed when the first edition of this book, *Teaching Young Gifted Children in the Regular Classroom,* was published in 1997. Some teachers worry about forcing younger students to learn curriculum content that they used to explore at higher grades. And the increased use of testing has brought anxiety to some classrooms, as teachers wonder what will occur if their children's year of in-depth, multidimensional learning and exploration does not result in high scores.

---

[1] Carson, Rachel. *The Sense of Wonder* (New York: HarperCollins, 1998): 54.

Despite the greater focus on minimum competency and content mastery in modern classrooms, we still find creativity to be the most effective way to enable even reluctant students to engage in, understand, express, and own new knowledge. We believe, as Rachel Carson did, that "it is more important to pave the way for the child to *want* to know [emphasis ours] than to put him on a diet of facts he is not ready to assimilate."[2] This edition of our book remains faithful to its original aim: to help you foster a creative classroom environment in which learning is interactive, process oriented, and nurturing to young children.

Teaching Young Gifted Children in a Standards-Driven Era

Teachers of young children today find themselves under unprecedented pressure to increase the academic achievement of their students regardless of the diverse linguistic and cultural backgrounds and special learning needs to be addressed. Standardized testing, the Common Core State Standards (CCSS), full-day kindergarten, and universal preK can provide more students access to good-quality education. But as teachers have told us, the term *good-quality education* often means "intensive academic education." As standards rise, each grade has to master the curriculum of the one that follows; preK becomes kindergarten, kindergarten becomes first grade, and so forth.

Some schools offer ongoing support and resources for teachers and provide a comprehensive and developmentally appropriate curriculum. But in the large number of schools that do not, students (including the gifted) stand little chance of developing their potential. A focus on mandated standards in literacy and mathematics narrows the field of learning and inhibits growth and development for all young learners. The need for young children to explore ideas and themes across disciplines, to engage in projects using multiple media and materials—in essence, to create, experience, construct, imagine, and invent—goes unanswered in many early childhood and primary classrooms today. Since the first edition of this book was published, many schools have turned away from play, drama, music, movement, art, and exploration.

With tighter controls on their time and planning, teachers may adhere to a more rigid curriculum and a more structured setting; they may not evaluate student progress as they once did or adapt as creatively to individual learning needs.

Our intent in revising this book is to address the needs of teachers who currently face many demands in schools and who feel less free to offer creative choices for their students. Many gifted young children hunger for any opportunity to experience intellectual challenge, accomplishment, and delight in learning. They come to school brimming with excitement and curiosity about the world around them. Creativity preserves that world and enables teachers to target CCSS and any other articulated goals without feeling constrained by them. This book focuses on practical ways to identify and assess gifted learners, work with families, and ignite meaningful learning in a variety of subjects. What is more: the ideas in this book are creative and adaptable, so they apply to learners of all ability and knowledge levels.

In this new edition of our book, we'll share updated strategies and techniques that will help you identify the high-ability children in your classroom, encourage their talents, and help them grow. Typically, young gifted students come to us already *knowing* a great deal. Yet, regardless of their advanced knowledge, they enter our classrooms with intellectual and emotional needs that are universal: to be recognized, to be accepted, and to experience the challenge and joy of learning. To meet these children's needs, we need a curriculum that offers developmentally appropriate opportunities for challenge, discovery, mastery of new skills, and sharing of new knowledge.

Young gifted children—even four- and five-year-olds—are often hungry to make sense of the world in ways we may not expect from most preschoolers and early elementary students. These children have the desire to exercise and expand their minds intellectually and creatively. In our extensive work with highly able and talented children, we have found that the most effective approaches evolve in an environment that is rich in critical and imaginative thinking, one in which learning is an interactive process. We have also found that these approaches can be successfully implemented within the regular classroom, to the benefit of *all* children, through curriculum practices appropriate to each child's development.

In 1996, the National Association for the Education of Young Children (NAEYC) adopted the

---

[2] Carson. *The Sense of Wonder*: 56.

position statement "Developmentally Appropriate Practice in Early Childhood Programs Serving Children from Birth through Age 8." In 2009, NAEYC published an updated version of this position statement.[3] While not diverging from the fundamental commitment to teaching based on understanding how young children develop and learn, the new statement increased focus on the importance of doing more to address the achievement gap in the earliest years of school. It articulated ideas on a curriculum that would recognize and respond to the unique rate and pattern of each child's learning and would work toward an integration of practices between preschool and the early elementary grades.

While the new 2009 NAEYC statement responds to more current realities and concerns of young children in the classroom, it merely complements earlier position statements. NAEYC proposes that developmentally appropriate practice includes the following key elements:

- **Creating a caring community of learners:** learning as an interactive process; supportive relationships fostered between teacher and students as well as among students; individual and group explorations; engaging, lively activities; rich variety of materials and resources; representations of children's cultures, languages, and interests in the classroom

- **Teaching to enhance development and learning:** stimulation, direction, and support to ensure growth; knowledge of children and how to translate learning goals to students with specific developmental needs; creation of meaningful activities—creative, explorative—that involve them in learning experiences beyond mandated domains; differentiated complexity and challenge in response to students' level of skill and knowledge

- **Planning curriculum to achieve important goals:** integration of children's physical, emotional, social, and cognitive growth; adaptations to children's developmental progress (based on teacher assessments), interests, and cultural and linguistic differences; mandated goals targeted through careful sequencing and pace based on children's needs, abilities, and knowledge; study that allows in-depth and cross-disciplinary focus

- **Assessing children's development and learning:** ongoing assessment that measures children's progress toward most important goals (developmentally and educationally); methods appropriate to age and range of differences in classroom (cultural, linguistic, and knowledge and ability levels); use of information from families; assessment of performance in a variety of contexts

- **Establishing reciprocal relationships with families:** collaborations that increase understanding and communication for the benefit of the children; shared responsibility and respect between teachers and families; deeper insight into the lives of individual children; greater awareness of family concerns and preferences and opportunities to link families with services for and information about children

In a nutshell, these principles underscore that to *teach* a child, you must *reach* the child. And the best way to reach the gifted children in your classroom is to design differentiated experiences that extend their creative and analytical thinking. Despite the increased demands for academic rigor and, in many classrooms, the loss of elements that once made early schooling so much more child-centered and flexible, preschool and primary grade teachers are among the most inventive educators around. Differentiation is not new to them! With the range of ability, readiness, and background in their rooms, they have to think on their feet and improvise. They notice that Abdi is struggling to read, but Marta is standing at the bookcase pulling out a book in the biography section. This edition provides strategies for developing and extending the abilities and talents of your gifted children that benefit all students in your class.

About This Book

In arranging the content of this new edition of *Teaching Gifted Children in Today's Preschool and Primary Classrooms*, we've approached our task in much the same way you might approach yours as the school year begins and your program unfolds:

Chapter 1 helps you identify high-ability children in your classroom in an affirming way. It draws on the most current understanding of giftedness in

---

[3] The position statement is published in Carol Copple and Sue Bredekamp, eds., *Developmentally Appropriate Practice in Early Childhood Programs Serving Children from Birth through Age 8* (Washington, DC: NAEYC, 2009). Write to NAEYC, 1313 L Street NW, Suite 500, Washington, DC 20005, or call 1-800-424-2460. The position statement is also available at www.naeyc.org/files/naeyc/file/positions /PSDAP.pdf.

young children, focuses on talent development, and presents a range of strategies for gaining a more complete and accurate picture of what your students can do.

Chapter 2 explores the learning environment as the foundation for learning. It includes information on using brain research to set up the environment and using learning centers that draw on students' preferred learning modalities. We explain how to create a classroom setting that makes young children feel safe and also entices them to energetically and constructively pursue their interests.

Chapter 3 focuses on planning for curriculum and extending learning in response to the needs of high-ability children, who often know much or even most of what will be presented in the classroom for the entire year. With timely information and examples, we explain how you can use compacting, tiered groups, interest groups, and other strategies to expand students' learning opportunities and school success.

Chapter 4 explores creative, integrated approaches to the study of environment, history, and culture and provides up-to-date sources and materials. We detail specific strategies that will enhance the discovery process in these subject areas and describe activities you can use or adapt for your own classroom. All subject chapters aim to help teachers burdened by demands to raise academic achievement levels adapt and/or develop more freedom and flexibility in their classrooms.

Chapter 5 provides an exciting range of creative strategies for teaching language arts. Drawing on a wide range of visual art, dramatics, music, photography, film, video, and technologies as catalysts, we show how you can generate and sustain the imaginative process in young people, enabling them to produce original and creative work.

Chapter 6 offers a variety of original activities and strategies to help children imaginatively investigate mathematics and science through story making, design, role play, and other explorations. Up-to-date sources and information offer a wealth of ideas for engaging young gifted learners, including the use of technologies that promote greater interactivity.

Chapter 7 examines the use of standardized testing and looks at ways to determine what the young gifted child needs to know, how the child's needs can

be documented, and how to advance the child's skills and talents. It focuses on the effects of current testing practices on gifted young children, and clarifies the limitations of tests, the misunderstandings that can result from testing, and the vital importance of assessment through multiple measures. It also offers information on tests more suitable for gifted learners from culturally diverse backgrounds.

Chapter 8 discusses response to intervention (RTI), along with other techniques for enabling children with high ability to find consistent challenge, accomplishment, and growth through group work in the regular classroom.

Chapter 9 shows how you can build partnerships with parents that will enable you to gain support and assistance where you most need it. It includes ideas on reaching out to parents and working with them to provide the kind of learning experiences your gifted students need.

Chapter 10 presents the unique social and emotional characteristics and needs of young gifted children, offering perspectives that will broaden your understanding of the challenges and difficulties talented students commonly experience. The chapter focuses on understanding and fostering social and emotional characteristics in a positive way to help families, teachers, and students.

Chapter 11 investigates the experiences and needs of diverse populations among gifted learners, including children from minority cultures, talented girls and boys, and students who are twice exceptional. The chapter offers information on current demographic trends and strategies for responding to the demands of increasingly more diverse classrooms.

Each chapter includes a "Questions and Answers" section with responses to questions we commonly hear from educators.

References and Resources recommends useful books, periodicals, and other materials related to the chapter topic.

Appendix A lists and describes standardized tests that can be used to identify young gifted children.

Appendix B lists and describes resources for teachers.

Appendix C lists sources for gifted education materials.

The general bibliography, which lists sources we consulted in writing and revising the book, might also be of interest to you as an additional source of practical references for boosting your background in the many facets of teaching the gifted child.

The ideas we share with you in this book are wholly *doable*. They will work for your students, their families, and you. As you use them, you will offer the talented and bright young children in your classroom many wonderful opportunities to:

- discover new possibilities for themselves
- delight in fresh challenges and the excitement of learning
- think of school as an exhilarating adventure of intellectual and aesthetic discovery
- thrive in a setting you have created to respond to their individual needs

In our experience of teaching, counseling, consulting, and talking with thousands of children, parents, and teachers, we have found that early awareness and knowledge of a child's unique abilities will make for a highly motivating educational experience throughout the school year and the child's school career. At the heart of it, we know that all children are looking for a conscious sense of their own value. A priority of this book is to affirm children's self-worth. We are certain that the strategies included here will create an environment that will benefit each student. In using these strategies, you can take pride in the knowledge that you're doing what you need to do for *every* child in your classroom: providing an appropriate educational opportunity for growth and success in school and life.

Just as a poem comes alive when it is read aloud, the activities and suggestions we've developed and described in this book will come alive for you as you try them out in your classroom. These ideas will enhance your work with all your students while enabling you to support the unique needs of the young gifted children in your charge. This book will also show you how to encourage family members, community members, and colleagues to share their time, skills, and expertise in developing classroom projects to broaden the realm of learning possibilities.

We believe that the most exciting and dynamic teaching in the world often happens in preschool and early elementary classrooms. No one is more sensitive to new ideas than the preprimary and primary teachers who devote themselves to working creatively with young children and who preserve their own sense of wonder and joy in learning. We know, too, that as one of those teachers, you welcome exhilarating challenges that will spark fresh inspiration in you and in all your students.

This book is designed to be that spark: to enable you and each student in your classroom to discover a new, individualized level of critical and imaginative thinking—to take greater risks, to dare more, and to attempt more. Young children love to stretch beyond the limits of conventional knowledge. Their natural responsiveness to creative catalysts and hands-on, participatory activities will ignite their enthusiasm, extending their discovery and inventiveness.

The impact of this book will arise from how you use it to expand your own repertoire of teaching strategies, especially in the face of greater expectations at the school and district levels. Our hope is that it will embolden you to explore new ways to nurture the development of your young students and to share in the joy and wonder of creative learning in different fields.

Let this second edition of *Teaching Gifted Children in Today's Preschool and Primary Classrooms* be a springboard for you. We encourage you to experiment and improvise with the book's insights and strategies, adapting them to the unique needs, interests, and talents of the children in your classroom. As you do this, many of your own ideas will emerge. Teaching and learning in your classroom will take on a new dimension—a stimulating climate of thinking and discovering, creating and originating.

We'd like to hear about how you use the activities in this book and about any new ideas our book generates for you. Please write to us at:

Free Spirit Publishing Inc.
6325 Sandburg Road, Suite 100
Golden Valley, MN 55427-3629
help4kids@freespirit.com

An adventure awaits us all!

Joan Franklin Smutny
Sally Yahnke Walker
Ellen I. Honeck

CHAPTER 1
Identifying the Young Gifted Child

Emily was a highly verbal child. She asked lots of questions and wondered how the world worked. She had a difficult time starting a task because she would much rather be engaged in conversation. Emily was involved in her own ideas and appeared absorbed in her own thoughts. When the teacher was providing directions, the classroom distracted her. Tasks provided to her were difficult for her to complete—she wanted to know the purpose and wanted to move past the directions to adding her own ideas.

During center time and free exploration, Emily directed the other classmates on what they should do and how they should play. She would get frustrated with her peers when they did not want to play the same things that she wanted to play or when they didn't want to play a game or activity the way she thought it should be done. She appeared bossy and uncooperative

When Emily was on the playground, she often sought out older children to play with. Relationships with these students appeared to be much different from her relationships with her classroom peers. The teacher was concerned that Emily would not have

same-age friends and was frustrated with Emily's lack of compliance on assigned classroom tasks.

This teacher struggled to engage Emily in classroom learning. In the preschool and primary years, most teachers are trained to focus on helping children acquire social skills and meet readiness markers. Yet, in this situation, one thing was clear: Emily's creativity and intellect were not being appreciated or developed in school. To help Emily experience learning and fit comfortably into the class, this teacher needed to recognize Emily's giftedness and look for ways to accommodate her unique learning needs.

On Being a Pioneer Teacher

Giftedness can be an uncomfortable topic for many adults. Many people have strong reactions when they think a teacher is favoring one child as intrinsically "better" than another. Much of the problem here lies in perceptions of giftedness. In the classroom and at home, *each* person develops with some qualities that are similar to those of other people and some qualities that are unique. Gifted children are not *better* than other children; they are *different* from other children. But it is vital to understand that a gifted child has unique characteristics and learning needs that should be fostered. These unique needs are important to recognize and program for both at school and at home.

Teachers who recognize and identify giftedness in the earliest grades are pioneers. Usually children are not formally identified as gifted by a school system until the third or fourth grade. This can be too late if the children's learning environments have not met their unique needs.

Why Is Early Identification Important?

Children's brains are highly sensitive and susceptible to new experiences; this is especially true up through about age five. If young children don't receive appropriate recognition and response during this sensitive period, potential skills may deteriorate. By fourth grade, some of the most intelligent children are resentful of waiting for the other kids to catch up. These high-ability students often find little meaning in a school day and may have fallen into a pattern of low performance. Since they're required to do only general classwork that may be far below their ability level, some have come to think of themselves as "the best." At times, they are bored and unchallenged, which may lead to depression or anger. These emotions may be turned inward, or they may be expressed outwardly—most often as behavior problems. The earliest school years are critical for finding gifted children before their eagerness for and joy in learning have been conditioned out of them.

Recognizing and rewarding giftedness in young children helps develop their confidence, self-esteem, and enthusiasm for learning. When children are encouraged to use their special abilities for worthwhile results, the outcomes are generally positive.

To recognize giftedness, we need to notice and accommodate ability and interest with appropriate opportunities. If parents and teachers respond enthusiastically to a child's exceptional abilities and interests, these qualities will continue to be expressed. A young child who is provided with appropriately challenging, stimulating schoolwork

can show substantial gains in achievement, motivation, and self-concept.

It is within your power to catch these children before they learn to hide their abilities or decide that school isn't worth their effort. You have the opportunity to become a pioneer in identifying and cultivating giftedness among the young children you teach.

What Are You Looking For?

Determining what it means to be gifted is a challenge. Several definitions of giftedness exist. The definitions are based on various intelligence theories, schools of thought, and perspectives in gifted education.

DEFINITIONS OF GIFTEDNESS

In 1972, the Marland Report by the U.S. Commissioner of Education to the U.S. Congress defined gifted children as children "who by virtue of outstanding abilities, are capable of high performance. These are children who require differentiated educational programs and/or services beyond those normally provided by the regular school program in order to realize their contribution to self and society. Children capable of high performance include those with demonstrated achievement and/ or potential ability in any of the following areas, singly or in combination:

- general intellectual ability
- specific academic aptitude
- creative or productive thinking
- leadership ability
- visual and performing arts
- psychomotor ability"[1]

More contemporary theories reach beyond cognitive ability to describe giftedness in broader terms. Joseph Renzulli's three-ring conception of giftedness, Abraham Tannenbaum's psychosocial model of giftedness, Robert Sternberg's triarchic theory of intelligence, and Howard Gardner's theory of multiple intelligences are some of the common theories and definitions embraced by professionals in the field of giftedness.

The three-ring conception of giftedness designed by Joseph Renzulli is based on the idea that an individual has three factors that converge in order to create the potential for creative, productive giftedness.

---

[1] S. P. Marland Jr. *Education of the Gifted and Talented: Report to the Congress of the United States by the U.S. Commissioner of Education, Volume 1* (Washington, DC: U.S. Government Printing Office, 1972).

The three factors include above-average ability, creativity, and task commitment. Renzulli also addresses the idea of schoolhouse giftedness, or high technical competence and skill level. Ideally, however, teachers following the Renzulli model would focus on the idea of creative, productive giftedness with high levels of innovation and expression.[2]

Tannenbaum's psychosocial model of giftedness includes five factors. These factors are general intelligence, special aptitudes, nonintellective factors, environmental influences, and chance or luck. These factors converge, thus leading to great performance or great productivity from the individual.[3]

Yale psychology professor Robert Sternberg's theory defines intelligence by how it is applied in real-life situations—through intelligent behaviors. As indicators of giftedness, Sternberg looks for effective approaches to both identifying and solving problems and for the ability to make the best use of an environment.[4]

In his 1983 book *Frames of Mind: The Theory of Multiple Intelligences*, Howard Gardner first identified seven intelligences: linguistic, musical, logical-mathematical, visual-spatial, bodily-kinesthetic, interpersonal, and intrapersonal.[5] In later research he added a naturalistic intelligence and is considering the possibility of a ninth intelligence: existential giftedness.[6]

In 2012, the National Association for Gifted Children (NAGC) reexamined its definition of giftedness and released the following statement: "Gifted individuals are those who demonstrate outstanding levels of aptitude (defined as an exceptional ability to reason and learn) or competence (documented performance or achievement in top 10 percent or rarer) in one or more domains. Domains include any structured area of activity with its own symbol system (e.g., mathematics, music, language) and/or set of sensorimotor skills (e.g., painting, dance, sports)."[7]

Using the NAGC definition, the task for educators is to recognize the student's optimal development and provide differentiated educational experiences targeted to the domain(s) of strength. The purpose of this approach is to focus on strengths instead of weaknesses, which in turn will minimize the barriers to identification. Barriers to identification can include socioeconomic status and access to early education experiences, acceleration opportunities, and appropriately trained educators. Focusing on children's strengths provides teachers the opportunity to meet and challenge children in their strength areas while still addressing their areas of weakness.

With many children, particularly those from minority cultures, it's important to be sensitive to the varied emphases and expressions that special abilities can take. Knowing the characteristics of giftedness and understanding the various definitions of giftedness will help educators observe all children with a wider lens and more easily recognize exceptional skills and interests.

Defining giftedness is a challenge, because no two children—including gifted children—are the same. Regardless of which definition you or your school or district prefer, it is important to identify the characteristics of giftedness that your students manifest. The characteristics are identifiable in children at a young age. The characteristics will be present no matter what; the definition just helps you focus on those that are the most important for your setting.

It's exciting and rewarding to be the person who makes a difference to exceptional children and their families. You can make your classroom a safe place that has enough understanding and flexibility for children to exhibit the unusual, idiosyncratic, and even esoteric qualities that make them extraordinary. In doing this, you invite gifted children to identify themselves.

[2] Joseph S. Renzulli. *The Enrichment Triad Model: A Guide for Developing Defensible Programs for the Gifted and Talented* (Mansfield Center, CT: Creative Learning Press, 1977). This is the initial work introducing the enrichment triad model and the three-ring conception of giftedness.

[3] Abraham Tannenbaum. "Giftedness: A Psychosocial Approach." *Conceptions of Giftedness* edited by Robert J. Sternberg and Janet E. Davidson (Cambridge, UK: Cambridge University Press, 1986).

[4] Robert J. Sternberg. *Beyond IQ: A Triarchic Theory of Human Intelligence* (New York: Cambridge University Press, 1985). This book provides information for understanding and appreciating intelligence as demonstrated through intelligent behavior.

[5] Howard Gardner. *Frames of Mind: The Theory of Multiple Intelligences* (New York: Basic Books, 1993). This is a provocative exploration of intelligence that broadens our conceptions of giftedness.

[6] Howard Gardner. *Intelligence Reframed: Multiple Intelligences for the 21st Century* (New York: Basic Books, 1999).

[7] National Association for Gifted Children. "Redefining Giftedness for a New Century: Shifting the Paradigm" position statement, March 2010. www.nagc.org.

ASYNCHRONOUS DEVELOPMENT

Many gifted children are out of sync with developmentally expected behavior for their age. To find these children, you need to look beyond what is usually considered "normal" and into the individual child. Consider this explanation:

> "Giftedness is *asynchronous development* in which advanced cognitive abilities and heightened intensity combine to create inner experiences and awareness that are qualitatively different from the norm. This asynchrony increases with higher intellectual capacity. The uniqueness of the gifted renders them particularly vulnerable and requires modifications in parenting, teaching and counseling in order for them to develop optimally."[8]

Please reread the passage quoted above and think about how much it refers to qualities that are immeasurable and emotional. You may find that you need to adjust your expectations for children's mental and chronological ages. The example of Emily at the beginning of this chapter illustrates this need. Rather than trying harder to fit Emily into the classroom structure, the teacher might win more enthusiastic cooperation by expanding opportunities that challenge and engage Emily. The fact that Emily is the same chronological age as most of her other classmates doesn't mean that her mind functions at the same level. As a second-grade boy once said, "What does size have to do with what grade you're in? Shouldn't it be about how much you know?"

ENIGMATIC BEHAVIOR

Gifted children can be difficult to understand. They differ from one another more than they are alike. For any trait that might describe one gifted child, the opposite will define another. Defining giftedness is like trying to describe a symphony; giftedness, like a symphony, encompasses a spectrum of qualities. Children with the same IQ will have different interests, personalities, abilities, and temperaments. Each gifted child is intricate, paradoxical, and complex; the brain that drives this child intensifies everything the child does. This intensity gives energy to intelligence and abilities, heightening and expanding these capacities even more.

Some aspects of giftedness present a real challenge to a teacher's traditional training. For example, astounding precocity can appear with gaps in physical, social, and emotional development. At times, it's just not convenient to accommodate a gifted child's special needs. To meet such challenges, you'll need to keep foremost in your mind the goal of supporting *all* children's growth and learning.

SHIFTING PASSIONS

It can be hard to keep up with a gifted child's ever-evolving passions. The passion may be dinosaurs, then creative cooking, then a computer game, then slime mold propagation experiments—until the child moves on to astronomy.

CHALLENGING BEHAVIOR

It is important to recognize that the characteristics of giftedness can manifest themselves both positively and negatively. Negative manifestations are more difficult and challenging; however, they do not render a child less gifted. It is easy for teachers to overlook exceptional abilities and instead focus on problems of immaturity, socialization, and discipline. Parents, too, may be inclined to focus on the perceived negatives of giftedness. As a result, adults may sometimes misdiagnose giftedness as a behavioral disorder. The table on page 10 provides a sampling of potential benefits and strengths as well as challenges that can come with the characteristics of giftedness. This is not meant to be an inclusive list.[9]

Getting to Know Your Students

How might you begin to see a child's passion? Giftedness goes beyond the confines of a classroom. To learn what excites a gifted child's curiosity and imagination, you need to look into the child. Here are some tools you can use to get to know your students better.

---

[8] Linda Kreger Silverman. "The Gifted Individual." *Counseling the Gifted and Talented* edited by Linda Kreger Silverman (Denver: Love Publishing Company, 1993): 3.

[9] Barbara Clark. *Growing Up Gifted: Developing the Potential of Children at Home and at School* (Hoboken, NJ: Pearson, 2012). This classic text familiarizes educators with information and processes for understanding and teaching gifted children. And Gary Davis, Sylvia Rimm, and Del Siegle. *Education of the Gifted and Talented* (Hoboken, NJ: Pearson, 2010). This textbook focuses on the history of gifted education, definitions, characteristics, and programming.

Characteristics of Giftedness: Potential Benefits and Challenges*		
Characteristic	*Potential Benefits*	*Potential Challenges*
Long attention span and intense concentration	Long periods of uninterrupted work time; depth of exploration in personal passions and interests	Transitions may be difficult; ignores others or activities
Preference for older playmates	Finds peers that have a similar style of play or passion for a topic	Older peers may not be easily accessible; exposure to content that may not be developmentally appropriate
Early and extensive vocabulary	Able to participate in advanced conversation; exploration of word play	May use words to manipulate; dominates conversations and discussions
Excellent memory	Remembers facts, previously taught or encountered information	Frustrated with repetition; remembers everything
Extreme curiosity	Real-world learning opportunities and applications connect to various areas of learning	Excessive interests; asks embarrassing questions
High activity level and unusual alertness	Likes to learn through movement	Frustrated with inactivity; may appear hyperactive
Rapid learning ability	Rapid pace of instruction; limited repetition	Impatient with others; frustrated with perceived inactivity
Excellent sense of humor	Able to understand puns and playful language	Peers may misunderstand the humor; may use sarcasm (which is often hurtful)
Keen sense of observation	Joy and recognition in little changes	Nothing goes unnoticed
High degree of sensitivity	Ability to understand various aspects of information	Sensitive to feedback or criticism; becomes overwhelmed (sensorial)
Abstract reasoning	Able to focus on bigger picture and not just the small details	Continues to question; wants to know more and why

*Barbara Clark. *Growing Up Gifted* (Hoboken, NJ: Pearson, 2012). And Gary Davis, Sylvia Rimm, and Del Siegle. *Education of the Gifted and Talented* (Hoboken, NJ: Pearson, 2010).

Interviews

One of the best ways to learn how to motivate a child is to have a conversation with the child. Ask the child questions about likes, dislikes, interests, passions, feelings, family, friends, school, and learning. The child's answers will give you insights that will help you differentiate lessons and activities to make them engaging and meaningful to each child.

Early in the year and as often as you are able, create time for a short interview session with each student in your class. Tell your students that you want to get to know them and will be spending some special time with each of them.

A few days before you begin interviewing students, send home a copy of the family letter titled "Your Child's Pictures" (page 18). When you schedule a child's interview, ask the child to bring about six photographs or pictures to share with you. (These are requested in the family letter.) This contribution gives the child a personal stake in the meeting, which enriches the discussion. Usually children have a wonderful time selecting or drawing pictures, and so have an initial positive association with your meeting. They also have some control over the image of themselves that they present to you.

This one-on-one time with you can have an enormous impact on the child and on your teacher-student relationship. The child feels more valued and liked by you. You are likely to see some marvelous ripple effects later in your classroom. Feeling liked by a teacher is one of the most important elements influencing children's school success.

Here are some conversation starters and questions that might help you structure your student interviews:

- What are some things that you do best?
- What are some things that you like to do?
- What are some things that are hard for you to do?
- What do you like best in school? Why?
- What don't you like in school? Why?
- What do you wish you could change to make school better for you?
- What do you like to play or do (such as a game, activity, or sport) outside of school?
- What are some things you would like to be and do when you are grown up?
- If you had three wishes that could come true, what would they be?

Portfolios

Another excellent way to identify young gifted students is to collect and examine evidence of giftedness by creating portfolios. A portfolio is a collection of products and observations about the child. It reaches beyond the confines of a classroom, integrating what the child is capable of at home and elsewhere, too.

Portfolios provide *authentic assessment*—evidence of actual witnessed behaviors. Such evidence is valuable in determining instructional plans, especially for young gifted children. Portfolio assessment has many advantages. It:

- validates your observations and hunches about a child
- enables you to talk more decisively about your plans with parents, guardians, caregivers, and support staff
- builds a concrete bridge between you and family members so that each can see what the other is talking about
- helps you document and evaluate the child's progress
- guides you to a more child-centered and responsive curriculum
- broadens your ideas and the choices you have to offer to all the children in your class
- becomes a learning tool for you by helping you identify giftedness in other students
- creates a source of pride and accomplishment for the child

Another advantage of portfolio assessment is that it gives you a means to find talents that may not be evident when children "perform" in front of other students. A portfolio can help you identify advanced or unique abilities in children who are culturally different from the majority of students. A child who feels different from most others in the class might be reluctant to directly reveal unusual abilities that could further emphasize difference. However, when children work and play uninhibitedly, their special gifts are likely to become apparent.

Portfolio work samples can be selected by the teacher, the student, or both. The materials selected should document both the process and the products of the child's work in order to demonstrate growth. In other words, not all materials should be final products; some should be drafts in various forms. When creating a portfolio, focus on the growth and strengths of the child.

NOTE STRENGTHS

Collect evidence of gifted behaviors and characteristics. Create a file for each child that includes succinct anecdotal statements of notable strengths. Aim for one entry a week. Yes, this takes time, but it's well worth it. Most teachers find that this process improves their perceptions of students. Equally important, when you look for and interpret behaviors as exceptional abilities, you're likely to get a payoff from your students, too. Children will be aware that you are watching for and responding to strengths. A positive reaction from students is a natural outcome.

Because expressions of giftedness vary among children and cultures, you will be looking for and noting evidence that corresponds with some characteristics of giftedness. Use the "Checklist of My Child's Strengths" (pages 22–23) as a guide, and also consider the following categories.

Use of language (early and extensive vocabulary): Things to note include vocabulary range, precision in word usage, and sentence complexity. Example: "Maya asked if she would be 'permitted' to take home her project 'in the foreseeable future.'"

Level of questioning (extreme curiosity): Is there more to the child's questions than the usual who, what, where, when, and why? Do the questions show depth of understanding or an unusual level of complexity? Example: "Luís asked if there was another two-dimensional universe beyond this one."

Problem-solving strategies (generating original ideas): How does the child attack difficult or novel problems? Does he persist? Does he seem to have a system or strategy for solving the problem? Can the child change his thinking if his strategy is not working? Example: "Bobby found answers when he had manipulatives and visuals to guide his learning."

Depth of information (rapid learning ability): Sometimes a child is a profound expert in an area. This can indicate a high level of curiosity, resourcefulness, and understanding. It also points to an excellent memory. Example: "Grace was able to explain the theory of extinction using several views."

Breadth of information (excellent memory): Sometimes a child is interested in everything. A child like this has a variety of interests and also an excellent long-term memory. Example: "I offered a choice of watercolors or colored pencils, and T.J. asked for the acrylic paints we used several months ago, because he liked their vivid colors."

Creativity (thinking outside the box): Is the child original in her creations? Can she elaborate on simple details? Are there instances in which you see creative or expressive movement, art, dramatization, or music making? Are any examples unusual for a child of this age? Example: "Shantelle makes her own products by reimagining materials and using them in different ways."

Focus on or absorption in a task (task persistence): When working on a task or problem, is the child so engrossed that he's unaware of all else that is going on around him? Are there times when the child doesn't hear that it's time to pick up? Does the child resist distractions? Can the child tune out others? Example: "Harry gets so involved with his projects that I sometimes need to sit down next to him and speak directly to him to interrupt his focused concentration."

Profound interest in existential and spiritual questions (moral development): Some children's thoughts and questions are intensely spiritual. They express a deep concern with the existential reasons for things. Example: "Clara said, 'It doesn't matter that I was born because Mommy would have had another little girl that she would have loved just as much as me, so why was I born?'"

Self-evaluation (perfectionism): Does the child appear to have an inner set of standards that he sets for himself? Is the child self-critical or impatient with his ability from time to time? Is he sensitive? Example: "Maruf revised his neighborhood map four times because he couldn't proportion the spaces to accommodate the elaborate details he envisioned."

Preference for complexity or novelty (abstract thinking): Does the child prefer to work on tasks that are difficult or challenging, rather than on simple ones? Given a choice, would the child choose an unusual or complicated game instead of an easy one? Example: "It's hard for Mei to find playmates at recess because she comes up with play ideas so complicated that the other children get confused and walk away."

Ability to synthesize, interpret, and imagine (making connections): Another way to collect information for your notes is by reading simple, lavishly illustrated stories and asking students questions about the pictures. Use questions that require creative imagination, such as: "What else could the dog be thinking?" or "What might Kai be doing if he lived on the planet Mars?" Listen for and make note of:

- elaborate vocabulary
- use of contextual clues
- logical reasoning to arrive at answers
- integration of factual knowledge
- intense emotional involvement in answers
- vivid imagination

OBSERVE SENSIBILITY

When you are creating portfolios, observe *sensibility* as well as sense. Sensibility is a child's capacity to be involved with something. It is a deep, internal, emotional response to what other children might not even notice. With gifted children, things matter a lot. Catching a snowflake summons up a keen, intense response. Learning how long it would take to travel to Jupiter evokes awe and excitement.

You can focus on sensibility by observing children and asking yourself: How acute are Kavon's feelings when he sees frost patterns on the windows? Is Libby totally immersed in stacking the blocks? Does Brendan talk to the books he organizes? Does Rachel anxiously try to find some food when she sees the guinea pig's dish empty?

At the end of her kindergarten year, five-year-old Katja's teacher-created portfolio included the following:

- photocopies of her work on math puzzles in workbooks brought from home
- samples of her paper folding in elaborate and inventive three-dimensional shapes
- the teacher's summaries of conversations with classmates demonstrating Katja's efforts to intervene as a peacemaker
- notes on the teacher's observation that Katja often chooses to play by herself with blocks and boxes, creating her own involved world of shapes and scenarios
- Photographs of her "block world," dramatic play interactions, and math problems solved through manipulatives
- drawings done at the beginning, middle, and end of the year

It also included the teacher's summary note:

"Katja's fine motor development and social progress are well documented. The math puzzles in the workbooks she brought from home and worked on during her free play time established that her math level is several grades higher than what will be offered in first grade. Katja appears to enjoy working alone, yet she is exceptionally sensitive to other children's needs and feelings. It is likely that Katja is a visual-spatial learner who learns best when concepts are shown to her and when she is manipulating materials. Her use of expressive language is developmentally appropriate."

CHILD-CREATED PORTFOLIOS

Portfolios that you compile are one kind of ongoing assessment. Another valuable window on a student's talents, abilities, and growth is a portfolio created and maintained *by the child*. Child-created portfolios help you foster children's passion for learning and gain insights into how children view themselves and their work.

Provide a space, folder, box, or bag for each child to use to collect favorite and special work. Encourage children to label their containers (example: "Mikiko's 'I Did It!' Collection") and decorate them however they wish using photos, drawings, or artistic designs.

You may want to make the initial selection for this portfolio. Start with a standard sample of a piece of work that everyone in the class has done, originating in the curriculum and grounded in instruction. This first example gives you a baseline from which to judge children's ability relative to their classmates' growth. From there, invite children to select the work they want to save, using criteria they have established. Guide children who need assistance in determining the criteria. They might select work that is special to them or that they feel represents their best efforts. The best portfolios are the ones that are created when students feel the importance of gathering and sharing their work. A helpful way to organize this process is to identify a space in the classroom for portfolio work. A file box with a hanging file for each child is a space-efficient way to house the portfolios. Not all work samples will fit into a hanging file, so you may need to take photographs of them or find an alternative location.

When children enter pieces of work in their portfolios, have them explain why they selected these particular items. They can write their explanations on attached notes or dictate them for you or another student to transcribe, as in this example: "I included this sheet because I got every answer wrong, but I learned a lot. This was really hard but I now know each right answer."

With child-created portfolios, each child has a special personal space in the classroom. This communicates to the children that they can make decisions. It lets them see that their work has value. It also encourages them to think critically about what they have done. At the end of the year, you have an illustration of each child's development—from the child's point of view.

Dynamic Assessment

In looking for learning potential—eventual ability development—one way to find outstanding qualities is to arrange for a child to demonstrate her learning capabilities. This method enables you to measure what a child knows and can do and helps you offer the next increment of challenge—what the child is ready to do or could do with a little instruction. Here are the steps for this kind of dynamic assessment:

Pretest: This establishes the current competency and skill level.

Instruction: Lessons should be designed to teach just beyond that level.

Assessment: Assessment should be ongoing throughout the instruction and also may be summative (after the lesson or unit).

These steps are particularly effective for children who may be socially awkward, inhibited, or shy. Exceptional abilities can be harder to detect in children who are introverted or less adept in revealing their thoughts, ideas, and feelings. The strengths of extroverted, socially confident children are more conspicuous; these youngsters get our attention and tell us what they know. Introverted or shy children can be inhibited, slow to warm up, and reticent in their responses. Often, teachers expect less of these children, who may appear to be immature or may seem to have less to offer. But some introverted children only *seem* less able, when in fact they simply prefer to understand and mentally rehearse activities before experiencing them.

Chapter 7 gives an in-depth discussion of assessing children's ability and development. See pages 113–132.

Enlisting Parents as Colleagues[10]

Parents can be of great help in your effort to identify gifted children. Parents (and other family members) tend to be realistic predictors of their children's abilities and needs. Since about 80 percent of parents of gifted children can identify their children's giftedness by age five or six,[11] a shortcut to finding young gifted students is to ask the parents.

When Grandmother brought four-year-old Maurice to preschool, she told the teacher that her grandson thought differently from other children his age. Grandmother owned a laundromat, and Maurice spent countless hours there with her. To occupy himself, he read magazines. He liked to read National Geographic *and* People; *he liked to learn what was going on in the world. Maurice had also mastered an important task: making change. Grandmother knew*

---

[10] Throughout this book, we use the word *parents* to refer to mothers, fathers, grandparents, guardians, or any other primary caregivers.
[11] Elizabeth A. Meckstroth. "Guiding the Parents of Gifted Children: The Role of Counselors and Teachers." *Counseling Gifted and Talented Children: A Guide for Teachers, Counselors, and Parents* edited by Roberta M. Milgram (Norwood, NJ: Ablex Publishing, 1991): 95–120.

that her own son had been very bright, but she felt that her grandson was more than bright. He was "different."

This grandmother may not have had the skills to judge the extent of her grandson's precocity. Nonetheless, she recognized that he had abilities unusual for a child of his age. She was able to accurately report his behavior and bring it to the attention of the preschool teacher.

How can you enlist families' help in identifying children's special talents and abilities? Your goal is to obtain insight into children's strengths that might not be apparent in the classroom. To do this, we suggest that you start the school year by requesting three things from families: pictures, information, and examples of products the child has made at home.

Request Pictures

As close as possible to the first day of school, send home the family letter titled "Your Child's Pictures" (page 18). You will want to do this before you interview each student. Use the letter we have provided, adapt it, or write your own request for family pictures. Having students bring in a family photo for display in the classroom is also a wonderful way to help the students feel ownership of the classroom.

Request Information

Have families complete the family letter titled "Information, Please" (page 19) and invite parents to complete the forms titled "About My Child" and "Checklist of My Child's Strengths" (pages 20–23). You can send these sheets home at the same time as or after the request for photos. You will need to gauge your population and determine the best time to send home various requests. If a family marks most of the characteristics on the checklist, you might want to take a closer look at their child's potential giftedness.

Request Products

After you have received the written information about children, you may want to follow up with a homework assignment for students to design a personal exhibit that includes examples of the child's home activities. Younger students often enjoy the idea of homework. Designing this as a homework task will give you information about the home support the child will have with task completion. Ask parents to help their child assemble a collection of items that demonstrate the child's particular interests and abilities. In making your request, you may wish to use or adapt the family letter titled "Your Child's Personal Exhibit" (page 24).

Depending on your population, it's likely that some children won't bring pictures or other materials from home. You may want to allow time in class for *all* children to draw pictures of themselves and their families and to draw or cut pictures from magazines of their favorite activities. This will provide the opportunity for every child to share something with the teacher and the other students and will provide a foundation for creating a personal exhibit.

A personal exhibit has dimensions to reveal a child's special skills and interests through real evidence that the teacher might not discover in the classroom. It can include photographs, art projects, video or audio recordings, writings—whatever captures the child's extraordinary interests and abilities. The personal exhibit can be stored or presented in any suitable container—perhaps a shoe box, a small unused pizza box, a stationery box, or a grocery bag. Make sure if video or audio recordings are used, you have a way to share them in the classroom.

A personal exhibit has great additional value if the child can briefly present it to the class. If you don't have enough time for class presentations, arrange a time for individual children to share and describe their exhibits to you. We suggest that you write a note about the exhibit to be added to the child's portfolio.

Seven-year-old Josh's personal exhibit, which he shared with his second-grade class, included the following:

- a map he used to locate several Civil War battles
- a replica of a Confederate dollar bill
- pictures of military uniforms and weapons

Josh's teacher wrote this note for his portfolio:

"Josh seemed to enjoy and take great pride in showing his exhibit to the class. He was completely engaged and enthusiastic as he shared his knowledge of the Civil War. We learned that he has participated in reenactments and that he knows weapon types, strategies, and the locations of many battles. He demonstrated a keen sense of technical knowledge and interest as well as logical and sequential knowledge. Josh's exhibit itself was small and simple, as he prefers to spend his time learning more information rather than creating projects."

Chapter 9 provides more information about communicating and working with parents. See pages 142–153.

What About Testing?

The earlier children's special needs are identified, the better it is for their development. Currently, the focus seems to be on finding very young children who have delayed development. Federal programs and money are available to identify any delay or learning difficulty and give these children optimal opportunities to meet their exceptional learning needs. It is equally important to recognize young gifted children. In general, test scores, checklists, and developmental scales are used for identifying giftedness.

Formal intelligence testing instruments may include the Stanford-Binet Intelligence Scales, the Wechsler Preschool and Primary Scale of Intelligence, or the Wechsler Intelligence Scale for Children.[12] Each instrument provides an objective appraisal of a child's abilities. These tools are not perfect, but they do assess a *minimal* level of ability. A child might not demonstrate optimal performance, for many reasons, but the child can't pretend or fake a score such as 133; you know that the child with this score has abilities that are at least this high.

Multiple forms of assessment exist to identify students' abilities. When you are interpreting test scores, look for the ability areas in which the child's performance is most advanced. Highly advanced performance often points to exceptional abilities and potential strengths. This perspective helps identify gifted children who might be overlooked if only the full-scale IQ test score—which is an average of several scores—is considered.

For young children, physical, social, and cognitive development is rapid and variable. Cognitive and motor skills develop suddenly—one moment the skill is not observable, then it miraculously appears! This is just one reason why you should use a multifaceted assessment approach. The variety of assessment tools utilized can include nonverbal assessments or checklists.

You'll find more detailed discussions of assessment and testing considerations in Chapter 7 (page 113) and Appendix A (page 215).

---

[12] For more information about these and other formal assessment instruments, see Appendix A, page 215.

Questions and Answers

"Zach often says something odd, not related to my lesson plan or the class discussion. How can I handle this?"

Gifted children could be described in three words: *more, more,* and *more*. They can be divergent thinkers. They consider information and make intricate, often unusual connections. They need appropriate opportunities to experience intellectual challenge, accomplishment, and satisfaction. You might ask Zach to draw a picture about his idea at home and share it with you or the class the next day. Or arrange to talk with him about his comment later in the day, so he has an opportunity to explain himself.

"I've read about gifted individuals, but I've never had a gifted child in my classroom. "

Sometimes, when adults think of gifted individuals, they imagine prodigies. That's probably because stories about prodigies, people who possess extreme talent or astonishingly rare qualities of intelligence, are memorable. Most gifted children are not prodigies. But gifted children can be in every class and school.

Teachers and administrators have made enormous progress in becoming aware of gifted children and their needs. In 1972, 57.5 percent of school administrators reported that they had *no* gifted children in their schools. By 1994, thirty-five states mandated the identification of gifted and talented students, thirty-one mandated required services, and twenty-three allocated funds to service these students.[13] According to the Davidson Institute, currently four states mandate and fully fund gifted education; twenty-three states mandate gifted programs and are partially funded; seven states mandate programming but do not fund it; five states do not mandate programming but do provide some funding; and eleven states have no mandate and no funding.[14] Despite this increased awareness, many thousands of gifted children are still unidentified or underserved. Depending on how giftedness is defined, the percent of identified gifted and talented children at the elementary level is 7.8 percent.[15]

To identify gifted children, we first have to want to find them. Then we must know what characteristics we're looking for and deliberately seek to find them.

"I don't believe in singling out gifted children. Isn't every child gifted?"

Every child is special and unique. However, when we use the term *gifted*, we are describing children who, compared to their age-mates, have an ability or a depth and breadth of awareness that is far beyond the norm. Although many children may have a particular talent, the designation *gifted* indicates a child who has unusually high abilities in some area and, because of that, has unique educational needs that are different from the norm. The gifted child experiences your classroom and your program in different ways than the other children in the class do. If we don't identify children's needs, we can't help them use their strengths to meet their potential. As teachers, our goal is to provide learning and growth opportunities for every student. To do this, we must identify any gifted children and their characteristics in order to respond appropriately to them.

"One of my students, Eli, is extremely smart— but he still cries in school. How can he be so immature?"

Asynchronous development is a trait of giftedness. For gifted children, physical, cognitive, emotional, and social developmental levels don't evolve at normal rates and don't keep pace with one another. These various aspects of development are out of sync. We can think of gifted children as being several ages simultaneously. These developmental abnormalities can cause confusion for adults who try to formulate reasonable, appropriate expectations for children. They also create inner tension for the children who experience them. It's common for gifted children to have highly sensitive, intense emotions. When gifted children experience a stressful situation, many react with a degree of tension, anxiety, and concern that seems excessive.

When Eli is able, he will stop crying in school. Until then, try not to be impatient. You might help both him and the other children by using the situation as a teachable moment for demonstrating compassion and empathy.

[13] The 1994 State of the States Gifted and Talented Education Report. Austin, TX: Council of State Directors of Programs for the Gifted, 1994.
[14] Davidson Institute for Talent Development. "Gifted Education Policies." Last updated December 23, 2014, www.davidsongifted.org/db /StatePolicy.aspx.

[15] Carolyn M. Callahan, Tonya R. Moon, and Sarah Oh. "National Surveys of Gifted Programs: Executive Summary 2014." Accessed June 11, 2015, www.nagc.org/resources-publications/resources /key-reports-gifted-education.

"How can Julia be gifted when I can't even read her handwriting?"

Giftedness does not apply to all aspects of the child. Some children may be able to create elaborate models in their minds but may not yet have the fine motor control or skill to define these designs on paper. Other children may have sophisticated ideas but similarly, don't yet have the motor skills to write down those ideas. Handwriting can be an obstacle to a child's expression, and she may react with frustration. If Julia finds handwriting cumbersome and tedious, she may resist laboriously reproducing her thoughts letter by letter. You can help her by putting less emphasis on the mechanics of handwriting and focusing instead on the capabilities she demonstrates verbally or in projects. By assessing her knowledge and accomplishments, you can create a less restrictive environment in which she can reveal her abilities. For example, if you ask Julia to *write* about her summer vacation, she might produce something like this: "Summer was fun. We went places." If, instead, you ask her to *tell* about it, she may describe every detail and nuance of her summertime activities.

"Ricardo has skipped a grade and now is in my class. The quality of his work is not what I would expect, and he is not developing high-quality products. What should I do?"

For many gifted students, acceleration is very beneficial. Grade skipping is one type of acceleration. (For additional information related to academic acceleration, download a free copy of *A Nation Deceived* and find information about *A Nation Empowered* at www.accelerationinstitute.org.)[16]

Ricardo skipped a grade, and it is important to recognize that he has not been taught the content from the grade skipped. He may need a few simple instructions about a specific technique you are requiring, because that may not be in his repertoire.

Before giving up on Ricardo and becoming frustrated, get to know him better. Discover what his strengths are, learn why he was accelerated, and find the areas where he may need support. Remember that he may need an introduction to a skill he has not been taught.

"Sara's abilities are at least two grade levels above her age peers, but in the classroom she shows little creativity or initiative. Why does she just do what is asked and nothing more?"

Very bright children are often socially aware and concerned with peer acceptance. For example, a child may read out loud fluently at home but in school, may move her finger slowly along the lines of type and pause after every word she reads. She explains, "This is how we're supposed to read in school."

You might be able to help Sara by connecting her with at least one child who is her peer academically and intellectually—if possible, someone in your classroom. This will create a safe space in which Sara might feel more comfortable revealing her abilities.

Conclusion

As a preschool or primary teacher, you are in a position to be a pioneer—a catalyst in discovering and nurturing gifted young children. To do this, you need to infuse your classroom with an atmosphere of wonder and an attitude of acceptance, flexibility, and understanding. Giving a child permission to reveal diverse and exceptional qualities welcomes and honors the whole child.

How do you find gifted children? Look for them. Encourage them to show you their uniqueness. Invite the adults in their lives to help you. In the process, you will discover and experience countless hidden assets—in your students and in yourself.

[16] Nicholas Colangelo, Susan G. Assouline, and Miraca U. M. Gross. *A Nation Deceived: How Schools Hold Back America's Brightest Students.* Iowa City, IA: University of Iowa, 2004; and Susan G. Assouline, Nicholas Colangelo, Joyce VanTassel-Baska, and Ann Lupkowski-Shoplik. *A Nation Empowered: Evidence Trumps the Excuses Holding Back America's Brightest Students.* Iowa City, IA: University of Iowa, 2015. www.accelerationinstitute.org.

Your Child's Pictures

Child's name: _____

Dear Parent/Caregiver:

In the next few days, I will be meeting individually with each child in the class. This meeting will give us the opportunity get to know each other.

I plan to meet with your child, _____(name),

on_____(day and date).

On or before that day, please send along five or six pictures that are special to your child. These could be photographs, pictures your child has drawn, or images cut from magazines or printed from the Internet. The pictures might be of your child, your family, your child's friends, a pet, or other things or activities that your child enjoys. Sharing pictures will give your child a chance to tell me about some of the people and experiences that are important to him or her.

Thank you for your help. If you have any questions, please call, email, or stop in to talk. I look forward to working with your child!

Teacher's signature: _____

Phone: _____

Email: _____

Information, Please

Child's name: _____

Dear Parent/Caregiver:

In my effort to get to know every child better, I'm asking all parents to complete the attached forms, "About My Child" and "Checklist of My Child's Strengths," and return them (via email or hard copy) by_____ (day and date). The information you provide will help me understand and respond to your child's unique emotional, social, and academic needs.

Thank you for your time and help. If you have any questions, please call, email, or stop in to talk.

Teacher's signature:_____

Phone:_____

Email:_____

About My Child

Child's name:_____

My child loves:_____

In her/his free time, my child usually: _____
_____

My child's favorite activities are: _____
_____
_____
_____

My child (can) _____ (cannot) _____ tell time.

My child creates or solves math problems such as: _____
_____
_____

My child reads books such as these on his/her own (this may include just reading images and talking through the book, actual reading of text, or reading by memory): _____
_____
_____

My child has these special abilities and talents: _____
_____
_____

Special concerns I have about my child are: _____
_____
_____

My child enjoys:

Math	yes _____	no _____	Writing	yes _____	no _____
Puzzles	yes _____	no _____	Dramatic play	yes _____	no _____
Games	yes _____	no _____	Creating projects	yes _____	no _____
Reading independently	yes _____	no _____	Physical activity	yes _____	no _____
Being read to	yes _____	no _____			

Use the space below to write some examples of your child's most notable moments during the past year or so. These might be memorable comments or questions, favorite projects or stories your child has made up, activities you have or your child has found interesting, or behaviors you have wondered about. If you need additional space, please attach an additional sheet.

_____

_____

_____

_____

_____

_____

_____

_____

_____

_____

_____

_____

_____

_____

_____

_____

_____

_____

Parent/Caregiver's signature: _____

Phone: _____

Email: _____

Checklist of My Child's Strengths

Child's name:_____

Please check any items that *usually* or *often* apply to your child:

_____ Is very aware of physical surroundings.

_____ Needs less sleep than other children of same age.

_____ Moves around a lot. Is very active—sometimes seems hyperactive.

_____ Talked early.

_____ Has a long attention span for activities that interest her/him.

_____ Is extremely concerned and curious about others.

_____ Reacts intensely to noise, light, taste, smells, or touch.

_____ Craves stimulation and activity. Is rarely content to sit idle.

_____ Is very emotional—cries, angers, excites easily.

_____ Has an excellent memory.

_____ Insists that people be "fair." Complains when things are "unfair."

_____ Is extremely curious—asks "Why?" "How?" "What if?"

_____ Becomes so involved that he/she is not aware of anything else—"lost in her/his own world."

_____ Explains ideas in complex, unusual ways.

_____ Is very interested in cause-effect relationships.

_____ Reasons well. Thinks of creative ways to solve problems.

_____ Is very interested in calendars, clocks, maps, structures.

_____ Asks questions about abstract ideas like love, feelings, relationships, or justice.

_____ Has vivid imagination and may have trouble separating real from unreal.

_____ Is extremely creative—uses materials in unusual ways; makes up elaborate stories, excuses; sees many possible answers/solutions; spends free time drawing, painting, writing, sculpting, or singing.

_____ Has spontaneous and/or advanced sense of humor.

_____ Likes to play with words. Uses advanced sentence structure and vocabulary.

_____ Likes to tell jokes and use humor.

_____ Is often singing, moving rhythmically; may tell stories or communicate by singing.

_____ Memorizes songs.

_____ Often prefers playing with older children or being with adults.

_____ Creates complicated play and games.

_____ Gives complex answers to questions.

_____ Becomes extremely frustrated when body can't do what mind wants.

_____ Has strong sense of self-control; wants to know reasons for rules.

_____ Is eager to try new things.

_____ Can concentrate on two or three activities at one time.

Describe any other strengths that *usually* or *often* apply to your child: _____

_____

_____

_____

_____

_____

_____

_____

_____

_____

_____

_____

_____

_____

_____

_____

_____

Parent/Caregiver's signature: _____

Phone: _____

Email: _____

Your Child's Personal Exhibit

Child's name: _____

Dear Parent/Caregiver:

As I get to know your child better, I want to do all I can to support your child's development. One way I can do this is by documenting abilities and accomplishments that may not be demonstrated at school.

Your child will be sharing a personal exhibit in class. Please help your child gather items to include in his or her exhibit. Many types of items can be included; please include only those items that your child wants to share. The items should fit into a container such as a shoe box, unused pizza box, grocery bag, or a stationery box. Here are just a few examples:

- a photograph of a completed project, or the project itself
- a video or audio recording of an exceptional activity or performance
- a poem or story your child has written
- a piece of artwork your child has created
- items that represent a special interest or knowledge

Please collect the items with your child and bring them to _____ (place)

on or before _____ (day and date).

Please remember that these items are to be shared with the class. If an item is breakable, valuable, or extra special, a photograph may be a better option.

Thank you for your time and help. If you have any questions, please contact me.

Teacher's signature: _____

Phone: _____

Email: _____

CHAPTER 2
Creating the Learning Environment

Shaundra peeks into the classroom prior to entering. She's unsure about this place. Will it be safe? What lies ahead? What is expected of her? She's talked about going to school, but now that she's here, she wants to be very sure that it is a good place.

Marcus bursts into the kindergarten classroom with unbridled enthusiasm. He has waited for what seems like forever for this day to finally arrive. His excitement is hard to contain. He wants to learn, to play, and to meet new friends. What will this new place hold for him?

Why Is the Environment Important?

Most young children can hardly wait to get to school. They love—or want to love—the school, the teacher, and the learning. School seems like an exciting place, filled with discovery and learning. Brightly colored posters, pictures, letters, words, calendars,

children's artwork, activity stations, and books all beckon the child.

School *should* hold a special joy and promise for every child, no matter what neighborhood, community, or region the child lives in. As a teacher, your challenge is to keep the promise of learning something new every day alive for all students—even the gifted children who may have already mastered the material you are planning to cover.

The Challenge of Designing Your Classroom

Some children have anxiety about the new environment and enter it cautiously, much like entering a cold swimming pool. Others may jump right in with their whole bodies. Your goal is to create a safe atmosphere that welcomes children of all attitudes and aptitudes and opens the door to discovery and learning. Make the entry to your classroom welcoming and inviting. Use lots of bright colors to highlight pictures, words, and children's work. Child-size furniture is a must, with centers or stations placed strategically about the room. You will want designated areas for quiet time, play, drawing, experimenting, and exploring.

It's essential that school be a place that guarantees at least one year of growth in each subject for every student. Learning needs to be challenging and rigorous, not repetitive and boring. But when a wide range of abilities and personalities arrive with your students at the beginning of a new school year, you face a dilemma. How do you even know where to begin?

In particular, what do you do with the five-year-old who is reading chapter books or with the budding paleontologist who is interested only in dinosaurs and has a theory on why they became extinct? What do you do with children who finish their work in a flash and then go about disturbing the class with silly antics? These children may be gifted and may have learning needs that differ greatly from those of others in the class.

Gifted students, along with all their classmates, deserve to have challenging learning experiences that provide opportunities to grow. If given work that's just more of the same, or extra busy work just to keep them quiet, gifted children may soon decide that school is not an exciting place where they want to be. If they adapt to typical classroom expectations, gifted learners may lose interest in school, may not develop their abilities, and might never reach their potential. Or they may act out or disrupt others. Neither result is desirable, and neither needs to happen.

You can avoid such results by responding to gifted children's needs. Balance group and individual activities. Pre-assess students so that you know where they stand in different subjects. Look at ways to extend the curriculum with the three Rs of risk taking, rigor, and relevance. Risk taking involves thinking outside the box, applying creative thinking, and exploring new ideas related to the content. Rigor involves going deeper into the subject or topic or going beyond the grade-level curriculum to examine more challenging content. Relevance looks at important, applicable extensions to the given topic.

How Does the Environment Feel?

When we talk about learning environments, we often think about the part we *see*: activity stations,

materials for thematic units, tables, chairs, and so on. To tailor your learning environment to respond more effectively to your gifted students, you also need to think about how it *feels*. For a few minutes, shift your focus away from your whole class and place it squarely on your gifted students. Examine your typical expectations and responses.

The learning environment needs to be intellectually stimulating, challenging, and emotionally safe. In an environment without these key components, learning will not happen. If gifted children are made to relearn what they have already mastered, the elements of stimulation and challenge are missing. The children's minds shut down, and boredom kicks in. In order to keep gifted learners learning, the material must be engaging. Students must want to learn the information because it has value and meaning to them. Students may ask, "Is this something that I can do? Does it make sense? Will I be able to use it? How will I use this?" If we ask students to learn information that doesn't seem connected to their lives, the information lingers in their minds for only a short time.

It's equally important to examine what the experience of being in a class of students with diverse abilities feels like to gifted children. For example, a gifted child may process new information far more quickly than most children. This means the child may become bored while waiting for classmates to master information and skills. Young gifted children have talents beyond their years, but patience and diplomacy typically aren't among these talents. Preferring to chat with you about new ideas or information with little regard for your other obligations, a gifted child may seem (and become) demanding. Frustrated, some gifted children react by seeking attention with silly antics, by challenging authority, or by developing other undesirable classroom behaviors. Other gifted children may grow quiet and withdrawn as a response to feeling that they don't fit in.

Helping Children Be Successful

At four and a half years old, Margo was able to add, subtract, multiply, and divide to find answers for real-life questions. She could calculate on the spot how many oatmeal cookies her preschool teacher needed for a classroom party or how a group of children could be divided into equal teams.

One day, after Margo had finished a math domino activity quickly and correctly, the teacher rewarded her with a sheet of simple addition problems. Margo took the sheet and sat quietly at the table. When the teacher asked her for the completed worksheet, the child burst into tears. "What's wrong, Margo?" asked her teacher in surprise. "I can't do this!" Margo sobbed. Pointing to an addition sign, she cried, "What are those little t's supposed to mean?" Margo had not yet been formally introduced to the mathematical symbol for addition.

Two years later, as a first grader, Margo had a teacher who recognized her advanced analytical abilities and provided her with a "math challenge packet" to work on at home or during free time in class. The packet gathered dust at home. Meanwhile, Margo's efforts on much simpler math activities in class appeared uninspired. When her teacher finally asked Margo why she didn't pursue the challenge packet, Margo replied, "I hate math." In subsequent ability testing, Margo breezed through discussion problems requiring advanced math but stopped halfway through a simpler series of written math calculations, saying she couldn't do them.

For any student, being able to visualize and solve problems is the important task. Margo had that skill. In fact, like some other gifted children, Margo appeared to have an uncanny ability to grasp and solve complex real-life problems. What she lacked was the understanding of how her mental calculations related to the symbols she saw in math books or on worksheets. Once aware of this, what might her teacher do?

A few minutes of basic, private instruction with questions and answers may be the lifeline a child like Margo needs. When a child has such a markedly advanced ability to solve complex problems, we sometimes simply assume that she knows the underlying fundamentals. Often, the child has never been shown how to do the work, has not understood its significance, or doesn't know how to express the work using math notation. If you have a Margo in your class, you may want to start by asking her to write the hardest math problem that she knows how to solve. Explain that the math symbols are a quicker, easier way of writing the problem. Talk through a real problem and show how it can be expressed and solved with mathematical symbols.

If the child finds the symbols boggling, remind her of the related tasks she is already able to do.

Real-life situations and manipulatives can provide a bridge between what the child can do and what confuses her. Remind children that math symbols can be read like letters of the alphabet. You might say, "You know how to read letters and words. Reading numbers and multiplication signs is like reading words."

Parents can be a valuable source of information about a child like Margo. What has this child's parent observed? Has the child discussed her feelings about math at home? Does the parent have any insights into the problem?

Application of Theory to Practice

Harry is a very precocious young child, but he is also extremely sensitive. He is cheerful, alert, and insistent on things being "right." Although he is advanced academically, he struggles with certain fine motor skills, such as handwriting and using scissors. He tends to focus on what he can't do well and labels himself accordingly: "not very good at art," for example.

Harry's attention span is short unless he is doing something that interests him. He loves computers and tablets. These devices can make up for his poor penmanship, help him find all sorts of information, and enable him to create the glitz that he wants to present in his projects without the need for artistic talent. If asked to write something on a specific topic, he turns in a few sentences. But if he is using a computer or tablet, he can create pages of information and even put together a PowerPoint presentation.

Harry's teacher, by allowing Harry flexibility in the way he presents or shares what he knows, helps him experience success and build upon it. It's also vital, of course, that Harry and other students learn basic, required skills such as handwriting and cutting with scissors. When you're faced with how to present any new skill or information, or when you're considering how to set up your classroom, keep brain research in mind.

Our learning is dependent on our brain. Our brain's structure and function depend on both genetics and experience. Children need experiences to grow their brain capacity. Intense actions within a stimulating environment can rewire learning in parts of the brain. The human brain experiences windows of opportunity for learning. If the right stimulation happens at the right time, the learning occurs and the brain grows stronger. Without the stimulation, the window closes and the opportunity to learn that skill may possibly be lost or impaired.

The neurons may atrophy or attach to other neurons and assume new functions. One example of this process is our ability to see. Humans need visual stimulation by the age of two years. If kept from seeing until age two, a child may become blind. The child may have other heightened senses and abilities, but vision will be impaired.[1]

For information to stick in one's mind, it must be planted in one's memory. The human working memory sorts information into meaningful bite-size portions and strings it together. The memory then puts the information into context. Storytelling is an excellent way to provide context and imbue information with meaning. If information seems random or appears to be useless trivia, it won't remain in one's memory. Humans need a personal connection to information in order to remember it. Emotion is the glue that makes information stick, the key to long-term memory. Emotion answers the question, "What's in it for me?" Emotion ignites the imagination, motivates a hunger for knowledge, and inspires curiosity. The deeper the emotion is, the richer and stronger the memory of the event or material will be.

Intelligence is the ability to form connections among chunks of information. The more synapses, or connections, between neurons the brain has, the more information it stores. A stimulating environment produces synapses. The brain makes more synapses than it will use and selects those that are most meaningful. The brain prunes or eliminates synapses that are not essential. An example of pruning is a young child's ability to learn languages. Children are born with the ability to distinguish sounds from every language that is spoken. Children learn and remember sounds they hear. If they do not hear a certain sound, their brains prune the ability to distinguish that sound. That is why as adults, we may have difficulty learning all the nuances of a foreign language.

So what are the implications of brain research for the primary classroom? Here are a few tips:

- Create a stimulating environment. Use colorful visuals, interesting sounds, and movement.
- Find ways to involve your students by using a variety of approaches. Use different learning modalities (visual, auditory, and kinesthetic). Take a concept you want the students to learn and watch a video, read about it, act it out, play a game using the information, do an experiment, draw it, sing about it, or put it to music.
- Encourage students to move their bodies. Sitting for long periods of time does not help retention. Movement does!
- Have a strong ending to every lesson. Minds remember best what they learned last.

Helping Children Work Together Comfortably

Tonya is very bright, but she has trouble with peer relationships. She gets upset when someone responds to a question with the wrong answer, and she corrects others when they make simple mistakes. She often blurts out responses instead of waiting to be called upon for an answer. No one wants Tonya for a partner, and some children ridicule her on the playground. Tonya's teacher is concerned that Tonya is setting herself up to be bullied. The teacher wants to know what she can do to help Tonya interact successfully with her peers.

First, Tonya's teacher needs to talk privately with Tonya. The teacher can say that she knows teasing and rejection hurt, and she can suggest some coping skills. She can explain that often children tease because they feel jealous or inferior or don't know a better way to say, "I like you." She can also discuss strategies Tonya could use, such as ignoring the teasing, laughing along (if that's fun for her), or telling the children who tease her how the teasing makes her feel.[2]

The teacher knows that Tonya is extremely bright. The teacher can confide that she understands Tonya knows lots of things and wants to share them. The teacher can suggest ways for Tonya to do that without taking away the joy of sharing that others need. To help Tonya develop relationships with peers and learn to listen as well as express her own ideas, the teacher might try grouping Tonya with other children who have similar abilities or interests. One way to do this is by using the name card method. Developed by educator Frank T. Lyman Jr. as a no-excuses way to get everyone in class participating, the name card method can also help a child like Tonya build social bonds. Here's how it works:

---

[1] Stanley N. Graven and Joy V. Browne. "Visual Development in the Human Fetus, Infant, and Young Child." *Newborn and Infant Nursing Reviews* (December 2008): 200.

[2] Ideas for helping children understand and cope with teasing are adapted from Judy Galbraith, *The Survival Guide for Gifted Kids: For Ages 10 & Under* (Minneapolis: Free Spirit Publishing, Inc., 2013): 83–87. Used with permission.

1. Write each student's name on a 3" x 5" card or on a clothespin.
2. Pair each student with a discussion buddy. Some discrepancy in ability is fine, but try to avoid a huge gap.
3. Use the think-pair-share strategy:
   - Ask a question. Give the class ten to twenty seconds to *think* about it.
   - Have students *pair* up with their discussion buddies.
   - Tell the pairs to talk about the question together. So that everyone has a chance to talk, tell the students that each person in the pair should have thirty seconds to talk while the other one listens.
4. Using the cards or clothespins, call on students to *share*. They may share their own responses or their buddies' responses. If they don't have an answer, offer hints or choices. Don't call on anyone to help a student. Instead, tell the child that you will return soon to ask the question again. Don't tell students that any response is correct or incorrect.
5. After responses have been given by several children, ask for volunteers who have something to add that has not already been said. Then call on those with hands raised. Wait until several students have answered before saying that a response is correct.
6. As you finish with each card, place it in the middle of the stack. Shuffle the stack and draw again. If you are using clothespins, place the finished one with all the others in a box or bag and shake the container. This gives everyone a fair chance of being called on and lets no one off the hook after answering. This also helps make sure that no child dominates the talk time.[3]

By using these suggestions, you can provide opportunities for all children to interact comfortably. Interaction can make a huge difference in learning. Sharing what you know reinforces your learning while you help another person learn. This does not mean that bright children act as unpaid tutors. It means that students share with others who have similar abilities so that concepts become clearer for both of them. To facilitate the feeling of success, have students summarize what they've just talked about or describe in their own words what they learned.

Responding to Children's Needs

The examples of Margo, Harry, and Tonya point out how important it is that you approach the gifted children in your classroom with *compassion*, *communication*, and *creativity*.

- *Compassion* lets you put yourself in children's shoes in the classroom to see how it feels for them.
- *Communication* of expectations and perceptions needs to take place between you, the student, and the parent.
- *Creativity*—in lesson content, in the configuration of the classroom and the student groups, and in modes of instruction—allows opportunities for gifted children to blossom.

In the simple structure and naturally creative environment of most early childhood and primary programs, the tools for responding to a gifted child are already in place. The key lies in understanding how to use these tools to craft effective responses to the special needs of children with high ability. Consider the following crucial aspects to create a successful environment for gifted children in your classroom.

A Balance of Structure and Creativity

Young children need some structure and rules to organize their thinking for learning. For the gifted child, it's essential that structure be used not to define learning goals but, like a sturdy ladder, to provide the stability and direction the child needs to reach as high as possible. Creativity provides the spark of intellectual energy needed for the climb.

Individual Learning Modalities

In addition to striking a balance between structure and creativity, it's important for teachers to identify a gifted student's learning modality and to provide opportunities for the child to work and learn in that modality. A student's learning modality is the predominant way in which the student learns and

---

[3] Suggestions for using the name card method are adapted from "Think-Pair-Share, Thinktrix, Thinklinks, and Weird Facts" by Frank T. Lyman Jr. in *Enhancing Thinking Through Cooperative Learning* edited by Neil Davidson and Toni Worsham (Columbia, NY: Teachers College Press, 1992); and *Teaching Gifted Kids in Today's Classroom* by Susan Winebrenner with Dina Brulles (Minneapolis: Free Spirit Publishing, Inc., 2012): 14–16. Used with permission of Frank T. Lyman Jr., Ph.D.

processes information. We all learn in multiple ways, but most humans have a preferred way in which they process and learn. This does not mean that they cannot learn in other ways; rather, it simply means that learning in other ways may not be as easy. Here are three basic learning modalities you may see among your students:

Auditory learners prefer to listen to information rather than read about it. A lecture or discussion about a topic will help these students learn the content. Auditory learners may like to have background music playing while they study or may be easily distracted by background noises in the classroom or environment. These learners may prefer to repeat words or ideas aloud and engage in discussions or debate. They also enjoy being read to or being told stories. Auditory learners think analytically. We often consider a child who is an auditory learner to be a "good" student. Usually an auditory learner's learning needs are readily met in the classroom as the child follows directions and moves sequentially from task to task.

Visual learners learn best by reading information; by looking at pictures, charts, and graphs; and by taking notes so they can "see" what the teacher is saying. These children typically like color and may highlight points to remember so that those ideas stand out. Drawing ideas and mapping out timelines can help visual learners see ideas and understand them. Children who learn visually tend to be holistic thinkers. They want the big picture, not individual pieces. Visual learners can learn logically and analytically, but may need to do this by working backward from the bigger picture. These are the students who prefer pictures to words, who look for visual clues (photos, charts, and graphs), who write or draw about what they are learning, and who want to view what the product of their work will look like.

Tactile-kinesthetic learners need to move, feel, touch, make, and do in order to learn. They understand much better if they can act out a story, rather than just reading the words. They want to *do*, not just see or listen. They prefer hands-on projects over reading or hearing about a topic. Field trips and role playing make their learning feel real. They may prefer to act out what they know. They need to move. They are holistic thinkers, like visual learners, but they need hands-on activities in order to understand the big picture. These children learn by doing. They

tend to dislike lectures, preferring to develop their own system of organizing information. Many tactile-kinesthetic learners move around while they are thinking. To learn math and symbols, these students use fingers and manipulatives.[4]

By observing a child's preferred style of interaction with new ideas and materials, you'll be able to determine the child's preferred modality. Learning modalities are not permanent and may change as circumstances change. There is no right way or wrong way to learn. And learning modalities are only one framework for understanding the different ways in which people learn.

In fact, over seventy different frameworks have been devised for understanding how people learn. Numerous catalogs, guidebooks, and tests are devoted to learning styles. The frameworks range from Bloom's taxonomy to Howard Gardner's multiple intelligences. No one way is the best way to teach, but a range of methods can help teachers meet the diverse needs of young students. The goal for educators is to discover how the content information can best be taught and how individual children process the information.[5]

Teaching to the Learning Modalities

By using a variety of approaches to present new information, and by allowing children to interact with information in different ways, you can help your students learn successfully through their preferred modalities. Most classrooms are highly verbal; yours may already include many features that help auditory learners succeed. To meet the needs of your auditory learners, you will want to teach through talks, reading aloud, and class discussions as well as small-group discussions. Provide recorded stories and music, too. Have conversations with individual children. Use scheduled activities and

---

[4] Some of the learning modality characteristics and the teaching suggestions in the section that follows are adapted from Susan Winebrenner, *Teaching Kids with Learning Difficulties in Today's Classroom* (Minneapolis: Free Spirit Publishing Inc., 2014), 44–57. Used with permission.

[5] J. D. Bransford, A. L. Brown, and R. R. Cocking (eds.). *How People Learn: Brain, Mind, Experience, and School* (Washington, DC: National Academy Press, 2000); F. Coffield, D. Moseley, E. Hall, and K. Ecclestone. *Learning Styles and Pedagogy in Post-16 Learning: A Systematic and Critical Review* (London: Learning and Skills Research Centre, 2004); Harold Pashler, M. McDaniel, D. Rohrer, and R. Bjork. "Learning Styles: Concepts and Evidence." *Psychological Science in the Public Interest* 9.3 (2008): 103–119.

give step-by-step instructions. With reading, help children analyze word sounds.

For students who learn visually, include in your instruction pictures, demonstrations, handouts, videos, computers, and tablets. Provide opportunities for children to write or draw about what they know or to create videos or slide show presentations on a computer. Help visual students see the big picture by mapping out a story or using graphic organizers. Use color. For children who are visual learners, color is important. Make humor and excitement part of their learning experience.

Keep in mind that tactile-kinesthetic learners need to *touch* and *move*. Help them learn by providing manipulatives, floor games, and task cards. Give these students concrete examples. Provide opportunities for both dramatic and physical play. In their reading, your tactile-kinesthetic learners love action, adventure, and excitement; they may fidget while listening to a story. Having play dough or clay available may help fidgeting children keep their hands busy and minds attuned to the story. You may want to have a digital recorder, tablet, or a computer available to record their thoughts and learning. A website or app that allows children to create mind maps can help children organize their ideas with words.

With awareness, sensitivity, and flexibility, you can teach to every learning modality. Later in this chapter we'll suggest ways to approach your students and arrange your classroom in order to support every child's preferred ways of learning. (See "Making Every Child Feel Welcome and Valued," page 32.)

Knowledge Base

Many gifted children easily know, or can quickly absorb, much of the content you plan to cover. It's clear that they need additional resources and encouragement to experience the benefits of learning in a school setting. However, although gifted children may grasp the big picture, they may lack a few of the smaller, yet still important, puzzle pieces that fit together naturally with age or experience to create the big picture. Use careful observation and curriculum compacting (see Chapter 3, pages 41–56) so that you can design activities that allow gifted learners to demonstrate mastery of concepts, gain the necessary knowledge and skills, and then move on to an appropriate challenge level.

Intellectual Risk Taking

Most children find comfort in competence. Competence comes easily to young gifted children—but learning happens only when children take intellectual risks. Gifted students may need special encouragement to venture into unfamiliar territory. Watch for signs of any young perfectionists. Children who are perfectionistic:

- are often dissatisfied with their work
- start over and over again (and may destroy work that doesn't measure up to what they feel they "should" do)
- are self-critical
- look for mistakes in others
- tattle
- procrastinate
- are afraid to try new things or take risks

Teach the value of mistakes and experimentation. Communicate with parents about ways to encourage intellectual risk taking at home. Ask them for insights that might help you more quickly identify areas in which the child needs extra encouragement to experiment with learning.

Make an activity more challenging by adding an extra measure of creative problem solving. For example, ask, "If you were the fourth little pig, what would you use to build your house? Why?" Or, "In studying pollution, how could we reduce waste in the school lunchroom? Create a plan and describe how you might put it into practice."

A Balance of Group and Independent Activities

It's important for gifted children to learn to work productively with children of all ability levels. It's also vital that highly able children be able to experience intellectual challenges and the companionship of other children with similar appetites and aptitudes for learning. One of the greatest gifts you can give your young gifted students is the confidence to become activists in their own education—to identify and articulate areas of interest and pursue them independently and productively through available resources.

Emily was a dream first grader. She complied with all that was asked of her. She did the required work and always finished quickly and accurately. Her manner was pleasant, and other children were drawn to her.

Emily did not boast or indicate that the work was easy for her. She gave no indication that her knowledge extended far beyond the information that was being presented in her first-grade class.

When Emily's teacher held a conference with Emily's mother, Emily's mother asked if the teacher realized that Emily had been reading chapter books for several years. She currently was reading Harry Potter books at home. Emily's teacher was stunned to hear this.

What might you do to avoid a similar oversight? How can you recognize, early on, the special abilities and interests of reticent children? You might try a creative strategy such as printing exciting news or information on chart paper and asking if anyone in class knows what it says. This can help you identify those children who are reading.

Once you've identified early and advanced readers, consider allowing them to read with children in a higher grade. Have a reading specialist meet with them on an individual basis, or group and regroup them as necessary to teach missing skills and allow for independent work.

Often, children who have learned to read at an early age have gaps in their learning. They may know many sight words, but lack the skill to figure out a new word phonetically. Or they may be able to memorize information, but not to apply it to new situations. It's essential that you identify and fill these gaps and teach the necessary skills a child may have missed. This is not to say, however, that the child should sit through every skill-and-drill lesson. Many gifted children will quickly and easily acquire the basics of printing, spelling, punctuation, and phonics. Assess children's needs, then provide opportunities for them to learn and master skills within the whole class, in small groups, and independently. Once students master the skills, encourage them to enhance and expand these skills as they work on more complex projects and activities.

Working with Parents

Parents, guardians, childcare providers, or others who know your students can supply a wealth of information about them. These caregivers know the quirks and unusual abilities of their children. It is helpful to have them share what they want you to know at the beginning of the year by using the "Help Me Help You" form at the end of this chapter. What are some special skills or observations that they note? Throughout the year, continue an open

dialogue with parents. This does not mean that you have to respond immediately to every email, text message, or phone call. It simply opens the door for communicating information that may be helpful in programming for your students.

See Chapter 9 for more information about working and communicating with parents.

Making Every Child Feel Welcome and Valued

Now, look around your room and think through your program. When the following features are a part of your classroom, you've created a child-friendly environment for all your students—including the gifted ones.

Nine Features of Your Child-Friendly Classroom

1. **The classroom invites learning.** Bright, colorful pictures are posted. Items from nature are displayed. Books with a variety of reading levels are arranged on a ledge or table or are available electronically. At appropriate times, music is playing. These elements all help frame the curriculum and let children know basic expectations.

2. **You use thematic instruction so the connections among content areas occur easily and naturally.** For example, when you are talking about a concept like change, you can connect the change in science with weather or seasons, change of characters or ending in a story, change in neighborhoods in social studies, change in math when using different operations or different numbers, change of sounds with the same note and different musical instruments in the orchestra, or change of color in an artist's picture. You can point out that change also occurs socially and emotionally as feelings shift with different circumstances and events. We can be scared or challenged in a new situation and then, when we find the situation is safe, we become more comfortable.

3. **You make available a wide range of materials.** These include materials that go beyond the average range of grade-level interests, such as sophisticated computer and tablet apps, three-dimensional puzzles, mazes, and magazines. Bulletin boards and other displays are not only attractive but also rich in content. You might

display collections, charts, posters, or cultural artifacts.

4. **Your activity centers invite self-initiated, hands-on experimentation.** They are well organized yet simple, so students can take responsibility for handling and putting away materials.

5. **Seating arrangements are flexible.** This way, you can easily make periodic changes based on different grouping needs. Your classroom allows space for independent study groups to gather as well as for individual students to work alone.

6. **You offer attractive, lesson-related activity options for students who finish work correctly with time left over.** These options include a daily balance of large-group, small-group, and independent activities. For fun, you also post special "super challenge" questions from time to time. (These are not only fun, they also help you identify children whose responses reveal advanced reading, math, or other abilities.)

7. **In evaluating students, you identify areas of strength, areas that can be improved, and areas in which the student needs more challenge.** When a student excels in a particular area or subject, your evaluation includes this question: "What can be done to provide this child with an appropriate opportunity for challenge?" (Chapter 7 gives an in-depth discussion of assessing children's ability and development.)

8. **You maintain a portfolio of each child's work.** The purpose of the portfolio is to document the child's growth and skill levels. The portfolio, which includes your personal observations, is used as a basis for discussion during parent-teacher conferences. (Chapter 1 includes information about creating and maintaining portfolios. See "Portfolios," page 11, and "Child-Created Portfolios," page 13.)

9. **Parents play an integral role in their children's education.** You welcome parent communication and invite it regularly.

A Balanced Structure

The class structure and schedule should allow for balance among whole-group activities, small-group activities, and individual activities.

WHOLE-GROUP ACTIVITIES

Whole-group activities allow time for forming a cohesive group, presenting information that all students need to hear, discussing ideas, or celebrating events. Following are some examples of whole-group activities.

Calendar: Look at the day, the month, and the year. Talk about the weather. Discuss important things that happened today or on this day in years past. Note birthdays or special events.

Attendance: When taking attendance, have students answer with their favorite color, a pet's name, a parent's name, a friend's name, or a favorite book, video, app, or game. Carry attendance-taking further by discussing similarities and differences within your group of students. Does your class consist of more boys or more girls? How many students' shoes have laces, how many have Velcro fasteners, how many have snaps or buckles, how many are slip-ons?

Music: As you sing songs, have the words to the songs visible on the board, on chart paper, or on an interactive whiteboard so that children can follow along. This helps children begin to identify words as they are singing. Those who are already reading or are beginning readers can recognize familiar words and learn new ones.

Brainstorming Activity: Brainstorming stimulates creativity and divergent thinking. Divergent thinking generally relates to having multiple ideas on the same topic. Following are some starter ideas. Challenge students to name:

- yellow (green, purple, red) items found in the grocery store
- ways to show someone you care about them
- things to do with water (an old tire, a clothespin)
- kinds of hats
- things that are cold (hot, invisible)
- ways to lift a heavy object
- ways we can save energy
- things to do at home instead of watching videos or playing computer games

Group Sharing Time: Take time regularly for children to share news and information. ("My brother fell and broke his arm." "My cat had kittens.")

Storytime: Select stories related to the content of group discussion. Ask questions that hook the children: "Have you ever done that?" "Did you know that?" Such questions invite children to become involved. If the story includes a pattern, have the children join in. Stop the story and ask, "What do you think will happen next?" Reading or storytelling should be enjoyable for you and your students. Make it fun, comfortable, and friendly. Ham it up. Don't be afraid to move, add actions, and change your voice. For a change of pace, have a puppet tell the story. You may want to use soft background music to set the mood. Enjoy what you are reading—your enjoyment is contagious.

You might also build whole-group activities around a topic or a theme. For example, you might focus on the theme of *patterns* and how they help us predict. In class activities, you could address the theme in a variety of ways.

You could look at the patterns of the *seasons*, asking children questions: "What do we know about the seasons? What pattern do they follow? What holidays are in certain seasons? Which season is your favorite? Why?" Ask children to brainstorm all the things that come to mind when they think of winter, spring, summer, and fall. Sings songs related to the seasons or learn the months of the year in a song.

Discuss and track patterns of *weather*. Chart the weather daily. Talk with children about high and low temperatures. Discuss appropriate clothing. Compare the weather in one part of the country or world and another.

Math is full of patterns. Demonstrate patterns using manipulatives—or by using the children themselves. (For example, you can do the latter by having the children arrange themselves in a boy-girl-girl-boy-girl-girl pattern.) Have the children add onto and continue the patterns. Discuss *color* patterns: Introduce the color wheel. Learn primary, secondary, and complementary colors. Create patterns with colors. Listen for patterns in *music*. Move to the music. Repeat the movement when the music stops.

Stories have patterns. Pick out the patterns for characters, settings, and plots. In reading, show children that *letters* have patterns, too. Talk about how we can predict the way words will sound when we look for letter patterns. Brainstorm *words* that rhyme and show how they can establish a pattern.

Other themes appropriate for young children are change, community, celebrations, and growth. Topics can revolve around food, seasons, holidays, colors, animals, weather, space, or regions.

By introducing themes, you create complexity beyond what is possible when addressing only a single subject, and you open the door for children to expand their learning and think divergently and

critically. The interdisciplinary connections and extensions among specific subjects lead to complexity. For example, the topic of *food* can lead the class into a discussion of food scarcity in different countries and of food for people who are homeless. You can connect this social studies discussion to science and the study of nutrition. A discussion of *weather patterns* might lead to tornadoes and how they can be predicted. From there, you might ask: "What happens when a tornado touches down? How can you be safe? Why? What if people's homes are hurt by a tornado? What help will the people need?" A focus on *cities* can incorporate literature, history, and economics. Questions you might discuss include: "What's good about living in a city? What are the advantages? What's not so good—what are the disadvantages? What problems do cities have? Who works to solve the problems?" You could use pictures or stories to compare and contrast a modern city with the way it was one hundred years ago and move to a discussion of inventions and of changes in transportation, dress, food, entertainment, family life, and school.

SMALL-GROUP OR INDIVIDUAL CENTER TIME
Young children spend much of their time at activity stations or learning centers in early childhood and primary classrooms. In order to accommodate their learning modality preferences, you can set up stations or centers based on content topics with differentiated activities representing the different learning modalities. In this way, the children can learn about a specific topic or topics through multiple modalities. Children may rotate through all the centers, or they may choose which center they wish to visit, depending on the child, the time available, and the lesson.

Setting Up Centers Using Multiple Intelligences
Learning centers are used in many classrooms and are designed to introduce, reinforce, extend, and enrich the curriculum. Children can learn, practice, and improve skills through purposeful work in centers. You can set up centers for a day, a week, or the duration of a specific topic. They work best if tiered with a variety of choices to match or reinforce the skills and content.

Learning centers can be set up in many ways. One way would be to base the centers on a particular learning framework. Howard Gardner's ideas on multiple intelligences offer a model that enables you to address a variety of learning modalities. For example, a student might learn a story best by reading it, seeing the story performed in a play, or hearing it read on an audio recording. The options address different learning modalities, but all are available at the reading center for the linguistic intelligence.

LINGUISTIC CENTER (READING AND WRITING CENTER)

The linguistic learner prefers to learn through words, so the materials at this center have to do with reading and language. The linguistic or reading and writing center should be located where it is quiet, away from noise and activity. Have available comfortable floor pillows, chairs, and tables. Materials for this center might include:

- books (a variety: picture, easy-read, and simple chapter books)
- magazines
- e-readers or tablets
- dictionaries
- storybook character puppets
- stories written by children, displayed on the bulletin board or bound in book form
- paper for writing or drawing stories
- audiobooks
- digital recording device for recording children's stories
- magnetic letters with board
- overhead projector with letters for children to project on the whiteboard and trace to create words or sentences
- wipe-off boards
- laminated sentence strips and nontoxic wipe-off pens or dry-erase markers
- word searches
- crossword puzzles (simple to complex)
- spelling materials and games
- phonics cards
- pizza wheels with pictures on the outside and a letter in the middle—children clip clothespins on the words that begin like the letter in the center of the wheel
- alphabet games
- games for matching uppercase and lowercase letters
- word cards for matching, rhyming, alphabetizing, and storytelling

- sentence blocks with articles, nouns, verbs, adjectives, and adverbs—children roll the blocks like dice to form different sentences
- apps for word processing and story writing

MUSICAL CENTER (MUSIC CENTER)

The child with musical intelligence may have the ability to learn through rhythm and melody. The child may be able to hear not only the melody, but also the parts of a musical piece. Children with musical intelligence may be auditory and kinesthetic learners who learn by singing songs, humming, rapping, or tapping a pencil, foot, or finger to a rhythm. Activities for the musical center might appeal to all learning modalities. They include reading stories or poems with music in the background; adapting nursery rhymes or poems into songs; teaching spelling, grammar, or math through rhythm, rap, or song; drawing pictures of images that come to mind while listening to music; holding sing-alongs; and matching instrument pictures to instrument recordings. Your options for musical activities and materials will depend on the degree of noise that's acceptable in your classroom, as well as on your budget. Materials for this center might include:

- piano, keyboard and headset, or MIDI keyboard for linking to a computer or tablet
- other musical instruments (ukuleles, harmonicas, recorders)
- drums
- rhythm instruments, both purchased and homemade (maracas, castanets, spoons, blocks, sandpaper-covered blocks, rice between taped paper plates, bones with a hole in the middle on a wire ring)
- device for recording music and playing recorded music, such as an MP3 player and recorder or a tablet
- instrument picture cards

LOGICAL-MATHEMATICAL CENTER (MATH CENTER)

The materials in this center deal with mathematical problems, symbols, and logical thinking. Children who are logically or mathematically inclined love to question, explore, and think about things. Math materials for this center might include:

- felt board with felt objects and numerals
- pegboards with colored pegs
- pattern cards (simple to complex)

- puzzles (simple to complex)
- dice
- number cards for sequencing and matching
- items for matching numbers (symbols) to sets of objects
- math facts cards
- number games, projects, and puzzles
- calculators
- tangrams
- attribute blocks
- beads of various sizes
- interlocking blocks, such as Legos
- beans, painted on one side so children can create patterns or estimate quantities
- junk to classify (keys, shells, rocks, buttons, bread tags, tickets, letters, tiles, old game tokens, magnets, pictures)
- Venn diagrams, graphic organizers, and matrices
- codes to decipher
- rice table or large container with measuring cups and spoons
- pentominoes
- math and logic games and apps

VISUAL-SPATIAL CENTER (ART CENTER)

Visual-spatial learners learn through pictures and through visualizing, designing, drawing, or doodling. Materials for this center might include:

- paints, paintbrushes, and easels
- finger paints
- clay
- cookie cutters or sponges to use with paint for making prints
- markers, crayons, colored pencils, and stamps
- paper in various sizes and colors
- scissors
- scraps of ribbon, fabric, and yarn
- glue, paste, and tape
- old catalogs and magazines
- loads of pictures
- photographs
- mazes
- recyclable materials
- picture puzzles
- artwork displays
- posters
- digital camera
- illustrated books
- maps, charts, and diagrams
- interlocking bricks, such as Legos

- video player and educational videos related to classroom topics
- websites or apps showing famous works of art or museum tours

BODILY-KINESTHETIC CENTER (BUILDING/DRAMA CENTER)

Children with bodily-kinesthetic ability learn through modeling, through hands-on activities, and by *doing*. They love touching, building, and moving; if required to sit for a long time, they often fidget or twitch. A kinesthetic child may accurately mimic other people's gestures and may be regarded as dramatic by other children or adults.

When you observe children playing, you gain a wealth of information about their abilities. It is in a bodily-kinesthetic center that young gifted children often demonstrate their capabilities. They may build complex block structures, use advanced vocabulary, and combine materials in imaginative, inventive ways. They may play roles that imitate real life and solve problems by using their imaginations.

Skills that are addressed in play are skills that will be needed for success in school and in life—cognitive skills such as problem solving, creativity, dealing with abstractions, and acquiring new knowledge; and social skills such as interacting, sharing, and showing consideration, tolerance, and self-control.

Basic equipment for this center might include:

- trucks and cars
- equipment, tools, and materials for crafts such as sewing, woodworking, and mechanics
- large blocks
- interlocking blocks, such as Legos
- cardboard bricks
- dress-up clothes and props for different work, play, ages, and cultures
- a variety of hats
- masks
- kitchen equipment, dishes, pots, and pans
- straws
- tape
- workbench and tools
- dolls representing both genders and a variety of races/ethnic groups
- puppets
- stuffed animals
- manipulatives to sequence
- puzzles

Beyond the basic equipment, materials that extend and enrich information or themes from a large-group discussion give children the opportunity to take information they have learned, explore it, and make connections. At different times, depending on the topic being studied in the class, the kinesthetic center may look like:

- a grocery store with boxes, cans, various containers, a supply of bags, a cash register, and play money
- an undersea world with blue netting, shells, flippers, and goggles
- a campsite with tent, firewood, mess kits, and flashlights
- a tropical forest
- a restaurant, garage, or community gathering place

You may also wish to include holiday and seasonal items in this center. An MP3 player with music that the students can move or dance to is an enjoyable addition, although volume is a consideration in a small, confined room.

INTERPERSONAL CENTER (GROUP CENTER)

The child with interpersonal skills is a "people person." In all centers, look for the child who leads, organizes, mediates, and relates well to other children. Take note of the child who befriends a classmate who is usually alone or who may lack friends, the child who helps others when needed, the child who offers suggestions when warranted, the child who excels in a specific area or in several areas. The interpersonal center is for group activities. Whole-group work and general instruction occur here. Activities might include:

- brainstorming
- cooperative tasks
- collaborative problem solving
- mentoring and apprenticeship
- group games

Author and consultant Carolyn Chapman suggests five rules for this learning center:[6]

1. Use six-inch voices (voices that can be heard no more than six inches away).
2. Listen to others in your group.
3. Stay in the group.

---

6 Adapted from Carolyn Chapman. *If the Shoe Fits: How to Develop Multiple Intelligences in the Classroom* (Palatine, IL: IRI/Skylight Publishing, 1993): 182.

4. Look at the speaker.
5. Don't hurt someone else's feelings.

INTRAPERSONAL CENTER (QUIET CENTER)

Because children with an intrapersonal bent have a strong will and sense of independence, we sometimes regard them as loners. These children know themselves well; they have a sense of both their strengths and their weaknesses and are capable, even at a young age, of expressing their feelings. They are usually quiet and enjoy working alone. For this reason, the intrapersonal area contains desks or carrels for individual work. This area is designated as quiet space for:

- independent assignments
- metacognition (thinking about thinking)
- journals
- self-paced projects
- problem solving
- time alone
- reflection
- writing or typing

NATURALISTIC CENTER (NATURE CENTER)

Children with naturalistic intelligence love to sort, classify, order, and categorize. They love nature—plants, animals, fish, rocks—and the natural order of things. These children enjoy collections of objects from nature as well as those that are not in the natural world. Materials for this center might include:

- a variety of rocks
- seeds, pots, and soil for planting
- garden area (potting soil in suit boxes lined with plastic)
- live animals (fish, hamsters, an ant farm)
- a variety of leaves, fossils, and seeds
- pictures of a variety of plants and trees for classifying and comparing
- pictures of a variety of mammals, reptiles, birds, fish, and insects for classifying and comparing
- a variety of plastic creatures or dinosaur models
- paper and pencils for drawing or recording data
- simple database software

Helping Children Use Learning Centers

Sometimes students can choose centers where they want to work, and other times the teacher may assign students to certain centers. A center may offer a choice of activities in which to engage, or it may have a single assigned activity. In either case, the children should know what is at each center and what they are expected to do for the allocated work time.

Some children will gravitate to certain activity stations and avoid others. To an extent, this is fine; students need opportunities to choose the centers they will work in. All students, however, need to experience all the centers over time and participate at a level appropriate to their ability.

To gain insight into a child's area of intelligence, learning modality, or interest area, ask the child, "What did you do today that you liked?" Note whether the child's response includes writing, singing, counting, drawing, playing, talking, thinking, or observing. Consider, too, what you already know about a child's learning modality. In general:

- *Auditory learners* will gravitate toward the linguistic, logical-mathematical, interpersonal, intrapersonal, or naturalistic centers.
- *Visual learners* will choose the visual-spatial, logical-mathematical, intrapersonal, or naturalistic centers.
- *Tactile-kinesthetic learners* will prefer the bodily-kinesthetic, visual-spatial, musical, or naturalistic centers.

Use this information to guide individual children toward both the learning centers and the types of activities that engage them.

Try to provide choices of approximately three or four activities at each center. All the activities will revolve around the content or theme your class is studying or around students' interests. When you present several options, children will usually choose the activity that is best suited to and most developmentally correct for them. Creativity, communication, and balance are the keys. Keep the activities available until the topic is completed or until children appear bored or restless. They will let you know when it's time for a change.

Structured experiences at each of the centers will give you a chance to observe which children have strengths within which areas. Then you'll be able to provide extended activities in each student's area of strength.

One of the main goals of school is to create lifelong learners. This occurs when children are given the chance to take responsibility for their learning and make decisions. You'll be amazed at the decisions children make about what they want to learn and how they wish to learn it.

Planning Lessons Using Multiple Intelligences and Learning Modalities

When you are creating lessons, feel free to address any skill, instructional outcome, or theme. Students can have their strongest way of learning addressed while working to develop an area of need. Begin by selecting a topic or theme or outcome. Ask yourself how it can be taught in different ways for different types of learners. Select and plan center-based activities from your ideas. Gather materials and carry out your plan. Modify your lessons as needed. Allow children to demonstrate mastery and make choices. Document how children learn and what they are able to do.

Questions and Answers

"How can I create this kind of classroom on my limited budget?"
It may not involve purchasing anything new, but rather rethinking and reorganizing what you already have. Inform parents of your plans and needs; invite them to contribute small and large items for your centers.

Be sure to open your doors to the community. Invite the local press to celebrate your accomplishments and to keep the public informed of the wonderful things your class and school are doing. You might adopt a sponsor in the community. Connect with service organizations, such as Kiwanis or Lion's Club, or with local businesses. Let them be aware of your larger needs. Do they have partnership grants available? Could they donate old computers, tablets, or other devices when they purchase new ones? Do they have scrap materials that could be used for art projects? Or people who could donate time and talent?

"If a bright child is at the head of the class in a subject area, why not let her take it easy and enjoy her success instead of looking for ways to make every moment at school more challenging?"
While children don't need to be challenged *all* the time, they must be challenged *some* of the time. The question you need to ask yourself is this: "What is the child learning?" *All* students deserve

to learn—and no real learning occurs without some struggle. Perseverance is an important skill learned by facing difficulty without giving up. Gifted children can become accustomed to getting the right answer and the top grade with little or no effort. If their work is consistently easy, they learn to equate giftedness with effortlessness. Too many bright children never learn how to study or how to use struggle or failure as a building block rather than a stumbling block. When they eventually encounter hard work (and sooner or later they will), bright children who have not been challenged may give up.

"With children of this age, how can I place greater demands on them intellectually when emotionally they're still so young?"
Children *are* children, even if they sometimes think like miniature adults. Your purpose is not to push children, but to respond to their needs. Young gifted children need the experience of learning. This can be creative and enjoyable for them. It's not a matter of *demanding* more from them, but of *inviting* more—of opening more doors to learning opportunities. This is not pushing, but recognizing and responding to the child's intellectual appetite.

"I know that many schools have all-day kindergarten, but our program is just two hours long. Those hours are so busy and full, there's barely enough time for the planned activities. How can a child fit in extra work under these conditions?"
In this situation, you may need to practice selective abandonment. What is essential? What core curriculum *must* you teach? What can you eliminate? Can you assess whether the children already know some of the information so that you can compact the curriculum? (Compacting is discussed in Chapter 3. See page 41.) Instead of spending one month on

a topic, one week—or even one day—might suffice. You might also consider designing units thematically, including activities from several subject areas. This holistic way of looking at curriculum can help you be more creative and build an environment that offers variety, play, and exploration even though your day is short. Instead of viewing activities as "extra" work, think of them as "instead of" work.

"There's obvious resentment among my first graders toward a highly gifted classmate who finds everything easy. How can I keep the situation from making the others feel bad about themselves?"
Using the multiple intelligences is a wonderful way to alleviate this situation. Gifted or not, all children are good at something! Recognize and build on their strengths. Invite children to share their interests, passions, and areas of expertise. When your students see that their different abilities are valued, their focus is likely to shift away from resentment and toward sharing.

Conclusion

Designing your classroom can be an exciting way to begin your school year. The preschool or early elementary classroom is no place for a one-size-fits-all program. To create an environment that offers a fit for young gifted children, you are called upon to be sensitive, creative, and flexible—and to develop a program that fosters the same qualities in your students. In a classroom brimming with opportunities, special care must still be given to ensure that gifted children find challenge and opportunity to develop their potential.

Help Me Help You

Child's name: _____

Dear Parent/Caregiver:

If you ever have a question or concern about what's happening for your child at school, I hope you'll feel free to contact me personally. I also invite you to let me know about anything happening at home that might affect your child at school.

You can reach me directly during the school day at _____ (phone number)

or by email at _____(email address).

Or, if you like, complete the brief form at the bottom of this sheet, place it in an envelope, and mail or deliver it to me at the school office: _____

_____ (address).

Thank you for keeping the lines of communication open!

Teacher's signature: _____

- cut here ✂- -

To: _____

Date: _____

I would like to talk to you about my child, _____.

I can be reached during the day at _____ (phone number)

or in the evening at _____ (phone number)

or by email at _____(email address).

Comments: _____

_____

_____

Parent/Caregiver's signature: _____

CHAPTER 3
Planning Curriculum and Extending Learning

Will exudes enthusiasm wherever he goes. His loud, energetic curiosity shows that he wants to grab onto all the knowledge he can so he can master his world. In class his hand waves wildly, his mouth is usually open, and his body gyrates. He's consistently the first one done with each assignment, and his work is usually correct—although barely legible. His knowledge extends far beyond the classroom and greatly exceeds expectations for his grade level.

Will's teacher finds it exciting to have this bright, ebullient child in her class. She wants to nurture his enthusiasm for learning. But she also says he wears her out. She's not exactly sure how to keep him occupied productively and not bothering the other children.

Time and the Gifted Child: A Banking Metaphor

Time is like money: it seems precious itself, but its true value lies in what is done with it. Time,

like money, can be spent wisely or wasted. Dr. Joseph Renzulli at the University of Connecticut's Neag Center for Gifted Education and Talent Development suggests that we allow students to "buy back" time we had planned for them to "spend" in one way and let them spend it in a different way.

You can take this metaphor further by imagining a "time bank" in your classroom with individual "checking accounts" and "savings accounts" for children. A child's checking account is the amount of time that child needs to learn basic information—time spent in whole-group instruction and activities. Some children will need more or less time in their individual checking accounts. A child's savings account is the time that child saves by documenting knowledge of the basic information. You need to ask yourself:

- How will I know who has some savings?
- How will children spend their savings?
- How will I organize the curriculum so children's savings yield the best "returns"?

How Will You Know Who Has Savings?

How can you tell who has savings, or who knows the content that you are about to teach? Certain strategies can give you information about students' knowledge. You may look at past work or projects, interviews, testing information, portfolios, videos of the children with their creations or books they read, parent perceptions, and dynamic assessments (if any of these are available). These forms of documentation can help you identify and evaluate prior knowledge.

How Will Children Spend Their Savings?

Once you have confirmed that students have advanced skills in one or several areas, you need to consider how best the children can build on these skills. Observing the children—the learning centers they choose, what they do there, and how they do it—will assist you in providing appropriate options on which children can spend their savings. (Chapter 2 discusses setting up learning centers to accommodate children's individual learning modalities. See page 34.)

Observe the child's interests and behavior. One good indicator of a child's abilities is how the student spends free time. What does the child do with choice time? Does the student gravitate toward books or the computer or tablet? Build with blocks? Act out a story? Solve puzzles? Work math problems? Draw or paint? Socialize?

If a student can read and write, you may wish to ask the child to complete the "What I Like" interest survey (pages 49–50). Explain that the child can read each entry on the first page of the handout and circle the preferred options. On the second page, the child can write or draw a picture about something he or she is especially good at. To use the form with a child who is not yet reading, an adult can read the entries aloud and assist as needed in completing the form. This form provides another way to look at the child's strengths and interests.

Observe the child's misbehavior. Misbehavior can also provide valuable information about the child's abilities. Does the child:

- Blurt out answers and speak out of turn? The child may be an auditory learner and may need to talk about the topic in order to process the information.
- Daydream or seem spacey? This might mean the child is visualizing ideas.
- Repeatedly ask, "Why?" The child could be digging for deeper meaning or wanting to know causes and effects.
- Fidget or have trouble sitting still? The child may be a kinesthetic learner and may need something to touch or may need frequent movement breaks.

Sasha was in constant motion. When she moved down the hall, she would bounce from one wall to the other. During group time, she simply could not sit still; she moved around the floor touching everyone and everything. Her teacher, Mr. Nguyen, tried keeping her next to him while he taught. Sasha sat more quietly then, but later, when her teacher asked her questions about the lesson, she recalled very little.

One day, after teaching a new math concept while allowing Sasha to move around as much as she wished, Mr. Nguyen quizzed her on the lesson content. Sasha's responses told him that she had heard and recalled nearly all of the lesson. Realizing that Sasha was a kinesthetic learner, he decided to teach math to her and some of the other "movers and shakers" using music and movement. The results were revealing: within a few days, the children had mastered math facts that many had struggled with when taught in traditional ways.

As this example illustrates, sometimes we can learn about children's strengths by paying attention to what they're telling us in moments of "weakness."

Don't forget the parents. Parents have a wealth of information about their children that they can share with you. You stand the best chance of developing an ongoing dialogue and winning cooperation when you communicate with parents in a variety of ways—through letters, phone calls, emails, texts, social media, and in-school activities. Chapters 1 and 2 include family letters and forms to assist you in communicating with parents. Chapter 9 provides more information about enlisting parents' support.

How Will You Organize the Curriculum?

First, you need to understand the children in your classroom. Who are they? What are their strengths and weaknesses? Next, you need to balance this understanding with your curriculum. What are your students expected to know and be able to do as a result of being in your class? What skills are they supposed to learn? What are the Common Core State Standards (CCSS) or other state standards that apply to your grade level? How do these standards align with the regular school or district curriculum?

With knowledge of both the content standards and your students' needs, you are ready to organize curriculum. Plan curriculum with the end in mind. That is: What do you want the children to know and be able to do? What goals do you have for each child? What outcomes do you strive to reach? How will you know if the children already have specific knowledge or skills? If students demonstrate that they already know and understand the content, they don't need to relearn it; instead, determine the best next step for each child. Now you can differentiate instruction by *compacting the curriculum* and *extending learning.*

Compacting lets you individualize one or more parts of the curriculum to facilitate and challenge gifted children's learning. When you compact, you compress your basic curriculum into a smaller time frame, thus adding time to the child's savings account. The idea is to compress the essentials, making sure skills are mastered and concepts understood without belaboring or excessively repeating what the child already knows and can do. You compact only in those areas that represent the student's strengths.

You might begin by looking at assignments you give to reinforce what the child knows. These can include practice work, center time, and group work that focus on skill development. If children already know how to do the work or have mastered the skill, they may not need the skill-and-drill practice other children in your class require. Ask gifted children to demonstrate that they can do the work by completing just a few of the problems. Use discussion, observation, or testing to confirm that children have the skill. If they do, they're ready to move on to other activities.

Then you'll want to provide extensions—opportunities to extend and expand learning in the area of strength. Extensions are meant to be "instead of" work, rather than "more of the same" work.

Extending Curriculum for Young Children Working in Groups

All children benefit from having time to work with others as well as having time to work alone. Neither type of work means that the work the students are doing is the same for all. Even if the students are all studying the same topic, their work can vary in content, process, and product. The following options for group work may help you vary the choices for your students and extend learning for those who are gifted.

Tiered Groups

Instead of having every group do the same activity, differentiate instruction by varying the assignments. You can plan three or more tasks that revolve around the same content but differ in difficulty and complexity. This works particularly well in the classroom that has a wide spread in ability. Group children according to the level of mastery they have achieved. Be flexible in placing children in skill groups. You can change the makeup of the groups to fit the lesson content and the needs of the children.

In *reading*, one group of first graders might be working on letter recognition, another on combining letters to make new words, and a third on writing stories. A fourth group (or even a single child) can be reading independently.

In *spelling*, one group might be learning their words while a second group is using the words to write sentences. A third group might be creating a word search, and a child who is exceptionally advanced could be using a thesaurus to look for synonyms and then composing sentences or rewriting nursery rhymes with the new words.

You can also form tiered groups based on children's *abstract thinking* development. In teaching a lesson on money, this might mean that some children count pennies while others learn the values of different coins. Those children who already know this information could set up a play store, decide which coins could purchase chosen items from a catalog, or practice making change.

In *math*, children who have not yet been exposed to numbers might work on some one-to-one correspondence. Those who are familiar with numbers might do simple addition problems. The children who know how to work addition problems could learn about subtraction. The most knowledgeable children may be ready to learn how to regroup with multidigit numbers.

Interest Groups

At times, you may discover that several children have a similar interest in a particular topic. Once they have mastered the required content, you can allow them to work as a group to pursue that interest. Interest groups encourage conversation and discussion among members. Groups may form to work on a particular puzzle for a day or longer, to research a question that they want answered on a common topic, or to read and share stories on a topic.

Interest groups in reading might focus on a particular author or area of reading, such as fairy tales, bears in literature, or mystery stories, or on a reading activity such as crossword puzzles. In math, interest groups may work with puzzles, tangrams, pentominoes, attribute blocks, number squares, sudoku, graphing, mazes, dot-to-dot puzzles, and so forth. Science interest groups might include favorite topics such as dinosaurs, astronomy, and animals.

The "Tic-Tac-Toe Menu" (page 51) works well as a planning tool for interest groups. The menu on the handout is a model that you may want to adapt. The sample menu shown here illustrates how you can use this tool with a group of students to extend learning after reading or listening to two familiar stories: *Blueberries for Sal* by Robert McCloskey and the fairy tale *Goldilocks and the Three Bears*.

USING THE TIC-TAC-TOE MENU WITH GROUPS OF STUDENTS

1. Create—or help each group create—a menu of possible activities.
2. Select activities that you believe meet the children's interests and abilities and write the activities in the menu format. Children may provide input.
3. If you wish, leave some blank spaces in the menu and invite the children to think of and write down other related activities they would like to pursue.

TIC-TAC-TOE MENU IDEAS

Here are some options you may want to incorporate in your own tic-tac-toe menus:

- sorting, classifying
- sequencing
- counting
- logic puzzles
- board games
- computer or tablet apps such as those from eLearning Industry and Edutopia (See "References and Resources," page 191.)
- working with a clock or stopwatch
- charts, graphs, diagrams
- science materials, equipment

- manipulatives
- calculators
- brain teasers
- mental math calculations
- problem-solving situations
- creating codes or decoding messages
- using play money, making change
- Venn diagrams
- mental mapping
- attribute blocks
- tangrams
- pentominoes
- twenty questions
- polls, surveys
- hidden pictures
- mazes
- constructing, building
- kaleidoscopes
- optical illusions
- visualization

SAMPLE TIC-TAC-TOE MENU:
BLUEBERRIES FOR SAL AND GOLDILOCKS AND THE THREE BEARS

For Students

Tic-Tac-Toe Menu

1.	2.	3.
Write a new ending to either story.	Make a chart that shows how the bears are alike in the stories and how they are different.	Tell another person one of the stories in your own words.
4.	**5.**	**6.**
Ask other students which story they liked best.	Describe how the bears in both stories compare to real-life bears.	Act out one of the stories.
7.	**8.**	**9.**
Compare and contrast the two stories.	Make a poster or video to advertise your favorite bear story.	Find out where bears live on your continent. Show their location on a map.

We choose activities #_____, #_____, #_____, and #_____

Names: _____ Date: _____

_____

_____

- picture library
- picture metaphors
- photography
- video recording
- color wheels
- using telescopes, microscopes, binoculars, magnifying glasses
- color coding
- keeping a sketchbook
- cartoons
- drawing
- doodling
- modeling with clay
- play experiences
- puppets, miniatures, stuffed animals
- simulations
- crafts
- creating collages
- pantomime
- relaxation exercises
- creating letters of the alphabet with the body
- communicating with hand signals
- creative movement
- blocks
- learning through music, rhythm
- using singing to learn facts
- time to learn musical notation or to play an instrument
- playing music on a keyboard, tablet, or computer with earphones
- creating melodies
- chanting
- mentorship with older children or adults
- organizing an event
- cooperative learning
- teaching a peer
- team projects
- reading in pairs
- small group discussion
- simulations
- sharing knowledge, experiences with peers
- group brainstorming
- buddy system
- cross-age tutoring
- thinking, explaining from different points of view
- allowing for discussion on a topic
- keeping a log or journal
- writing stories
- creating role plays
- websites such as Education.com and Iowa Public Television (See "References and Resources," page

191. Please review any website you suggest to make sure it is appropriate for your student and relevant to the content you wish to teach.)

Branching

Branching encourages children to explore content through different disciplines, themes, and learning modalities. It provides richness and depth. For instance, instead of just looking at autumn leaves, examine the process of photosynthesis. Note changes that different seasons bring. When teaching about color, introduce primary and secondary colors. Look at the color wheel. Examine cool and warm colors. Discuss shades and hues.

Discuss and explore more than the basic colors; for example, when discussing red, introduce ruby, scarlet, cerise, russet, and crimson. Look at artwork by Wassily Kandinsky. Read *The Red Balloon* by Albert Lamorisse. Create or follow a recipe to make a dish that's red. Estimate the number of dried red beans in a container. Brainstorm things that are red: sunburn, blood, chili peppers, apples, tomatoes, ketchup, cardinals, ladybugs, stop signs, and so on. When you're discussing blue, explore navy blue, aqua blue, sky blue, powder blue, royal blue, and periwinkle. Listen to blues music. Look at a painting in the *Blue Dog* series by George Rodrigue. Talk about what it means to feel blue and what makes you feel blue. Read *Blueberries for Sal*. Estimate the number of blueberries in a pint container.

Extending Curriculum for Young Children Working Independently

Of course, you can initiate branching with individual instruction as well as with group instruction. Here are some other suggestions to extend learning for children who are working independently.

Point of View

This is an extension that fits easily into any literature study. Upon reviewing a story, you may discover that one or two students already know it well. They can tell you in detail what happens and when. These children don't need to hear or read the story again unless they would like to.

While the class reviews the story, give a child who is already familiar with it the chance to consider it from a different point of view. For example, if Cinderella's stepmother told Cinderella's story, how would it be different? If the troll told *The Three Billy Goats Gruff*, what would it say? If Little Red Riding Hood lived in the inner city, who would she visit? What dangers might she face? Who might save her? Who might she save? If you could rewrite Judith Viorst's *Alexander and the Terrible, Horrible, No Good, Very Bad Day* as *Alexander and the Super, Wonderful, Terrific, Very Good Day*, what would it be like?

If a child has difficulty writing, let the student record ideas orally instead, using a computer with a microphone, a tablet, or a digital recorder. The child can illustrate the story while playing back the recording.

Resident Expert

For primary gifted students who already know most of the information in a unit of study, independent study aimed at becoming "resident experts" may be the answer.[1] These students need the flexibility to explore an area of interest. Given the chance to satisfy their curiosity, they're likely to cover a vast amount of information.

Inform parents when their children are working on alternative assignments to become resident experts. Help parents understand that such projects are their children's work, not theirs. This work is an opportunity for their children to extend their learning and explore new information as well as the format for reporting it. If young children need parental help, suggest that the children offer to "pay" parents for their help by doing a household task such as setting or clearing the table, putting the dishes away after they are washed, sorting and folding clothes, emptying wastebaskets, taking out garbage, and so on.

STEPS TO BECOMING A RESIDENT EXPERT

1. Interview or observe the student to determine the child's preferred learning modality.
2. Help the student find or refine a topic to explore. (You may wish to use the "What I Like" form on pages 49–50.) Prompt the child to think about where to find information on the chosen topic. For example, the student might read, search the Internet, talk to people, take a field trip with a parent, or conduct interviews or experiments. Help the child find and collect books and other materials about the topic.
3. Provide a space for the student to keep and use the materials.
4. Encourage the child to look through the research materials during free time.
5. Give the student a copy of the "My Plan to Become an Expert" form (page 52) and demonstrate how to write ideas for "what I want to learn about" and "how I will learn."
6. As the child goes through possibilities and materials, meet with the child to discuss them.
7. Ask the student to select one topic or area of interest.
8. Help the child make a plan to assemble information and share it with the rest of the class. As this plan firms up, demonstrate how to write it in the "how I can share" section of the form.
9. Schedule meetings with the student to check progress.
10. Help the child plan and deliver a presentation of the project.

To clearly establish expectations and goals, develop a contract with the child. Your contract will depend on the topic and the degree of independence and understanding the student has. Help the child determine realistic goals for the research, the product, and the approximate date the product will be complete. Make the end date somewhat flexible. (A word of caution: If the project takes too long, the child may lose interest.) Check in daily to see how the child is progressing. You'll find sample "Resident Expert Contracts" for younger and older children on page 47 and reproducible versions of these contracts on pages 53 and 54.

Tic-Tac-Toe Interest Areas

The "Tic-Tac-Toe Menu" (page 51) is a helpful model for planning and carrying out independent study as well as for group study.

USING THE TIC-TAC-TOE MENU WITH INDIVIDUAL STUDENTS

1. At the bottom of the form, cross out the word *We* and write *I*.

---

[1] The concept of a resident expert and the steps to becoming one are adapted from *Teaching Gifted Kids in Today's Classroom* by Susan Winebrenner with Dina Brulles, (Minneapolis: Free Spirit Publishing Inc., 2012): 76, 171. Used with permission.

2. Create or help the child create a menu of possible activities.
3. Ask the child to select activities from the menu and write those choices on the form.
4. If you wish, leave some blank spaces and invite the child to think of and write down other related activities the child would like to pursue.

Trust the Student

Independent study projects can be relatively unstructured. Trust that gifted children will use independent study time productively. They are learning that school is a place where they can be passionate—where they have the opportunity to learn a great deal about topics that interest them and to develop their intelligence and creativity.

Documenting Mastery and Planning Extensions

To document children's strengths and plan learning extensions, you will want to keep records of your observations and your plans. The form on page 55, "Plan for Compacting and Extending the Curriculum," provides a model you may wish to use or adapt.

Remember: Parents need to be kept informed about what you are doing in the classroom. One teacher's experience tells a valuable story:

It didn't occur to the teacher to tell students' parents what she was doing the first year she tried compacting. One parent noticed that his child had very few papers. When he asked his daughter what she did in school, the child responded, "I play." This activated the rumor mill, and a group of parents went to the administration wanting to know why the teacher wasn't teaching their children the same things.

Before you begin compacting and extending the curriculum, send home a letter explaining what you'll be doing and inviting input from parents. If you wish, use the "I Thought You'd Like to Know" family letter (page 56). Once parents know what's happening in the classroom, most are comfortable—even impressed—with what their children are doing and learning.

FOR YOUNGER CHILDREN

For Students
Resident Expert Contract

Name: _Joe_
I want to learn about: _teeth because I lost one_

I will make this: _model of a tooth_

I will have it ready by: _Friday_

Student's signature: _Joe Milnes_   _October 11_ Date
Teacher's signature: _Mr. LaFrenz_   _October 11_ Date
Parent's signature: _Elaine Robb_   _October 11_ Date

FOR OLDER CHILDREN

For Students
Resident Expert Contract

Name: _Sandy_
I want to learn about: _poisonous snakes_ (topic or subject)
I will need/use these materials and equipment: _books, trip to the zoo, camera, computer, conduct interviews, maps_

The product I will make is: _model snake (papier-mâché) with map where it lives and story of what it does, what it eats, where it lives_

I will have the product ready by: _2 weeks_ (approximate date)
Student's signature: _Sandy Ramirez_   _October 11_ Date
Teacher's signature: _Ms. Linse_   _October 11_ Date
Parent's signature: _Ray Ramirez_   _October 11_ Date

Questions and Answers

"Isn't it better to wait until the child is older to begin compacting?"

When you being compacting and extending the curriculum in preschool or kindergarten, children learn early on how to work independently and manage their time. They become enthusiastic about school, rather than bored and frustrated by continually doing what they already know.

"Jocelyn doesn't seem able to work independently, and she disturbs the other children. What can I do?"

First, make sure that Jocelyn understands what her options are and that she has all the supplies, materials, and resources she needs. Go over work rules with her, being clear and firm about your expectations. Make certain that she fully understands her task. Also, make a point of spending time with Jocelyn. Even though she has advanced abilities, she still needs your attention as much as the other children do. If her disruptive behavior continues, contact her parents for additional insight and support.

"I group flexibly by ability. Is it still necessary for me to compact the curriculum?"

Yes! Even within a group of high-ability children, you will find differences in learning rates and interests. By compacting what each child already knows or can learn easily, you help meet each child's individual needs.

"What if the child does nothing during 'instead of' time?"

Many children have much of their days scheduled for them, both in and out of school. They may have experienced little or no free, unstructured time and may not know how to manage it productively. Offer these children a wide selection of choices. You may need to explain that doing nothing is not an option.

"If I don't cover every item in our curriculum, isn't there a danger that the child will miss something?"

It is important that children master the objectives, not simply make their way through a textbook or other curriculum resources. In fact, many children who do work through a resource page by page still don't master the material. Textbooks and other resources are tools for presenting and reviewing information, one vehicle by which students can learn. If the child has already learned what is in the resource, it's inappropriate to use it with that child.

"Won't compacting, extending, and documenting require a lot of extra time?"

This strategy does front-load your instruction. But it makes *more effective* use of time overall. Assessing what the child knows, documenting it, and selecting alternative activities saves time later in fewer papers to correct, fewer discipline problems, and fewer disruptions. Teaching becomes less time-consuming as you become comfortable with this strategy.

"Should I start with one student or a group?"

In some cases, it may be easier for you to start with one student who is really advanced and would benefit from compacting. In other cases, students may feel more comfortable if they begin with a group, so that no one is singled out. Which strategy you choose depends on several factors. What space do you have? How comfortable are you with each option? How many different types of extension activities do you have? Do you have the support of the administration? Is the media center available? Do you have parent helpers or a classroom paraprofessional?

Conclusion

Looking at the different ways children learn and demonstrate their knowledge can help you identify compacting and extension opportunities for both group and independent study. It's hard to let go and trust young children to use their time wisely. But by providing these opportunities, you open the door for gifted children to be passionate about a subject, to explore it by a variety of avenues, and to present their findings in ways that take them beyond traditional paper-and-pencil tasks.

What I Like

My name:_____

Circle all the things you like:

I like to count.

I like to make patterns.

I like colors.

I like to draw.

I like to build things.

I like to invent things.

I like to explore things on the Web.

I like to dance and move.

I like to act out plays.

I like music.

I like to sing.

I like books.

I like to listen to stories.

I like to be with other kids..

I like to work alone.

I like to collect things.

I like to help others with their problems.

I like to sort and arrange things.

I like to play video games.

Use this page to write or draw a picture about something you are good at.

Tic-Tac-Toe Menu

1.	2.	3.
4.	5.	6.
7.	8.	9.

We choose activities #_____ ,#_____ ,#_____ , and #_____

Names: _____ Date: _____

_____

_____

_____

My Plan to Become an Expert

Name: _____

Subject: _____ Date: _____

Here's what I want to learn about:

Here's how I will learn:

Here's how I can share this with the class:

Student's signature: _____ Date: _____

Teacher's signature: _____ Date: _____

Parent's signature: _____ Date: _____

Resident Expert Contract

Name: _____

I want to learn about: _____

_____

_____

_____

_____

_____

I will make this: _____

_____

_____

_____

_____

I will have it ready by: _____

Student's signature: _____
                                                            Date

Teacher's signature: _____
                                                            Date

Parent's signature: _____
                                                            Date

Resident Expert Contract

Name: _____

I want to learn about: _____
(topic or subject)

I will need/use these materials and equipment: _____

_____

_____

_____

The product I will make is: _____

_____

_____

_____

I will have the product ready by: _____
(approximate date)

Student's signature: _____
Date

Teacher's signature: _____
Date

Parent's signature: _____
Date

Plan for Compacting and Extending the Curriculum

Student's name: _____

Learning Objective

_____

_____

Level of Mastery

Date demonstrated: _____

How demonstrated: _____

_____

_____

_____

_____

Strengths

Preferred intelligences or learning modalities: _____

_____

_____

Other strengths: _____

_____

_____

Extension Options

_____

_____

_____

_____

For Parents

I Thought You'd Like to Know

Child's name: _____

Dear Parent/Caregiver:

I want to let you know about something exciting we're doing in class.

Because some children already know some of the material we're covering, and some children learn new material more quickly than others, I'm giving students the chance to do "instead of" activities. If they can show me that they've mastered an idea or a skill that I'm teaching, then they can work on other projects and assignments for a period of time. These "instead of" activities are meant to keep school interesting and challenging for all students.

I know that parents are sometimes concerned if they hear that their child isn't doing the same work as other children in the class. That's why I wanted to let you know about the "instead of" activities. If you have any questions, be sure to stop by, email, or call.

Teacher's signature: _____

Phone: _____

Email: _____

CHAPTER 4
Promoting Creativity, Discovery, and Critical Thinking in the Social Studies Curriculum

Maya is seven years old. She loves geography. When her grandmother and cousins journeyed up to Chicago from Mexico, she wanted to follow their route on the map. Maya asked her cousins about the places they stayed at, the cities and towns they traveled through, and the animals, foods, and smells they encountered. She created her own map and traced their journey, complete with little sketches and notes on the green hills they traveled through; the roadrunner, eagle, and coyotes they saw; the skunk they smelled; the pink hotel run by a banjo player; and the diner where they ate eggs and grits for breakfast.

Children love to investigate new geographic environments, cultures, and wildlife, all of which give them fresh opportunities for exploration and discovery. Imagination and curiosity emerge in the earliest years of childhood, leading children to a deeper understanding of the world around them. In our early childhood and primary classrooms, we can draw on the same creative process our students have used

outside of school to keep learning alive for them—to make it interactive, participatory, and stimulating.

Creative Learning and Critical Thinking

This chapter and the next two chapters focus on creativity as the natural way young children learn. Creativity is fundamental to enabling all students, including gifted children, to expand their learning beyond prescribed standards or curricula. The approach presented here can inspire and encourage higher-level thinking in *all* your students while simultaneously providing incentives and opportunities for your gifted ones. Your goals are to help children:

- use creativity (including the arts) as a channel for critical thinking and research
- explore a range of subjects creatively and make discoveries they might not ordinarily reach

- make connections between their imaginative work and real-world contexts
- become participants in and contributors to a subject, rather than passive spectators or recipients

We're using creative thinking in a special way here—as a link to intellectual discovery. Activities that call on children's imagination and creativity can do more than jazz up the curriculum. You can use creativity *as a means to promote critical thinking and discovery.* Creative thinking stimulates children's curiosity to discover the world in ways that other methods don't.

In addition, creative thinking enables young children to make personal contributions to whatever subjects they undertake. This is an important dimension of learning, especially for talented students. If we expect gifted children to contribute to the world in meaningful ways, we need to nurture their creative potential and their confidence that they can make a difference. Students who have a "growth mindset"—who believe that everyone can change and grow through effort—are more likely to succeed, according to Stanford University psychology researcher and professor Dr. Carol Dweck. She urges adults to stress for children the link between willingness to work hard and achievement of goals.[1] The classroom is the ideal place for this process to begin. (For more information on mindset, see Chapter 10, page 154.)

The Creativity Challenge

Primary school teachers who want to use creativity in the classroom face greater challenges today than ever before. The Common Core State Standards (CCSS) and high-stakes testing can hamper the more open style of teaching and learning used in many kindergarten through third-grade classrooms. Values that have long been the hallmark of teaching young children—play, child-centered and hands-on learning, imagination, and so forth—have given way to a new mindset emphasizing core skills and knowledge. This emphasis, though intended to develop students' knowledge base, skills, and thinking abilities at a deeper level than previous methods allowed, has encouraged a phenomenon called curriculum narrowing in which other disciplines, such as the social studies and the arts, retreat into the background. This is a disappointing and debilitating prospect for young learners of all ability levels, who come to school so hungry for new adventures in learning about the world around them. Certainly, children need core skills and knowledge at the level CCSS and other standards outline, but children need to experience these skills and knowledge as part of a larger journey—as tools for discovery, invention, and imagination.

Creative teaching approaches ensure that young children's learning not only includes the standards but also expands *beyond* them. Teachers sometimes feel unqualified to do anything too creative or artistic and resist the prospect of more work added to an already full schedule. Primary school teachers may be forgetting that they are already among the most inventive professionals in the field; they are constantly thinking on their feet, improvising with materials, and orchestrating class activities to meet different needs. It may help to remember that creative improvisation is already part of their job—and also that in these chapters, creativity is not an add-on to the curriculum but the means through which teachers teach and children learn core knowledge and skills. It is the means through which you can inspire greater and more meaningful discovery, unique expression, and critical and original thinking in all your students.

Creative Processes for Classroom Use

E. Paul Torrance, a pioneer in the study of creative thinking, describes four basic components of creative thinking that we use as a guide for teaching young children: *fluency, flexibility, originality,* and *elaboration.*[2] To this list we have added *evaluation*—an element we feel brings an important dimension to creative work. The "Taxonomy of Creative Thinking" table on page 59 gives examples of how you might use these five components in your classroom.

Fluency: In creative expression, fluency is the ability to produce many ideas with ease. We encourage fluency when we ask students to respond to problems or assignments by producing an abundance of ideas.

Flexibility: Flexible thinkers view problems or assignments from different angles—often ones that

---

[1] Carol S. Dweck. *Mindset: The New Psychology of Success: How We Can Learn to Fulfill Our Potential* (New York: Ballantine Books, 2006): 6–7. This book introduces the positive psychology approach and provides research, examples, and strategies to help readers use a growth mindset.

[2] E. Paul Torrance. *The Search for Satori and Creativity* (Buffalo, NY: Creative Education Foundation, 1979). Used with permission of E. Paul Torrance.

are unconventional or untried—and march to the beat of their own drumming. We encourage flexibility when we invite students to think of alternative ideas and solutions.

Originality: Original thinking is highly innovative and unique. Students often use fluency and flexibility in the early stages of their work; to foster originality, we encourage them to discover ideas and concepts uniquely their own.

Elaboration: With elaboration, students add details to make their ideas more useful and practical. More than a mere extension of creative work, elaboration often requires students to use fluency, flexibility, and originality to develop concepts beyond the idea stage.

Evaluation: Evaluation is an ongoing process of analysis, investigation, experimentation, and synthesis. As students evaluate their own work, they exercise judgment; analyze the different parts of their idea; see what does and doesn't work; consider new adjustments, refinements, and developments; and then reintegrate these new or changed parts into the whole.

As you can see, these five components often overlap. It's never easy to contain creativity within artificially imposed parameters. Nevertheless, you can still emphasize different mental processes at different points in your work with your class. We recommend that you use whatever ideas most readily apply to your students and to the subject area. As new possibilities emerge, both your students and you will be rewarded.

A Map of Creative Activities

Within your social studies curriculum, you can develop lessons and activities so all students can participate, learn creatively, and learn at their own level. Include advanced activities and opportunities that appeal to high-ability children while guiding the rest of the class in the more fundamental processes of creative work. In the end, you will inspire all your children to shift into more advanced thinking as they engage in the projects that interest them.

If you are in a school that is actively implementing CCSS or other rigorous standards, you may feel concerned that creative work will divert the class from what students need to learn in core subjects. To resolve this tension, begin the process with the learning goals of a lesson or unit and explore how creativity can address the diverse learning needs in

Taxonomy of Creative Thinking				
Category	*Focus*	*Process*	*Example*	*Outcome*
Fluency	Generate many ideas.	Free association; brainstorming	Children name different ways animals can help people.	An abundance of ideas for creative work
Flexibility	Think of alternatives to the conventional.	Imagining; integrating subjects	Children imagine some other unusual ways animals *could* help people.	Alternative, divergent ideas; limitations overcome
Originality	Conceive innovations unique to context.	Reviewing alternatives; imagining; combining	Children use their ideas to create a unique solution for a species (wild or tame) that is in need.	Highly novel, unique ideas
Elaboration	Extend new ideas: provide details for application.	Testing; analyzing; synthesizing	Children expand on their idea; explore whether/how it might work.	Ideas tailored to fit new contexts
Evaluation	Assess performance; examine gaps; exercise judgment.	Analyzing; comparing; experimenting; fine-tuning	Children compare their idea with actual current practices; they analyze strengths and weaknesses, anticipate problems, and make adjustments.	New perspectives on ideas and application

Adapted from E. Paul Torrance, *The Search for Satori and Creativity*. Buffalo, NY: Creative Education Foundation, 1979. Used with permission of E. Paul Torrance.

your classroom. Creativity can enable more students to reach and exceed the goals of CCSS. Here are some questions to consider as you think about how you can make best practical use of creativity and the arts in your curriculum.

- What fundamental concepts and skills do all students need to master in this class or unit?
- What learning modalities, experiences, and strengths do your students have that would lend themselves to a creative or arts-based activity?
- How could creativity (for example, divergent thinking, imagining, art making, art interpretation, or diverse materials and media) best enable students to master and exceed required concepts and skills?
- In what ways would creativity advance learning for all students, including gifted ones?
- What activities engage young learners and enable them to make discoveries and form new ideas? Do the students enjoy moving? Interpreting visual images? Doing things with their hands? Imagining they are someone else? Imagining they are somewhere else? Brainstorming ideas? Expressing their knowledge in costumes, sketches, or short poems?

As you read this chapter and consider how to use these ideas and suggestions in your classroom, we recommend that you:

1. Start a creative thinking process as soon as the class has some general knowledge of a topic; this will equip students to embark on more creative explorations.
2. Treat the examples on the following pages as creative project ideas that align with standards and learning goals and also inspire the children to work at a higher level of thinking.
3. Read through the detailed description of each process to gain an overview of how it works and how you might adapt it to your own classroom.
4. If you prefer, focus on specific activities within a process and extract segments that seem most responsive to the academic needs and abilities of the children in your classroom.
5. Use the ideas offered here as a guide to create alternative learning experiences in other subjects.

In other words, we hope the chapters ignite your own creativity and that you feel free to improvise!

Fluency: Imagining Environmental Solutions

Jackson loved everything about this unit on endangered species. He liked how his teacher brought to class a friend dressed in brown fur who introduced himself as a wombat—and not just a wombat, but a hairy-nosed wombat. The teacher had the class ask the wombat questions. Where did he live? How big was he? (This was funny, as the teacher had taken out her ruler and said, "Well, this wombat isn't quite the right size.") What did he use his claws for? What did he eat? And most importantly, why was he endangered? Jackson loved the words—marsupials, herbivores, burrowing mammals, and so on. He wanted to learn everything he possibly could about wombats and other endangered animals. His enthusiasm for researching them far outstripped that of his classmates.

The teacher's imaginative introduction to wombats caught Jackson's interest, but he eventually became frustrated with the pace and level of the class. By incorporating the process of fluency, Jackson's teacher could invite him to delve into the study of disappearing animal species more broadly and deeply.

In *fluency*, you ask children to generate as many ideas as possible, even outrageous ones. The focus at this point is on quantity, not quality. Gifted children like Jackson may enjoy the shift from gathering already established facts to generating their own ideas. The more you encourage your students and acknowledge the ideas they offer (recording each one on the board), the more eager they will be to take greater risks and use their own imaginations.

1. SET THE STAGE

Ask the children to choose an endangered animal species *they* would like to explore in class. When possible, offer a few choices and concentrate on a specific geographic area. This will allow students some choices and at the same time deepen their understanding of a region and its ecologies. Some teachers like to build environments and allow students to add what they've discovered about the various fauna and flora. Be sure to have plenty of resources available for them to use once they make their selection.[3] Find a high-quality source that you can use to reinforce basic concepts and

---

[3] You'll find some resources related to the activities discussed in this chapter in the "References and Resources" section beginning on page 189, in Appendix B beginning on page 217, and in Appendix C beginning on page 227.

inspire interest in the creatures and their world. An excellent and stunningly rendered one is Steve Jenkins's *Almost Gone: The World's Rarest Animals*. This book's vivid display of little-known creatures, together with concise descriptions of their habitats, food sources, and threats to survival, is sure to spark the curiosity of your young students, including the gifted ones. Though the subject may be sad for some sensitive students, the book offers hope in its descriptions of habitats and animals protected by human effort.

We recommend that you choose sources on the basis of their ability to inspire interest, communicate main concepts clearly, and engage children in many ways—through their senses, intellect, imagination, art, language, and so forth. For example, you might choose:

- books with vivid photographs and paintings
- short videos or films for children that give a direct impression of the animal and its circumstances
- fictional stories, poems, and pictures—anything that provides images, impressions, and facts about an animal
- animal posters that include factual information
- environmental sound recordings
- maps
- resources available via software, apps, or Web downloads

For older children or gifted children with advanced abilities, provide more challenging materials.

Give the children time to respond to these stimuli through discussion, acting, drawing, or writing. Ask questions such as these:

1. What are the needs of your animal species? What is its habitat? Its food? Its shelter?
2. What are the greatest threats to your species?
3. What kinds of threats are these? Are they environmental (such as pollution or loss of habitat)? Are they predatory (such as being hunted, fished, or trapped for food or other human needs or wants)?
4. Why is your animal important to other flora and fauna? (This is a question for more advanced students.) Here are a few examples: bees struggling to survive are indispensable for food production; moose, whose numbers are in serious decline in some states, create nesting material for birds through foraging; wolves reintroduced to Yellowstone National Park have had a beneficial impact on the rivers and life around them.

These questions can turn the children toward identifying both the sources of the animals' problems and the *types* of threats to survival faced by the species.

2. GENERATE SOLUTIONS

The children can now generate their own solutions—ideas for saving their animal species. You could start them off by saying something like this: "Now that you've explored the problem a little, imagine that you have all the power, money, and people in the world to help this animal. Anything at all is possible to you. What would you do?"

Animal Interviews

To help children organize their thoughts, you could have them pretend to be their animals and interview them about the habitats they live in, the types of food they eat, and some of the wonderful words they've learned. (Young children love saying things like "I am a small marsupial and omnivore from Australia.") Younger students can draw the animals, the different foods, and the environment. Students skilled in reading and writing may describe more features of the species they've chosen, how it fits in with others, and what problems they are having in their habitat.

Current Solutions

Young children need to learn about some of the solutions people have created to assist endangered or threatened species. Many existing solutions came from creative minds. For example, people use large puppets to raise young whooping cranes in captivity, and people teach the young cranes the proper migratory routes by piloting small aircraft in the shape of birds. They also work on breeding programs and habitat conservation. In a similar vein, volunteers who want to save migratory birds from crashing into glass buildings have changed the policies of some cities, which now dim all lights during migration, saving thousands of birds' lives. Others rehabilitate injured migratory birds, releasing them to safer areas to continue their journey.

To stimulate fluency, be open to both probable solutions and improbable ones. One child might wish to start a website on the plight of the monarch butterfly, where elementary students can share projects to address the problem. Another child might want to create a monarch sanctuary full of milkweed to help prevent extinction or might want to start a milkweed growing campaign from Canada to Mexico.

Imagination Exercises

Children who aren't used to fluency activities may need encouragement. Asking them to pretend they are a member of the species they have chosen is an especially useful encouragement strategy. Identifying with an animal is effortless for young children, and it will help them grasp the animal's needs and problems. After you've asked a child to pretend to be the chosen animal, offer one or more of the following activities.

Describe the animal's life. Say, "Tell us about your *habitat*. Where do you live? How do you feel about your home? Tell us about your animal community. What is your *flock or pack or herd or colony* like? What do you love about being this animal? How do you protect your young? How do you look after one another? How do you work together to find food?"

Create artworks. Invite children to draw a picture, create a collage, or collaborate with others to make a mural of their adopted animal family and its home.

Write about it. Suggest that children write a description of their life as their animal. Encourage them to turn their writing into an illustrated booklet. Share short poems about animals and encourage those who can to try their hand at writing a poem. Artist and teacher Susan Kapuscinski Gaylord presents a number of wonderful book-making projects for young children that are easy to implement. (These free projects are available at www.makingbooks.com.)

Write a letter. Say to the children, "Write a letter to humans and tell them how you feel about what they are doing to your species. Is it hard for you to find food? Is your air or water unsafe? How is your family being hurt? Tell the humans what you would like them to do to save your species."

Hold an animal rally. Have the children hold a meeting of the members of their species to protest what is happening to them and to make demands for their survival. This can evolve into a meaningful drama, where students apply what they've learned to make the first step in causing change—communication. Students could make posters bearing messages like *Share the planet!* or *Hairy-Nosed Wombats Unite!* Students can experience a little of what it means to be part of a rally. Children can take turns speaking on behalf of their animals or, more generally, on finding ways to keep species from disappearing due to human activity.

Encourage children to let their imaginations run free. To get the most out of this exercise, they must pretend that they have no limitations and no lack of resources. Anything is possible! You can give a few examples to prod their thinking, such as starting a mass media campaign to discourage people from buying anything with ivory or using satellites to guard the remaining whale population.

3. MAKE THE LINK TO CRITICAL THINKING

At any point in this process, you can always improvise other activities you feel will solidify children's ideas, inspire new ones, or prompt a deeper inquiry into the issues involved. Your gifted children will probably be ready for a more critical inquiry earlier than other students. For those ready to make this leap, you can easily provide small projects similar to the following ones.

Create posters. The purpose of creating posters is to make the public aware of the problem. What aspect of the situation would the students like to emphasize? What do they care most about? A student may show where a species is on the index from threatened to extinct, noting how many of the species are left. (To find this information, children can visit www.iucnredlist.org or www.fws.gov/endangered.) Another student may combine a painting, photograph, or drawing with a list of the species' assets (describing traits such as beautiful, industrious, curious).

Create poems, songs, or skits. Performing these works offers another way for children to teach others about the plight of an animal species.

Use Earth's perspective. Say, "Pretend you are Earth. Write a letter to humans defending the endangered animal. As Earth, explain how much you want to keep your water, air, and soil clean and all your creatures living in harmony with one another."

Organize a group mural. Children can organize, plan, and create a mural that highlights the special qualities of the species they are studying.

Plan installations in public places. Explore places in the community where pieces of work by all the children can be displayed—poems, paintings, collages, maps, designs depicting the decline in certain species, posters, and so on.

Throughout this process, your goal is to inspire as many creative responses as possible, thereby stimulating deeper inquiry or research. Keep asking questions: "How else could you save the habitat? How else could you protect the species against overhunting? How else could you meet the needs of your species and at the same time supply humans with what they need? What other approaches would you use to stop humans from harming the animals? What sorts of people would be able to help this animal—biologists, oceanographers, ecologists, environmentalists?" Word lovers will enjoy all the wonderful words that come with this study.

With a long list of solutions in front of them, students have a wealth of catalysts for a more critical analysis and investigation. For example, once they decide that overfarming is the greatest threat to whooping cranes, they will want to know more about the kind of habitat this species needs. This in turn will prompt them to research in response to their own interest, rather than to simply perform a task demanded by the teacher. They become more invested in their own ideas and, therefore, in their own learning.

When creativity through fluency is used as a link to critical thinking, children reap several benefits. They learn to tackle a problem from a standpoint of *possibility*. Beyond what already exists, they see what alternative solutions *might be*. The solutions, even the outlandish ones, give children an investment in the research they undertake. Because they have already imagined ways to tackle the issue, they will want to discover how workable their ideas are, what adjustments they may need to make, and what plans they may have to undertake to see their ideas through. Perhaps most important, they will learn the value of invention. Tell them not to toss out ideas that may appear unreasonable at first—those ideas may have components that could work in an unexpected way. Many inventions and innovations appear unreasonable and unrealistic at first.

All young children, including gifted learners, need to feel confidence in their ideas. When they launch into the study of a subject without engaging in any creative work, they miss the opportunity to make a personal contribution to the discovery process.

Flexibility: Alternative Histories

Amanda loved history this year. Her teacher erected a big, funny sculpture with an archway, and he called it his time capsule—"the place where history is made." The teacher asked, "Are you ready to travel back in time?" And everyone yelled, "Yes!" The teacher would then get out his coat and hat and transform into a detective, because he said detecting is a large part of a historian's job. There were mysteries about the past to be solved, the teacher explained. Amanda felt the thrill of adventure overtake her. Amanda disliked learning chronologies of events, but she loved it when she put on her own detective cap and stepped through the time capsule to another time.

For a gifted child like Amanda, learning basic historical facts isn't challenging enough to hold her interest for long. The conventional approach to learning history can feel inhibiting to a child with a big imagination. The tasks of memorizing distant dates, putting events in sequence, and studying remote characters are too simplistic. Even challenging students with more in-depth questions and explorations does not go far enough. Young children (including gifted ones) need to be *inside history*—to taste it, feel it, follow it, listen to its language, wear its clothing, walk on its streets, and join its struggles and problems and hopes. Incorporating flexibility into the teaching of history invites children into different, more interesting dimensions.

In the process of *flexibility*, you ask children to diverge from an established sequence, fact, norm, formula, or phenomenon in order to explore alternatives and gain new perspectives. Applied to history, flexibility means exploring the what-ifs of the past. It asks the child questions such as "What if you were in that village during that time? Who would you be? What would you see that others might not? What would you experience? What does the past have to do with your life in the present? How are historical figures similar to you and your friends?"

A flexibility process departs from the deterministic view of history as a series of events that just *happened*. Instead, it shows that people make history. When you put your students into a past and let them imagine how they lived, what they did, and what they aspired to, you help them see history as it moves forward in time—as a process that is alive and relevant.

1. SET THE STAGE

To begin studying a historical period, first select an engaging and informative book—either nonfiction or historical fiction—that will reinforce what the children have learned so far and also interest them in the story.

As an example, let's suppose the children are studying the Pilgrims. *The Pilgrims at Plymouth* by Lucille Recht Penner is a good source for this period. Read the book aloud to the class and use it to create a conceptual base for the subject, to build vocabulary, and to generate discussion and questions. Show pictures or sketches of Plymouth Colony. Share artwork, posters, and maps that will help children imagine the hardships of the Pilgrims' journey from Europe to North America and give the class visual images of the land, the architecture and design of the town, the style of dress, and some of the main historical figures.

After covering some basic ground through the Pilgrim story, you can move on to more creative activities. Have a collection of books, pictures, sketches, maps, and other materials available for children to use as they explore the subject imaginatively. Begin by posing a few questions. Ask students to imagine they lived four hundred years ago and took a ship across the ocean for many weeks to come to a completely unfamiliar land. Then ask them:

- How did you feel about taking such a trip?
- What did you experience on that long trip across the ocean?
- What hardships did you face? How did you deal with them?
- Who else was on the ship with you? How did you get along?
- What did you do for fun? Did you play? How?
- What were your hopes as you waited to reach shore?
- Why did you make the trip?
- What did you take with you? Why? What did you leave behind? Why?
- What did you eat on the ship? What did you wear? Where did you sleep?
- When you landed, how did you go about making a home?
- How did you survive the first terrible winter?
- Were you surprised to find other people already living in the New World? How did these people feel about your coming?

Children will enjoy learning about the Pilgrim experience much more if they do it within the context of imagining themselves living in the colonial village of Plymouth as the first generation of European settlers there. Have them choose roles for themselves in the village—servant, carpenter, weaver, soldier, farmer—and think of the kinds of families and friends they would have. Let the children choose names from the list of passengers on the *Mayflower*. Display common English words and phrases used back then to help students talk like Pilgrims. In this way, they can begin to inhabit the lives of actual historical figures. They can imagine and produce a variety of stories about the Pilgrim experience—stories that reflect the historical world they are exploring. Some classrooms may choose to build a few models of Plymouth houses and shops common at that time, or create murals, maps, or wall hangings depicting the community.

It is vital to also expose the children to Wampanoag life and culture, which predated the Pilgrims by thousands of years. *The Wampanoag* by Kevin Cunningham and Peter Benoit offers a vivid portrait of these indigenous people—their customs, beliefs, and way of life. Another excellent source is *The Children of the Morning Light: Wampanoag Tales as Told by Manitonquat*.

Some students may want to explore the Wampanoags' experience by imagining what they thought of the foreign newcomers from across the sea. Children could draw a Wampanoag village scene, construct a Wampanoag dwelling, make a list of words in the language of the Wampanoag people, or create a collage or sculpture representing their experiences of the new settlers. Guide them with critical questioning:

- What do your people eat? Do they farm? Hunt? Fish?
- How do you dress? How do you make clothes?
- What is your home (*wetu*) like? How did you build it?
- What do you do for fun? What games do you play? What are your favorite foods? What activities do you like most—fishing, swimming, running in the woods, acting out stories?
- What special celebrations do you have?
- What do you think of the Pilgrim people? Are they strange to you? In what ways?
- What are some of your experiences with the Pilgrims?

- How did your people help the new settlers survive and build their community? How did the settlers help protect your people from tribes attacking them?
- What are the things you like about being a member of the Wampanoag that the settlers do not have (for example, matrilineal society; communal concept of territory; knowledge of flora and fauna in the land; growing squash, beans, and corn—the "three sisters")?

Very young children with limited reading or writing skills could draw or paint pictures of a scene they have imagined. Or you might use pictures and posters as catalysts for the students to examine what is happening and to imagine what Pilgrims and Wampanoag thought and felt about each other's customs and cultures.

2. IMAGINE

The focus of the flexibility process is different from that of fluency. The persistent question in flexibility activities is "What else might have been?" You and your students will approach the past as a territory full of unknowns—a place where students can gain new insights. By putting themselves back in time, they begin to discover what's important to *them* as participants in this unique period of history.

Identifying with the Pilgrims or native peoples gives children perspective they wouldn't acquire by reading a book or listening to the teacher. Exercising their imagination allows them to find some common ground with people of times past—ideals that many people still value centuries later, such as freedom from political and religious domination.

Children can empathize with the fears and concerns the Wampanoag felt about losing their world to foreigners. They can understand how a mother might worry about her children's uncertain future with the Pilgrims, or how a father might fear losing the land on which his ancestors lived and worked. It's important for the students to understand, too, that though the Wampanoag suffered many losses and disappeared from history books, populations still exist today and members are working to bring back their language.

In this way, children see that history isn't dead and gone, but correlates with the present in unique ways. Students can discover many histories—they can imagine stories of the past happening in a particular place and time long ago.

Tell children you're sending them back in time, and explain that in the 1600s North America was mostly wilderness. Be sure they understand the unique circumstances the Pilgrims faced in this early period—the terrible first winter there, the unknown and enormous natural world around them, the native people they did not know and who looked strange to them. Visuals, stories, videos, and so forth can help them enter into this world. For their part, the Wampanoag had made this wilderness their home and created their own unique way of life, means of food production, style and construction of housing, dress, and other customs. Some of your students can "go back in time" to one of these environments and look at life from their perspective.

Try to locate sources about both Pilgrims and Wampanoag that are authentic accounts of people who lived then. Children can use these resources to create their own narratives of life in Plymouth and surrounding territories. They will enjoy collecting vivid impressions of the environment of the 1600s—the homes, furniture, clothing, tools, ships, buildings, and landscapes of Plymouth Colony. Have diagrams of the village of Plymouth and scenes of Wampanoag life available. These will feed children's imaginations and provide personal contexts for creating stories that diverge from the more prosaic versions of the Pilgrim experience.

What kinds of sources do we mean? A child's story. A mother's story. The story of Susannah White (later Susannah Winslow), who gave birth to a child on the *Mayflower*, survived the hardships of the first winter, and lived eighty-five years, a rare age at a time when so many women died young. The story of Samoset's first meeting with the Pilgrims, or of the first treaty concluded between the Pilgrims and Massasoit, the *sachem* (leader) of the Wampanoag. The stories of Tisquantum (Squanto), who assisted the Pilgrims after their first winter, enabled them to survive in a wilderness they knew little about, and acted as an interpreter between the Pilgrims and Massasoit. The tale of the first Thanksgiving. The story of a new settler expelled because he played games in the streets on Christmas Day, or of another who got caught in a deer trap. The tale of John Billington Jr., who wandered into the woods and lived among the Nauset people for a month. The story of how Billington and his brother Francis almost blew up the *Mayflower*. The story of impulsive Myles Standish, the leader of the Pilgrims' tiny army.

Here are some questions to get students started thinking.

For Pilgrims:

- What did you and your family hope to find in the New World when you came?
- Did you find it?
- What is Plymouth like? What do you miss from towns, villages, or cities you knew before?
- How do you learn when you don't have a school? What are you learning?
- Do you have friends?
- What do you wear? What do you eat?
- Where do you travel? How do you get there?
- What chores or jobs do you have to do?
- What do you like better about your new home than your old one?
- What do you miss about your home country?
- What do you find difficult in your new home?
- What kind of world are your family and other families trying to create in this new land?
- How do you relate to the Wampanoag?

For the Wampanoag:

- What did you think when you first saw a European settler?
- What do you like about your own home's structure?
- What do you wear in the different seasons?
- What are your chores?
- How did you learn to swim? How did you learn to play toss-and-catch games, shoot arrows, make clay pots, or fashion dolls out of cornhusks and cobs?
- What are the old stories of your village and who tells them?
- What do these stories teach you?
- Have you spent any time in Plymouth? What did you find there that was different from where you live?

3. MAKE THE LINK TO CRITICAL THINKING

Critical thinking plays a key role in this questioning process. You can either write the children's answers to the aforementioned questions on the board, or ask the children to write down their own answers. Break students into groups and ask them to work on the questions together, using what they have already learned as well as the resource materials you have provided. Here are a few other activities you might incorporate:

Create visual depictions. Ask children who are not yet reading historical materials to think of one main response to a question. They could then create a visual image that represents their idea—a painting, collage, cartoon, or model. Later, invite the children to share their work as a catalyst for class discussion.

Draw maps. Mapping provides a more complex visual-artistic and tactile-kinesthetic project. Tell children: "You live in a Pilgrim (or Wampanoag) village. Draw a map of the village. Include as many details as you can: the Pilgrim homes, the Wampanoag *wetus*, the streets, the central square for councils and ceremonies, the shoreline, the paths, the streams, and so on."

Tell stories. Have students imagine that they are reporters sent back in time to interview people about what's been happening in Plymouth. Ask them to think about what questions they most want to explore. Use resources such as pictures of a wild area in the Northeast, sounds of birds in the woods, constructions made by the students, myths, or diary entries to inspire a tale. Visuals are especially popular with young children. They quickly respond to and interpret what they see and enjoy talking about what they imagine might be happening.

Create biographies. Have the students create short biographies of themselves and their families. The biographies can be written, oral, theatrical, or visual. Children can accompany these with drawings of their homes and families, maps or sketches of their neighborhood, and examples of their tools, games, clothing, or foods.

Provide options for biographies. Some children will want to explore famous historic figures like Massasoit, Tisquantum, Myles Standish, and governor William Bradford. They could write, describe, or dramatize an event in this person's life or imagine a day when they met one of these people and describe what they felt and saw.

Provide Opportunities for Sharing

Provide opportunities for the children to share their work. Hang their pictures and biographies on the wall, and guide the students around the room to see each other's work.

Walk around the room with children and talk about the representations. As you discuss the various pieces of work, there will be many opportunities for you to refer to historical events and conditions. As you do, ask questions such as "Could this event have happened to this family in the 1600s? What means of transport did the Wampanoag use (for example, canoe or walking)? How did they send messages to other villages? How did the Pilgrims get around? Did the Wampanoag act as guides to this new world?"

Encourage Editing and Refining

Whether the histories take the form of visual art, maps, dramas, or written works, give children a chance to refine, polish, and edit. This is an ongoing process of exploration, not an exhibit of final products.

Connect the Past to the Present

As a conclusion to this process, you might also ask the children to write letters to people in our present time. These letters could tell families, members of the school community, public officials, and others what part of the Pilgrim experience is important for people of today to know. Help the children reflect on values such as tolerance for differences in culture, language, or religion and cooperation in the face of contest or disagreement. In the time of the Pilgrims, it was unimaginable that such a vast wilderness would disappear or that entire species would become extinct. How native peoples treat the natural world might be another lesson for today; even a little of their respect, honor, and care might help us safeguard the few remaining natural preserves in the world. What would the children like today's history teachers to teach about that long-ago time? What do they feel is most important for parents to know? What aspect of life among the Pilgrims or the Wampanoag could be applied to improving or changing today's world?

The children could write or dictate these letters; you could transcribe as necessary and attach the letters to the students' work. This gives the students a chance to distill in their minds what *they* have found unique and special about the Pilgrim experience and how that experience contributed to the world in which we live today.

Originality: Cultural Invention

When Jimmy moved with his mother to the city, he noticed all the different languages in his class. He would hear them in the hall, in the neighborhood, and on the streets with his mother. Different sorts of script appeared on shops for those who spoke Hindi, Arabic, Korean, Chinese, and each culture seemed to inhabit a particular section of town. Jimmy and his mother lived near an Indian shopping district, and there he feasted his eyes on shops full of foods, teas, spices, electronics, and many other things. The smells of cooking spices wafted over Jimmy as his mother led him into the take-out restaurant of her friend. The owner would give him a small packet of sweets— nothing like he'd ever had in his small rural town. Outside, they passed a shop displaying a beautiful sari, where a man and a woman were talking. Jimmy broke away and stood near them just so he could hear their language. As he walked home with his mother, he said, "I feel like we just visited India." Jimmy wondered what Indians felt about living in North America. Does this neighborhood make them feel like they're not so far from home? Why do some of the women wear such long dresses and the men wear such long shirts and jackets with their pants? What are their celebrations like? He was enthralled with the music and a video showing a traditional dance performed at a wedding.

Jimmy is an original thinker with keen sensibilities who needs to know the reasons for what he observes. Identifying customs, languages, and cultural practices would never feed his inquiring mind. The child who has to know "why" all the time is a child already on a higher level of thinking, more interested in what makes things the way they are than in the characteristics of those things. Jimmy's tendency to imagine India while walking through local Indian shops also reveals a desire and ability to invent a world based on what he is learning.

Students like Jimmy thrive within the framework of originality. Like the other two processes we've explored, originality has a distinct emphasis. Fluency produces a large quantity of ideas; flexibility seeks alternatives to the commonplace. *Originality* is a little different. Children may draw on the other two processes, yet they are creating something uniquely their own—something that not only stands apart from established inventions but also *exceeds* the status of an alternative or digression. An original idea may or may not use any known thing as a reference point. It may temporarily use something already established as a way of exploring a range of alternatives, but eventually it assumes a distinct shape of its own.

1. SET THE STAGE

Nothing delights most young gifted children more than discovering that they can create something completely unique. The study of culture offers many opportunities for this to happen.

Let's say that you approach the whole subject of human cultures by involving the children in researching their family backgrounds.[4] This kind of inquiry is very beneficial for young children. While learning about their own cultural heritage, they can also contribute to the class's pool of knowledge about human cultures in general. The students become producers as well as recipients of knowledge. For children in the younger grades who may not be reading much, this is an ideal approach to a very basic kind of research. You could ask children to interview family members and collect answers to the following questions:

- Where did your mother or father come from? What about your grandparents? Other relatives?
- Who in your family first came to the United States or Canada? Or, who first came to this state (province) or community?
- When did they come? How did they get here?
- Why did they come here?
- What hardships did they face?
- What language did they speak? Does anyone in your family still speak this language? Do you know some words you could teach us?
- What is the architecture like in your family's home country or community?
- What is the environment like—the climate, flora, fauna, sights, and smells?
- What clothes are commonly worn there?
- What foods do people in your family eat that others in our class might never have tasted?
- What are some of your family's customs or traditions? Do you celebrate special holidays? Eat special foods? Sing or dance to traditional music? Light candles? Tell stories?
- Does your family have any special artwork—like paintings, pots, dolls, or baskets—made by people who come from the same place your family came from?
- If you're from another country or a different kind of community, how do you feel about life away from your country or community? What do you like? What don't you like?

Be sensitive to the fact some children may not relate to this type of research project. They could be members of Native American groups; they might be adopted, in the care of foster parents, or live in stepfamilies or blended families; or they may be unsure of their cultural background due to the fact that their ancestors have lived in the United States or Canada for generations. In this case, they can still explore the culture of the places where their family has lived—or the culture that a relative recalls experiencing as a child. They may want to research their family backgrounds, or they may not. Offer alternatives for those who don't. For example, they could focus on any culture close to them in some way—in their experience (travels, friends, neighbors) or in their connections to other students (through child-safe Internet sites, and so forth).

First, write a few key questions on the board and go over each one. Make sure the children understand them. We also recommend sending some questions home; if you wish, use the "Your Child's Cultural Heritage" family letter (page 77). Also, ask the children to bring in pictures or other artifacts that represent the country, culture, or environment they come from.

2. EXPLORE AND SHARE PERSONAL BACKGROUNDS

Get an extra-large map to hang on a bulletin board or the wall. Write out the children's names and ask the children to tack their names to the country or area where they or their family originated. (If their roots involve several places, which is often the case, ask them to pick the ones they know most about.) Then follow through with other activities, such as the following.

Explore maps. Have children explore a map of their country or geographic area and then draw it, filling in landmarks such as towns or community gathering places, lakes, forests, and oceans that surround it. Some children may feel that their areas of origin are less identifiable. Assure them that they may identify a general area. For example, they might mark out a geographic area such as the Arapaho lands on the Great Plains, which cover parts of Kansas, Nebraska, and Colorado. If the maps are large enough, children can make a living history out of them, identifying where a parent or relative was born or grew up, the travel routes from one place to another, and symbols that indicate various happenings along the way.

---

[4] Be sensitive to the needs and feelings of children who are adopted, are in the care of foster parents, or live in stepfamilies or blended families. They may want to research their family backgrounds, or they may not. Offer alternatives for those who don't.

Students could create their own legends at the bottom of the page.

Tell stories. Next to their maps, children could write stories describing their family backgrounds: how people were related, the town or area in which they lived, what work their ancestors did, how and why life changed for the family.

This assignment can be as simple or complicated as you like. You can ask children who are just learning to read and write to tell their stories using a few very simple sentences. Encourage others, especially those of higher ability, to describe their families' lives vividly, as in a storybook. Children who don't yet write can create a drawing that tells their story, with an arrow on the map pointing to the place where they lived. They could also dictate captions for you, a parent volunteer, or another student to write.

Share customs. Ask the children to talk and then write about the language, dress, and some of the customs of their family (or of another family whose culture they know well). Again, offer the option of drawing, painting, collage, or dictation.

Share words and written language. Gifted students are often fascinated by the sounds of different languages, mysterious styles of writing, and foreign words that have crept into the English language. A word, phrase, sentence, or poem in the native tongue of other peoples comes alive in creative expression. Languages with different writing systems—Arabic, Chinese, Nepalese, Russian, and Greek, to name a few—become puzzles, irresistible to explore.

Share artifacts. Assure the children that these are *their own* stories of their families' cultures. The children can add all sorts of things to make their stories more vivid, including family pictures, images and articles from magazines, traditional stories and poems that reflect their heritage, and small objects, tools, or mementos that mark important events in their history.

Each product or presentation can be unique—different in size, style, medium, and so forth. The children should feel free to draw upon their creative strengths. Those who are more confident in the visual arts, for example, may feature visual images more than written ones. Other products may include dance and dramatizations. While there may be certain required elements, students should be allowed to integrate them in their own way so they can take possession of the process.

3. MAKE THE LINK TO CRITICAL THINKING

Once the children have completed their work, display their presentations around the room so the class can see them. Encourage students to walk around and look at the different countries, cultures, and environments represented. Invite children—especially those who haven't written on their maps—to talk about their work. This will give them an opportunity to elaborate on whatever they wrote or depicted, describing customs and cultural practices in more detail to the class.

Compare Cultures

After a systematic tour around the room, ask the children to select a culture other than their own. Many young gifted students become quickly drawn to anything new and different, and will often home in on particular ideas or customs that particularly interest them. It might be the way a culture responds to animals and nature, the brilliant colors and textures of the clothing displayed in an ethnic neighborhood (as in the case of Jimmy), or the stories and ballads of city-dwelling migrant families, whose elders still long for the places of their youth. Opportunities to peek into other worlds are often irresistible to gifted children and fuel their need to know more.

Ask the children to write down at least two things about their selected culture and its people that interest or inspire them the most. Give each child a copy of the "Me in a Different Culture" handout (page 78). Using primary and secondary sources (direct interviews of peers, photographs, video footage, text, picture books, musical recordings, foods, tools, and so on), have children compare how the culture differs from their own. Young gifted students love the mental challenge of discovering other ways that people live in the world. This challenge can sometimes lead to an understanding not only of customs, geography, and language, but also of values. What do the people care about? What do they think about the rearing of children? The treatment of the earth and animals? The role of the family and community?

Some children might focus on how people in a culture greet each other. It could be by bowing slightly with hands folded together, by giving a light kiss on each cheek, or by doing no physical action at all. The greetings could be lengthy, ritualized ones in which each person asks about the other's well-being and the health of the family. Children might find it strange to take so much time with a greeting or they might feel that it's appropriate because people are very important to each other. If you have children in your classroom from distinct cultures, they will relate to this process and can share experiences either of their own (if they are new arrivals) or of family members demonstrating what they or relatives found difficult or odd about living in America.

Now have the children focus on the same areas of interest and imagine that they belong to the culture they just explored. Knowing what they do about this culture, what might they find strange about the way people act in their homes, on the streets, or in shops? How do they treat each other during games, in celebrations, or in public? Some students might notice that the culture they're studying values a quieter vocal level than the energetic, sometimes loud one in mainstream American culture, and so the idea of yelling someone's name or whistling to get their attention would seem very rude. Similarly, hospitality may be a highly prized cultural value, to the point where you always welcome a hungry neighbor—regardless of whether you feel that you have enough food to share. Looking through the eyes of people from other cultures helps children understand that culture is something that influences the way we live in the world and the way we view other cultures, and that each of us may seem strange to someone else.

Observe Commonalities

Young children also need to explore commonalities. A farmer in Ethiopia and a teacher in New York City may seem oceans apart in language, life experience, customs, and traditions. Yet they both care about their families, want their children to live well, and desire to live in a peaceful nation. Also, while the behavior of someone from one culture may seem disinterested or overbearing to another, this does not make that appearance true. Americans and Canadians are from many lands and tongues and so tend to respect others despite differences. What makes culture interesting to gifted children is not merely the differences or variations they observe, but the meanings and values behind them.

As an example, let us choose how cultures celebrate the birth of a new child and subsequent birthdays (or special milestones in the child's life). Have the children interview a family member, relative, or family friend about the process of preparing for and celebrating the birth of a new life into the world. Being an observer close to the event would be ideal. Explore questions that look at the child's own culture and another culture, such as:

- How did the baby shower tradition start?
- Why is this party called a shower?
- What is the name used in another culture?
- What happens after the child is born?
- Do the family and community meet the child informally after a certain amount of time?
- Is there a formal celebration introducing the child to society?

Students can use the "Custom Observation Form" (page 79) to record memories they have of the births of siblings or relatives.

Young children find this topic fascinating: what are the different cultural views about twins, and what do people do when they have twins? Among the Baganda in Uganda, for example, a mother of twins adds another word to her name: *naalongo*, which means "mother of twins." A father adds *saalongo*, or "father of twins."

What do the different people in a baby's immediate family do after a new baby arrives? How much time do other family and friends give them to be alone with their child before visiting and celebrating? How do those whose family structure is larger—an extended family, a clan, a tight-knit neighborhood—introduce the newest member? What are the customs, celebrations, and rituals?

How do these customs express the love and care people in different cultures feel toward children? Exploring birthday celebrations can also give young students insight about how other cultures make children feel valued and important.

Other areas where children can discover commonalities include:

- games
- instruments
- weddings
- meals
- schooling
- homes (architectural design, interior design, paintings, colors)
- art

Through this process, children learn that different cultures have different traditions for even the most ordinary events, like sharing meals, playing games, or designing the interior of a home—yet these differences do not make any of the traditions wrong or weird. They also realize that there is no single way to live in this world, and that what seems strange to them becomes less so once they understand it.

Resources for observing commonalities could include visitors from different cultures; the sharing of different foods, dress, or songs from students' families; Internet links between classrooms across the globe so children can ask questions, share information about their cultures (not personal pictures or videos that could place them at risk); emails; footage of cultural performances by star musicians, actors, and dancers; visual, text, and video sources on architecture showing the practical, aesthetic, religious, spiritual, and other reasons behind design.

Learning about how cultures other than their own approach fundamental areas of life enables gifted students to look at their own world *through another's eyes.* They might consider some of the spoken and unspoken rules connected with mealtime in different cultures, or how greetings, politeness, and hospitality function in their own and other cultures.

Ask children to observe their day through the eyes of someone from another culture. They should just watch what happens and try to make sense of it by describing in a journal (or a letter to a friend) what people are doing and how they're behaving. The idea is to help students see how familiar things in their culture may seem strange to those outside it. A simple example might be the volume and expressiveness with which people speak. A child who lives in the crowded, noisy city might wonder if all the noise and commotion would be overwhelming to those from a different country or community. She pretends to be a newcomer from a remote mountain village. She focuses on this topic throughout her day. Encourage the children to be creative in their descriptions. They can create a scrapbook, adding pictures, sketches, photos, collages, or anything else that brings their experience to life. They could collect things—a label or receipt from an ice cream shop; a list of some of the cars zipping by and the way people are driving; hats, wigs, and shamrocks from a Saint Patrick's Day parade.

Through this wonderful, mind-bending process, the children filter the reality of their own culture through the eyes of another culture's customs, traditions, and values. Gifted children in particular will likely enjoy the challenge. Many will love sharing the scenarios of what they found "foreign" and the conclusions they made based on what they saw. At the same time, you'll be encouraging the whole class to think more critically and creatively about culture. By assuming the position of someone outside their own cultural world and trying to imagine what might seem strange or foreign, children will begin to see the deep connections between culture and meaning.

Create a Fictional Culture

To extend this process to a more complex level, high-ability students who show an interest could take on a project of imagining an entirely fictional culture. The best fantasy fiction, whether in text or on film, features rich cultural worlds that take readers or viewers far from their own world—though not so far that they cannot relate to underlying needs and practices. This type of project offers several benefits:

1. It gives gifted children an opportunity to draw on their understanding of how any culture invents a unique system of commonly held values, communication styles, and customs.
2. It challenges creative, artistic children to think and work in a way they love as they invent worlds and decide how the societies within these worlds will organize their lives.
3. It makes children "cultural experts" in their fictional worlds who can make sense of practices and customs that seem inexplicable to others.
4. It gives children the opportunity to envision culture in a way that addresses current world issues—for example, by inventing a society that deeply values the environment or one that is opposed to war.
5. It can foster an increased appreciation of cultural differences as children think more logically and sympathetically about cultures different from their own.
6. For imaginative students who particularly love reading and writing or who perhaps devote a lot of their time to sketching characters from their favorite fantasy worlds invented by others, this project will encourage them to invent a world of their own.

You could start the process of invention by encouraging children to think about what they value in their own culture and other cultures. Here are some possible questions:

- What kind of cultural world would you create if you had the power to do so?
- What would you name it?
- What behaviors would be common in this culture?
- What would be the celebrations and special holidays connected to historical events, anniversaries, and beliefs?
- What would the language sound like? What are some of the words or phrases?
- What would the people wear?
- What kind of geographical environment would the people of this culture live in?
- What would the homes and other buildings look like?
- What would the transportation system be like? How would people get around?
- What kinds of jobs or work would the people do?
- What would their food look like? How would it be prepared?
- What would be the history of this culture?

Drawing on cultural information from a variety of resources (the discoveries they have made so far, television programs, movies, videos, apps, cultural websites for children, books, and so on), the children will relish the opportunity to invent their own worlds.

If this process seems complicated or unmanageable, or if you would like to give a whole class of older children an opportunity to create a fictional culture, you might consider having the class work together to create a single culture. Divide the children into groups and assign each one a particular domain such as clothing, foods, political organization, architecture, history, or environment. To be successful, you'll need to spend some whole-class time setting a few parameters and allowing periodic sharing among groups to encourage a cross-pollination of ideas; continue to move from group to group, keeping track of what children are creating for their areas. If the group working on clothes invents attire at odds with the environment or traditions of the people, you may need to help them focus on how this culture's people might dress in different settings. What does the climate demand? Do some people have finer clothes than others? Does this culture have kings, queens, presidents, premiers, tribal leaders? How do they dress? What do women and men wear? Girls and boys? Are there strict rules about how people should be dressed? Have plenty of books, pictures, and videos available for the children to browse as their ideas evolve.

You can adapt this process for younger (preschool and kindergarten) children. Focusing on simple things such as clothing, language, food, and fundamental customs and celebrations, the children can first explore differences among real cultures. Maureen Cech's *Globalchild: Multicultural Resources for Young Children* and Mem Fox's *Whoever You Are* are wonderful resources for beginning this process. Or introduce fairy tales from other cultures—stories similar to those students might already know, such as Shirley Climo's *The Egyptian Cinderella,* Rafe Martin's *The Rough-Face Girl* (an Algonquin Indian Cinderella story), and Ed Young's *Lon Po Po: A Red-Riding Hood Story from China.* Many more resources, teachers' guides, and book titles are available through the Web, and they are keeping pace with the global environment young gifted children want to explore. Through these sources, young children can begin to conceptualize what culture is.

In devising their own fictional culture, preschool and kindergarten students could begin with the environment. Ask the students to choose a climate and geographical setting for their culture. This will lead to discussions of the clothing people make; the food they gather, grow, hunt, and prepare; and possibly the kinds of ceremonies and traditions they develop. Young gifted students can also consider the technology their imaginary culture has developed in response to environmental conditions.

As with older children, have younger students create cooperatively. Organize their work around some key questions:

- What do your homes look like?
- What do the children do for fun in this world?
- Do you go to school or do you learn some other way?
- What animals live near you, and what are they called? Do you have a pet?
- What are some of your celebrations?

Students can draw or dramatize a history of the people, explaining how certain customs evolved. They can paint or draw pictures of this world, create models of villages, and sketch different species of flora and fauna that live there.

Although you may feel reluctant to spend too much time on a fictional culture, building a world that makes sense unto itself—that has a history, an environment, and a way of responding to challenges and celebrating special events—teaches the class a great deal about the inner workings of culture.

Gifted children especially will appreciate the complexity of culture and enjoy its planning.

Here are a number of related activities you could consider as well:

- Create laws of behavior for this new world—laws you would value if you lived in it.
- Create a new kind of architecture for buildings in this culture.
- Write some patriotic songs.
- Design a flag.
- Design a map of the country or area that shows cultural landmarks.
- Devise a transportation system.
- Write or create murals depicting the culture's history.
- Design clothing.
- Develop recipes.
- Create the beginnings of a language.

After this sort of in-depth learning experience, the students will gain a deeper understanding of how culture pervades all aspects of human societies. Despite the apparent strangeness of certain customs or practices, they will perceive inner cultural consistencies—the links that connect a people's way of thinking and doing things into some understandable pattern.

Elaboration and Evaluation: Translating Creativity

Elaboration and *evaluation* don't necessarily occur separately from the processes of fluency, flexibility, or originality. Rather, they extend out from these processes, translating novel ideas into practice. We'll consider elaboration and evaluation together because they usually complement each other. To employ these processes in your classroom, you'll need either a problem-solving context (in which students are grappling with an issue in a new way) or a creative context (in which the product or idea works as a unique invention within the framework of certain requirements or standards, as in the case of a fictional culture).

It's not unusual for gifted students to have a difficult time pursuing their idea to the point of elaboration and evaluation. When an idea has taken them as far as they want to go, they may be impatient to move on to something new. Persisting with their idea may seem dull in comparison to the more exciting process of discovery and innovation they

experienced in creating it. However, evaluating their work to see what adjustments might be necessary, or what further developments might make it more useful, can present new and exciting challenges. As a teacher, the main points for you to remember are that gifted children tend to be harsh judges of their own work and they need guidance in elaborating and evaluating. Following are some useful practices to help *all* your students develop their ideas and evaluate their work in constructive ways.

1. SET THE STAGE

Even very young children—preschoolers and kindergartners—can benefit from this process. Let's say, for example, that the children have just created their own fictional cultures. You can walk the children around the room to examine and analyze the different projects. Original insights often emerge from this process, enabling students to elaborate in unexpected ways on what they have created. Young gifted students will likely enjoy this process, because it inspires critical and creative thinking.

Start by introducing elaboration and evaluation as phases of discovery. Gifted children may lose interest if they think that this process means aborting or severely altering their ideas to fit some external standard of what is reasonable and possible.

Whether the child is trying to devise a new language or test an idea for a new kind of car, you can use the same simple principles. Try introducing evaluation and elaboration like this: "Now I want you to try this out to see if it works. To do this, you need to be a true inventor. Don't give up on your idea if it doesn't work right away or if it seems impossible. Many inventors have felt just like that. To make this work, you need to stick to your idea, but feel free to make changes where you think you need them. Inventors keep trying new designs to see what works. If Thomas Edison had never experimented with his lightbulb to make it practical in everyday life, we might still be reading by candlelight today!"

Point out that even failed experiments have contributed valuable knowledge that has paved the way for other significant discoveries. The history of human flight is one great example. You could choose several examples of real inventors and pioneers to set an encouraging tone for your children's work. The process of putting their ideas into practice should be fun, leading to new ideas they might not have otherwise considered. To a large degree, a child's ability to see the elaboration and evaluation processes as satisfying and rewarding depends on *your* enthusiasm and engagement.

2. USE QUESTIONS TO GUIDE STUDENTS

Like fluency and flexibility, elaboration and evaluation are creative processes. To preserve this creativity, don't assign specific steps for children to take in order to make their ideas work. Doing so is likely to make students quickly lose investment in their own idea and in some of its most innovative features.

We've found that the best approach is to present students with a series of leading questions. The questions should prompt critical and creative student responses. You'll need to select and adjust the questions depending on the age and ability of the children as well as the project they have chosen. Are they seeking a solution to the extinction of a species? Attempting to create an original alternative piece of historical writing? Designing a new concept in transportation? Also bear in mind that elaboration and evaluation don't necessarily happen quickly; the process may need to span several days or even weeks.

To Begin

To put this process in context, let's say you have children who are developing a campaign to stop the destruction of a habitat important to an endangered species. Some children have composed songs, written poems or short articles for a newspaper, or created cartoons, slogans, small sculptures, or paintings. Others have devised plans to transport endangered animals to a new site in another country. Still others have created ads to increase awareness among consumers and to inspire them to take action. At this point, you might say to the students:

- Look at your idea (or product). Think about what you would like it to do. What might you still need to do to make it work?
- Tell us all you know about the role or setting you have planned for your idea. What problem does your idea solve? What sort of place will be good for your creation?
- What might still be missing from your idea to make it work in the place you've chosen?

These questions help children begin thinking of natural extensions to their ideas. Extensions can occur on different levels. For example, very young children who have invented a new environment for Brazilian tamarins can build models or draw sketches, adding details as they think through the questions. Older students who have written fictional accounts of their experiences in Plymouth or in a Wampanoag village can test their stories against the historical facts, developing and refining them from the new insights gained. You may not want to provide a lot of structured feedback at this point. Gifted students often prefer to elaborate on their ideas before receiving responses from you or other students.

To Continue

After students have worked for a while, some may be ready to share their ideas. To ensure that the class gives productive criticism, set three ground rules:

1. **Say what you like.** Have classmates first share what they like about a child's project or idea. Encourage the classmates to be specific. What meant the most to them? Why?
2. **Offer helpful ideas.** Ask the children to focus only on what they think would make the idea work better—not on what they think is wrong with it.
3. **Don't judge or criticize.** Don't accept or allow value judgments like "this is stupid" or "that won't work." If children foresee certain problems with an idea, ask them to state what they think might not work. They should do this without criticizing the idea itself.

Guide your students through this stage of the process with comments and questions such as these:

- What changes are necessary?
- How could you make the changes? Write down or brainstorm all the ways you can think of.
- Are there parts of your idea that don't work? Which parts? Can you keep these parts by changing the way you apply your idea?
- If you have to change part of your idea, can you create something new in its place?
- There are gaps between what you have made and what is needed. You can use your imagination to fill these gaps. Keep asking yourself, "Is there another way I can do this?"
- Stay focused. Ask yourself, "How else can I imagine my idea working? Who or what could help me do it?"

Encourage children to respond to the suggestions. This will stimulate critical and creative thinking, and will help the students see new possibilities for their work.

To Finish

After the children have spent some time experimenting, they can bring closure to their work. As you guide the class through the elaboration and evaluation process, you'll find that some students benefit more by collaborating, others by working independently. Be flexible and allow children to complete their ideas in the way they feel most comfortable. Here are some questions you might pose:

- What things do you need to have or do in order to complete your idea?
- Who might be able to help you? Do you have any questions for your teacher? For another student or group of students?
- Generally speaking, what do you need to reach your goal? Time? Materials? Space? A way to convince other people?
- Does your project require a team, or just you? If you need a team, what kind of workers do you need? How many? What do you need this team of helpers to do for you?

This exercise keeps the children's thoughts focused on their own vision and ideal for their work, which is very important at this point in the process. Children—especially gifted ones—are often extremely critical, highly sensitive about their work, and quick to abandon all or part of it if they think it will fail. You can support your students' efforts by helping them think about what is important *to them*. This will keep them from becoming distracted or overly concerned about how "good" their project looks on the surface or how other people see it.

3. CREATE OPPORTUNITIES FOR SHARING

Once the children complete their work to their own satisfaction, they should have a chance to share it with the rest of the class. It's a good idea to discuss the sharing of ideas beforehand and coach the class on positive ways to respond to others' efforts.

When students share their work, it's an extremely powerful and effective teaching and learning process for all—including you! From the children's perspective, it's revolutionary to be in a position where *they* are the experts, leading the class through their own discoveries and ideas. This alone often transforms the dynamics of the class. We've found that most young students are quiet, respectful, and willing to ask probing questions when their classmates make presentations. For gifted children who often fear what others will say or think about their work, it can be extremely beneficial to find that others respond well to their ideas *and* that others can be a valuable resource for their work.

Sharing isn't about deciding whether a child's creation is good or bad, right or wrong. It's about continuing the discovery process—acknowledging and praising the accomplishment, helping the child investigate where else to go or what else to do to carry the idea further.

Exploring children's work together as a class provides many opportunities for you to support creative learning, using the children's work as a catalyst for higher-level thinking. This kind of class environment will teach all your students that learning is a discovery process, that everyone has a role to play in this process, and that each of them has a unique contribution to make to the world around them.

Questions and Answers

"Wouldn't some gifted children prefer to work alone rather than share their work?"

The stereotype of gifted children as contented loners, capable and happy to work completely on their own, is a potentially damaging one. We should not regard isolation as an unavoidable aspect of giftedness. The brightest, most talented children need others just as much as anyone else does. Frequently they feel pressured to figure out everything on their own, and often they think that asking for help is a personal failing. Yet they want and need to ask for help and to get some honest feedback. These children need support—not just from the teacher, but also from their classmates.

It's a sad thing to see an older gifted child struggling on a project alone, afraid even to ask for assistance or to consult peers for fear of rejection or ridicule. Often, these fears are unjustified, based on a lack of experience in sharing with others. This is one of the reasons we believe in early intervention for gifted children. They need to learn that, although some people may disagree with their ideas or find them offbeat, others will welcome them and may have constructive criticisms to help improve them. They need to learn this as early in life as possible. If we don't teach them this vital lesson, how can we blame them later when they become uncommitted or underachieving, content with using only a fraction of their true talents?

This is why it's important that gifted students in the preschool and primary grades have opportunities to share their work in a relaxed, informal, and cooperative atmosphere. All through this chapter, we've emphasized the importance of encouraging students to strike out in new directions, to test new ground, to challenge the assumption that there is a right or wrong answer for everything. At the point of application and evaluation, it's vital that you maintain this same attitude and encourage it in your students.

"Are these processes and activities applicable only to environmental studies, history, and culture?"
No. As you'll see in Chapters 5 and 6, many of the basic principles also apply to other subject areas—language, visual and performing arts, and math and science as well. By the time you finish reading Chapter 6, you'll see that although the activities may differ to some extent, many of the processes translate easily from one subject to another. They also provide effective means for integrating subjects.

"What can I do if some students excel in these imaginative activities while others find them difficult or uninteresting?"
Rather than anticipate that children won't be interested, remember that creative teaching approaches enable a wider range of young students to learn in authentic and dynamic ways. Some children may not know that their special interests and abilities are the fertile soil for learning in the classroom. Or they may think they don't have abilities worth applying in

school, simply because they'd rather build something or sing and dance than read a book. Creative children may be sitting in your classroom right now, barely using their talents. Some children who have never shown a spark of interest in your class may suddenly come alive when you use creative instruction.

Although your students will move at different speeds and in different directions, you can inspire all the children in your classroom. Give them enough preparation time before the activities begin, then share and display student work at regular intervals.

Conclusion

Nothing excites young children more than discovery. The first lessons they learn are a function of this fundamental process and provide a powerful and natural incentive to explore. The entire world of the young child is creative—undivided and uncompartmentalized. Each new discovery leads to further inquiry and research, which in turn lead to more discovery.

The principle underlying many of the processes in this chapter is the simple act of *pretending*—of placing children in roles or giving them opportunities to invent stories and situations around the facts they are learning. This is a familiar process to young children. And it's this critical act of invention that enables young students—particularly gifted ones—to make unique discoveries that transform them into enthusiastic learners.

Your Child's Cultural Heritage

Child's name: _____

Dear Parent/Caregiver:

In school, we're discussing the children's cultural heritage. Your child will want to know many things about his or her ancestors. Here are some questions your child might want to talk about:

Where was I born? Where were my parents born?

Where did my ancestors come from? Why did they come here? How did they get here?

What hardships did they face?

What language did they speak? Can you teach me any words?

What customs do we have in our family now that came from our ancestors?

What can I tell my class about my family heritage? What can I show them to help them learn more about it?

Your child may also want to bring something from his or her cultural heritage to school: a picture, a decoration, or another memento. We promise to take good care of any items and return them on _____ (day and date).

We want to be respectful of each family's customs, beliefs, and culture. Please call or email me if you have any questions. Thank you for your help.

Teacher's signature: _____

Phone: _____

Email: _____

Me in a Different Culture

My name: _____

Culture: _____

What would it be like to be part of this culture? Write or draw your ideas.

Custom Observation Form

My name: _____

Observe some customs at home or somewhere in your community. Write or draw about what you observe.

Where I was: _____

What I observed:

CHAPTER 5
Promoting Imagination in the Language Arts Curriculum

Liz was always fidgeting during storytime. Her mother wondered why, even as a very young child, Liz wiggled off her lap whenever they started a book together, and why Liz kept asking questions outside the story line. Didn't all little kids like stories?

When a storyteller from Ireland and a blues singer from the south visited Liz's third-grade class to share stories, Liz felt electrified. Story became something different than she had ever experienced before. The cadences of the Irish storyteller sang in her ear, and his gestures and performance transported the whole class. The blues singer shared the lyrics of some early blues songs, described the stories they told, traced the evolution of the blues from the late nineteenth century to the present, and sang the blues while playing his guitar. Soon, the children were all singing and rocking to his music, belting out a travelogue of adventures across America.

Through this experience, Liz discovered that stories are not static. They live in all people and can take unlimited shapes and forms. The visitors ignited her
imagination, and she realized that stories lived in her, too. Suddenly she had an abundance of story ideas.

Creative Learning as a Link to Imaginative Thinking

Liz has not yet realized her gifts in reading and writing because she loses focus quickly when an activity doesn't allow her to leave the beaten path. How can we inspire young children like Liz to express themselves creatively? To answer this question, this chapter will:

- present creative strategies that stimulate students' imaginations in language arts—poetry, fiction, readers' theater, and biography
- show how integrating the visual, theatrical, and language arts with children's multiple talents serves as a catalyst for children's writing
- guide you in developing creative projects that meet the needs of children at different levels of ability and experience

While Chapter 4 focuses more on using creative processes for intellectual discovery, this chapter places more emphasis on using creativity for *imaginative* discovery—to tap into the world of ideas within children themselves.

Integrating the arts, a strategy used frequently in this chapter, is a powerful catalyst for creative work. It's a strategy that involves the whole child. The arts give children multisensory experiences—images and ideas they can see, hear, feel, and embody, rather than just observe. Throughout the creative process, we encourage mixing arts media to achieve a multi-dimensional learning experience.

Take, for example, a multimedia activity conducted with young students using the classic Disney film *Fantasia* as a catalyst. The children can watch and listen to the segment based on Igor Stravinsky's *The Rite of Spring*, which depicts the origins of the universe and follows the progress of Earth from a molten mass of gases through the passing of the dinosaurs.[1]

To begin, students may focus on the rhythms, melodies, and instruments or sound sources. They can think and talk about where the music or sound takes them. They can beat out the rhythms on their desks and sing or hum along or imitate the sounds.

Children can imagine themselves catapulted back to an era when dinosaurs roamed the earth. They can write, draw, or paint about how they feel there. The teacher might ask the children, "What was it like to see the dinosaurs? To move around them? To feel their heavy breath? To sense their giant shapes?"

The children can move to the music, dramatizing the behaviors of the dinosaurs or the motions of Earth's elements. After watching the segment, they can listen to it again with their eyes closed. Then they can either write about or draw some of the qualities and images that have come to them.

Any type of musical or environmental sound recordings can serve as a springboard to multi-dimensional learning. Teachers can use such recordings to guide young children through an imaginative process. The award-winning CD series Putumayo Kids provides an extraordinary range of songs for children from around the world. Putumayo also offers a World Playground Activity Kit, and many Putumayo CDs include useful information for

teachers as well as activity ideas. (See "References and Resources," page 198.)

Another possibility is to explore how Jon Schwartz, a second-grade teacher and blues musician, uses blues songs to get his students engaged in learning, singing, and interpreting lyrics. (Visit edutopia.org and search for "kids like blues.") In Schwartz's classroom, the children listen to blues music, explore the rhythms, learn about where this music comes from, apply technology, and perform the music through singing, dancing, and dramatic movement.

Each artistic medium adds another layer or dimension to creative work. Visual images in paintings and photographs, combined with music recordings, offer textures and colors for environments or characters, helping children formulate creative ideas for self-expression. Georgia O'Keeffe's painting *Music—Pink and Blue No. 1* resulted from this kind of multimedia experience. As she explains:

> "I never took one of [professor] Bement's classes at Columbia University, but one day walking down the hall I heard music from his classroom. Being curious I opened the door and went in. A low-toned record was being played and the students were asked to make a drawing from what they heard. So I sat down and made a drawing, too. Then he played a very different kind of record—a sort of high soprano piece—for another quick drawing. This gave me an idea that I was very interested to follow later—the idea that music could be translated into something for the eye."[2]

Children don't need to wait until they reach college to benefit from a creative multimedia activity. We've presented combinations of different kinds of art prints with a variety of music—classical recordings, movie soundtracks, and popular tunes. These presentations enable children to feel and sense a creative work as a live, full-bodied reality. While feeling their way through these different creative media, your students can experiment with writing, drawing, movement, and drama. This process exposes children to a broad range of stimuli and helps them form very specific images and textures for their ideas.

[1] You'll find some resources related to the activities discussed in this chapter in the "References and Resources" section beginning on page 189, in Appendix B on page 217, and in Appendix C on page 227.

[2] Georgia O'Keeffe. *Georgia O'Keeffe* (New York: The Viking Press, 1976): 14.

Integrating the Creative Processes to Stimulate Imaginative Thinking

Chapter 4 presents five components of creativity that are essential for nurturing creative thinking: fluency, flexibility, originality, elaboration, and evaluation. In that chapter we focused on these components separately, but here we will integrate them under four general processes: *creative response, creative divergence, creative exploration,* and *creative composition.* Each process emphasizes one particular medium (such as story, painting, music, poetry, or drama) but also combines this medium with other media to provide a multidimensional catalyst for students' creative expressions. The processes are somewhat progressive (that is, they advance in complexity and involvement as you work your way through them), but not exclusively so. As the teacher, you can easily pick and choose from among these activities without having to conduct them in sequence. The "Taxonomy of Imaginative Thinking" chart gives

examples of how you might use these processes in your classroom.

As with the "Taxonomy of Creative Thinking" in Chapter 4, use this taxonomy more as a general guide than as a formula or recipe. We suggest that you select ideas and activities from any of the processes according to the needs, strengths, and interests of your students. The purpose of this chapter is to help you nurture creative development in *all* of your students, enabling you to meet the needs and interests of gifted children as well as those of other students.

Young children have two fundamental needs in creative work: *catalysts* and *guidance.* A multimedia approach fulfills the need for catalysts. Your students need a range of resources—literature, prints of works by great artists, photographs, posters, technology, music, rocks, shells, found objects, and so forth—with which they can craft their own inventions. Your students also need guidance, or specific steps and sequences that structure and support the students' work. All children, including those who are gifted, need teachers who provide workable contexts

Taxonomy of Imaginative Thinking				
Category	*Focus*	*Process*	*Example*	*Outcome*
Creative response	Free response to catalysts	Exposure to art, music, film, theater, photos, and interpretation	Children listen to or read a story.	Awareness and expression of creative ideas
Creative divergence	Variation of an existing creation	Changes made to stories, myths, and art to create new pieces, embellishments	Children create an alternative ending or add another ending to the existing one.	Adaptations of existing works
Creative exploration	Discovery of many dimensions to an idea; intuitive insights	Development of an idea in depth through structured imaginative activities	Children consider aspects of the story in new ways; they reimagine the text, ask "what if?" questions, and experiment with plot and character to build a new story idea.	Interpretive expressions (theatrical productions)
Creative composition	Unusual, novel invention	Creation of unique images and perspectives	Children write, draw, or narrate a new version of the story; create a dramatization to interpret it; compose a poem; or work with peers on a literary magazine to include story, poems, artwork.	Original compositions (poems, stories, theater, songs, and art)

and reachable goals. These contexts and goals help children formulate unique ideas and then develop them into poems, stories, theater, or whatever else they choose to create. Without that structure and support, many creative ideas fall by the wayside because the children feel uncertain about how to proceed with them. When there's no one standing by to provide constructive criticism and encouragement, even highly creative children may abandon a promising idea.

We have included here a philosophy for teaching art written by Marji Purcell Gates, an itinerant art teacher. We feel that you can apply its basic principles to all creative teaching.

Taxonomy of Teaching[3]
(The Job of a Traveling Teacher)

Take a deep breath.
Dramatic entrance; intriguing tools.
Unfurl exemplary creative expression.
Examine its power.
Teach technique.
Tell true stories.
Engage imagination.
Bestow possibilities.
Protect incubation and reflection.
Respect evidence of flow.
Reward striving.
Steady each stumble.
Encourage, nourish, reinforce.
(Learn to whisper, "Yes.")
Bestow more possibilities.
Return to earth.
Clear debris.
Step back.
Promise more.
Tiptoe out.

A Map of Imaginative Activities

As you use ideas from this chapter, we recommend that you:

1. Choose the process you feel will be most accessible to the whole class (and most relevant to the curriculum) to try first; encourage your gifted students to go further with it. One of the advantages of creative processes is that you can easily

adjust them to the talent and experience levels of individual students.
2. Improvise in unique ways with the activities outlined here. This might include combining processes you feel would work together well in your curriculum.
3. Use as many media as you can. Children benefit enormously from the integration of art, video, music, literature, magazines, dramatics, and creative movement.
4. Incorporate these activities into lessons on entirely different subjects. For example, you might have children create stories out of a historical event or write poems on an environmental issue.

Creative Response: Interpretive Expression

Prints of artworks and photographs depicting a variety of landscapes drew clusters of children. José said, "I can't decide whether I want to write about the animals that live by the river or imagine a story about an eagle who fishes there every day." Naomi had a different idea. She said, "I'd rather draw another picture showing what you can't see in this painting—the train that zooms by the river a little farther down—and then write an adventure story." David thought a minute and said, "Well, I think it would be more fun to write about this place from the river's point of view. I would explain how the river came here and tell about all the animals that use it—the muskrat and beaver that swim and build homes near it, the fish that swim through it, the people who fish near it, and the birds that fly above it."

1. CATALYSTS

José, Naomi, and David reveal several different ways young students can make a *creative response* to visual images. To demonstrate how to involve children in creative interpretation—responding to the images they see in unique or unusual ways—we can use the example of trees. Painters and photographers have shown great love for trees; children can explore tree-related works by Vincent van Gogh, Ansel Adams, and many other artists pictured in books and nature magazines and on websites.

Such sources may explore not only the beauty of trees, but also the great diversity of trees on our planet. For example, *Tell Me, Tree: All About Trees for Kids* by Gail Gibbons is a fun, fact-filled book that unravels the scientific secrets of different trees. *Are*

[3] Marji Purcell Gates, Art Teacher, Palatine, IL. Used with permission of Marji Purcell Gates.

Trees Alive? by Debbie S. Miller explores species all over the world.

Through various sources, some children experience the strange beauty of a cactus while also learning how it survives in its desert environment. Other students choose a group of deciduous trees, their brilliant orange-leafed branches reaching up into a violet sky, and wonder why the leaves change color. They learn about *photosynthesis,* a process in which the green pigment *chlorophyll* helps a tree's leaves convert energy from the sun into sugar for food. As the daylight hours decrease in the fall, the tree stops producing chlorophyll, allowing the tree's own natural pigments to brighten and transform the leaves from green to red, yellow, and orange. Books like Robin Bernard's *A Tree for All Seasons* and Gina Ingoglia's *The Tree Book: For Kids and Their Grown-ups* feed curious minds. Providing different catalysts gives children a broad range of creative choices in responding to the concept of trees.

2. QUESTIONS

With encouragement, all the children in the classroom can respond by writing a story, by describing trees in novel ways, or, if they are inexperienced writers, by creating paintings, drawings, or illustrations of their own. You can help them by asking questions such as these:

- What do you see in the pictures or videos?
- What colors, shapes, and textures do you see in or around the trees?
- Are these the kind of trees that change color from summer to fall (deciduous), or are they evergreens? How do the trees live and grow as seen through the pictures or videos?
- What animals live on or around the trees?
- If you were a tree pictured, how would you feel about other trees, rivers, streams, the weather, and the families and animals who live there?
- If you were a tree pictured, what stories might you have to tell about the world around you?
- If you were a scientist looking at the trees, what would you notice? Would you notice something different if you were an artist painting or a photographer taking a picture?
- If you lived nearby, what stories would you have to tell about the trees? What animals hide in them, build nests inside them, or drill the bugs out of them?

- When you look carefully at the picture or video, what does it tell you about the heat or cold of the day? The wind and the rainfall?
- What sounds do you hear in the picture or video? Do you hear any birds? Is there anyone or anything else that might be making noise around the tree?
- Do you think a tree moves? How would you move like a tree?
- How would you describe your favorite tree? What words would you use if you wanted to describe it to someone who couldn't see it? What movements would you make?

These questions represent different ways you can use rich visual images with your students. Feel free to adapt this kind of questioning to the materials you have. Keep asking the students for their own ideas about trees: the tree as a part of nature, as a person, as a story. Exposure to visual images, the questions about them, and follow-up discussions will help every student be able to respond in some way. When children give you words or phrases that describe their experience of the tree, write them on the board. Encourage them to use new words they've learned in their creative process—not just *photosynthesis, deciduous, evergreen, canopy, sap, germination,* and *pollination,* but also the evocative names of trees that captivate them: *sequoia, oak, cypress, red maple, weeping willow, Bodhi, baobab,* and so on. Eventually you'll accumulate a lot of descriptions, and the class can use these to aid or inspire their own drawings or compositions.

3. RESPONSES

Children will naturally respond in different ways. Help children with different abilities, talents, and preferred learning modalities recognize their strengths and use them to achieve more daring, imaginative responses.

Artistic Responses: Nonwriters or inexperienced writers and the artistically inclined may choose to respond visually through drawing, painting, or collage. These children may also want to focus more on the artistic quality of the painting. For example, how does the artist create the effects of wind, light, atmosphere, and mood? Or children may wish to paint a part of the landscape they imagine exists *beyond* the video or picture. Your discussion will bring oral language into the creative process, but since the emphasis here is on imaginative and interpretive response, you don't need to confine it to language.

Scientific Responses: Children who want to use scientific information in their stories or descriptions about trees will want to explore sources that provide such information. *Crinkleroot's Guide to Knowing the Trees* by Jim Arnosky and *From Little Acorns: A First Look at the Life Cycle of a Tree* by Sam Godwin stimulate scientific curiosity about trees. Gifted science buffs in your class could pursue the following questions:

- How does a deciduous tree stay alive in the winter?
- Where does maple syrup come from?
- How does a cactus stay alive with so little rainfall?
- How did the weeping willow get its name?

Children could draw diagrams that illustrate how the cactus survives or where sap comes from, or they could write brief descriptions or captions and tell a story of a tree from a cloud's or leaf's perspective. A book-making activity can allow students to combine images and text in a form that expresses their learning in an imaginative way, and this activity can become a source for more exploration. Susan Gaylord, mentioned in Chapter 4 (page 62), describes a variety of wonderful book-making projects that are suited to the needs of young children and easy to implement.

Kinesthetic Responses: Exploring the world of trees also draws on kinesthetic and auditory sensibilities. Students can imagine themselves to be trees. How would it feel to be perched at the top of the hill? To endure all the seasons? To sense the world around them—the motions of weather and animals and the stillness of the dawn? Questions like these will appeal to kinesthetic learners, who may be inclined to perform a scene or embody the tree through dance or creative movement set to music.

4. EXPANDING THE EXPERIENCE

To expand the experience of visual images, add sound. If you add music or sound to the tree image, children will experience yet another dimension—absorbing atmospheres, subtle meanings, and a variety of story lines. Some students will imagine themselves to be the tree, others wind or clouds, still others the people who live nearby. You could divide the class into children who will be trees and those who will be other elements. With the music and image present, the children can improvise. The

students playing wind, snow, moonlight, and other elements can weave around the students playing trees; the students playing trees can grow, bend with the wind, sag under the weight of the snow, and so forth.

You can extend this process even further with other activities, such as more writing and painting. Creative movement and drama tend to inspire imaginative thinking in children who feel comfortable in this kinesthetic mode. Those who don't can still imagine themselves in particular roles without actually moving to demonstrate or interpret the process.

Creative Divergence: Alternative Fairy Tales

Lakesha was giggling as she read Goldilocks and the Three Dinosaurs *by Mo Willems. The story featured three dinosaurs—a father, a mother, and . . . well . . . some dinosaur visiting from Norway. For no obvious reason, the dinosaurs cleaned up their home and made scrumptious chocolate puddings of various temperatures and left. Why did the dinosaurs suddenly leave? Were they perhaps setting a trap for a foolhardy but succulent little girl who couldn't resist chocolate pudding? Dreaming of chocolate-filled little-girl bonbons, the dinosaurs returned. The language in this picture book was full of irony, none of which was lost on Lakesha. She loved the winks at the reader as much as the story itself. Lakesha started reading the book aloud to the other children at her table and brought that ironic voice to life.*

At another table, Alex was enjoying Carmine: A Little More Red *by Melissa Sweet, a retelling of the story of Little Red Riding Hood. He loved the artwork and the wonderfully odd words that emerged from Granny's alphabet soup—words like clutter, surreal, and omen. By the time he finished, Alex was already busy cooking up ideas for his own fractured fairy tales. He couldn't wait to start!*

Lakesha and Alex were discovering how to fracture fairy tales through *creative divergence*—that is, through departing from the original tale in some way to invent another, often quite different, story. Teaching fractured fairy tales meets the learning needs of many young gifted students, enables everyone to create humorous and witty alternatives to the stories they know well, and also fulfills a number of standards in language arts. Children can explore point of view and consider other settings, times, and characters. They can analyze how these new elements allow them to create wonderful plot twists.

Fractured fairy tales abound, as do ideas on the Web describing how teachers have used fractured fairy tales. (See "References and Resources" beginning on page 196.) Teaching aids can be helpful, but we have found that imposing too much structure can sometimes hinder imagination. For example, one child may prefer to fracture a tale by point of view and character; another may discover that changing the nature of the main character or adding an entirely new character to tell the story actually changes the plot and offers surprise endings. You can guide individual students according to their interests, needs, and abilities.

1. CATALYSTS

You could use any of many delightful examples of fractured fairy tales as catalysts. Some of our favorites—besides *Goldilocks and the Three Dinosaurs* and *Carmine: A Little More Red* are:

- *Pondlarker* by Fred Gwynne
- Jon Scieszka's *The True Story of the Three Little Pigs! by A. Wolf*
- *Cinderella's Rat* by Susan Meddaugh
- *Falling for Rapunzel* by Leah Wilcox

All these fractured fairy tales alter the original tales in interesting ways to present new versions of the stories. Sweet's quirky retelling of Little Red Riding Hood's tale in alphabet book form is quirky and fun, and the comments Carmine and the wolf make about their circumstances—presented in cartoon balloons—provide a unique interpretation of the story. The rat who unceremoniously enters the Cinderella story encounters all sorts of mishaps as he finds himself transformed into a carriage boy, with his sister Ruth changed by a zany wizard into a girl who barks. And the frog in *Pondlarker* decides, after a long search for the princess of his dreams, that he'd rather return to live in his happy little pond than mess around with finicky princesses who hurl insults at frogs.

2. QUESTIONS

Reading such books with the children will suggest all sorts of possibilities for diverging from well-known tales. It may help if you also read the traditional versions as well, so that both renditions will be fresh in their minds. After reading the stories aloud, ask probing questions, such as:

- What's unusual about this story?
- Who is different in this story? Little Red Riding Hood? The wolf? Goldilocks? The frog? How is each character different?
- What parts of this new story don't exist in the old one?
- What events occur in both versions? How are these events alike? How are they different?
- Does the new version make you feel different? How?
- What do you think the writer is trying to say or do in the new story?
- Do you like the new version as much as the older one?

3. RESPONSES

This line of questioning will help children identify where changes occurred and give children ideas about where further changes are possible. As the children share their stories, they will discover more about how they can alter the characters or plot to transform one story into a different one.

This process accomplishes two goals simultaneously. First, it's an engaging way to teach children about the basic elements of a good story (character, plot, conflict, and resolution). Second, it gives the children opportunities to exercise their own story-making powers.

Create a class story. Before giving students the assignment of creating their own version of a fairy tale, you may need to create one—in abbreviated form—with the whole class. Gifted children are less likely to require this preparation; you can excuse them from sitting through this process by asking them to start on their own alternative fairy tales right away. For the rest of the class, we would advise an activity in which everyone *together* experiments with one tale.

Change characters. Begin by explaining to the children that they can change the characters or the plot and affect the story. Referring back to examples read in class, focus first on the main characters (for example, the three little pigs and the big bad wolf). Ask the class to change the descriptions of those characters. For example, the pigs could be big and mean, the wolf small and frail. Goldilocks could be cast as a thief, with the bears as sleuths planting her favorite treats to catch her in the act.

Once the children have changed the characters, ask, "How would this change the story? How would the wolf approach the pigs' houses? How would the pigs respond to the wolf?" As the children respond, write their answers on the board.

When you get to the end of the story, ask children to write or draw their own ending, keeping it private. Afterward, they can share their responses and the class will see how many different responses are possible, even when they all have similar characters and plot. Through this activity, students will understand how the simple process of changing characters will give them an alternative story.

Change the plot. Another approach is to focus on plot first. Children can choose to preserve the essence of the story in terms of characters, atmosphere, and meaning, but use these elements in a different way—for example, with a contemporary perspective or through a different cultural lens. An example of this is *The Rough-Face Girl* by Rafe Martin, a story based on Algonquin sources that has a plot similar to that of the Cinderella fairy tale. Other examples include Shirley Climo's *The Egyptian Cinderella* and Ed Young's *Lon Po Po: A Red-Riding Hood Story from China*. Share a few such stories so children can see other ways of creating alternative tales. Children from minority cultures will especially enjoy this.

Create conflict. Some of the choices children make may take the conflict out of the story. If, for example, they have the pigs and wolf become friends, then the tale will no longer have any suspense. This is not a problem as long as the children create a new conflict. What new problem could arise to threaten this unusual friendship? Since the wolf is not behaving in a way befitting a real wolf, perhaps his father who sent him off to bring back a pig for dinner is now angry and howling outside the door, accusing his child of being a vegetarian. "What kind of wolf are you?" The wolf now has a problem and may need to enlist the help of the pigs.

To get at this idea of conflict, talk to the children about what excites them in the original fairy tales. What keeps them listening? Ask questions such as:

- What made you feel excited when you heard or read about Cinderella?
- What's your favorite part of the story? Why?
- While you listen to the story, what are you hoping will happen to Cinderella?

- In your changed Cinderella story, what new problem do your characters face?
- Is there something in the story that your characters have to escape, hide from, or outsmart?

Some students may need to work through a fairy tale together to understand how to re-create the feeling of suspense in the original tales. Also, highly creative children will occasionally pack too many ideas in one story—changing so many elements that the plot becomes unmanageable. Help them select a few of their best ideas—those that allow maximum flexibility, wit, and humor. Beginning writers and English language learners can dictate their stories or draw illustrations of their favorite scenes.

Share stories. Once the children finish their stories, they can begin to share them with one another. This can be fun and humorous. The stories don't have to be long, elaborate creations. The process is designed simply to give children experience at improvising with an already existing idea in order to make a different one—something professional writers often do. Students will realize, "Wow! I made this story out of that one, and they are very different stories!" This creative process builds the children's confidence in their own imaginative powers by showing them what they can accomplish in an open, flexible environment.

4. EXPANDING THE EXPERIENCE

In order to convert this experience into a multimedia one, you can involve the children in both art and drama activities as extensions of their stories. Give them plenty of choice in determining what other dimensions they would like to add. You may find all sorts of hidden talents in your students as you go through this process with them. Musical children may like to compose something—a song or other short musical number—or even create a dance that evokes images from the story. Others may prefer the visual arts—sketching out illustrations or creating a painting or mural, a distillation of their story through a specific set of images. Podcasts and digital storytelling can also support extension activities. (For more on digital storytelling, visit the website Educational Uses of Digital Storytelling; see "References and Resources," page 197.) The theatrically inclined may prefer to dramatize their stories either by using a narrator and mime or by using readers' theater techniques. (These are described in "Creative Exploration: Readers' Theater and Playwriting," beginning on page 88.)

Some children will need more supervision and guidance than others, depending on their experience in these domains. Be sure that the children work well together and don't distract the rest of the class. Suggest alternatives, if necessary. For skits, the children could narrate their own stories, leaving the dialogue to actors, or the children could read their own stories from start to finish with several others miming the action. Other children in the class can then discuss how the story changed from the original and what they liked about the new story. The goal is to create a variety of new stories using different media for their expression—dramatizations, illustrations, written narratives, paintings, shoe-box dioramas of key scenes, songs, or whatever else the children may wish to create.

Creative Exploration: Readers' Theater and Playwriting

The children loved The World According to Humphrey *by Betty G. Birney. To encourage deeper reflection and to enrich the reading experience, the teacher decided to use readers' theater. Everyone would have a role to play. The children's response to this idea was electric.*

As the class reviewed and selected the most important scenes in the book, a group of advanced readers worked together on adapting biographical sources to their own readers' theater pieces. They had two ideas: Theodor Seuss Geisel (Dr. Seuss) and Jane Goodall. The children wanted to focus on Goodall's and Seuss's childhoods. What early clues could the children find about the people young Goodall and Seuss would become? What were they like as children? What led to their adult interests? Seuss gave his creative and light-hearted mother credit for introducing him to rhythms and rhymes as a young child. When he couldn't sleep, she would softly chant in catchy phrases the many pies she used to sell at her father's bakery. As for Goodall, long before she went to Africa to study the chimps, she spent her childhood observing, drawing, and taking notes on birds and other animals around her.

Readers' theater is a very effective way to instill in young children a deeper understanding of the elements of story—character development, plot, and setting. Readers' theater can work for nonfiction and fiction. (See page 90 for an example of readers' theater applied to biography.) The process can be as simple as just having students read expressively or as elaborate as directing them in costumes on a set

suggestive of the story. By embodying segments of a full-length book, selecting passages to narrate and perform for an audience, children acquire insights about the art of storytelling that they might not gain otherwise. This process of creative exploration is an excellent foundation for the students' own story inventions—developing full-bodied characters and believable plots, conflicts, and resolutions.

1. CATALYSTS

To start, try a readers' theater version of a familiar book or story collection. One child can take all the narration lines. (There's no need to speak the "said" parts of the narration.) Each of the other children can take a character. The narrator can probably take the role of leader. Gifted children who are quite young—even first graders—may be ready to take the narrator's part. With younger children, you can do the narrator's part yourself the first time.

After you divide the class into groups, have each group choose a different book or, if the class wants to tackle a longer work, different sections of one book. Either way, have the students familiarize themselves with the book, discuss it, and share ideas. You could begin by reading the book aloud or having one of the students do so.

A word to the wise: The first time you try this, don't get too ambitious and choose too much to perform. Perhaps a shorter book would be best until you and the children become experienced in readers' theater. If, after reading this section, you think it might be challenging to do in your classroom (for example, if your students have widely varying abilities and/or are younger than second grade or so), recruit some assistance in the form of paraprofessionals, parent volunteers, or other classroom helpers.

2. QUESTIONS

The first phase of this process is to identify the main elements of the story or book. To facilitate this phase, ask the children some fundamental questions to focus their thoughts, such as:

- What is this story about?
- Who are the main characters?
- Where and when does this story take place?
- What are the problems that the main characters face? How do they solve these problems?
- What are some of the most exciting parts? Why are they so exciting?

Choose a child in each group to record answers to the questions. If the whole class is doing one book, you can write their responses on the board for reference.

3. RESPONSES

Through your questions, you're encouraging your students to think analytically about the book and thereby heighten their own awareness of the key elements that hold the story together. This in turn will help them choose passages to dramatize in readers' theater.

Choose critical passages. Based on the children's responses to your questions, help students choose the chapters or passages that seem most critical to the book or story. For a book like *The World According to Humphrey*, this probably means the first few chapters (introducing the major characters and problem), the middle chapters that are critical to the story's development, and finally the chapters that solve the problem—particularly the last three or four. Have the children select the sentences and dialogue and descriptive statements in each chapter for the performance. Reassure children that no one has to memorize lines. Explain that they will do one of two things:

- plan a dramatization in which actors read lines or use their own words to reenact the scenes
- write narration for scenes that the actors will enact as the narrator reads them

As the children work through the book or story, keep them focused on the important or critical moments in the development of the plot. They could begin by listing the memorable scenes—those that most interested them as readers or listeners. After the group has compiled the list, have them put the moments in chronological order and review the list. You can write the list on the board as the children share. Tell students to look at each scene and ask themselves:

- Is this an exciting scene? Why?
- Is this scene necessary to understand the story?
- How important is it?
- How could we act it out? If we don't do that, is there a way we can retell the scene using mime and narration?
- What will we gain by keeping this scene?
- What will we lose if we don't use this scene?

Somebody in each group could keep a record of the selections the children wish to perform. Circulate among the different groups and mediate disagreements where they arise. Put a limit on the number of scenes allowed for each group. Otherwise, the process will quickly become complicated and unmanageable.

Choose roles. Each group can choose one child to be the narrator, and then the students can choose the characters they would most like to dramatize, read, or mime. The unique circumstances of your classroom (time constraints, number of children, students' needs and interests) will require you to be adaptable in determining children's roles. If more than one child wants to play a particular role, you can have them take turns. If you have more students than roles, consider distributing the role of narrator to several good readers. Another possibility is to expand the enactments by having children briefly mime parts of the plot that will not be dramatized, with narrators summarizing what happens in the intervals between dramatized selections. This solves two problems at once—what to do with children who don't yet have parts, and how to inform the audience about what has occurred between scenes. Some children may also wish to provide sound effects or work on props.

Become the characters. Readers' theater production encourages students to take ownership of a story. We have found that students of all abilities become more connected to their roles if they do more than read or write a brief summary of their characters. A kinesthetic learning process is at work here. In order to embody the story vividly, students need the freedom to imagine the lives of their characters based on the story. Ask questions to get at:

- specific characteristics ("Where do you sleep? What do you eat? How do you move around?")
- the emotions that drive the character ("What are you worried about? What do you want more than anything? Why do you want that?")
- the character's history ("How long have you been _____ or been in the situation you are in? What do you do every day? What do you enjoy about being _____?")
- how the character feels about the other characters and what they do ("What do you think about _____? Why?")

- the character's challenges ("What problem do you face? What problem is another character facing and what do you think about it?")

As they probe the characters, children begin to make the story *their* story. By internalizing the story in this way, they gain deep knowledge of it. Their discovery becomes a dynamic process rather than a finished product.

Stage it simply. Help the children keep their staging clear and uncomplicated and use simple props, costumes, and sound effects. Circulate among the different groups as they work, offering suggestions on staging and the selection of lines and summaries that operate as transitions from scene to scene or chapter to chapter.

Place the narrator to the side of the dramatic action. Encourage groups who plan to use any props, costumes, or sound effects to assign someone to keep a list of items required for the production. Remind the class that the main purpose of props, costumes, and sound is to *suggest* an environment, to *evoke* (give the feeling or sense of) an atmosphere that will inspire the imagination of both performers and audience.

Keep the performance relaxed. When the class reaches the performance phase of readers' theater, be as informal and relaxed as you can, and encourage the children to do the same. This process is not intended to produce a flawless theater event, but to expand students' experience and understanding of the great art of storytelling.

Be positive as the children perform. If a child makes a mistake, minimize it and offer encouragement. Before the performances begin, explain to children that the dramatic process is a way to give stories new life, not to criticize. After each performance, ask the performing group what new things they discovered about the story. Then ask the rest of the class for their comments and questions.

When children attempt to develop their own stories in this way, the readers' theater experience will generate untold benefits. Your students will create more developed characters—and plots that evolve organically from those characters. With performance experience, the children will develop a habit of examining issues of motivation in characters and how this relates to the creation of conflict and suspense in a good story.

4. EXPANDING THE EXPERIENCE

For gifted students, using readers' theater to dramatize the lives of great leaders or pioneers (scientists, writers, artists, and so on) draws on many talents in one process: interpretation, imagination, theatricality, analytical thinking, composition, and invention. One of the greatest benefits of dramatizing an exceptional life is that young children, especially those who may have problems writing, can still express their talents and inspiration.

General Principles for Teachers

- Begin with students' interests and questions. "What do I want to know about this person?" Feeding their own curiosity and imagination will motivate inquiry. They could approach this assignment as detectives uncovering clues about the experiences that influenced their subjects and about the people who inspired their subjects to take steps they might not have taken otherwise.
- Discuss the myth of greatness—that accomplished people become accomplished effortlessly. Offer examples the children might recognize (prominent people in sports, film, music, literature, and so forth) that show the difficulties and setbacks encountered by accomplished people.
- Provide a variety of biographies for children so they can see different ways of telling a true story. They do not have to start at the beginning or feel bound to a monotonous chronology. In fact, they can extract one or two key events as the core of their biography and use these to create depth and complexity in their dramatizations.
- Expose students to both primary and secondary sources and help them distinguish between the two. In addition, draw on materials from other media—sketches, portraits, documentaries, websites, and online interviews. Help students find the sources that best ignite their imagination and enthusiasm. Trusting that inner fire is highly important for young learners. Often it tells them, "Come over here, this will pique your curiosity; it will surprise, and delight you."
- Have students record their discoveries in writing or in voice recordings. Help them focus on what they like about the people they've chosen to study—the qualities that enabled their subjects to be open-minded, creative, hopeful, courageous, or motivated no matter what. What strengths and what events seem most important to students?

As the students immerse themselves in the lives of famous leaders and pioneers, they connect with their subjects and intuitively sense what else they need to know. Point of view shifts and deepens, and imagination begins its work of weaving a sequence of scenes that children would like to enact. For children who feel shy or intimidated, others can assist by miming or narrating. Gifted students tend to love doing their own blocking.

Sequence for Students

1. Become an expert in your subject (person).

    -   Find primary sources (diaries, letters, photos, notes, and recordings).
    -   Find secondary sources (books, stories, documentaries, and articles).
    -   Explore media representations (films, audio, video, and art).

2. Think of the qualities you most admire in this person. What do you believe made it possible for this person to do what he or she did?

3. Write down one or two questions that you want to answer about this person's life.

4. Experiment with point of view. How would this person's life appear to his or her dog, child, neighbor, tree, paintbrush, writer's pen, or old pair of walking shoes? The boots would notice the heavy tread of the owner's feet. The child would notice the parent's tone of voice and facial expressions.

5. Imagine being the person and answer the following questions:

    -   What was your childhood like? Who inspired you? Who challenged you?
    -   What difficulty or problem are you facing?
    -   What do you want to express? What event(s) do you want to share that relate to your message?

6. Write a biography focusing on the qualities and questions you've chosen to guide you. This will be the narrator's part.

7. Write your part—your words to other characters and to the audience, as well as the other characters' words to you. If possible, use direct quotes. Explore different media, such as recordings, visual images, videos, websites, and letters.

A key feature of using readers' theater to dramatize a person's life is that students often compose their own speaking parts (unless they find a biography or autobiography with direct quotes that they like). Using more sources increases the challenge of readers' theater, but this is exactly what gifted students love. Assure the children that if they work in pairs or small groups, they will have more choices in how they bring their subject to life. Some children excel more in writing, others in oral interpretation, movement, editing and blocking, and so forth. Working together under your guidance, they can create a powerful dramatization that synthesizes all the elements of their story and that uses their different talents.

Creative Composition: Free Verse

Mrs. Gromicek's second graders were studying biographies of great inventors and pioneers. They had already read together and explored and discussed the lives of pioneers in various fields, what made these people unique, and how each one dealt with obstacles. Now Mrs. Gromicek was giving the children an opportunity to use this information to create an original product or idea based on their study and the distillation of their deepest thoughts and impressions. She asked the class for ideas. Rafael suggested, "I want to write a poem. But I want it to also tell a story like a picture." Zoe sighed, "But I don't like rhymes at all. My ideas can't run free because I have to find all those tidy rhyming words." Jacob, who also loved poetry, piped up, "You don't have to rhyme, you know. A lot of poems don't rhyme at all, and they're great." Zoe mused, "So I could write a poem about Amelia Earhart flying around the world in an airplane, and I wouldn't have to worry about rhymes?" The answer, of course, is yes!

Creative composition uses many of the other processes already described in this chapter. It *responds* to many stimuli and reinterprets their varied images and textures. It *diverges* from and improvises with products already made, embellishing and altering them. It also *explores* the inner depths of a painting, a book, or a story to locate other meanings than the more apparent ones. Creative composition draws upon all these processes and then invents something unique—something more than a variation, a version, an interpretation, or a response.

1. CATALYSTS

You can design a creative composition process within any general topic you happen to be studying. In the scenario we use here, the children focus on the life stories of famous pioneers and inventors as catalysts for composing free verse.

Free verse is an ideal medium for enabling children to develop original compositions. Many gifted children enjoy the process of creating vivid images in poetic form. Poetry, like painting, combines feelings, textures, and ideas to create unique, multi-dimensional visions of human experience. Poetry has the power to help children distill their deepest perceptions and thoughts; it also acts as a springboard to other creative work. Children can use their poems as seeds for other inventions—for paintings, songs, stories, and dramatizations.

Expose children to poetry. Teaching children about free verse is a simple process, especially in the primary grades.

When Zoe expressed a keen interest in writing a poem on Amelia Earhart, Mrs. Gromicek distributed some poems as examples of free verse. She read one or two brief poems to the class and then led a discussion on how poets compose lines of different (and often uneven) lengths, vary the rhythms, and use no rhymes (although they may use similar sounds within the lines). Mrs. Gromicek also read a few poems written by children she'd taught in previous years. One of the poems was a response to a Monet painting, and she showed the class the painting as she read the poem aloud to them.

Create a joint poem. Working as a group to create a poem gives children the benefit of hearing a variety of ways they can use language to express ideas.

Mrs. Gromicek picked up a poster on Amelia Earhart and asked the students what they saw in this picture of a woman standing by her airplane, preparing for her solo flight around the world. She asked for one sentence describing the feeling, the atmosphere, the color, the excitement, or whatever else struck the children. One child began tentatively. Mrs. Gromicek wrote down the sentence and then remarked, "There is the beginning of our poem. Now can I have another sentence? What else do you see? What do you imagine you might hear or feel if you were hiding in the back of that plane?"

Emboldened by the first child's offering, more children responded. Soon, practically everyone in the group interested in Amelia Earhart had contributed a phrase. Then Mrs. Gromicek asked for a title for the new poem. Some discussion ensued before the children decided on "Flight to the Skies."

2. QUESTIONS

As with all the processes we have explored, asking questions helps children find and structure their ideas. Like Mrs. Gromicek, you could use a series of questions to set some general, loose guidelines for children's own representations. As the children respond and explore, be sure to have available plenty of books, magazines, biographies, autobiographies, historical fiction, pictures, posters, poems, and stories that offer a rich variety of images and perspectives for the children's compositions. (Several are suggested in "References and Resources," beginning on page 196.) Returning to the example of accomplished people, you might ask questions such as these:

- Who is the person you want to be? Why?
- What was the person's contribution to the world?
- What qualities about the person do you most admire? Bravery? Determination? A sense of adventure?
- What challenges and obstacles did the person overcome?
- Would you like to have known this person? Why or why not?
- What do you admire most about this person? Why?
- What facts about this person's life do you find most important?
- If you were to think of this person in colors, what colors would they be?
- If you were to think of this person as music, what would it sound like?
- What pictures, stories, or paintings help you find what was special and important about this person?

3. RESPONSES

After the children have written their poems, ask them to share their work. If they seem reluctant, you can read a few poems first and talk about the different images and feelings the poems evoke. Since there is no pressure for a rhyme scheme at the ends of lines, most students will feel free to manipulate the form in the way they want and will probably enjoy sharing their work.

In Mrs. Gromicek's class, one student decided to write a poem describing what was in the picture. Another child wanted to talk to Amelia Earhart as she stood by her airplane and write a poem that resembled an interview for a newspaper. Another preferred to be the plane itself and to talk about his life as a plane and the feats he would perform for this famous lady who flew so daringly in the sky.

Following are a few examples of free verse written by primary-age children.[4] The poems illustrate how talented young children can write from unique perspectives, creating images that are vivid and even rare:

Mona Lisa
Jessica, Grade 1

Maybe her smile
means she's sitting there
smiling and thinking,
or maybe just daydreaming,
or just thinking.
She's dressed up like
she who's going to temple.
Mysterious smiles,
mysterious looks, but
Da Vinci must have fallen
in love with Mona Lisa
and painted
a picture of her.

Sequoias
Sindhuja, Grade 3

The rangers call them the faithful couple
Those two-thousand-year-olds
Rising centuries above
Side by side, they'd grown so close
They finally fused into a single tree
A triumphant union of fiber, leaf, and cell
For they were blessed love
Sunlight spills down miles of bark
The rain sinks into the world
A longing so pure
Even heavenly in its silence

The Dark
Christopher, Grade 1

The dark,
pitch black,
roams in the night.
Trees and animals
feel a little bit scared
as they go into their cozy homes,
warm and toasty
like a nest.

Wishes and Dreams
Marlene, Grade 4

Your mind is but a dream
So let your wings spread wide
Youth is but an age
Wishes, dreams come to young and old
An unspent wish or dream is nothing
They come in unlimited quantity
Whenever you want or need them, they are there
Just on the other side of your imagination
Lying there unspent, waiting to unfurl . . .
Wishes and dreams

Here Is There
Craig, Grade 2

When here is there,
Then there is here.
When they come together
There is here and so is here
Then something is taken from the past,
But if here is there and so is there
Then something is taken from our time.

I Have a Dream
Noah, Grade 3

That I can make the world a better place somehow
That my family will not have to suffer like some
people do today
That my friends will always make hard times better

Oh, I Have a Dream . . .
That children will always flow with ideas and never
give up
That grown-ups, wherever they are, at whatever
age, even if they are gone, will always remember,
always, their little ones
That people will start forgiving for everything
and realize that P.E.A.C.E. is much more than
five letters

Oh, I Have a Dream . . .
That people will find war as silly as an apple with
a fruit hat dancing to the Cha Cha while holding maracas
That people will learn that you should not lie, like
you should not smoke
That there will be so much fun, peace, and love in
the world!

Oh, I Have a Dream . . .

---

[4] These poems are reprinted here with the permission of the children and their families.

Lonely Night
Whitney, Grade 4

Snow glistens in the moonlight
The world feels so empty and silent
Too quiet to be true
Winter's era is lonely
No birds chirping
The wolves and coyotes have ceased their howling
Even though the moon is full
Moon looks lonely through my window
She has no water to push and pull
And no wolves or coyotes to howl to her
Only clouds, dark and thick, surround her
But she cannot sleep or cease her duty
Sleeping deer, wolves, and others lie buried
Under a blanket of snow
But all will wake when spring comes.

4. EXPANDING THE EXPERIENCE

When you use creative composition in this way, chances are good that you'll find *all* your children eager—and able—to compose in vivid and evocative language. If you wish to extend your students' work to other media, encourage them to use their free-verse compositions as catalysts. The class can do a multimedia project around the poems—including stories, drawings, diagrams, maps, cartoons, songs, and dramatizations. Encourage children to choose whatever media they enjoy using or whatever media they feel best enhances their poems. You might ask, "What would be the best way to build on the feeling in your poem? What will help you share the mood of your poem? How can you show that heavy air? How can you make us feel that cold, fresh rain? Can you do it with a painting? A cartoon? A story? Another poem? A song? A skit?"

When creating with these other media, children don't need to confine themselves to merely representing their poems. They can also *complement* their poems in interesting ways. For example, take the poem "Mona Lisa" by Jessica, a first grader (page 93). Jessica could decide to write a story on what Mona Lisa is daydreaming about.

Sharing Creativity with Others

Children love to share the work they have done, especially creative productions. It validates their worth as originators and helps them believe that they have something unique and valuable to contribute. You can be creative yourself in orchestrating a variety of opportunities for your students to share their work:

- Ask the children for their ideas on how they would like to share their projects.
- Display pictures, poems, stories, and other works created by your students. If your class has a website, blog, or other presence on the Web, you can display student work there.
- Invite younger or older children into the class to see your students' creations.
- Have each group of your students present its work to the rest of the class or to another class at your grade level.
- Create opportunities for the performers in your class to present their readers' theater pieces, songs, dances, poems, and stories for the school.
- Invite parents to come in and see the children's work.
- Start a newsletter in your class where students can regularly report on their creative accomplishments. Distribute the newsletter to the rest of the school, as well as to parents, via paper or email.
- Present students' work at a Grandparents' Day event, or take the completed creations on the road to a hospital or senior center.
- Make a video of the children's work. Show the video at an open house or another appropriate schoolwide event. If your students have pen pals, make copies that they can send via mail or email.
- Investigate the venues your school or district offers for sharing student work on its website.

Questions and Answers

"I don't have much experience in the arts. Can I still teach using these processes?"
Yes! You are not training children to become authors, painters, or performing artists. Rather, you are using the arts to encourage children to freely explore their creative potential. The point of creative work is not the product, but the process of thinking flexibly. Start on a scale that feels manageable for you, and encourage your students to have fun.

"How can I set tangible goals for projects that seem so open-ended?"
It depends on how you are using these activities. Most teachers will want to integrate them into the existing curriculum. If you do this, your goals are already established. If you don't integrate these

activities into the existing curriculum, you can set tangible goals that still provide freedom for children to improvise.

For example, you may want the children to identify and understand the different elements of a story (characters, plot, setting, theme, and so forth). After introducing these elements and discussing them (perhaps within the context of a story or movie), you could allow your students to explore them creatively by inventing alternative fairy tales, brief dramatizations, or visual representations. Or you may wish to have students analyze the stages of a story: the beginning (often a descriptive paragraph), the introduction to the main characters, the conflict, the climax, and the ending. With students who choose to work more independently, you may wish to create a contract that will help them commit to their goals.

"What's the best way to manage situations in which children want to work in groups?"

We recommend grouping children according to their strengths—the talents they share. When your students start on creative projects, initially you may want to have them group themselves randomly. As the projects get under way, you will probably discover other, more useful ways of grouping the children based on mutual interests and motivations that become apparent. Gifted children tend to accomplish the most when grouped in this way. (You will find additional information about grouping children in Chapter 8, "Cluster Grouping: A Flexible Alternative" on page 135.)

"Does this kind of teaching in language arts also support skills such as critical reading, writing composition, and vocabulary building?"

Absolutely! In fact, these creative processes can accomplish more in the area of basic skills and advanced thinking than many more conventional approaches to language arts. The use of theater, painting, music, story invention, and creative movement encourages children to explore the world of words imaginatively. In the process, they also acquire vocabulary and reading skills. Arts integration has repeatedly proven its effectiveness as a catalyst for academic and creative growth in all subjects. "Artful Thinking," a program developed by Harvard University in collaboration with the Traverse City, Michigan, schools, integrates visual art and music into the curriculum. (For more information, visit the arts websites listed in "References and Resources," beginning on page 196.)

Conclusion

Involving young children in the creative arts can be beneficial to students at all points on the academic spectrum. Those who struggle with reading and writing will begin to discover that reading is not merely acquisitive, but creative; that writing is not just a skill to learn, but a way to think. Gifted children will likely love the freedom to stretch beyond traditional skill learning to activities that invite imaginative thought and expression.

An emphasis on creativity is valuable in all areas of study. Language arts, in particular, lends itself to this kind of focus. Students who seem lukewarm toward language arts will find new life in the subject when they realize *they* have something to bring to it. Through promoting imagination in the language arts, you have a valuable opportunity to turn your young students' focus away from what they *must absorb* to the unique strengths and abilities they *can apply* to the work at hand. All your students can expand their talents if they take this plunge into creativity now, when they are young.

You can help each child find the courage to do so. You can give children the confidence to believe that what they have to offer is valuable and worthy of sharing with the world. All students—including those who are gifted, those who have learning differences, and those who struggle with the discrepancy between their ideas and their writing or reading skills—need to believe this. Through the processes and activities we have shared in this chapter, students can experience breakthroughs in creativity and self-esteem.

Children need the opportunity to use language imaginatively—through reading, listening, discussing, writing, acting, and speaking—and to share the products of their creative efforts. Beyond this, gifted children need to know the purpose of their talents. Sharing is a first step to discovering what they have to give and the purpose of the giving.

CHAPTER 6
Promoting Discovery and Higher-Level Thinking in Math and Science

Simone was bending over the table she shared with four other second graders. They were adding two-digit numbers using a method of regrouping. Simone had finished her assignment and decided to help her friend, Jenna, who didn't understand place value.

Simone, a gifted child, told Jenna a story. "Think of it this way," she said, drawing a small house on a piece of paper. "Pretend a family moves into this house. They have two adults and three kids. So there are five people in this house. They have four more kids. Now nine people live in the house. The parents start wondering how they're going to fit all these kids in their house. They agree, 'No more kids!' But a year later, they have one more child. Now ten people live in the house. The wife says, 'This house can't hold more than nine people! We need a bigger house.'

"So," Simone said, "the parents build a huge house to the left of the smaller one." She drew another house. "It's divided up into ten-person apartments. Only

groups of ten can move in. The whole family moves into the big house to the left of the small house. They start renting the small house to families with nine people or fewer. Each time the small house gets more than nine people in it, ten people move to the big house and leave the remainder in the small house."

Simone looked at Jenna's addition problem: 25 + 27. "So," Simone said, "look at these two numbers—twenty-five and twenty-seven—and think about them as people living in the two houses. For twenty-five, you have twenty people living in the big house and five in the small house. Now twenty-seven people want to join the twenty-five, so how do you do it? First, let's put twenty in the big house and seven in the small house. When the seven try to join the five people already living in the small house, the group gets too big for the house—twelve people. So ten move to the big house, and two stay in the small house."
Simone made this diagram:

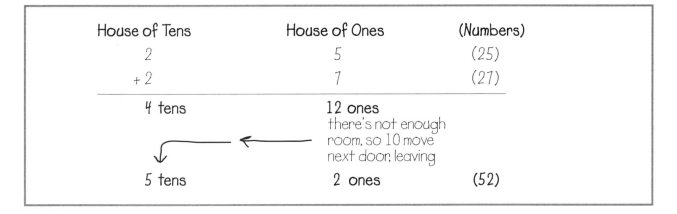

Then she went on, "So you add those ten people to the twenty plus twenty already in the big house, and you get fifty in the big house and two in the small house—fifty-two!"

Without realizing it, Simone used storytelling to help Jenna understand how to regroup in addition. Simone created an imaginary scenario of houses, each having a place value that corresponded with the actual place value Jenna needed to learn for her addition problem.

If Jenna understands Simone's house scenario, she will probably be able to transfer this understanding to the problem she's working on and will comprehend, in a concrete way, the kinds of operations she needs to perform to get her answer. Carrying a one over to the tens column will stick in her mind as another ten people moving from the small house to the big house.

Simone has also benefited from this process. In telling the story, she's gained new perspectives on an operation that she has grown used to doing mechanically.

Creative Learning as a Link to Higher-Level Conceptual Thinking

In order to translate a math or science concept in this way, a child first has to understand it fully. Many students—gifted and otherwise—who may feel disinclined to pursue a particular subject (or may be confused by it) often become motivated when they see a way to give life to it. Integrating language arts and other arts with math and science presents new perspectives on the concepts students are learning and new ways to manipulate the concepts. It's the difference between saying "Here's how the process

works—follow it like this" and "Here's how the process works—now see if you can perform it through a story (poem, painting, dance, skit)." For gifted children, this approach provides opportunities to explore relationships and test hypotheses in new ways.

In this chapter, we'll use some of the creative strategies discussed in Chapters 4 and 5 and demonstrate how you can apply them to primary math and science lessons. One of the greatest assets of creativity is its capacity to involve and motivate students. This is especially true in subjects that are abstract or seem to be confined within a rigid set of rules and principles. Imagination restores wonder to the world of math and science, revealing elements of surprise and adventure that delight young children and engage them in higher levels of critical and conceptual thinking.

Creative representations of mathematical concepts tend to make thinking more flexible. Take the example of Simone and Jenna. Knowledge of *how* and *why* certain rules work as they do can give children a stronger grasp of logic and the different ways to apply it. Math problems evolve from boring formulas children repeat and record into intriguing phenomena they can create and manipulate.

Creative thinking in a math or science class quickly lights up when teachers allow children to learn new concepts through other fields of their choosing—stories, art, music, design, and so on. Drawing on their strengths, children understand mathematical and scientific principles and ideas at a deeper level. Meanwhile, children enjoy the playful and expressive experience of using other media to carry out original projects.

We wholeheartedly believe that children need different ways of relating to math and science concepts. Primary math and science should not be merely sets of rules and procedures for children to memorize and follow. Rather, they should be "sense-making" experiences that invite students to create and contribute to their own growing knowledge. In this chapter, we suggest several avenues by which you might guide children to do this, including exploration of properties and processes in everyday life, experimentation, manipulation of ideas for new inventions, and imaginative translations of mathematical and scientific concepts. Our intent is to help you guide children to see the math and science all around them and to apply mathematical and scientific ideas in innovative ways.

To present these ideas, we've divided children's study into explorations of *properties* and *processes*. At times, these explorations overlap. For example, in a geometry lesson, students could learn the basic characteristics (properties) of two- and three-dimensional shapes and might then investigate more about both properties and processes by doing some of the following:

- Experiment with these shapes to create their own environments.
- Explore ways that geometric shapes can compose a wide variety of patterns.
- Express their ideas and insights about shapes through art, creative writing, and drama.

In a similar fashion, students could begin a science lesson by learning some of the basic characteristics of birds and then proceed with one of the following:

- Study one or several principles of flight, relating the flight of birds to that of aircraft.
- Write stories from the birds' perspective.
- Imagine how to construct wings for people to imitate the flight of birds.

Through this approach, math and science become more than means to understand the world; they become means to imagine it.

Discovering Properties

The creative imagination is a powerful source for exploring the *properties* of an object, a living thing, a concept, or even a symbol. In the last two chapters, we've seen the value of having students identify themselves imaginatively with someone (or something) they are studying. Pretending is a very natural activity for young children—one that expands conceptual thinking. When you empower your students to draw on their creative resources, you can deepen

what they've already learned and help them explore their knowledge in new ways.

As students begin to understand scientific and mathematical properties, you can encourage them (especially those who don't yet write much) to use a variety of media for their work—visual arts, short skits, mimes, or dictated stories and poems. Your goal is to allow students to step into the world of a math or science topic and explore its properties and attributes through the arts.

As a warm-up, you might want to begin with some "mind benders"—questions or activities that help children stretch their imaginations. Analogies are useful aids to innovative thinking. You can create them in isolation or relate them specifically to whatever the class is studying on a particular day. Here are some examples:[1]

- How are you like a flower?
- How is third grade like a tree?
- How is a flower like a star?
- How is a story like a river?
- How is a computer like an animal?

You can adapt this line of thinking to different grade levels and subjects within your math or science curriculum. For our purposes, analogies encourage children to make unusual connections between themselves and the subject they're studying. This will prove useful when the students begin to explore math and science concepts and to elaborate on many of the properties and processes they are learning.

Science: A Study of Animals

Kwami had always loved reptiles and amphibians. As a three-year-old, he'd pored over pictures of lizards, frogs, and snakes, asking for their names and learning to identify them himself. At four, he'd spent hours in the backyard looking for toads and garter snakes. In kindergarten, Kwami and his class were exploring a variety of animals and habitats. Kwami seemed less than enthusiastic about the activities the children were doing. During free time, he would head for the back of the room and absorb himself in picture books about amphibians.

With gifted children like Kwami, you might try a process that allows students to delve deeply into a subject they feel keenly about. In-depth creative and scientific work on a *single* animal can often impart

---

[1] Carol D. Creighton, primary classroom teacher, Northbrook, IL. Used with permission of Carol D. Creighton.

more knowledge to students than teaching them a few facts about a whole spectrum of animals.

Let's explore some ways in which you might undertake this type of study. You could begin by asking all the children to choose a species they would like to investigate. Tell the class they're each going to explore one animal and will then turn their knowledge into a creative story. In this story, they'll pretend they are the creature themselves. Provide books and magazines for the children to thumb through while they decide.[2] Like Kwami, the students should feel some curiosity, delight, or fascination for the creature they choose in order for this activity to work effectively. The value of creative exploration is its flexibility, allowing students of different ability levels to advance at their own pace.

1. SET THE STAGE: INVESTIGATE

Once the children have decided which animal they wish to investigate, have them write down or dictate any facts they already know about it. Even if they can report only what the animal looks like, and whether it has fur or scales or feathers, it's always a good practice to begin with the *students'* impressions and insights. You could have the children share some of their thoughts and begin to discuss basic animal categories according to habitats, types of food the animals eat, comparisons to different species, and other distinguishing features. Use questions such as the following to guide children before, during, and after their research:

- Is your animal warm-blooded or cold-blooded?
- Does it eat meat, plants, or both?
- Is it a mammal like humans? Why or why not? Does it belong to another animal group?
- What does your animal look like? Does it have hair? Is it big or small? Does it have claws or feet? A mouth or a beak? Does it fly, swim, crawl, jump, or run?
- What kind of place does it live in?
- What do you like most about your animal?
- What is your animal's most unusual feature?
- Is there something you don't like about your animal?

2. IMAGINE

Once the children have collected some facts they know about their animal, explain that you want

them to create a story about it. The point of the story is not for the students to make up a complicated plot, but to try explaining their animal's world from the standpoint of the animal itself. Here you're guiding children to use the art of story-making to enhance their scientific knowledge of the animal they select. Rather than simply gathering information for an assignment, they'll be seeking facts they need in order to write their story.

Two story starters we like to use are "A Day in the Life" and "What Would It Be Like?"

A Day in the Life

Make available a variety of books, posters, websites, videos, and other resources for students to use in learning about their animal. Ask the students to describe their day as if they were this animal. Encourage them to tell their story with the word *I*. To help them choose details to include, you might ask questions such as these:

- What kind of place do you live in? Is it hot or cold? Wet or dry? Above ground or below?
- What does your body look like? How does it feel to live in that body?
- What do you eat? Where do you find food? Where do you find water?
- Where do you sleep? What do you use to build your home?
- How do you spend your day? Do you gather food? Hunt? Sleep? Move from one place to another (migrate)?
- Are you a mother? A father? A child?
- How do you get along with other animals who live near you?
- What is the name of your group or species? Are you part of a pod? A herd? A flock? A school?
- How do you communicate with other animals in your group?
- What dangers do you face from other animals? From humans?
- How do you defend yourself? What do you do if you or other animals in your family are in danger?
- What's special about animals like you? Why is your species important in nature? In the world?

For students who can read, you may want to write these questions on the board. The children could follow them as they design their story. For younger children who aren't yet reading independently, you could provide resource books with fewer words and more pictures. Your focus for these children would be to help them acquire a number of

---

[2] You'll find some resources related to the activities discussed in this chapter in the "References and Resources" section beginning on page 189, in Appendix B on page 217, and in Appendix C on page 227.

scientific facts about the animal. Nature videos are another excellent resource for nonreaders. (See, for example, the large collection of videos at National Geographic Kids; "References and Resources," page 202.) With very young children, we often turn down the volume of videos and talk to the class ourselves—asking them questions and reviewing the concepts they are learning.

You can also encourage more creative thinking by asking the children to visualize their animals in unusual environments. For example: "If you were an elephant, how would you like living in a city? Where would you go? Where would you look for food?" "If you were an otter, how would you like living in a nearby stream? Would you be happy?" These alternative scenarios are fun and can help children use their imaginations to gain more precise knowledge and understanding.

Ask nonwriters to draw or sketch different scenes of a story. The story could unfold in steps or sequences, which students could then share with the class. Guide children as they explain their stories. Ask questions about their pictures, and encourage the other students to ask questions, too. For example: "How fast can you run (swim, fly)?" "What do you do when you're afraid and need to escape quickly?" "Where do you look for food?" "Where will you sleep tonight?" The whole class can learn from this process.

Occasionally, a few students may realize they don't know exactly how their species behaves in certain circumstances. Sharing their work and responding to questions will stimulate critical thinking and the desire to discover and know more. The children will enjoy using each new fact they learn as a source for additional artistic and imaginative details.

Allow for flexibility in how children express their ideas. This is a chance for them to think about and share science creatively. For example, instead of writing or illustrating a story, some children may want to compose some free verse to describe their animal. (For suggestions on helping children write free verse, see "Creative Composition: Free Verse" beginning on page 91.) Some children may want to use a computer or tablet to produce a slide show or video. Younger nonreaders may enjoy expressing their ideas through mime, dance, or some other form of creative movement. If you have several children working on the same animal, you could group them together so they can pool resources and ideas. They might also

collaborate: one could write, another draw, another compose a poem, and so forth.

Here are examples of how a couple of students translated their interest in nature into poetry:[3]

The Poem According to, and from the Perspective of, Tree
Christopher, Grade 2

Today I wear a warm cloak,
made of a great golden glare,
on the hill which I stand
in the melting wet day.
I hear the cracking of ice chunks
floating down the river
and scraping at the banks,
getting driven into the ground
by smiling, laughing kids who've
come to play.
They grab sturdy ice chunks and
sticks that have fallen from my branches
and row across the river to
their farm home.

Hidden
Angelina, Grade 4

It may always seem
that the grassy shades of emerald
are never enough
to spark the imagination of the sky
so that its canvas of cerulean
can never change
into the hopeful color
of misty tangerine
but in the early mornings
when you can only see a speck of periwinkle
covered by the light of the stars
there is always the hope
that daylight will come soon
so the forest will awaken
and while the sun rises
and gives off its rays of light
it does not take long to realize
that what your memories have seen
are not the same
as the others have
so as you breathe in the sunshine
the stars have already disappeared
into the brightness
but you are still there

---

[3] These poems are reprinted here with the permission of the children and their families.

waiting for a sign
of understanding.

What Would It Be Like?

This story starter will spark many children's imaginations. To give you a feel for how appealing this can be for students, we'll use the chameleon as an example.

The chameleon lives primarily in Africa and Asia. Because it's too slow to escape predators or chase insects, nature has bestowed on it a unique asset: camouflage. The chameleon's natural skin color blends perfectly with its surroundings, yet it can change in a matter of seconds when the chameleon needs to communicate with others in its species. Some varieties of chameleons can also alter patterns as well as colors on their skin's surface. For example, the skin of a Senegalese chameleon can change from a smooth, uniform green to black and gray with triangles and dots displayed on either side of the body. Nature has also provided the chameleon with an amazing prey-catching tongue that is long, sticky, and quick. The tongue extends in length farther than the animal's entire body, and its speed more than compensates for the chameleon's otherwise slow movements.

We've provided this description to illustrate how and why this imaginative process could appeal to young children. For an investigation of chameleons, students might create a story about what it would be like to wear the skin of a chameleon. Students could investigate ideas and questions like the following:

- A chameleon can use one eye to look at a juicy insect and the other to watch for danger. What is it like to have two eyes that can see different things?
- How does it feel to be able to change your skin color and patterns?
- How do you use changing colors to "talk" to other chameleons?
- What does it feel like to have a body temperature that matches the temperature of the air around you?

Most children will enjoy imagining being a chameleon or other animal. An experience like this gives life to the scientific facts they learn about animals. Gifted children may wish to go further with the activity, finding more facts on their animal and incorporating the facts into their stories or visual representations in different ways. Be flexible with your students' explorations. Just as you adjust your methods to the needs of children who struggle with reading and writing, you'll also want to adjust your methods to encourage discovery and growth in young gifted students. Let them pursue their research and creative representations to new dimensions.

Suggest to children that the more they learn about the *science* of their creature's life and habitat, the more interesting their stories will be. (To stimulate your own imagination, you might enjoy reading *The Color of Distance* by adult science-fiction writer Amy Thomson, who used her research on rain forests and lizards to create the novel. In her book, humanlike chameleons speak "skin speech," live in the canopy of the rain forest, and have an entire culture based on their unique physical needs and environment.)

3. EXTEND THE EXPERIENCE

Gifted children who quickly master the essentials of this process could attempt more challenging projects, such as the following.

An Animal Culture: You might suggest that students create a culture based on scientific facts of an animal species. The students can depart from strict fact into fantasy, but they must ground their created culture in actual biological and environmental attributes. (For more ideas on helping students do this, see "Create a Fictional Culture" on page 71.)

Balance of Nature: You might have students analyze what they (as their chosen animal) contribute to the balance of nature. One way to do this is by considering what would happen if the species disappeared entirely. Which other species might overpopulate as a result? Which species might also disappear? How would the air change? The plants and trees? The oceans? The weather? Have students consider the opposite possibility: what would occur in nature if their species began to overpopulate?

Animal-Inspired Language: Encourage children to consider the influences an animal or species has had on human culture. In a study of chameleons, students might explore what people mean when they refer to someone as a chameleon, or what is meant by the concept of camouflage. A wonderful source for this line of inquiry is *Nature Got There First: Inventions Inspired by Nature* by Phil Gates.

You can adapt this exploration of properties to a wide range of subjects and issues in the sciences. Transforming science into a fictional account motivates children by making learning personally meaningful. As they begin to take on the role of the animal species they have selected, they will naturally want to know more scientific details. Science then becomes a source for imaginative creation, and imagination becomes the engine for scientific discovery.

Math: A Study of Shapes

Desiree, a second grader, finished the class assignment and began fiddling with the shapes on her desk. She loved playing with geometric shapes. Soon she was constructing a scene of houses, yards, and cars out of the shapes in front of her. Watching Desiree, the teacher had an idea. Preschool and kindergarten children build with different-shaped blocks all the time. Why not extend that experience for her second graders by having them explore and construct with two- and three-dimensional shapes?

This is a wise teacher. The fun of geometry may disappear for a child like Desiree without more creative activities. And the possibilities for exploration are nearly endless. When learning basic principles of geometry, primary students enjoy investigating the different things they can do with shapes. Playing with shapes imaginatively invites critical thinking.

You can use role playing to explore properties in the mathematical universe as effectively as in the scientific one. Doing so offers a way for children to investigate the attributes of certain math concepts. At first, this approach may seem to be more of a stretch than the last one, since it involves making an environment out of inanimate shapes. As suggested earlier, you can use analogies to prepare children for the kind of flexible thinking they will do in this exercise. Ask the students to think of geometric shapes they like and think about why they like these shapes. Next, invite them to create analogies between themselves and a shape. For example, you could ask: "How are you like a triangle? How are triangles like people? If you became a triangle, how would you feel about yourself? What would you do with yourself?" We have found that, with a little encouragement, primary students easily make the mental leap that enables them to imagine their world in geometric terms.

1. SET THE STAGE: INVESTIGATE

To start the students on their imaginative journey, expose them to some books that will help them see the different possibilities of geometric shapes. Tana

Hoban's *Cubes, Cones, Cylinders, and Spheres*; Jerry Pallotta's *Icky Bug Shapes*; and the Metropolitan Museum of Art's *Museum Shapes* are all wonderful sources to help children make connections between geometry and the real-world shapes around them. Children could also consider how environmental objects resemble familiar geometric shapes. For example, children might think a tree looks like a rectangle with a triangle on top, or that a rounded bush looks circular.

You could also read and discuss math expert Marilyn Burns's *The Greedy Triangle*—a book that animates the life of a triangle in a way that provides a more creative approach to geometric properties. You could then invite students to write or tell similar stories. Have them begin with the statement "If I were a circle (triangle, square, rectangle), I would look like this." The children could draw themselves and go on to develop their story. Or they might begin in this way: "What I would like best about being a triangle is _____." Children could complete the sentence and diagram their ideas. Simple introductory activities like these are a good lead-in to creative projects in geometry. They provide some preliminary experiences for the class to explore mathematics imaginatively.

Continue by asking the children to choose a basic geometric shape such as a circle, square, or triangle. Group the students together according to the shapes they have chosen. Ask them to think of as many different uses as they can for their shape. At first, they'll probably list the obvious ones: a circle can make wheels, a square can make a box, and so forth. Keep encouraging new and unusual ideas. For example, discuss how they could make a shape with many sides and angles and why it would roll better than a square. You might say: "Imagine you have an unlimited supply of triangles. What would you make? What in your home or school or neighborhood would you change with this supply of shapes? How could you construct a merry-go-round made only of triangles? How could you have buildings, buses, or bicycles?" This will help students think flexibly about shapes that may seem—at first glance—inflexible and static.

Next, ask children to write down or talk about properties of the shape that they already know. Supply pictures of a variety of environments (both natural and human-made) so children can explore the different ways their shapes function in the world around them. Have three-dimensional shapes available for the children to handle while you ask questions such as these:

- Is this shape circular, or does it have sides?
- If it has sides, how many? Are they equal in length, or are they different lengths?
- What do you like about your shape? What can you do with it? Can you build or make anything with it?
- Why are many roofs triangular? What are some of the problems buildings with flat roofs might have? Why do you think more buildings aren't shaped like circles? Why are cans cylindrical—both round and straight—and not rectangular—straight on all sides?
- Can you imagine a world where all the doors are round and all the doorknobs are triangles? Where wheels are square? Where the sun and moon are square? Where cars and airplane wings and sailboat sails are round?
- Can you imagine inventing a triangular door? If a point were at the top of the door, what would it be like for people coming and going? What would it be like if a point were at the bottom?

These questions encourage the children to perceive the uniqueness of the shapes they have chosen and to experiment with this uniqueness.

2. IMAGINE A WORLD OF TRIANGLES

Using the triangle as an example, you could have your students imagine that they are triangular people. They will have begun exploring this through Marilyn Burns's *The Greedy Triangle* and may already have created drawings or stories about themselves as triangular beings. Now ask them to explore their shape further. Explain that there are many different triangular shapes, with a variety of angles and side lengths. Encourage children to explore the different possibilities of triangular bodies. Suggest that they sketch an entire family or a group of friends. Tell students that they may include arms, hands, legs, feet, and necks, but that the end result should be basically triangular human shapes.

Move on to a discussion of the furniture and living spaces for triangular people. Tell the class that the shapes we use in our own doors, chairs, tables, and beds are those that work best for our shape. You might ask: "How would you describe the basic shape of a human being? Are we most like a rectangle? A square? A circle?" To help children visualize this, have them trace a shape over a person in a magazine picture.

Then have students look at a door and see the relationship between a person's shape and that of a door. Explain: "Doors are made to allow shapes that are basically tall and rectangular *(oblong)* to move through them. But what if we were shaped like triangles—wide at the bottom and very narrow at the top? What would be the best shape for a door then? For a bed? For a whole room?"

Next, ask children to imagine they are designers. It's their job to design a room, a vehicle, clothing, or a space that will be uniquely suited to triangular people. Follow the children's interests. They may like to explore transportation systems, kitchens, or playgrounds. The point is to foster critical and creative thinking about spatial relationships—in this case, the relationship of the triangular body to the environments that surround it.

Keep the activity simple. If it helps, you could write on the board a list of objects or spaces for the children to explore in depth. Ask questions, such as:

- What are some of the main problems someone with a triangular body would have in our world?
- How would you like the rooms of your home arranged? Would you like a lot of rooms? Or would you like to have an open space with different sections?
- How would your house be shaped? What would your car look like?
- What would it be like to have a very wide bottom and a pointed head? What sort of clothes would you have? What sort of bed would you sleep in?

Be sure the students have enough visual aids and manipulatives so that they can experiment and explore. Offer assorted magazines with pictures of indoor and outdoor scenes as well as blocks, interlocking blocks such as Legos, and shapes made by the children. Give students some choice in how they represent their designs; they might draw, paint, model with clay, create shoe-box dioramas, or even write stories. An excellent tool for drawing and for creative thinking about design and shapes is an application called SketchUp. Gifted primary students can see their ideas quickly translated into three-dimensional shapes, which frees their imagination. (See "References and Resources," page 203.)

Have them label their creations: "Neighborhood of Triangular People," "Bedroom for Young Triangles," "Kitchen for a Triangle Family."

3. EXTEND THE EXPERIENCE

So far, the students have explored the properties of triangles by re-creating everyday objects and environments to fit the needs of triangular bodies. This is a fun way for young children to think critically about the basic triangular shape and its relation to other shapes and spaces around it.

To extend the experience, ask the children to pretend that the triangular people moved away. Now they need to re-create their objects and places for ordinary humans—using only triangles as building materials. Their job will be to try to build homes, furniture, vehicles, or other objects that resemble what people use in the real world, and build them entirely out of triangles.

Transform the World of Triangles

This activity demands flexible thinking. The children will need plenty of two- and three-dimensional triangles to play around with. To help the class see the range of possibilities for *non*triangular shapes made from triangles, pose a few problems such as these:

- How could you make a regular four-sided door out of triangles?
- How could you use different-shaped triangles to draw a tree with branches?
- How could you make a skyscraper out of triangles?
- How could you make a wheel out of triangles?

As they work on these problems, the students will begin to investigate relationships among different kinds of triangles and to experiment with ways triangles can be combined to make other geometric shapes.

When you feel they are ready to tackle a complete environment, guide students through the same explorative steps. First, give them plenty of options. They don't have to use the same idea they used when they made their triangle worlds—that's only one possibility. Some of your students may wish to try something completely different. To give them ideas, you might display children's work from the preceding activity ("Imagine a World of Triangles," page 103). Again, you can use pictures from magazines as well. Or ask the children to think of their own homes, neighborhoods, schoolrooms, and playgrounds as sources for their choices.

Give yourself options, too. You may decide that your students would benefit most by choosing one environment to work on together. You might even wish to start by asking the class to try a series of experiments. Let's say you choose the classroom as an environment to re-create with triangles. You could guide children by asking questions like these:

- Look at the tables or desks. Is there a way you can make a table out of triangles?
- What kinds of triangles can you use to make walls that look like our walls?
- How can you construct a door out of triangles?
- Can you make something nearly round—like a doorknob—out of triangles?
- If we had a huge plant in this room, what would it look like? Can you make the plant's leaves out of triangles?
- Can you make three-sided windows?
- Can you make a person—you, me, or another student—out of triangles? Can you make the person look like an ordinary human being rather than a triangular one?
- Can you draw a human face made of triangles? Is there a way you can draw the legs, arms, and other body parts so the person looks something like you or me?
- What might it feel like to live in a world where everything is made only of triangles? Would it feel different living in a world of circles? Of squares? Of octagons?

Allow children to work on other scenes or objects if they wish. Once they begin to experiment with triangles in this way, they'll be able to continue on their own. They can make cars, streets, or outdoor parks using triangles in unique ways.

Referring to artists is also helpful here. Picasso's cubist paintings are an obvious choice; Monet's landscapes offer another good visual reference. Calendars are a wonderful source of many artists' reproductions. You could use an interactive whiteboard to explore art with students. Tablets and computers also allow them to examine images in detail. NGAkids Art Zone at the website of the National Gallery of Art provides a wealth of interactive art activities, free apps, and free downloads of images. WebMuseum, Paris, with its exceptional range of images and mirror sites, is guaranteed to offer something for every child's interest. The Contemporary African Art Gallery in New York provides images of prominent artists from different countries who are experimenting with shape, light, design, and so forth. (See "References and Resources," starting on page 200, for more information on these websites.) Hang the calendar pictures and/or downloaded images around the room and have the children walk up close to the paintings, then back up slowly to see the overall effect. In the case of Monet, you could show the children how the artist created an entire landscape using nothing but dots. This may suggest ideas for creating similar "impressions" out of triangles.

These are all creative—and very instructional—ways for primary children to explore triangles. You can also have students follow this process for other polygons (such as squares, rectangles, or hexagons). The experience of moving one shape around in various directions and combining and recombining shapes gives children many insights into the properties of a particular shape and how it relates to other ones.

As much as possible, let the children choose the media for their projects. Some students may like to create models using three-dimensional triangles they've created. Others may prefer to paint or draw. Children could also cut out and glue different-colored shapes to create images of their ideas. Hang the models as mobiles; this will enable the children to see them from different angles. Display students' paintings and drawings so that the rest of the class can observe them. These displays will come in handy as you continue to work with the class on geometry. When you use children's work in this way, they'll feel that they are making a valuable contribution to the learning of the class.

Build a Bridge to Fractions

You can extend the reasoning the children are learning to other mathematical concepts, such as the relationship of parts to the whole. For example, when the students used triangles to form new shapes, they put parts together to make another kind of whole. From here, you could ask them to look at some of the new shapes they have made, particularly those that form rectangles or squares.

Suppose a few children made a rectangle or square with two triangles. You could show them that each triangle is one half of the rectangle or square. In the same way, the children could cut paper triangles into smaller ones, color in a few of them, and figure what portion of the whole square or rectangle each of the colored pieces is. Children will probably adapt easily to this activity after the earlier creative process, because they have already discovered how to place certain shapes together to create other ones.

Most gifted children enjoy the challenge of creating new and unusual shapes through one fixed type of shape. If they complete the process quickly and are ready to tackle a more difficult one, encourage them to draw or construct a scene using the shapes they've made and any others they like. The scene could be one from nature, school, home, community, or another place. If they have worked for the most part in plane (flat) geometry, have them draw or construct three-dimensional cubes, prisms, cylinders, cones, and spheres. Have the students experiment with three-dimensional objects, using whatever manipulatives you have in class or manipulatives the children bring from home. Talk about and explore how cylinders are like tree trunks, how houses are like squares or rectangles, and so on.

Another approach would be to ask children to look for the shapes they see (or can imagine) *inside* objects and forms around them—the clock, the chair, or even their own hand, which has curves, lines, and angles.

As you guide the class through this process, you can add another creative dimension by displaying some of Picasso's cubist paintings and sketches in which he configured human faces and other natural objects in striking geometric forms. A wonderful tactile activity is to have students examine and touch objects that have a lot of texture—trees, fabrics, certain kinds of wood, and so forth. The children could then try to reproduce the textures geometrically.

Discovering Processes

A similar creative approach can expand young children's understanding of scientific and mathematical processes. A *process* is a series of sequential actions or changes that produces a specific effect. When you bring creativity to bear on the study of a scientific or mathematical process, three immediate benefits result:

1. The children feel more motivated to study the process.
2. They tend to remember the process, and the logic or reasoning behind it, much better.
3. With this deeper understanding, students (especially those who are gifted) develop the confidence and freedom to apply the process to other contexts; they can then make discoveries of their own.

Science: A Study of Growth and Change in the Natural World

Colin was always very sensitive about the natural world. He loved sitting in trees, searching beneath stones and leaves, and studying how things grow. His mother taught him how to prepare soil, plant seeds, and care for the seedlings after they sprouted. Colin also enjoyed creating terrariums—natural environments he made in a number of large jars in his room. When his class began studying trees, Colin was excited. But he wanted to do more than the rest of the class, because he already knew much of what they were studying.

For children like Colin, who have already acquired some fundamental knowledge of what the class is studying, imaginative activity related to the subject will both sustain and propel their interest. Such activity will allow them to move from general principles and rules to specifics—specific trees, specific places, and specific circumstances. Rather than learn a few processes in given circumstances, the children can explore them in environments they choose and under conditions they imagine. As in other creative work, students become producers as well as recipients of knowledge—and producing knowledge is vital to their growth. All children can benefit from learning in this way; gifted children especially may enjoy experiencing the processes in a variety of contexts and creating hypotheses of their own.

In Chapter 5, we introduced a number of resources on trees that integrate science, art, and language in lively ways. In our workshops for young gifted students, we have found that the combination of imagery (art or photography) and narrative stimulates children's imagination and curiosity. The students absorb information, insights, and impressions from imagery and narrative through their senses, feelings, and intelligence, the same way they would if we were to walk them into the woods and have them touch the trees, listen to the birds, and explore probing questions. This experience encourages scientific inquiry, which in turn sparks creative response, which then inspires more inquiry.

Let's assume that you want to expand on the class's understanding of photosynthesis and of other related tree facts. The process of photosynthesis in particular is a rich and intriguing one. A tree uses solar energy to convert carbon dioxide from the air and water and minerals from the soil into sugars and starches for food to survive and grow. Trees, along with other green plants, not only produce their own food but also food and oxygen for other living things. The survival of all life forms on Earth (including people) depends on the great work of trees and other photosynthesizers.

Wonderful, evocative sources like *A Tree for All Seasons* by Robin Bernard can enhance what children understand about the science of a tree. Students can begin creating stories, writing poems, and rendering their ideas in sketches, movement, or drama. The purpose here is to give children the freedom to invent. Using the scientific facts you have taught them, they can build fictional narratives that enable them to deepen their study and research.

1. SET THE STAGE: INVESTIGATE

The easiest way to begin this process is to have the children choose a tree species they like. Students may want to delve into different environments for their trees—a tropical or temperate rain forest, a redwood forest, a boreal forest, and so on. Provide resources students can use to make their selection. You might display several pictures of different species of trees and discuss their unique features—the climates in which they grow, their colors, the shapes of their leaves, or their life spans. You could also ask the children to tell you about different trees they have seen in their neighborhoods or travels. Ask questions such as these:

- Do you have a favorite climbing tree? Why is it your favorite?
- What changes do you notice in your tree in spring? In summer? In fall? In winter?
- What's the most unusual tree you've seen? Why is it unusual?
- How is your favorite tree like other kinds of trees? How is it different?

Encourage students to think about what aspects of tree life they want to research. To do this, they need exposure to different kinds of trees, climates, and environments to see what interests them.

Once your students choose their tree, you can guide them through a series of leading questions. Ask them to pretend they are the tree they have selected. You could stimulate their imagination by asking:

- Where do you live?
- What kind of climate do you live in? Is it dry? Rainy? Cold? Warm?
- What kind of land surrounds you? Woods? Rocks? Desert? Hills?
- What kind of bark do you have? What do your leaves look like? How tall do you get?
- What kinds of animals live around you? Inside you? What crawls or hops around in your branches?

- What do you have that helps the animals around you?
- Are there other trees around you? How tall are they? How thick are their trunks and branches?
- What are the greatest needs of trees like you?

Give the children time to think through and sketch out whatever they already know about their tree species and its basic needs.

2. IMAGINE: STIMULATE FURTHER DISCOVERY

It's more difficult to pretend to be a tree than to pretend to be an animal. Catalysts are critical here. A book like Debbie S. Miller's *Are Trees Alive?* can help students make the imaginative leap. This book compares the different parts of trees to human beings and explores tree species around the globe, each with its own distinctive shape, color, seeds, and fruits. Using books, prints, and online sources, primary teachers can find many aids to engage their students in the daily life, ecology, and beauty of the world's trees.

A combination of science and artistry will enable young students to see the different possibilities of rendering scientific facts creatively. Pictures of trees will inspire them to draw some of their own, sketch environments, and write anecdotes or short poems from the trees' perspective. Students can represent the daily process of making food for themselves; of the kinds of animals, birds, and insects that surround them; and of their feelings about seasonal and other changes.

To successfully integrate science facts and creative imagination in a way that encourages critical thinking and discovery, you could ask your students to focus on several fundamental aspects of tree life in their representations. For example, they could choose a few of the following topics:

- How does the tree make its own food?
- What animals get their food, home, or shelter from the tree?
- How is the tree affected by climate and seasonal changes?
- How does the tree survive the hardships of its environment?
- How does the tree reproduce? What part do animals and birds play in this process?
- How are we dependent on trees to survive?
- In what ways might we have to change if trees changed?

3. EXTEND THE EXPERIENCE

You can help children extend these concepts artistically by asking them to think about trees in terms of color, feeling, story, and movement:

- What color would you give a tree in winter? What color would you make the sky?
- What feeling would you give the tree?
- What is a typical day like for your tree?
- Can you show us what your roots do when it rains?

You can also use analogies:

- How is the tree like the stars?
- How are branches of a tree like the arms of a person?
- How are leaves like clothes?
- How is bark like skin?

This kind of questioning will loosen the borders between science and art, between scientific principle and poetic or artistic expression, and between fact and fiction.

Ideally, you'll want to have a display of books or posters that show trees in diverse seasons, conditions, and environments. Besides those mentioned, other excellent resources include Thomas Locker and Candace Christiansen's *Sky Tree: Seeing Science Through Art* and Gail Gibbons's *Tell Me, Tree: All About Trees for Kids*. The students can begin simply and move ahead to more complex work according to their ability and understanding. To give them a visual image of the processes they describe, encourage children to make sketches or drawings with arrows that indicate the process they wish to represent. Depending on their ages and abilities, the students could add captions identifying the tree species they are depicting and what the tree is undergoing to make food; to store food for the winter; to protect itself against drought, wind, or frigid temperatures; or to reproduce.

Your gifted students will likely enjoy the mental exercise of using scientific processes to make creative tree stories. It will be a challenge for them to make the life of a tree—which appears on the surface to be static and even dull—lively and adventurous. To help all your students step into the role, guide them with these ideas and questions:

- Look down at the ground. See how far down your trunk goes. How do your roots feel? How deep are they? Feel the rain. Feel your roots soaking in the water. How does that feel? Can you feel the water seeping up into your trunk? Is the soil healthy? Can you make enough food to grow and be strong?

- Stretch up to the sky, as high as you can. Look up at the sun. Feel your leaves taking in the sun for you, taking in the energy and the carbon dioxide. What does this feel like? Like breathing? Like taking a shower?
- Feel the sun, the carbon dioxide, and the moisture in the earth combining to make sugars for food. Can you taste these sugars? Are there any animals that want some of this sugar?
- It's fall. How does the air feel around your branches and leaves? Is it warm? How long are the days now? What changes do you feel happening? (Here children could focus on the breakdown of green chlorophyll, allowing other pigments to become more visible.)
- How old are the trees around you? Are they ancient trees? Seedlings? Young saplings? How old are *you*?
- What animals live in your branches? Tell some stories about these animals. How do they help you and the other trees in your neighborhood?
- How long have you lived? What are some of the changes you have seen happen around you?

While they are thinking about these questions, the students can also integrate paintings or sketches into this exploration. Studying their tree in books, magazines, or outdoors will give them new insights to include in their drawings; they'll notice details they hadn't observed before. This experience will be especially rich if the students choose trees from different environments around the world. The whole class will benefit from studying these basic science principles in different contexts. Gifted students may enjoy comparing how trees function in diverse settings and how they develop unique responses to the challenges of weather conditions, seasonal changes, density, drought, and other climatic hardships.

Math: Turning Symbols into Stories

Mattie loved playing with numbers. When she went shopping with her dad, she liked checking the prices of items and adding them up. She also enjoyed comparing prices of various brands to see how much money her dad could save. Sometimes Mattie would pretend to be different characters who had come to the store to buy things. She would make up stories to herself as she

walked up and down the aisles. In the store, numbers had a real life for Mattie that they didn't always have in school. Mattie didn't like doing word problems as much as she liked creating them. She enjoyed inventing scenarios that took her to the limits of her mathematical understanding and posed new problems.

In children's earliest years, the world of numbers has a wondrous, almost magical quality. Who hasn't seen the earnest face of a toddler pointing and counting or proudly answering the question "How old are you?" with two or three fingers? Yet numbers often lose their appeal in school, where the priorities of acquiring certain skills overshadow creative play.

When you try more creative approaches, number processes can assume lively new dimensions for children. More than providing entertainment or diversion, these approaches give students an opportunity to analyze the processes in completely new ways. This in turn encourages students, especially those who are gifted, to pursue their understanding in new, more challenging contexts.

1. SET THE STAGE: TELL A STORY

At the beginning of this chapter, we saw how vividly Simone was able to translate the concept of place value into a concrete, memorable story (see page 96). Using stories to revitalize the number world not only breathes life into mathematical concepts and processes but also reframes them in familiar, understandable terms.

Let's say you're teaching children to regroup when subtracting two-digit numbers from two-digit numbers. The example you're using is subtracting forty-seven from ninety-five. You could use manipulatives if you'd like, but along with these you could add this explanation and story:

"Even though ninety-five is a bigger number than forty-seven, when you subtract it bit by bit, some of the numbers have to borrow from their neighbors. Okay, do you see Ms. Seven here? She wants to scare Mr. Five by taking his five ones and then asking for more. That would put Mr. Five in debt. So Mr. Five has to come up with a plan. He goes over to his neighbor, Ms. Nine—here in the tens column—and says, 'Hey, you have nine tens—ninety ones. Would you lend me some ones?'

"Now, anyone who wants to live in the tens column has to follow this rule that when they lend ones, they can only lend ten at a time—no more, no less. So Ms. Nine agrees to give Mr. Five ten ones (which leaves Ms. Nine eight tens, or eighty ones, which means Ms. Nine is now Ms. Eight). Mr. Five goes back with the ten ones and joins them to the five he already has, making him Mr. Fifteen.

"Now, when Ms. Seven comes back the next day, Mr. Fifteen won't be scared because he can give her the seven she wants and still have eight left over. Now we move over to tens column on the left. Mr. Four in the tens column comes to Ms. Eight in the tens column and takes *four* away, leaving four tens (forty ones). The final answer, then, is forty-eight."

A story is a wonderful way to make mathematical concepts more accessible to young children. You can draw a diagram on the board or have the children enact the story as you tell it. Through this experience, the students will begin to connect mathematics with story situations. Rather than remaining processes for children to perform mechanically, math problems become plot lines for stories. Before you invite the students to create stories of their own, begin another addition problem for the class to do together; work the problem and create the story for it together. The value of this method of teaching is that children learn certain concepts inductively. By exploring stories to the limits of their knowledge, they prepare themselves for the next logical development.

Gifted children may like to turn a problem into a story on their own and then add some additional elements to their story. For example, Simone might move more and more people into her house of tens, perhaps to the point where it fills up. As the teacher, you could use Simone's story with the class and guide children to move from two-digit numbers to computations with three-digit numbers. To do this, you could introduce a new column and a new "house"—the mansion of hundreds. Once students become comfortable with the three fictional houses, the principle of subtraction could evolve in similar story fashion. The idea of people moving out will seem as natural as that of people moving in. Keep reminding children that the people from the house of tens can only move in groups of ten. When the house of ones needs to borrow in order to subtract, a whole group of ten ones will have to move into the house of ones temporarily. Then students can subtract the numbers with the same logic they used for adding.

After children become more comfortable with these basic steps, they can invent stories of their own. This creative strategy tests and strengthens students' knowledge of the concrete process and gives them a chance to discover how it works in different fictional contexts.

Once you break out of the strict divisions between math and art, math and language arts, and math and creative thinking, you and the class will find yourselves inventing some wonderful stories around number operations. Gifted children will probably love this. They frequently seek new and innovative applications for the knowledge they so quickly acquire. They'll especially value the process of translating the representation of numbers and symbols into imaginary worlds.

2. CREATE FAIRY TALES WITH NUMBERS

An approach we like to use is to turn number operations into fairy tales. Fairy tales are an excellent genre for this purpose because they are so familiar to young children. Here are some ideas for getting your students started on number fairy tales:

A Fraction Fairy Tale

Once upon a time, there was a greedy detective who was looking for treasure in a field. Now, this detective *really* wanted to have this treasure all to himself. As luck would have it, he was also a magician. So he came up with a clever plan: he would divide himself into pieces and have each piece look in a different part of the field. This would ensure that the detective—at least, some part of him—would find the treasure before someone else did. The detective told the pieces of himself that whichever piece found the treasure should hop up and down to call attention to itself. Then the dividing began. The man divided himself in half, and then those halves divided themselves in half. Each of the four pieces went into a different part of the field looking for the treasure. Finally, one of the pieces found it! But instead of hopping up and down, what do you think it did? It grabbed the treasure and ran off as fast as a piece of a person could run!

Using this fairy tale, the children can play with the idea of fractions. Have them draw the story, perhaps in a cartoon frame format, so they can visualize it. Then have them make symbolic representations under the different segments of the story.

Beneath the picture of the detective dividing himself into four pieces, students could write one or both of these notations:

$$1 = \tfrac{4}{4} \qquad 1 = \tfrac{1}{4} + \tfrac{1}{4} + \tfrac{1}{4} + \tfrac{1}{4}$$

In the segment where one piece runs off with the treasure, they could write this:

$$\tfrac{4}{4} - \tfrac{1}{4} = \tfrac{3}{4}$$

A Division Fairy Tale

Once upon a time, there was a famous cookie maker who had a bakery called Twenty-Four Cookies. She made twenty-four cookies an hour—no more, no less. One day, eight hungry trolls came in and demanded all the cookies. The cook looked at her cookie sheet of twenty-four. She told the trolls, "I have twenty-four cookies. There are eight of you, so I can give each of you three cookies." But the eight trolls were hungry; they wanted more than three cookies apiece. So they started arguing with each other about who could have how many cookies. Four of the trolls got tired of arguing and ran off. "Now how many can we have?" said the trolls to the baker. "I still have twenty-four cookies," the baker replied. "But now there are four of you, so I can give each of you six."

The students can go on from here, inventing more and more operations. But you'll need to monitor this process to maintain a balance between invention and actual mathematical learning. Students may create plots that exceed their math knowledge considerably! In some cases, this can be counterproductive. The plots should stretch children's understanding and encourage flexibility in mathematical thinking, not overwhelm them with convoluted twists and turns.

Gifted children, on the other hand, may introduce all sorts of added complications that they are able to handle mathematically. For example, three instead of four trolls could run off, leaving five to divide up the twenty-four cookies. This would then lead to a remainder—four cookies for the baker! Or perhaps the five trolls would divide the extra four cookies up into smaller and smaller fractions. As before, you can have the students draw cartoonlike sketches and write the operations beneath their pictures. The fun of all this is that math operations occur in the course of a story, and there are infinite possibilities for the kinds of problems children can create.

A Multiplication Fairy Tale

Once upon a time, there was a young boy who could weave yarn into gold blankets. The boy was trapped high in a tower by six dragons. "Please release me!" pleaded the boy. "I must get home to my family!" The head dragon replied, "All right, we will release you—but first you must weave two beautiful gold blankets for me." So the boy wove two blankets. It took a little time, and when he was finished they were golden and beautiful. But when the other dragons saw the blankets, they each wanted two blankets as well. The head dragon said to the boy, "You must make all the blankets my dragon friends want, or I will not release you!" The boy cried bitterly, for he knew that if he made the blankets one by one, it would take him months to finish.

Just when the boy thought all was lost, a little elf appeared on the floor at his feet. The elf said, "Fear not, child, for I am the multiplier elf. If you have made the right number of blankets for one dragon, I can multiply that number for the rest." So the boy put the two blankets in front of the elf, who waved her hands six times. And, lo! Six piles of two blankets each appeared on the floor! The dragons took their twelve beautiful gold blankets, and the boy thanked the elf and headed home.

In the beginning, you'll need to give the students story ideas like these. Doing so will help them make the mental leap from math operations to fictional illustrations—which, in turn, will lead to more explorations. We have found that children have a wonderful time concocting stories about the multiplier elf—stories that lead to unexpected mathematical discovery and learning.

Given a start with a story like this, many children will quickly elaborate, inventing twists and turns in the plot that have corresponding mathematical formulas. At some point, gifted children (even those as young as four) will begin creating story ideas themselves.

You can also adjust the stories and operations for younger students who may be learning more basic math concepts than those described here. After children have learned a new concept, you can have them generate a fairy tale about it. To help students begin their stories, you might want to give them some starter ideas. Here are some situations you could pose:

- A mouse enters a bakery and finds five cupcakes and five cookies.
- Four hungry giants come to a school cafeteria asking for tacos.
- In a toy store, a row of twelve teddy bears hope that children will take them home.
- Four worms meet inside an apple; each of them wants to eat some of it.

Have children make their own suggestions. As different students offer ideas, write them on the board. In a short while, the class will have compiled a variety of scenarios for mathematical explorations. As they work on their stories, encourage students to sketch or dramatize their inventions. This will help them actualize the math plots they are inventing and identify the parts for which they may need help.

For young children just learning about numbers, you can use a simpler version of the fairy tale idea:

An Addition and Subtraction Fairy Tale
Once upon a time, four kangaroo moms went for a hop. Each had a baby in her pouch. The babies were happy while their mothers hopped along. But soon the moms met two friends in a field and stopped to talk. The grown-ups talked and talked. The babies started to fidget. Finally, two baby kangaroos jumped out of their pouches and hopped off into the woods to play. The other two followed them. Soon the moms realized their babies were gone. With their friends, they called and called, hopping all around the woods. They found the four babies in a shady glen, happily dancing and leaping. The four moms took their babies and put them back in their pouches. Then they said good-bye to their two friends and went home.

This is a very simple scenario for addition and subtraction. The children can easily act it out, or you can talk them through it while sketching the story on the board. Four kangaroo moms plus four babies equal eight kangaroos ($4 + 4 = 8$). Then they meet their two friends ($8 + 2 = 10$). For a while, there are ten kangaroos. Two babies leave ($10 - 2 = 8$). Then two more babies leave ($8 - 2 = 6$). The moms and their friends look for the babies, and find all four

playing ($6 + 4 = 10$). Then the two friends leave ($10 - 2 = 8$), and the moms and babies go back home.

Young children can easily add to this story. As they speak, you can write the plot in math form. Each time a child adds another piece to the story and the number of kangaroos changes, ask: "How would I write that? How many kangaroos did we have before this happened? How many are there now?" This process unites mathematics with imagination. It can involve even very young children in creative reasoning that enables them to explore math problems of their own making.

3. EXTEND THE EXPERIENCE
As the children become more involved in a story, they will find more and more elaborate mathematical situations they can create through the plot. At times, they may find themselves in a math scene they can't quite figure out. This gives you a natural opportunity to explore with students the complex mathematical dimensions their story has developed. Jon Scieszka's *Math Curse* is a wonderful example of a story that uses mathematics imaginatively.

Because the field of exploration is virtually limitless, gifted children will delight in this activity. It gives them the freedom to test their knowledge and integrate it with other math operations they have already learned, creating unique and complex scenarios.

Give all your students opportunities to explore their ideas through a variety of means. They can draw, create models, or even act out the processes with classmates to see how they can solve the problems they've invented.

When the activity draws to a close, be sure to display students' work. Sharing the many different scenarios the class has created will allow you to significantly extend children's learning. Through this process, they will become more flexible and innovative in their thinking and will be able to create as well as solve mathematical computations.

Questions and Answers
"What will I accomplish by using the creative arts to help me teach math and science?"
We know that children learn and master math and science concepts in a variety of ways. The more avenues we can find to help young learners grasp and really own their knowledge of a process, the better the chance that they will do so. And by integrating

lessons on new concepts with creative activities, we foster a higher level of critical thinking in children— and the flexibility to explore a whole new dimension in math and science.

Even students who are talented in math or science will explore new directions through this integration. It's an approach that can also create real breakthroughs for children who resist or struggle with either subject by enabling them to enter its world from a more imaginative, artistic framework.

There are many stimulating and imaginative new ideas for teaching math and science today. A number of the publications cited in "References and Resources" (pages 199–204) present rationales, teaching strategies, and activities for integrating the arts and sciences.

"What should I do if the children create mathematical or scientific problems beyond their ability to solve?"
This is a legitimate concern. An imaginative child could easily create a math fairy tale that involves concepts and activities far ahead of the curriculum. How you respond depends on the ability of the child and the level of the problem created. Sometimes you'll have to encourage students to make changes in their stories. There will be other times, however, when you may find it appropriate to teach the whole class a new concept, using a student's tale as a catalyst. Generally speaking, discourage the class from developing convoluted or irrational plot twists. Remind students that their creations need to occur within the bounds of the math and science facts they know.

"What can I do with children who have trouble making the mental leap from a math or science concept to a language arts context?"
Some children are so accustomed to the traditional approach to subjects that they may find imaginative approaches difficult. How can ordinary life be conceived in terms of triangles? How can we humans put ourselves in the position of a tree? It's one thing to get students thinking in interdisciplinary terms within general themes; it's quite another to ask them to convert a mathematical concept into a fairy tale, or to dramatize the inner life of an ordinary tree. However, if you provide sufficient catalysts— questions, suggestions, and examples—you'll find that children will begin to perceive relationships among concepts that once seemed unrelated. Be sure to give yourself and the class enough time and preparation to warm up to these ideas.

"Do you recommend these kinds of activities as enrichment or as a core part of the lessons?"
Both. We understand the pressures that all classroom teachers have in working within a set curriculum. We don't want to upset the natural rhythm you establish throughout the year. Start by trying a few simple integrated activities. You might spend several days teaching a basic math operation and then introduce a creative activity to enhance students' new knowledge. All of the examples we've described require a certain amount of prior knowledge of a property or process. They enhance the children's understanding of the new knowledge they have gained and prompt them to exceed that knowledge by applying it in new directions.

Conclusion

The creative imagination recaptures for young children the wonder they once felt for the fascinating world of science and math. Rather than merely jazzing up the subjects, imaginative approaches encourage higher-level thinking by allowing the children to invent their own contexts for the phenomena they study. Creativity softens the rigidity that students sometimes feel in math and science. It can transform those subjects into intriguing possibilities to be discovered and explored, rather than isolated facts to be memorized. Even word problems or lab experiments can be made more vivid and meaningful when children can take them beyond the confines of their specific subject matter. When science and math traverse the world of the arts, young children discover new possibilities and avenues for self-expression.

Creatively gifted children especially will benefit. These students can find release from the restrictions of narrow logic and rules, processes and principles. They are hungry for more—more exploration and discovery, more knowledge and mastery, more unique perspectives. Creative learning satisfies this hunger. Bright, imaginative children can discern the poetry of mathematical logic, the magical qualities of nature's rhythmic processes, the circuitous routes of number operations within fairy tales, and the amazing transformations of the geometric universe. As Albert Einstein so aptly observed: "Imagination is more important than knowledge."

CHAPTER 7
Assessing and Documenting Development

Nina felt anxious about her report card. Did her teacher remember all her work? Would she get a lower grade because she was sick one day? What did an S or U mean? What would her parents think? How would they react? She had no idea how report cards worked. She was worried.

The Assessment Conundrum

Tracking each child's work in the beginning years is very important. Documentation showing what the child *knows* and *is able to do* should be maintained and passed along from teacher to teacher. This assures continuity. Each new teacher can use the information to plan projects, avoid needless repetition, and find areas of expertise.

Assessment is a difficult undertaking, regardless of the subject, the student, or the teacher involved. Personal evaluation brings out a wide range of emotions in all the participants, from fear of failure to anticipation of praise.

Assessments have changed dramatically over time. In the past, the most common assessments were tests. Students' answers on the tests were either right or wrong. Educators have moved beyond that thinking and now often use assessments such as portfolios, observations, performances, student writings, presentations, visual displays, and so forth. While these assessment methods better demonstrate student growth, they are far from perfect at measuring what a student actually knows and can do. In addition, assessment reports present difficult questions for teachers and parents trying to interpret them. What does S (satisfactory) or U (unsatisfactory) really mean? What does a letter grade really mean? Does an A mean that the student has grown in the content area to exceed the student's grade level? Or does it mean simply that the student has mastered the content? Or that the student has worked as hard as possible to learn the content? What is fair? What about the child who does not have support at home, who has not had the advantage of being read to, taken places, or taught basic information?

Curriculum Standards and Related Testing

State and national curriculum standards further complicate the task of assessment. The U.S. education standards and accountability reform movement began in the 1980s, with the goal of setting high academic expectations for all students. This shift toward standards-based education translated into substantive change when it became law under President Bill Clinton as the Elementary and Secondary Education Act (ESEA) in 1994, and it was further expanded by President George W. Bush in 2001 as the No Child Left Behind (NCLB) Act.

With the onset of standards came the issue of accountability. Legislators, as well as the public, wanted schools to prove that *all* students were learning. NCLB was instituted to assure that all students would eventually perform at their designated grade level in all subjects. Tests aligned with the standards in each subject area were implemented to measure student growth. The assumption with NCLB was that all students would be at their grade level in reading and math by 2014. The problem with this assumption was that it ignored all the variables involved in raising student achievement. At any given age, but particularly in the primary years, students vary in cognitive development, skills, and abilities. Standardized achievement tests assume that such individual differences do not exist. NCLB also pushed teachers to focus more on the children whose achievement lagged behind grade-level expectations, rather than on children whose achievement was ahead of grade-level expectations.

School chiefs and governors developed the Common Core State Standards (CCSS) in 2009 in order to have clear and consistent learning goals across the states. CCSS sets the bar high for all students. These standards claim that all students should be college- or career-ready by the end of high school. The standards were designed to be rigorous and relevant to the real world, reflecting skills and knowledge needed for college and careers. As with NCLB, under CCSS, achievement tests are used as measures of students at a particular grade level to see how well they are performing. (The achievement tests that accompany NCLB and CCSS are different from IQ tests that measure students' potential. For more on the latter, see page 116.)

Curriculum standards and standards-based achievement testing ignore the fact that at any given age, students have different backgrounds, experiences, and abilities. Many educators are compelled to "teach to the test" rather than look at individual differences and adjust their instructional content, process, and products to the needed level of learning. For example, some students start the school year with knowledge and skills way below the expectations for their grade level; they need more than one year to reach that goal. Meanwhile, other students start out—or eventually surpass—the expectations for their grade level; with curriculum restricted by standards, these students do not learn anything new or challenging.

The standardized testing process itself raises sticky questions, too. How can we know whether subject-area tests actually measure children's knowledge and skills, especially in young children? For example, a child may not yet have the fine motor skills to mark responses correctly in small ovals or may not understand how the computer works. Does this mean that the student does not understand the content?

Planning Activities for Broad-Based Assessment

Although assessment can be a difficult and uncertain task for the reasons we've just explained, it's still an important one. Tracking what each child knows and can do is essential. Information gained from assessment can help educators establish plans for growth and end needless repetition of already-mastered curriculum.

A great starting place is documenting what students know and can do at the beginning of each year. The teacher can add to this information throughout the year. The documentation can follow students when they move on to new teachers, in order to assure continued growth.

In assessing young children, nontraditional methods that show *how the child is intelligent*, as well as *how intelligent the child is*, are essential supplements to standards-based achievement testing. As a teacher, you'll want to plan assessment experiences that show meaningfully what each child knows and can do. For best results, plan assessment activities that fit the following criteria:

1. **They are natural rather than contrived.** The activities need to flow with the lesson rather than being artificially added on.
2. **They are open-ended.** All the children need opportunities to show all that they are capable

of doing. Too often, assessment activities have ceilings. Gifted children may get all the answers correct, but you have to guess what they know beyond the questions asked. Open-ended assessment is more likely to elicit higher levels of response from children.

3. **They incorporate all areas of the curriculum.** In evaluating children's knowledge and abilities, we need to consider what the children can do in language arts, math, art, science, social studies, physical games, music, and drama (acting out what they know).

4. **They are age-appropriate.** In planning an assessment activity, ask: What's the purpose of the activity? Has it been taught, or have the children had the opportunity to learn it? Is it clear? Do the people reading or scoring the performance know what they're looking for?

5. **They reflect the many ways in which children learn.** Whenever possible, give children choices about how to present their knowledge: through drawing, writing, singing, role playing, speaking, or physically demonstrating. Choose experiences that allow the use of varied learning modalities and multiple intelligences. Chapters 1 and 2 describe different intelligence preferences and learning modalities and discuss ways to help children learn and perform within their most comfortable modes.

Assessment activities should include both *formative* and *summative* assessments. Ideally, both types should focus on growth and make use of learning modalities, allowing teachers to move away from rigid assessment situations toward those that are more flexible and open-ended.

Formative assessments are ongoing, informal daily assessments, reviews, and observations used to monitor and modify instruction. For example, a teacher might assign tasks or quizzes periodically to evaluate student progress. Or a teacher might observe that some students don't understand a concept and devise a review activity or an alternate teaching strategy.

A summative assessment, or evaluation, occurs at the end of a unit, topic, area, or year of study. Its purpose is to measure a student's mastery at the end of a given phase of instruction. It traditionally involves a test at the end of a lesson or unit. It is more product-oriented and concerned with producing a score or a grade.

Sound, authentic assessment provides the basis for building activities and experiences that challenge children who already know the information and can do the regular work. At the same time, it gives us information about which children need additional teaching or a different format in order to learn the material.

Sara didn't like things that were too simple. In fact, if something was too simple or too plain, she added details. It took her a long time to complete drawings, since she wanted to include every eyelash in her portraits and every stone in her landscapes. No detail went unnoticed by Sara. When asked to draw a picture of her house, she created an aerial view. She explained that she wanted to show where the rooms were located and to show not just the front yard, but the backyard as well. She explained that this is what birds see.

Sara did not do well on standardized tests. She took too long, thought too intricately, and pondered all the possibilities. Her creativity was remarkable, but

Moving Toward Open-Ended Evaluation*

Rigid evaluation relies on:	*Open-ended evaluation relies on:*
right or wrong answers	open-ended opportunities for multiple answers
quiet	appropriate level of noise
paper-and-pencil tasks	hands-on tasks
teacher talking	child participation
negative criticism	positive, growth-producing comments
desk activities	activities within a variety of settings

*Adapted from Joan Franklin Smutny, Kathleen Veenker, and Stephen Veenker. *Your Gifted Child: How to Recognize and Develop the Special Talents in Your Child from Birth to Age Seven* (New York: Ballantine Books, 1989): 97–98. Used with permission of Joan Franklin Smutny.

creativity was not a component of the standardized testing. Although Sara was one to two years above grade level academically, her poor test results did not show it. Portfolio assessments or observations would have portrayed Sara's abilities much more accurately.

This example points out three tools of broad-based, authentic assessment: intelligence testing, portfolio assessment, and observation. Let's look at each one more closely.

IQ Testing[1]

Children deserve to learn in school. In order to teach them, we need to find out how they learn best and at what pace they learn. We also need to find out what they already know. Testing offers a means for doing this. Testing complements and creates a basis for teaching.

Tests Don't Give the Whole Picture

STANDARDIZED SUBJECT TESTS ARE NOT IQ TESTS

Some schools and districts focus heavily on standardized subject-area tests rather than on the actual learning of individual children. Communities use such tests as indicators of how good their schools are. Property values are determined in part on how well the students in area schools perform on these tests. School scores are published in regional papers, and schools may be listed as desirable or undesirable based on test scores.

But standardized subject-area tests do not measure background knowledge, interests, or cultural or linguistic factors. These tests do not care if a child is well or ill, has a learning disability, or is a perfectionist who is afraid of making a mistake. These tests also may not measure how much beyond grade level a gifted child may be in one or more content areas. Most state tests, for example, measure content areas only at one particular grade level.

Standardized tests can be misused. Often, achievement tests for specific academic subjects are interpreted as IQ tests. However, these tests usually record only what children can do with pencils in hand. That leaves out many components of achievement, ability, and intelligence. Another limitation

of these tests is that they're likely to penalize highly gifted children by not measuring the full extent of their abilities. On these tests, a gifted child may score in the 98th or 99th percentile—but this score does not demonstrate how much the child knows and can do beyond the level at which the test is aimed—especially if it's normed for the student's grade level. In fact, any test that is "on-level" for the child's age or grade is probably inappropriate for a gifted child. An "off-level" test, one designed for older students, has a higher ceiling and is less likely to limit the highest possible score.

IQ TESTS AREN'T PERFECT EITHER

Pablo was very bright and seemed to have exceptional math ability. When the tester was administering an individual IQ test to Pablo, he gave an answer that was wrong according to the scoring guide. The tester asked Pablo to count backward from ten. He looked curiously at the tester, got out of his chair, which was facing the tester, and turned the chair around. Pablo's back was now to the tester. He then proceeded to count "ten, eleven, twelve, thirteen, fourteen," and so on, until the tester stopped him.

Pablo's story illustrates how children can easily misinterpret test directions. This misinterpretation can produce an answer that is not correct according to the scoring manual, but *is* correct according to the child's interpretation. The directions were not clear to Pablo, and his score did not reflect his mathematical knowledge.

When Brandon was four, his first individually administered IQ test score was 139 on the Wechsler Preschool and Primary Scale of Intelligence–Fourth Edition (WPPSI–IV). When he was six, his school used a group test, the Otis-Lennon Mental Abilities Test–Eighth Edition (OLSAT 8); Brandon scored 132. Further testing, this time with the individualized Wechsler Intelligence Scale for Children–Fifth Edition (WISC–V), resulted in a score of 152. Then Brandon scored 180 on yet another individually administered test with a higher ceiling—the Stanford-Binet Intelligence Scale–Fifth Edition (SB5). How could he keep getting such different scores? And what could it mean?

Brandon's experience illustrates how scores may vary from test to test. This variation can produce confusion for both educators and parents. Commonly, the first IQ scores obtained through a school are determined by group testing. Many

---

[1] For a list of standardized tests and their descriptions, see Appendix A, page 215.

group tests given in schools measure academic aptitude or achievement more than abstract reasoning abilities. Such group tests generally require one right answer; they sometimes confuse children who consider many possible answers. Also, group tests usually include only a few items at the higher ranges of difficulty. This creates a ceiling that tends to limit children's possible scores.

Measuring children's intelligence is complex, because children express intelligence in many ways. Intellectual differences among young gifted children are vast and varied. That is why standardized intelligence tests designed to accommodate the majority of children give only a limited view into gifted children's capabilities and ways of functioning.

Although an individually administered IQ test is usually more comprehensive as a single measure of intelligence than a group test is, scores for individualized tests aren't completely reliable either. And these need to be considered within a range of five to ten points above and below the given score. (For example, a specific score of 130 means that the child's IQ is between 124 and 136.) Most individually administered IQ tests measure many abilities and then find the average of those diverse skills for a single score of *general* intellectual ability.

Regardless of whether a test is administered within a group or individually, there's much that an IQ score *doesn't* tell about a child. For example, if a child has extremely high verbal skills but lags somewhat in spatial and fine motor development, the child might attain an IQ score in the average range, despite having many intellectual abilities that are far above average.

It's usually safe to assume that any test score is probably an *underestimation* of a child's abilities. There are many reasons why this might be the case. At the moment of a testing situation, a child might:

- say "I don't know" rather than risk saying something wrong
- wonder what a parent or sibling is doing or what's on TV
- be distracted by the noise in the next room
- want to avoid creating higher performance expectations in parents and teachers
- want to avert the possibility of being placed in a gifted program that will separate the child from friends
- have an ear infection and not hear clearly

- be ill (or becoming ill), hungry, tired, or low on energy and therefore not fully alert
- be reacting to an allergen, known or unknown, and thus feel tired, hyper, or unable to fully focus

By the same token, it's safe to assume that a test score is never an *overestimation* of a child's abilities. It's impossible for children to perform on a test *beyond* what they know or can do. A child can't fake a right answer or a skill. A student can't pretend to say a series of numbers backward. A child can't cheat on putting together a puzzle.

Other factors are also involved in testing any child. Sound IQ testing must look for specific abilities and strengths and test for the limits of those abilities and strengths. Learning and thinking modalities must also come into play.

At age five, Mario was a complex thinker. He questioned everything. His powers of observation were fantastic. However, he didn't perform well on standardized tests. Sometimes his thoughts went beyond the test. He thought of different answer options that should have been given but weren't. In many instances, the choices on the paper seemed too simplistic. At other times, Mario read more into the question than the test maker had intended, so his responses were frequently "wrong." One test question asked, "What is the color of coal?" The choices were black, purple, or gray. Mario marked all three. When the examiner asked him why, he responded, "It's black when I see it inside, it's purple when I see it in the sun, and after it's burned, it's gray."

In this situation, the examiner needed to ask Mario how he arrived at his answer. By Mario's reasoning, the answer was logical and correct—but according to test regulations, it would be scored as wrong.

THE ROLE OF THE EXAMINER

In order to obtain a reliable and valid score for a young child, the examiner needs to have a rapport with the child. Children need to feel safe in order to show the examiner what they know and can do. When children feel safe and encouraged, they're more likely to risk showing examiners who they are and what they know. They're more likely to guess—and to tap into their subconscious—when they're not absolutely certain about an answer.

But what if a child simply doesn't like the examiner? Perhaps the adult reminds the child of someone the child doesn't like. Perhaps the child is even afraid of the examiner. Keisha offers a good example of the latter.

Keisha was a quiet girl. She was unsure of this new situation and the new lady who was asking questions. Her mother had told her not to talk to strangers, and she had never met this lady. Therefore, Keisha decided that she would be safe and not talk to the lady. She sat silently while the lady kept asking questions. The examiner finally stopped and asked Keisha why she was not responding. Keisha told the examiner that she did not talk to strangers.

The examiner asked her if she knew Kermit the Frog. Keisha said that she did. The examiner went to her cupboard, where she kept a Kermit puppet. Kermit asked the questions, and Keisha responded. The skilled examiner was able to allay Keisha's fears and make her comfortable enough to respond to test questions.

Here are some ways to create a more comfortable situation for both the child and the examiner:

- Before the scheduled examination, explain that the child will do activities with a man or woman to find out how the child learns best.
- Request that the child bring a snack to eat during the testing process. This might provide essential brain fuel, or it might be comfort food.
- Be flexible enough to reschedule at the last minute if necessary. This flexibility is important. The child might not feel well; noisy construction work might suddenly begin just outside the window; the child might receive an invitation to a birthday party scheduled for the same time as the examination. In any of these cases, the child's scores may not be valid.
- Have the child bring a favorite toy or stuffed animal to share with the examiner.
- To establish an easy give-and-take between child and examiner, ask the child to select and bring several photographs or pictures to show the examiner. This invites the child to invest something in the process, to quickly become accustomed to how the examiner interacts, and to start off with a positive association.

TESTING CULTURALLY DIVERSE CHILDREN

Nearly all tests have some bias toward the dominant culture. When a child from outside of the dominant culture is tested, the results of standardized IQ tests should not serve as an absolute sign of cognitive ability. Instead, they should serve as a general estimate of the child's current level of measurable

functioning and as a benchmark for further testing. Testing can also help teachers identify the best learning approaches for the child and plan procedures that will engage the child's strengths.

Some children from cultural minorities may have fewer test-taking skills and different problem-solving strategies. Some may even sabotage themselves by working slowly, to avoid competition and gain acceptance. Here are some suggestions to consider when assessing a child from a cultural minority:

- Determine the child's preferred language.
- Use a multiple-method assessment approach. Don't assume that a single score or a small collection of scores can fully portray the child's intellectual abilities.
- Integrate other types of assessment, such as informal observations or actual work samples and anecdotes from the child's portfolio. (Portfolios are discussed beginning on page 120. You will find information on informal observation on page 122, and forms to use for this purpose on pages 124–130.)
- If possible, compare the child's scores with those of other children from the same culture. National norms are likely to be inappropriate for judging most children who belong to minority groups.
- Take into account the child's degree of acculturation.
- Be cautious about drawing generalizations from any test score.
- Try to be aware of any personal biases you might have, and guard against letting these affect your interaction with or assessment of the child.

A few tests are less culturally biased than others. Here are some we recommend. (The tests are fully described in Appendix A, beginning on page 215.)

Wechsler: The Wechsler Preschool and Primary Scale of Intelligence–Third Edition (WPPSI–III) is designed for children ages three years to seven years and three months. Children who are seven years and older are able to complete the Wechsler Intelligence Scale for Children–Fifth Edition (WISC–V). WISC–V has been translated or adapted to many languages, and norms have been established for a number of countries. The Wechsler Verbal Comprehension Index (VCI) and Perceptual Reasoning Index (PRI) are also independently appropriate gifted program selection tools for culturally diverse, bilingual, and twice-exceptional students or visual-spatial learners.

Stanford-Binet: Use the Visual-Spatial Processing subtests of the Stanford-Binet Intelligence Scale–Fifth Edition (SB5).

Kaufman Assessment Battery for Children–Second Edition (KABC–II): This test is culturally fair and individually administered.

Cognitive Abilities Test, Form 7 (CogAT): CogAT measures students' acquired reasoning abilities in Verbal, Quantitative, and Nonverbal categories, which are closely linked with achieving academic success in school. None of the items on the three Quantitative tests require comprehension of oral language, thus resulting in a more meaningful assessment of every student's reasoning ability.

Naglieri Nonverbal Ability Test–Second Edition (NNAT2): This test uses thirty-eight questions of four types: Pattern Completion, Reasoning by Analogy, Serial Reasoning, and Spatial Visualization, which do not require verbal skills. The test uses geometric shapes and designs to measure reasoning and problem-solving abilities.

U-STARS~PLUS: This acronym stands for Using Science, Talents, and Abilities to Recognize Students~Promoting Learning for Underrepresented Students. This test uses a science-based model for recognizing and nurturing students with hidden potential in kindergarten through second grade. It is intended for students from economically disadvantaged and culturally diverse families, because it is not heavily dependent on early language experiences.

Scales for Rating the Behavioral Characteristics of Superior Students: These are commonly referred to as the **Renzulli Scales** or **Renzulli-Hartman Scales.** The Renzulli scales are designed for teachers to use the scales to rate students, with easy-to-follow instructions on how to establish local norms in a school or district and a practical plan for identifying students for gifted and talented programs.

Scales for Identifying Gifted Students (SIGS): This is a comprehensive observational instrument for identifying gifted students ages five to eighteen years old. It consists of two rating scales (Home and School) that can be used independently or together. A Spanish version of the Home Rating Scale is available.

Note that the Peabody Picture Vocabulary Test–Fourth Edition–(PPVT–IV) is a measure of receptive vocabulary only. It should *not* be used to determine intelligence of preschool and kindergarten children of Hispanic-American descent, because these children may wrongly interpret words, not understand the meanings of words, pronounce words differently, or use other words with similar meanings.

Ethnicity is only one type of difference. Children of *any* ethnicity who have a low socio-economic status are likely to test differently than the cultural norm. Children in poverty are the most vulnerable. Their adaptive strategies may not fit well with the tests. Children with learning or physical differences and those with personal problems may also test differently.

Another important caution in interpreting IQ scores: Gifted children, because of their exceptional cognitive abilities, may exhibit great discrepancies between their measures of performance and fine motor abilities and measures of verbal and other cognitive skills. For example, using the WPPSI–IV or the WISC–V, differences of twenty, thirty, and even forty points between Verbal and Performance scores indicate learning difficulties in most average and high-average children. *This may not hold true for gifted children.* Such disparity *does* alert educators that gifted children might be frustrated by their fine motor lag and might need alternative ways to express what they know.

OUTSIDE CONSULTANTS

Sometimes it's necessary to use outside help to become aware of children's exceptional learning modalities and needs. Few schools will provide this. It is usually the parents who are responsible for finding and paying for a qualified examiner and making arrangements for the testing. When a private professional assessment is made, consider these questions before and after testing:

- Is the agency or examiner/interpreter (usually a licensed psychologist or a school counselor) widely experienced in testing young gifted children?
- Does the examiner/interpreter have a respected reputation among those in your gifted community?
- Did the child enjoy the testing experience?
- Were the scores adequately interpreted to the parents? Were behavioral, emotional, social, and academic recommendations discussed? Were

parents told clearly what the numbers mean and don't mean?

- Do the test scores accurately reflect the child's abilities?

What Intelligence Tests Tell Us

Intelligence tests give information about some areas of strength and weakness. They help us know how a child compares with others of the same age. However, they often don't assess the wide range of talent or abilities of the child and may focus only on intellectual development, reading ability, visual-spatial acumen, or thinking skills. For some children of minority cultures or economic groups, the test may cover material with which they have no prior experience, thus placing them in an invalid assessment situation.

QUESTIONS TO ASK ABOUT DISCREPANCIES

Any discrepancies between test scores and classroom performance need to be carefully analyzed. The following questions may give you helpful information about the validity of a particular test.

When the child performs far better on a test than in the classroom, ask:

- Are the lessons too easy, or are they repetitious? Is the curriculum too meager?
- Is the child not challenged in the classroom?
- Does the child usually or often feel stressed or fearful in the classroom?
- Are there problems outside of school that affect the child's learning?
- How is the child's health? Could there be a physical problem? Is the child getting enough rest?
- Are the directions given in the classroom clear?

When the child performs far better in the classroom than on a test, ask:

- Was the test appropriate for the child?
- Was the child motivated to take the test?
- Did the child feel anxious about the test or testing environment?
- Was the test administered by a stranger in an unfamiliar environment?
- Did the test involve only paper-and-pencil tasks?
- Are the child's strengths obvious in areas not covered by the test?
- Was the child tired or ill during the test?
- Is the child a perfectionist or a slow, methodical thinker? This child may need more than the allotted time to perform the tasks.

- Was the child distracted during the test? (Sometimes being with other children or in a stimulating environment may pull the child's attention away from the task at hand.)
- Did the child appear to think with more complexity than the test required?

Using Portfolios to Document and Evaluate Progress

For some children, tests will be inappropriate. Mario's case (page 117) provides an example. Mario's low score was in no way indicative of his knowledge. A simple interview documenting his responses needs to replace or append the test score. Real-life assessment is much more appropriate for the child whose ability far exceeds the boundaries of the testing situation. If a test or examiner does not fit well with a child's personality, or if a test is not designed to measure the full extent of a child's knowledge, it will not show the child's abilities accurately.

Even when testing is appropriate, more broad-based, authentic assessment is an important and useful means of documenting children's abilities and progress. One of the most promising methods for collecting and evaluating the child's work is a portfolio. Author and gifted educator Bertie Kingore defines a portfolio as "a systematic collection representative of a child's work that the teacher and student select to provide information regarding each child's developmental readiness, learning profile, interests, achievement levels, and learning growth over time."[2]

Chapter 1 discusses creating portfolios and using them as a means of getting to know your students (page 11). The same portfolio you compile for this purpose can also be an excellent tool for ongoing assessment. Its effectiveness requires careful planning and clear organization. It must be more than a random collection; you'll need to establish goals for the portfolio and make decisions about what it will contain in order to serve its purpose of helping you evaluate a student's progress. The portfolio should reflect the child's growth and learning over time.

You might consider including a small collection of work that represents the young child. For

---

[2] Bertie Kingore. *Developing Portfolios for Authentic Assessment, PreK–3* (Thousand Oaks, CA: Corwin Press, 2008): 14.

example, at the start of the school year, you might ask the child to create a self-portrait or a family portrait. Then you could have the student repeat the task in the middle of the year and again at the conclusion of the year. This will show growth and be affirming for the child.

The same type of assignment can be given in other subject areas—each showing how the child grows in ability. You might also choose an item that represents a student's unique characteristics or interests. For example, a child may love horses and draw pictures of them during all available free time. One of those drawings, included in the child's portfolio, can be a kind of snapshot of the child's special love.

Involving Children

Save children's work or pictures of their work. Each week, have them select a piece that they wish to put into their portfolio. Some teachers find it easiest to have children start with one or two content areas. Encourage students to select not only work they're most proud of, but also things that were hard for them to do or required a lot of effort. Add to the portfolio work that represents new information that the child has just learned. Include any "draft" copy or copies along with the finished product; you'll then have excellent examples of multiple stages of growth.

You might also include products students have done in their free time or at home. These spontaneous products will be different for each child and will be a prime source of information about the child's special interests and abilities. They may show excellence or indicate areas where the child needs special help. Not every child will have a spontaneous product; some children may have several.

Involving Parents

If you like, suggest to parents that they maintain their own portfolio for their child. Parents could, for example, collect:

- items that commemorate special occasions
- notes about firsts for the child
- photographs of the child at different stages
- drawings the child has made
- pictures of, or notes about, the child's collections or hobbies
- a list of books read by and to the child
- medical notes
- anecdotes or observations made by childcare providers

- videos of books read by the child, counting and math problems solved, constructions made with interlocking blocks such as Legos, cooking done, crafts made, games created and played, sculptures made, plays produced, sports played, and so on

Keeping a home portfolio gives parents a way to share with you what the child is like or has done at home. Chapter 1 includes several family letters and forms to assist you in learning more about children at home: "Your Child's Pictures" (page 18), "Information, Please" (page 19), "About My Child" (pages 20–21), "Checklist of My Child's Strengths" (pages 22–23), and "Your Child's Personal Exhibit" (page 24).

Children can make and maintain their own portfolios. (See "Child-Created Portfolios," page 13.) A child-created portfolio can complement the one that you keep, offering a window to what the child enjoys and values and to the ways in which the child is excelling or growing.

Maintaining the Portfolio[3]

Date each new entry and file it at the back of the portfolio. This allows you to see growth and to keep a chronological record of the work. You can teach the child to do most of this filing. It then becomes the child's responsibility to add to the portfolio. You may need to write the date in a visible place or provide a stamp that the student can use to date work. To be meaningful, portfolios need to be manageable, easily identifiable, and readily accessible for the child.

Each entry should include an explanation of why the piece was selected. Young children who aren't yet able to write can dictate their reason to an older child or an adult. This can be a simple note: "I chose this because _____." This aids the decision-making process, and you and any portfolio reader can see why the work was considered significant enough to be included.

Talking with the Child About the Portfolio

It's very important that you talk with children about their portfolios. Portfolio conferences give you the opportunity to highlight work and give students a chance to value their work and see progress. You're

---

[3] Many of the suggestions included here for maintaining students' portfolios are from *Portfolios: Enriching and Assessing All Students, Identifying the Gifted, Grades K–6* by Bertie Kingore (Des Moines, IA: Leadership Publishers, 1993): 3. Used with permission of Bertie Kingore.

building on success and providing encouragement and motivation to keep on learning.

Open the lines of communication with statements and questions such as the following:

- Tell me about your work.
- How did you do that?
- Explain what you did.
- How did you figure that out?

A portfolio conference is a time for sharing information, not for interrogation. Recognize effort as well as any end result. Be positive. Build on what the student has done, and set goals for what the student will attempt to accomplish next. This encourages the child to take responsibility for successes and needed improvements. Self-esteem is a natural byproduct here—it thrives on growth and success. The conference also opens a door for increased understanding between you and the child and provides an opportunity for you to become more sensitive to the child's needs and strengths.

Conferences need to take place apart from other children, yet still in clear view of the rest of the class. We suggest that you meet while the remaining students are working in learning centers or using free time. Help the others in the class understand and respect that this is your special time with one student. Knowing that they, too, will have time alone with you will support them as they develop this understanding and respect.

Effective Portfolio Assessment

For portfolios to be educationally effective, they must emphasize content, process, and product as well as effort and achievement. They also must include student ownership and self-evaluation. Bertie Kingore writes:[4]

"Portfolios must be developed so they:

- are a natural part of daily classroom activities rather than contrived
- are thoroughly integrated into the instructional program
- encourage student responsibility, ownership, and pride of accomplishment
- allow students to polish and refine their craft—to build upon what they are learning to do well

- focus discussions about learning and development among students, teachers, and parents
- incorporate learning tasks and also students' ideas, interests, and attitudes
- invite challenge and complexity in students' thinking and in the works they produce
- encourage student metacognition and increase their awareness of their capacity for self-reflection and making judgments"

Children become so proud of their portfolios that they need the opportunity to share them. You might want to arrange a portfolio party. Children can display their portfolios and explain what they have done and learned to parents, relatives, neighbors, and community members. This is a chance to inform stakeholders in your school about the wonderful things your students are doing—things that aren't adequately reflected in test scores alone. The portfolio party might occur in conjunction with parent night, parent conferences, open house, or a school learning fair. Be sure to invite the local press and get media coverage!

Documenting Development Through Observations

Observations are yet another way you can assess the young child. To make accurate, reliable observations that are objective, fair, and consistent, you need to establish what you are looking for and the degree to which a particular behavior or skill is evidenced.

A checklist is an easy and efficient way to document what you have observed. When the child shows evidence of a behavior or skill you note it along with the date. You can record and date more detailed observations on note cards and file them in the child's portfolio.

Checklists are especially effective when they not only list behaviors and skills, but also provide brief descriptions and standards by which to measure them. For example:

Includes detail in writing
Not yet evidenced: *Gives no detail.*
Developing: *Includes some detail.*
Age-appropriate: *Includes appropriate detail.*
Outstanding: *Uses elaborate, descriptive, rich detail.*

---

[4] *Portfolios.* Used with permission of Bertie Kingore.

This gives bright children who have achieved the level of "age-appropriate" a goal or direction to grow in so mediocrity won't be established as the norm. You'll want to date your notations; then you can reassess the child periodically, each time noting both *what* level has been reached and *when* the child reached it.

The "Student Observation Forms" (pages 124–130) are detailed checklists. They can help you evaluate young children's performance or skills in specific areas.

When children have finished a piece of work or when an area of study comes to a close, they may be able to give you valuable information about what they have learned. You may want to have children report on this by using the "What I Learned" self-evaluation form (pages 131–132).[5] Older students will be able to complete the form on their own. With younger students who aren't yet comfortable reading or writing, ask the questions on the form that you think will give you helpful information.

Questions and Answers

"My children want to take their work home with them. How can I keep it for their portfolio?"
If the children really want to bring their work home, make photocopies for them. However, you may find that once the children get into the portfolio process, your problem may not be about what goes home, but about how to limit what goes into the portfolio. Be sure to communicate with parents so they understand that not everything the students work on in class will be coming home. And make an effort to share children's portfolios with parents at conferences and open houses. You can also make electronic copies of the work for the portfolio.

If you like, and if your school's policy allows it, you can send the portfolios home at the end of the year for families to keep. Some schools save portfolios from year to year, and others send them home at the end of each year. Some schools save selected works from year to year and present the portfolio when a student graduates or moves to a different district.

"What if children want to put many examples of the same thing into their portfolio?"
Explain to the children that you value their ability to do that particular thing very well, and you recognize that they're trying to perfect their skill. Say that you'll keep one example of that favorite subject each month, or that they can choose one example for September, one for January, and one for May. Then make it clear that you expect them to also select other items that represent other areas of learning.

"Won't all this assessment and evaluation take time? How can I do it all?"
It will take time, but time that is spread across the school year. Your goal is to have ongoing information to aid you in designing classroom instruction. It's initially time-consuming to teach children portfolio management skills, but as children master these skills, your burden lessens. It's also important that you structure your time for what's important.

Tests take time to give and to score. Portfolios can be integrated into the lesson and classroom routine so they don't necessarily take *more* time, but instead take *different* time. Practice selective abandonment of tasks that are time-consuming and unproductive.

Also, think creatively. Do you have a parent, a community volunteer, an older child, or an aide who's willing to help you do some one-on-one student evaluation? Could you work with *one* child for a few minutes each day during students' free time? Keep in mind that this process is continuous and comprehensive. By doing a little bit each day, you can help yourself stay on top of things.

Conclusion

When young gifted students come into the school setting, they are excited about learning new things. Your task is to make sure that you extend the excitement and nourish the curiosity, without leaving gaps in children's knowledge and skills. To do this, you need to constantly assess and evaluate what each student *knows* and *can do*. Documenting growth validates achievement and rewards excellence. Your own payback comes when you observe children thrilled at learning, busy working on new projects that match their abilities and potential.

---

[5] The "What I Learned" form is adapted from a self-evaluation tool developed by Dodie Merritt, a teacher of gifted children at Genoa-Kingston School in Genoa, Illinois. Used with permission of Dodie Merritt.

Student Observation Form I

Learning and Cognitive Development

Student's name: _____

To the teacher: Use this form several times throughout the year. On the line beside the appropriate item, write the date on which you assessed the child's level of development.

KEY TO LETTER SYMBOLS
N = Not yet evidenced
D = Developing
A = Age-appropriate
O = Outstanding

Analytical Thinking

Analyzes tasks:
_____ **N:** Approaches tasks with no evidence of prior thought.
_____ **D:** Begins tasks after some thought.
_____ **A:** Shows ability to think through tasks.
_____ **O:** Thinks through and analyzes tasks; can apply learning to new tasks.

Sees cause-and-effect relationships:
_____ **N:** Has no idea of cause and effect.
_____ **D:** Occasionally sees what caused reaction.
_____ **A:** Sees cause and effect when it occurs.
_____ **O:** Understands (and can explain) cause and effect.

Ability to take apart and reassemble things:
_____ **N:** Is unaware of parts.
_____ **D:** Can disassemble, but has difficulty putting things back together.
_____ **A:** Can take apart and reassemble basic things or ideas.
_____ **O:** Is able to disassemble and reassemble things and ideas in novel, workable ways.

Expresses relationships between past and present experiences:
_____ **N:** Able to see only the present.
_____ **D:** Beginning to distinguish between past and present.
_____ **A:** Can distinguish past and present.
_____ **O:** Expresses relationship between past, present, and future events.

Makes up stories, songs, plays about experiences:
_____ **N:** Does not tell stories, sing songs, or enact plays.
_____ **D:** Repeats stories, songs, or plays as told.
_____ **A:** Can make up short stories, songs, or plays.
_____ **O:** Tells stories, sings songs, or acts out plays with elaborate details.

Organizes collections:

_____ **N:** Does not see any organizational schema.

_____ **D:** Is beginning to see simple organizational patterns.

_____ **A:** Can organize simple collections in standard ways.

_____ **O:** Is capable of organizing complex collections in different ways.

Motivation or Task Commitment

Keeps at task until it makes sense:

_____ **N:** Flits from thing to thing; has short attention span.

_____ **D:** Is able to stay with task for short while.

_____ **A:** Stays with some tasks when they are of interest.

_____ **O:** Shows persistence and commitment to getting task completed.

Asks penetrating questions:

_____ **N:** Does not ask questions; asks unrelated questions.

_____ **D:** Asks questions that relate to topic.

_____ **A:** Asks questions that show evidence of understanding the topic.

_____ **O:** Understands topic in depth; asks questions that reflect thinking.

Is curious:

_____ **N:** Has difficulty focusing on item.

_____ **D:** Asks standard questions (who, what) relating to items.

_____ **A:** Wants to know how things work.

_____ **O:** Asks why and what if.

Displays unexpected depth of knowledge in one or more areas:

_____ **N:** Shows only superficial knowledge.

_____ **D:** Has an area of interest.

_____ **A:** Wants to know more about an area of interest; asks questions or searches for more information.

_____ **O:** Is a resident expert in a specific area.

Remembers:

_____ **N:** Has difficulty recalling information or details.

_____ **D:** Remembers some details while other information may be hazy or lacking.

_____ **A:** Recalls details of things that pertain to self.

_____ **O:** Can clearly recall and recount past events, promises, and minute details.

Displays energy and excitement when learning:

_____ **N:** Is reluctant to try anything new; shows little enthusiasm.

_____ **D:** Shows interest in learning.

_____ **A:** Is energetic about topic that interests him/her.

_____ **O:** Becomes very enthusiastic about learning; does not want to quit.

Wants to do things on own; shows independence:

_____ **N:** Wants teacher to do things for her/him.

_____ **D:** Does some things on own.

_____ **A:** Prefers to do things on own.

_____ **O:** Does not want help; asks to be left to do things in own way.

Learning

Number of repetitions needed to learn:

_____ More than thirty

_____ Fifteen to twenty-five

_____ Ten or fewer

_____ Five or fewer

Categorizes by more than one attribute:

_____ **N:** Does not see attributes.

_____ **D:** Observes attributes but has difficulty categorizing.

_____ **A:** Can categorize one or two simple attributes.

_____ **O:** Is capable of seeing and categorizing multiple attributes.

Is able to read and explain meaning of what was read:

_____ **N:** Recalls a few details.

_____ **D:** Knows literal meaning.

_____ **A:** Comprehends written material.

_____ **O:** Makes inferences and/or analyzes reading.

Comprehends symbols (note all that apply):

_____ Letters

_____ Numbers

_____ Maps

_____ Music

Understands these mathematical concepts (note all that apply):

_____ One-to-one correspondence

_____ Addition

_____ Subtraction

_____ Regrouping

_____ Multiplication

_____ Division

_____ Making change

_____ Telling time

_____ Measurement

_____ Graphs and charts

Student Observation Form II

Writing and Language Development

Student's name: _____

To the teacher: Use this form several times throughout the year. On the line beside the appropriate item, write the date on which you assessed the child's level of development.

KEY TO LETTER SYMBOLS
N = Not yet evidenced
D = Developing
A = Age-appropriate
O = Outstanding

Writing Skill Development

Writes sentences:

_____ **N:** Does not write in complete sentences.
_____ **D:** Writes in complete sentences.
_____ **A:** Writes fully developed sentences.
_____ **O:** Writes exemplary sentences well above those of age peers.

Includes detail in writing:

_____ **N:** Gives no detail.
_____ **D:** Includes some detail.
_____ **A:** Includes appropriate detail.
_____ **O:** Uses elaborate, descriptive, rich detail.

Predicts:

_____ **N:** Thinks and predicts inaccurately.
_____ **D:** Predicts some with minimal accuracy.
_____ **A:** Has made a prediction based on thinking through information.
_____ **O:** Shows thoughtful reflection; makes reasonable, accurate predictions.

Shows comprehension:

_____ **N:** Shows foggy comprehension.
_____ **D:** Shows some comprehension.
_____ **A:** Comprehends information.
_____ **O:** Shows strong, complete comprehension; applies comprehension beyond lesson and to other situations.

Language Development

Is able to do the following (note all that apply):

_____ Use multisyllabic words.
_____ Use similes, metaphors, and analogies.
_____ Modify language for less mature children.
_____ Use language to teach other children.
_____ Express similarities and differences among unrelated objects.
_____ Use time concepts.

Student Observation Form III

Social and Emotional Development

Student's name: _____

To the teacher: Use this form several times throughout the year. On the line beside the appropriate item, write the date on which you assessed the child's level of development.

KEY TO LETTER SYMBOLS
N = Not yet evidenced
D = Developing
A = Age-appropriate
O = Outstanding

Sensitivity

Takes action to help someone in need:

_____ **N:** Is not aware of others' needs.

_____ **D:** Sees others' needs but is not sure what to do.

_____ **A:** Sees others' needs and attempts to respond.

_____ **O:** Is sensitive to others' needs and responds with appropriate action.

Shows nonverbal awareness of others' needs:

_____ **N:** Is not aware of others' needs.

_____ **D:** Sees others' needs but is not sure what to do.

_____ **A:** Sees others' needs and attempts to respond.

_____ **O:** Is sensitive to others' needs and responds with appropriate action.

Shows sensitivity in these ways (note all that apply):

_____ Uses empathic statements.

_____ Has a sense of justice.

_____ Has high expectations of self.

_____ Has high expectations of others.

Sense of Humor

Catches on to subtle humor:

_____ **N:** Does not get the point of jokes.

_____ **D:** Laughs at simple jokes.

_____ **A:** Understands jokes.

_____ **O:** Understands puns and subtle jokes/humor.

Likes to play with language:

_____ **N:** Understands only literal language.

_____ **D:** Understands simple riddles and jokes.

_____ **A:** Makes up simple riddles and jokes.

_____ **O:** Makes up puns, riddles, and jokes with double meanings; shows mature sense of humor.

Personal-Social Development

Does the following (note all that apply):

_____ Expresses feelings in words.

_____ Works and plays cooperatively with other children.

_____ Participates with others in large groups.

_____ Takes turns and shares.

_____ Shows concern for others and their property.

_____ Takes initiative in learning.

_____ Pays attention and concentrates on a task.

_____ Consistently completes a task.

_____ Works cooperatively with adults.

_____ Feels good about self.

_____ Is courteous to others.

_____ Resolves peer conflicts with language.

_____ Can separate from parent and engage in activity.

_____ Reunites well with parent.

Student Observation Form IV

Fine Motor Development

Student's name: _____

To the teacher: Use this form several times throughout the year. On the line beside the appropriate item, write the date on which you assessed the child's level of development.

_____ Follows top-to-bottom progression.

_____ Follows left-to-right progression.

_____ Folds paper into halves.

_____ Folds paper into quarters.

_____ Folds paper into diagonals.

_____ Uses crayon or pencil with control within a defined area.

_____ Controls brush and paint.

_____ Uses scissors with control to cut a straight line.

_____ Uses scissors with control to cut a curved line.

_____ Connects a dotted outline to make a shape.

_____ Pastes using one finger.

_____ Holds a pencil correctly.

_____ Works a previously unseen puzzle of ten or more pieces.

_____ In drawing a person, includes a major body part and features.

_____ Traces objects.

_____ Copies a pattern from board to paper.

_____ Writes basic strokes.

What I Learned

My name: _____ Date: _____

This is what I studied:

Here's what I did:

Here's what I learned:

Here's what I enjoyed most:

Here's what I enjoyed least:

If I did it all over again, here's what I'd change:

Here's how I rate what I did (circle one):

Needs More Work   OK   **Good**   **Excellent**   **The BEST**

Here's the grade I would give myself: _____

CHAPTER 8
Flexible Grouping to Help All Children Learn

Rosa came home from school and told her mom about how her teacher always moved her from one group to another. Rosa enjoyed certain groups more than others. In some groups she was a "teacher," while in other groups she was a "learner" and learned new things. Rosa explained that sometimes teaching was fun, but that she really liked learning new things better.

Grouping for Learning

Every few years, it seems, a new education initiative claims that it will solve our classroom problems. Some initiatives last longer than others. Some initiatives are more effective than others.

These initiatives often include new or different ways of grouping students. Some initiatives even suggest that we don't need to group students, that a one-size curriculum can fit all. This approach doesn't work for clothing, and we believe it does not work for the classroom either.

Educators group students for many different purposes. No single form of grouping works well for all

purposes with all students. Rather, the goals of the lesson and the characteristics of the students should determine the composition and the size of the groups. We recommend grouping students according to the content they are learning, the process they are using, the product they are creating to demonstrate their learning, and the abilities, interests, and motivations of the students involved.

Cooperative learning was once seen by some educators as a solution to the problem of teaching ever-larger groups of students with ever-widening ranges of ability. Traditional cooperative learning divides students into groups comprising of one child with high ability, two with average ability, and one with low ability. Many schools and teachers have used this arrangement in an effort to help students learn efficiently and to improve socialization skills.

But for gifted children, being placed in traditional cooperative learning groups can present problems. Rosa's feelings about "teaching" and "learning" illustrate this. Students learn better by motivating one another—by sharing ideas and pooling resources toward a common learning goal. Gifted students, therefore, perform better when they are with other students of similar ability.[1] By contrast, placing gifted children in the role of "teacher" can eliminate many opportunities for their own discovery and growth.

Drawbacks of Traditional Cooperative Learning

For all students, traditional cooperative learning produces mixed results. A child who is highly able may provide some leadership and help the other students in constructive ways; however, the child may also become frustrated by having to do most of the work. In practice, the brighter students and the more assertive ones (who aren't necessarily one and the same) often end up doing most, if not all, of the decision making and work.

This arrangement is unfair to everyone. In many cases, it teaches the group leader how to dominate a group. This can reinforce a sense of superiority, which can be intimidating to others in the group. A gifted or bright child may perceive concepts more quickly and comprehensively and may become impatient with other students' slower pace. We need to guide assertive and bright children to learn tolerance, humility, flexibility, and patience. At the same time, we must find ways to meet these students' needs for academic, creative, and intellectual fulfillment.

Meanwhile, students in the middle—those with average ability—may lose their chance to shine. These children may feel intimidated by or resentful of the gifted students in their groups. Children with lesser ability, meanwhile, may have their weaknesses reinforced. In a supportive learning environment, children with generally lower ability often show unexpected strengths at surprising moments. But when they are grouped with students who are so much faster than they are, they may learn not to try. It's discouraging and even painful to work with a classmate who thinks more quickly and who is looked to as the source of all the best ideas.

Response to Intervention (RTI)

Response to Intervention (RTI) is a strategy for identifying and supporting students' learning and behavior needs. RTI uses the model of a triangle showing different degrees of academic support for students with specific needs. This model has been widely accepted as a schoolwide initiative because it specifies degrees to which the curriculum can be adapted based on the specific needs of the students.

Tier 1 is the base, or the core curriculum presented to all students at a given grade. Students receive differentiated instruction; assessments are administered regularly to screen for learning difficulties.

Some students need support in addition to the basic curriculum. **Tier 2** reflects interventions and targeted teaching methods geared to students who are struggling and at risk of failing.

Tier 3 is for those students who are not succeeding with Tier 2 interventions and need more intensive interventions in order to learn and advance. Tier 3 interventions are intended to support students who have the most severe academic needs.

Response to Intervention

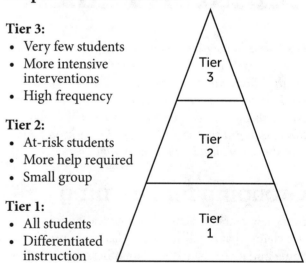

Tier 3:
- Very few students
- More intensive interventions
- High frequency

Tier 2:
- At-risk students
- More help required
- Small group

Tier 1:
- All students
- Differentiated instruction

Some educators have proposed reconfiguring the RTI triangle into a diamond so it addresses students at *both* ends of the learning continuum—those who struggle to learn and those who are gifted—and shows the need to serve all students with curriculum geared to their needs. In the middle of the RTI diamond (Tier 1) are students for whom the regular curriculum with differentiation is appropriate. Left

---

[1] Karen Rogers. *Re-Forming Gifted Education: Matching the Program to the Child* (Scottsdale, AZ: Great Potential Press, 2002): 208.

RTI and Differentiation

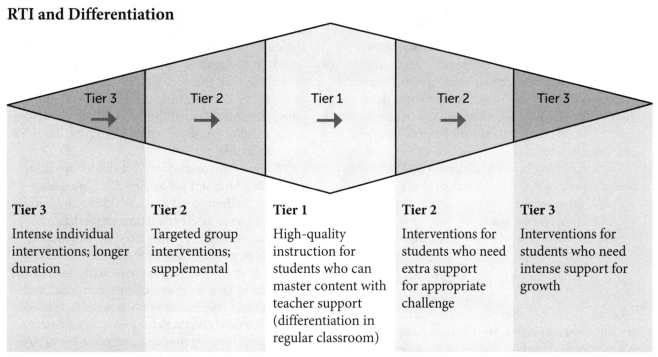

Tier 3

Intense individual interventions; longer duration

Tier 2

Targeted group interventions; supplemental

Tier 1

High-quality instruction for students who can master content with teacher support (differentiation in regular classroom)

Tier 2

Interventions for students who need extra support for appropriate challenge

Tier 3

Interventions for students who need intense support for growth

of middle (Tier 2) are students who need special help or adaptations to make the curriculum meaningful. Right of middle (Tier 2) are students who master the basic curriculum rapidly, who learn rapidly and need fewer repetitions, and who need extensions of depth, pacing, and complexity. On the far left (Tier 3) are students who need intensive, individualized interventions. The core curriculum must be presented in a manner that is individually tailored, appropriate, and engaging to these students. These children struggle and need explicit, step-by-step instructions and assistance. On the far right (Tier 3) are students who have intense needs that extend far beyond the curriculum of their grade level. They already know the content or can learn it with ease in a short time. Their needs are just as intense as those of students in Tier 3 at the other end of the learning continuum, but their knowledge stretches beyond the required content mastery. Because they already know the content, they need and enjoy the chance to grapple with new information, delve deeply into the content, explore new areas, and/or accelerate their learning.

The more differentiation that occurs in Tier 1, the better for all concerned. For students in Tier 2 on both sides, some adjustments to the regular curriculum are needed for growth to occur. Students in

Tier 3 on both ends of the learning continuum need major changes in the regular curriculum in order for growth to occur.

Cluster Grouping: A Flexible Alternative

Six-year-old Mark's mother called the teacher. She was distraught. A few months ago, Mark could hardly wait to start school. Now he was crying and feigning illness so he wouldn't have to go. His mother couldn't understand what had happened. Mark was a serious boy who loved learning. He had been reading since the age of four. His math skills were exceptional. Mark enjoyed watching the evening news and discussing current events with his parents. At times, his questioning skills and level of understanding made him seem like a miniature adult. Why wouldn't he love school?

Mark's teacher, Ms. Costino, was also upset. In her classroom, she used cooperative learning a good deal of the time. But Mark was uncooperative in his group. He had little patience with the other students. Sometimes he tried to take over the group and boss the children, who in turn grew resentful. At other times, he became quiet and sullen. Ms. Costino spent much of her energy trying to coax Mark to be more cooperative. It was a situation in which everyone seemed to be losing.

After talking to Mark's mother and consulting with some of her teaching colleagues, Ms. Costino decided to try a new approach. She grouped Mark with other high-ability students, matching their experience with a separate, challenging task. At the same time, she kept the rest of the class in mixed cooperative learning groups.

Although Ms. Costino had worried that the groups would founder without a role model, to her surprise and delight, new leaders emerged—in both Mark's group and the others. And Mark's mother reported that her son's attitude toward school was greatly improved.

Originally, Ms. Costino was using a group strategy that didn't allow Mark to grow beyond what he already knew. Mark was frustrated and felt he had to either tutor the other children or adapt to them by withdrawing. When Ms. Costino grouped Mark with other highly able children, the teacher saw many benefits—not only for Mark, but also for the rest of the class.

Experts in the field of gifted education agree that children with high ability need to spend at least part of their day interacting and learning with other children who have similar ability. To make this happen, the experts recommend using cluster grouping. Cluster grouping allows you to place gifted children together while simultaneously placing the other students in heterogeneous groups. This approach provides the best cooperative grouping situation for all children.

With cluster grouping, children who have been identified as gifted are placed in a small group of four to six students and are clustered in one teacher's class. While clustering can be done within a single classroom, ideally, cluster grouping is done schoolwide or gradewide. (If your school does not use gradewide or schoolwide cluster grouping, the following information will still be helpful. On page 137, under "Guidelines for Grouping Young Children," you will find information on grouping within a single classroom.) The teacher with the gifted cluster (Tier 3, far right in the diamond-shaped model) does not also have the children who need specialized individual instruction (Tier 3, far left in the diamond-shaped model), as this would create too wide a range of abilities in one classroom. Instead, the gifted children are grouped with students of average and below-average ability. The students with above-average ability are not grouped with the gifted students, but are grouped with students of average ability and those who are struggling. Using this approach, the teacher with the gifted students can extend the curriculum as well as manage the social and emotional implications of working with the gifted students. Meanwhile, the children with above-average ability can shine without being outshone by the gifted students.

With very young children, when identification of giftedness has not yet occurred, it is possible to group children based on their skill levels, work styles, and interests.[2] For example, a kindergarten child who is already reading needs to be grouped with others who are reading at a similar level, so their instructional time is spent *learning more* rather than coasting while other students learn readiness skills. A child who already knows math facts needs to be grouped with other children who understand more complex math concepts and can solve problems on an advanced level. It's deadening for children to repeat simple reading and math tasks that provide no opportunities for growth or creativity. These children need challenging "instead of" work (see Chapter 3, page 43)—related work that sparks their curiosity, interest, and motivation.

Cluster grouping provides the best learning situation for children at all ability levels. Gifted children feel less isolated or different and more free to take risks and rise to the challenges of further learning. Meanwhile, other students feel less intimidated or dominated and more encouraged to contribute ideas and effort. Everyone wins.

Some teachers worry that this arrangement is somehow elitist. It truly isn't. With cluster grouping, we recognize that children don't all learn in the same way or at the same rate. We aren't providing something better for the gifted students; we're creating appropriate opportunities for all the students to experience challenge, to learn, and to grow. This is what we want to provide for every child and what most programs already provide routinely for the majority of students. Children with high ability simply require something different at times.

---

[2] We encourage early identification whenever possible. See Chapter 1 for ideas on working with parents and others to identify unique abilities and talents. Chapter 2 discusses learning modalities. Chapter 7 presents information on testing and ongoing evaluation.

Guidelines for Grouping Young Children

Most teachers find that cluster grouping provides the most productive situation for young gifted children. Research has shown that cluster grouping provides benefits for the entire class, including the gifted students.[3] However, there may be times when other arrangements will also work. These other arrangements might include interest groups, cooperative learning groups in which the children's strengths complement one another well, or groups formed to focus on creative or imaginative processes. Following are some guidelines you can use to help all children gain the most benefit from working cooperatively.

Provide Variety

Provide opportunities for children to work with a variety of other students on many different subjects. If at all feasible, each child should have the chance to work with several others in the class. This will ensure that no one is stuck with a difficult combination of individuals over and over again. It will also open opportunities for children to collaborate in unexpected ways.

The approach you use to group work (structured, open, creative, divergent, or content-based) should serve the learning goals you've established for each classroom activity. The first question to ask yourself is "What kind of learning process have I planned for the children?" Your answer should direct you in determining the types of groups you'll create. For example, group processes can be more flexible and open-ended in interdisciplinary units in which students explore a subject from multiple perspectives. If the class is studying the ecology of the rain forest, you can organize groups according to interests (what aspect of the forest children wish to explore), study sources (such as science books, stories, paintings, or drama), ability levels, motivations, or a combination of all four.

Feel free, too, to use group work as a catalyst for individual projects. Sharing ideas can provide an impetus for students to achieve in unique ways. Periodically, you can use instructional groups as a resource to reignite the class when children run out of ideas or need inspiration to consider other approaches to their study.

---

[3] Susan Winebrenner with Dina Brulles. *Teaching Gifted Kids in Today's Classroom* (Minneapolis: Free Spirit Publishing Inc., 2012): 195–196.

Offer Choices

Grouping may work better when children help choose group mates and topics and assist in designing the project's structure. For practical reasons, you'll sometimes need to make these decisions. Whenever possible, however, try to offer the students as much input as possible. At the very least, consider their personal preferences. Children will be far more invested in the project and excited about the process if they have helped choose partners, subjects, and format.

It's fine to negotiate with students in setting up activities. This doesn't mean that you should simply let children have their own way, or that you should avoid areas in which they really need practice and experience. But it's both appropriate and desirable to offer students some degree of input in designing and defining a task or project. Start by deciding where you can be flexible and where you need to set limits. How you use group work and the kinds of parameters you set will depend on the time available, the nature of the task, and the composition of your class (children's level of maturity, their strengths and weaknesses, and so forth). For example, if you want your students to master certain math concepts, you can encourage them to choose resources, activities, and media for exploring their ideas. But you'll also need to set limits on the amount of time they spend experimenting, the number of options they explore, and the media they use.

Feel free to make adjustments as you go along. For example, sometimes you may find that children benefit from occasionally working on their own rather than completing their ideas together. This is fine. Remember, group work should serve the learning needs of the class, not create a situation in which you and the class are constrained by the group work.

Set Clear Parameters

Young children are used to spending time with other children, but they are not necessarily used to working cooperatively within a group to meet individual and group goals. As mentioned before, you'll need to set parameters that are clear, but not stifling. You have three objectives:

1. To provide a specific framework in which children can operate confidently without feeling overwhelmed, confused, underdirected, or discouraged.

2. To allow as much latitude as possible to accommodate individual strengths and interests.
3. To encourage and accommodate a wide range of decision making and plenty of creativity.

GROUND RULES FOR CHILDREN WORKING IN GROUPS

By the time they begin school, most children have a wealth of experience playing in groups. You can draw on what your students have learned from this experience while you prepare them to work in learning groups.

Take some time to discuss behavior expectations. One way to begin this discussion is by asking students to think of times when they most enjoyed playing with their friends. Try to get them to identify what made those play activities work for them, using questions such as these:

- How did your friends act while you were playing?
- How did you feel when they acted like that? Why did you feel that way?
- How did you act?
- How do you think your friends felt when you acted like that? Why?
- Did anyone lead your group of friends in your game? Or did everyone share in leading?

In the same way, you can invite children to consider an experience they *didn't* like. Use questions such as these to help students think about what they found difficult:

- Did you feel overwhelmed—lost or alone—in the group?
- Did you feel bored or left out? Why do you think you felt that way?
- Did anyone take over the game?
- Were everyone's ideas respected?
- What happened when friends disagreed?

The questions and discussion will help your students identify *specifically* what has and hasn't worked in their experience with others. This process serves two additional purposes: It informs you about students' sensitivities and experiences, and it puts the children in touch with qualities they value in themselves and others when working or playing in groups.

Exploring these questions will prepare the class for a discussion of ground rules. We recommend that, in setting rules, you use children's ideas and suggestions wherever possible. Students are more apt to follow rules they feel they've helped create than ones that appear arbitrarily set by the teacher.

In essence, you're modeling the very behavior you want children to adopt in their own groups. While setting the rules together, keep referring back to children's own play experiences. Explain the importance of finding ways to make groups fair for everyone. Let your students think of ways to monitor themselves, to prevent anyone from taking over the group, and to ensure that everyone has opportunities to explore ideas. Gifted children often are particularly sensitive to issues of justice; they may suggest policies that even you haven't considered.

We use the following ground rules. Feel free to adapt them to your students' ideas and to the ages, abilities, and unique circumstances of the children in your own classroom:

- Decide what you want to do.
- If you can't all agree, see if you can try more than one idea.
- Take turns sharing ideas.
- Listen to others in your group.
- Make your best effort.
- Help each other.
- If you don't understand or agree about something, talk about it with your group.
- Get the teacher's help if you need it.

You may find it useful to create a role of group monitor—someone in the group who has the job of upholding the ground rules. The student who has this role will feel empowered to speak up. Having a group monitor also helps keep the volume down; there won't be a cacophony of voices every time a child breaks a rule. Allow children to take turns with this role. That way, no one becomes the group boss—and all the children have the experience of upholding the rules they helped create.

WHEN A GROUP DOESN'T CLICK

Sometimes a group simply won't click. Two or more children may be significantly mismatched in temperament or ability. If you have done your best to help them stick together productively and the group simply is not connecting, let the students (and yourself) off the hook. It's particularly important to do this if the learning goal is an academic one.

Separate the children who are in conflict and allow them to finish alone. Do this matter-of-factly, without condemnation or punishment. Simply say to the students, "I feel you could do a better job if you each finished this project on your own." Often, conflict can be legitimate and can indicate the need for students to move in separate directions. Let the children know you honor this need. They will probably complete the work far more effectively. Forcing groups to stay together is usually counterproductive. There will be plenty of other opportunities to insist that children carry through and finish projects together—projects in which it's not essential that major academic learning take place.

We have found that one of the most effective ways to use group work, particularly for gifted students, is as a catalyst for individual learning. This is often true when group members are struggling to agree on what to do. You can expect them to share ideas and coordinate their efforts for part of the assignment. Then offer children the option of following through by working in pairs or threes or by pursuing their ideas on their own. Be flexible at all stages of the learning process. Forcing groups to stay intact when they are not functioning well will hinder success. Instead, improvise with your students. If, at any point, group work stops producing results for children, conclude the joint activity and allow each student to continue working independently.

Evaluate Students Individually

When children work in groups, it's important that you assess the degree to which each child has met the academic goals for the activity and what new learning has taken place. Whatever methods you use (mastery tests, portfolios, checklists, oral responses to questions, or others), you'll need to document that each student has acquired new learning through the group's project. Be sure that every child has plenty of opportunities to design and develop ideas. Even if your students are producing a project together, provide some way that the children can write, draw, or sketch their own individual ideas so you can see how each student has responded to the assignment.

This is a situation in which group grades aren't appropriate. At best, a group grade on a project intended to produce individual learning, creative expression, and discovery is unfair; at worst, it's damaging to future motivation, self-esteem, academic progress, and confidence. Working in groups is an aid to the learning process. Obviously, those who take full advantage of group work will acquire more ideas than those who do little or who never

even attempt to participate. Evaluations, however, should focus on each individual's learning and growth rather than on how much the student contributed to the group. Otherwise, you'll be grading the child on group learning skills rather than on knowledge and conceptual growth.

When evaluating, remember that appearances can be misleading. Shy children may not say very much in a group, but they will still learn a great deal from listening to the ideas of others. Creatively gifted children may misbehave because they're bored or because they want to approach an assignment differently than the more academically gifted students.

The last thing you want is for group work to decrease students' motivation to stretch their knowledge and imagination because they think doing so will affect their group grade. Be sure students understand that they will be evaluated on what they, as individuals, learn and produce.

Avoid Group Homework

We strongly recommend that you not give cooperative learning assignments for homework unless they are truly optional. These assignments can be unfair to children and parents alike. Families are busy; many parents will find it difficult, if not impossible, to arrange the time, transportation, and supervision young children's group homework requires. Students can collaborate without having to do off-site work together. Your students gain the most when you closely monitor group or partner work in class. There, you can circulate from group to group to ensure the ground rules are met. You can observe, check for understanding, help iron out difficulties, and ensure that children are learning ways to collaborate. You're able to teach the skills students need to work with others, and you can assess whether individual children are getting the activity's full benefit.

Let the Goals Determine the Group Size

Let the goals for each activity determine the group's size and scope. If the major goals are for children to learn to work together and make group decisions, the activity should be one that calls for group problem solving, such as planning a science experiment, producing a puppet show or simple play, or creating a picture or mural. While individual students will take responsibility for the various components of projects such as these, group cooperation is still important and appropriate.

If the goals involve learning cognitive skills, understanding advanced concepts, or mastering complex subject matter, grouping children in pairs will be more effective than forming larger groups. In partner learning situations, each child will have more ownership of the outcome and more accountability for learning. There won't be so many distractions and personality conflicts, and the mastery of the material will be more manageable. It is easier, too, to compatibly pair students of similar interests and abilities than it is to arrange a whole class of fully productive groups.

Most important, allow plenty of opportunities for the children to work on their own. Children need to do this for many reasons: to learn accountability, self-discipline, and responsibility; to build a sense of self-worth through achievement; and to grow in self-reliance. Working independently is highly important for both gifted children and students with average or lower ability. The team spirit resulting from working cooperatively has many benefits, and much learning can take place in a group setting. But the sense of self-worth that a student gains through *individual* achievement is absolutely essential for every student's continued personal progress.

Questions and Answers

"With young children, is ability grouping always the best approach? Aren't there times when I will want to group for other reasons?"
If the group's topic is of great interest, children of various levels can come together and learn productively, each contributing individual strengths, curiosity, enthusiasm, and creativity. Sometimes, too, children of widely varying abilities will choose to work together and will engage in creativity. Through art, music, creative writing, and drama, children with diverse abilities may express their knowledge in multiple ways at different levels of understanding. If a keen interest or a close friendship exists, the children often instinctively supplement one another's weaknesses and complement one another's strengths. It will be up to you as the teacher to use your intuition, observation, and judgment in arranging groups that bring out the best in everyone.

"With cluster grouping, won't gifted children feel singled out?"
If they're grouped with children who have similar abilities, gifted students will feel more a part of a group than if each student is the only one who is different in a traditional cooperative learning group. Gifted children *know* they're different, even if no one says anything. They may wrongly perceive that to be different is "bad," and they may try to hide or play down what they know so they'll fit into the class. If this happens, they may never realize their potential.

"What kinds of activities can I provide for high-ability children?"
It's important to provide every child with appropriate opportunities to learn and grow. You'll first need to look at the objective of the learning task and then assess whether each child has met the objective. If a particular child or group of children has already mastered a concept or skill, you can assign something connected to that concept that is more advanced. You'll find many ideas for doing this in Chapter 3.

"It sounds like cluster grouping means putting all the gifted children together in one classroom. At my school, each teacher has one or two gifted children. How can we make cluster grouping work?"
Schoolwide or gradewide cluster grouping does place gifted students together in one class. Cluster grouping is best done schoolwide or gradewide, with the assistance of the principal and gifted program coordinator, who monitor the program and assure that differentiation and compacting are taking place on a regular basis.[4] Research has shown that gifted students learn more when grouped with other gifted students. Gifted students are more willing to take risks and to delve into the depth and complexity of the content when working with others who have similar ability. Meanwhile, students with above-average ability excel when grouped without the gifted students, who already know the answers. When gifted students are grouped together, the other classrooms have fewer ability levels of students.

If you teach at a school that does not use cluster grouping schoolwide or gradewide, and you have only two or three gifted students in your classroom, you can still create a cluster group within your room. Place the gifted students together in a small group, or join them with other gifted students from other classes when time and content allow.

---

[4] Winebrenner with Brulles.

Conclusion

Any kind of instructional grouping must serve the educational needs of the children involved, regardless of their ability level. While heterogeneous grouping can sometimes benefit everyone, it frequently fails to meet the needs of students on either side of the ability spectrum—especially those who are gifted.

In this chapter, we have recommended *flexible* grouping based on ability, interest, and motivation. We advocate the use of instructional groups solely as a means to promote growth and learning. As new requirements arise, you should feel free to improvise with the group process by making adjustments and creating different kinds of groups. It's also important that you give students opportunities to work independently to develop the ideas that spring from their group collaborations.

With instructional grouping, students' learning is what is most important. Always ask: Are *all* children benefiting from the experience? Are they growing as a result of their collective efforts? Individual student achievement is more critical than the successful performance of the group. Cooperative groups may work together well and yet not result in significant individual learning. A more creative and flexible approach to grouping will inspire students to develop their abilities freely. Rather than stifle children's ideas, flexible grouping can encourage them to expand in a context that does not impose inhibiting roles or restrictive boundaries, but instead gives students the confidence and freedom to be themselves.

CHAPTER 9
Building Partnerships with Parents

It was the first day of third grade. Down the hall marched Ms. Johnson with her third grader, Charlie. She walked into the classroom and unpacked his backpack and supplies. As the teacher asked Charlie questions to get acquainted, his mother answered for him.

For the first six weeks of third grade, Charlie seldom spoke. Every morning, his mother hovered. Every week, she called the teacher or wrote notes touting Charlie's abilities. Ms. Johnson was already known among the school staff as an extremely pushy parent. Just the mention of her name made the principal's eyes roll. Charlie, however, had always been quiet in school. Due to boredom, he tended to daydream. When called on, he rarely knew the answer because he never paid attention. Though his kindergarten, first-grade, and second-grade teachers recognized that he was bright, none of them saw proof of his mother's claims that he was highly gifted.

But Ms. Johnson was right about her son. Charlie was brilliant. Before long, his astute third-grade teacher could clearly read the signs. She met with Ms. Johnson and assured her that she, too, recognized

Charlie's gifts, and that she would challenge him in her class. Ms. Johnson was happy and relieved. She gradually eased up on her hovering, bragging, and interfering. Charlie began to speak for himself and to use and expand his many intellectual gifts.

Charlie's story shows how critical it is that teachers build partnerships with parents. Parents know their children best, and we need to rely on them to provide us with information about their children. When teachers proactively build positive relationships, parents tend to be more willing to address any concerns that arise.

What It's Like for Parents

Parents of gifted children often feel lost in a maze of conflicting emotions. They may feel proud, excited, and awed by their children's abilities. At the same time, they may feel doubt and anxiety over how those abilities will play out, may worry that they are being pushy, or may fear that they're not equipped for parenting a gifted child.

Parents of young gifted children often are unsure what to expect and share common concerns with other parents of gifted children. Typical worries focus on common aspects of giftedness, such as:

- characteristics of giftedness (perfectionism, sensitivity)
- the child feeling different
- motivational issues for child (underachievement)
- community resources for help (emotionally and academically)
- peer relationships (lack of friends)
- feeling overwhelmed as a parent (parent perception of childrearing abilities)[1]

Many parents of gifted children know that their child is somehow different and perhaps bored at school, but are uncertain how to go about obtaining the educational experience they intuitively feel their child needs. And once a gifted child is identified, parenting can suddenly seem a good deal more complicated. When children have uncommon qualities, conventional wisdom about childrearing often falls short of their unique parenting needs. Parents can experience confusion and anxiety about resources (of their finances, intellect, or time) and about their parental roles. Although studies show that giftedness has a strong genetic component, most gifted children's parents don't view themselves as gifted.[2] Yet, quite often, these parents share some of the qualities of their children:

- acute sensitivity and focus
- intense feelings and reactions
- strong internal sense of control
- keen awareness
- creative imagination
- probing, analytical curiosity
- extraordinary memory
- high intelligence

Parents wonder and worry about many things: about the effects of labeling their children as gifted; about socialization, acceleration, emotional well-being, and sibling relationships; about their roles and responsibilities as the parents of gifted children; about the many aspects of gifted programming; and about understanding the programming options.

Like their children, parents need to understand the reasons for practices and policies. They, too, need to feel a sense of justice and fairness. They're confused about what it means to be gifted—and about what it doesn't mean. Sometimes, when told that their children have scored in the top 5 percent of all students, parents develop an array of new expectations for the children. Parents (and teachers, too) often confuse intellectual precocity with emotional maturity, organizational abilities, or the level of responsibility they expect from children. It isn't easy to deal with a second grader who can discuss world politics at dinner but acts the silliest of all the children at a birthday party.

Parents of gifted children face particular stresses that require some focused guidance:

- What they experience may contradict everything they've ever heard about childrearing. Faced with challenging children, these parents may not know where to turn, may have no readily accessible resources or experts to consult.
- Their children may oppose or undermine every assertion of parental authority in such persuasive ways that the parents are rendered speechless or confused. Gifted children may have perfectly rational answers for every reprimand and seemingly logical reasons for doing everything they're asked not to do. Parents and other adults often perceive highly verbal children—especially those with a flair for the dramatic—as arrogant, a pain, or starved for attention.
- Parents may expect too little or too much of their gifted children, or they may find it difficult to reconcile disparities in the children's intellectual and emotional development.
- Often finding expert advice conflicting, these parents may feel unable to create or choose effective options. Which teacher or school administrator should they believe after hearing varying explanations for their children's unusual, inadequate, or troublesome school behavior?
- Families may become overwhelmed by seeing their children's special needs poorly served, and they may feel unable to help or to find help.

Parents of gifted students need support from other parents and from educators and other professionals who understand the challenges of living with highly able and creative children. They need to know that they are not alone and that there are people who are willing to help them. As a teacher, you can be one of those people. These parents already know

---

[1] Linda Kreger Silverman. "Counseling Families." *Counseling the Gifted and Talented* edited by Linda Kreger Silverman (Denver, CO: Love Publishing, 2000). This is a seminal text on the counseling and psychological aspects of giftedness.
[2] Kathryn S. Keirouz. "Concerns of Parents of Gifted Children: A Research Review." *Gifted Child Quarterly* 34:2 (1990): 57.

their child isn't perfect and can be extremely difficult for the teacher and the school to deal with. Parents are usually glad to receive suggestions for dealing with the downside of giftedness, as long as their children's positive traits are recognized and academic needs are met.

Success at school is more likely if parents are understanding and encouraging with their children at home. To cultivate this understanding, schools and teachers have a role to play in informing parents about characteristics of gifted children. As the teacher, you may be parents' first (and possibly only) source for this information. After one father learned that some of his son's troublesome behaviors also characterized giftedness, he sighed with relief and explained, "Now instead of reacting to him as someone who's always trying to drive me crazy, I can see him as someone special who has ideas that are different from mine."

Examining Your Own Feelings

With many students and much to teach, it's easy to feel impatient or even resentful sometimes about the special needs of gifted students. After a long and frustrating day, you may find it challenging to consider new strategies for dealing with a particular child or to talk with a concerned parent. Keep in mind that without a conscious effort on your part to show empathy and interest, any underlying irritation you may feel is likely to come through. Something in your body language, facial expression, choice of words, or tone of voice will probably reveal your feelings. This can hurt the relationship you are working to cultivate.

If you struggle from time to time with negative feelings about gifted students and their parents, you are not alone. Yet you want to treat all children and families with respect, and to open all possible doors to children's growth and learning. To help yourself maintain and communicate a positive perspective, you may find it helpful to examine your feelings and the self-talk you use when your enthusiasm begins to wane:

- When a student knows more than you do about dinosaurs or can recite the Latin names for flowers, how do you feel about yourself as a teacher? Do you hear yourself thinking, "How on earth does Darryl know all that?" Try to shift that

thinking: "How exciting that Darryl knows and cares so much about that! How can I challenge him to learn more?"
- What's your mental attitude toward children's uneven development? Instead of thinking, "Maisie can't be gifted—she is too forgetful," you could ask yourself, "I wonder what's going on in Maisie's head. How can I help her explore and express all of her ideas and be less forgetful?"
- Are you ambivalent about labeling and providing special support to gifted children? Try reminding yourself of the importance of helping all students reach their full potential. Also, remember that without a label, additional support often will not be provided.
- How do you feel when parents criticize or offer suggestions? Uncomfortable? Irritated? Defensive? Try to find a way to productively redirect your thinking: "Mr. Jones cares so much about Callie's education. Is there a way he can help me work more effectively with her?"
- Do you become defensive when parents disagree with you regarding assessment, methods, or advice? Could you focus instead on acknowledging your shared concern for their child?
- When a child constantly asks questions, do you find yourself frustrated that you can't finish a sentence? Instead, ask yourself, "How can I capture Tamara's wonder and excitement for learning in a way that is not disruptive for the class?"

If you've made an effort to grapple with these attitudes and feelings honestly, you should congratulate yourself. By working through these kinds of issues, you'll be much better prepared to build a positive relationship with parents of gifted children. If you find yourself feeling stuck, you might want to return to the first two chapters of this book or to some of the suggested readings in the "References and Resources" section for Chapter 1 (page 189), Chapter 2 (page 190), and Chapter 9 (page 205). There you may find the inspirational boost you need.

You Can't Overcommunicate

Parents are likely to be your most enthusiastic and valuable sources of support and resources. Since parents tend to be most involved with their children's education during the early primary grades, they can provide you with abundant information and assistance. Connecting with parents helps you become acquainted with children's interests and abilities outside the boundaries of your classroom. As each person shares and receives ideas, everyone benefits: you, the parents, and the children.

Opening a Dialogue

You can open and sustain a dialogue with parents by inviting their input and offering a variety of ways for them to provide it. Chapter 1 includes several family letters and forms to help you communicate with parents about their children's abilities, interests, and needs: "Your Child's Pictures" (page 18), "Information, Please" (page 19), "About My Child" (pages 20–21), and "Checklist of My Child's Strengths" (pages 22–23). To invite parents to communicate easily and regularly about concerns for their child, Chapter 2 suggests that you send home the "Help Me Help You" family letter (page 40) at the beginning of each month or school term.

For students in early childhood, home visits are a common practice. These visits are meant to provide you with information about the children's likes, dislikes, and interests. During a home visit, it is important to get to know the child and parent within their environment, where they feel most comfortable.

For students in kindergarten and first grade, an intake interview is common. Here's your opportunity to excel as a good listener. Ask parents to tell you about their children's special interests and abilities. Take notes. Also, find out how much parents know about what goes on in your classroom. Pay attention to body language and stay alert. Even offhand comments may give insights into family dynamics. Although intake interviews are less common in older grades, they can be very helpful—especially when information from previous teachers isn't consistent with a child's behavior and performance in your classroom.

During second and third grade, family interviews generally do not occur, as these students are not new to the school environment. Many schools believe that teachers can use their time more efficiently in other ways. Therefore, you will need to consciously build relationships with parents and provide them opportunities to share information with you about their children. This information starts a conversation that will help you meet the needs of the children.

To promote parental cooperation, helping must be reciprocal. This means that you'll want to update parents on your current projects, goals, and needs.

Weekly or monthly newsletters or email blasts or a class blog, website, or Facebook page will be helpful in updating parents on what is happening in your classroom and will provide a way to communicate the need for assistance. (You can keep Web-based communications private by using a password or setting them up for participation by invitation only.) If you don't identify your needs, parents are less able to support you. Parents can loan or donate materials, share skills, and help you connect to others in the community; they can be your best cheerleaders when they are aware of the extensive and exciting learning going on in your classroom. To invite this kind of participation, you can send home either one of the "Can You Help?" or "Can You Share" family letters. Use the first letter (page 148) to ask for materials and assistance for your general classroom program; use the second letter (page 149) to request contributions to a particular theme or topic of study. Send either letter as often as you feel it's appropriate and necessary.

The Parent-Teacher Conference

The parent-teacher conference is an opportunity to communicate with parents about the identification of each child's particular abilities and social-emotional characteristics. Give parents enough notice so they can prepare for the conference. You might want to send home a copy of the form "Questions for Your Child's Parent-Teacher Conference" (page 150).

GUIDELINES FOR PARENT-TEACHER CONFERENCES

The Harvard Family Research Project published "Parent-Teacher Conference Tip Sheets for Principals, Teachers, and Parents" in October 2010. According to this document, the following are good conference practices. (It is possible that the guidelines for your school or setting may vary slightly.)

"Prior to the conference:

- Send invitations for conferences.
- Review student work.
- Prepare thoughts and materials.
- Send reminders.
- Create a welcoming environment.

During the conference:

- Discuss progress and growth.
- Use examples.

- Ask questions and listen actively.
- Share ideas for supporting learning.
- Seek solutions collaboratively.
- Make an action plan.
- Establish lines of communication.

After the conference:

- Follow up with families.
- Communicate regularly.
- Connect in-class activities."[3]

It would be hard to overemphasize the importance of being positive. Parents want to be assured that you know and like their child. Begin with a look at what's going well, emphasize the positive throughout the conference, and invite parents to talk first or early on. But do not minimize problems. Glossing over situations that need immediate attention isn't wholesome for the child or you and only perpetuates a bad situation. Even so, the conference should be a positive experience overall for the parents, or you risk losing them as your best allies in helping their child. If a child has a host of problems, choose one or two to focus on. Help parents view the problem as solvable, not overwhelming. By the end of the conference, make sure you have said several positive things for each negative one. This will lay firm groundwork for good parent relations over the remainder of the school year. At the close of the conference, summarize the main points, concerns, or agreements you've discussed.

CONFERENCES WITH PARENTS OF GIFTED CHILDREN

For the gifted child, the purpose of the conference is not to glorify giftedness, but to explore the child's particular abilities, needs, sensitivities, personality, and interests. It is important to discuss both the positive and the negative. Being gifted and talented does not excuse poor behavior. You'll encounter in parents a vast range of responses and emotional reactions to their child's giftedness, from insecurity about acknowledging special abilities to clear assumptions that *of course* their child has exceptional qualities. Remember that parents know more about their child's life out of school than you do, and that you know more about the child's life at school. Share that knowledge with one another, so that together you will all know more about the child than you did before.

Depending on the age of the student, formal identification may or may not be an option. Either way, it is important to focus on the characteristics of giftedness, which provides the opportunity to be more inclusive in acknowledging exceptional qualities. If a gifted program is available, it is important not to limit your focus to only those abilities served by the program. If the program starts in a higher grade, remember that children don't begin to be gifted when they enter the program; they have the characteristics of giftedness well beforehand.

In most cases, parents come to you as the expert. This is especially true for parents of young gifted children. Sometimes these folks are having an unusually difficult time. At worst, they may be experiencing difficulties in disciplining or handling an active, creative, inventive, strong-willed child; at best, they are scrambling to keep up with their child's insatiable curiosity, drive, thirst for knowledge, and hunger for novel experiences. The parents are likely to look to the school (and thus to you, the teacher and first point of contact) for advice, validation, coping strategies, ideas, and guidance in finding additional resources.

You will want to be able to give them information that will be helpful. This chapter includes two reproducible forms with information for parents: "Books for Parents of Young Gifted Children" (pages 151–152) and "Organizations and Online Resources for Parents of Young Gifted Children" (page 153). You may want to make copies of these forms before the parent-teacher conference and offer one or more of them to parents who seem interested. In addition, research state programs and organizations for parents of gifted and talented children.

The more you know or can learn about giftedness and related resources in your school and community, the more you can help parents and, ultimately, the children you serve. Can you refer parents to any local parent groups, enrichment programs, counselors with expertise in giftedness, or local organizations?

Because the general awareness of giftedness is relatively low, you may find that you're the first person ever to suggest that misbehavior or other problems might be due to the fact that the child is extremely bright.

By third grade, Ramón already had a notorious reputation in his school for clowning around, wisecracking, and leading other kids astray. Ramón was

---

[3] Harvard Family Research Project. "Parent-Teacher Conference Tip Sheets." October 2010. www.hfrp.org.

always getting in trouble on the playground. He had lazy study habits and generally showed little interest in school. Ramón's parents thought he was just mischievous. His perceptive third-grade teacher, however, thought he might be bored and so assigned him higher-level work. With a good deal of discipline from the teacher, Ramón's attitude and schoolwork began to change markedly. It became evident that he had an extraordinary talent for creative writing. The teacher had few behavior problems with Ramón for the rest of the school year.

"Smartness" is often associated with children who think quickly, speak articulately, and always have the right answer. Because of this, many children's intellectual gifts remain unrecognized by both parents and teachers.

At a conference with her daughter Sun's second-grade teacher, Ms. Kim explained that Sun seemed to be having trouble in math. She wondered if Sun needed a tutor or should be tested for learning disabilities. The teacher, Mr. Marquette, asked Ms. Kim for some more time before making a recommendation. He began to pay particular attention to Sun's behavior during math. He soon realized that Sun was very bright in math, but lacked confidence. Though she couldn't do computations quickly, she had fantastic reasoning abilities. Sun was clearly intimidated by a few boisterous children in the class, who shouted out correct answers almost immediately. Sun wasn't aggressive in that way, and so she had concluded that she was "dumb" in math.

Mr. Marquette made some changes by providing small wipe-off whiteboards for each student. Students could answer the questions individually on their boards, so they no longer shouted out answers. Mr. Marquette was able to wait until students had answered the questions individually before calling on anyone for solutions to problems. Gradually, Sun began to excel. Her confidence returned. Months later, she became the first child in the district to achieve a perfect score on the state achievement test in math.

Sun's gradual transformation provides a wonderful window into the value of parent-teacher communication. Without hearing Ms. Kim's concern, Mr. Marquette might not have stopped to observe Sun more closely and may not have changed his classroom procedures. Without her teacher's thoughtful intervention, Sun's unusually high ability would probably have gone unrecognized and unchallenged.

Questions and Answers

"If I go to the trouble of asking parents what they think their child needs, how will I find the time to manage my regular curriculum?"
Any change in your style or approach will take some time at first. But if children are given the opportunity to pursue their interests and to be challenged at a level that engages their thinking processes, your job is likely to become easier. With parent support, children often become generally more cooperative. Also, you don't need to accommodate all of the suggestions and requests a parent makes. Start with a small adjustment, and see if the child's day—and yours—gets any better.

"I have a parent who really wants to get involved in gifted education. What should I suggest?"
Here are a few ideas. You might suggest that the parent:

- learn about gifted children and different ways to enhance their development
- research the resources available at the school and ask how the school needs to be supported—ideas may be to spearhead the development of a gifted child resource library or to create a parent support group
- identify and contact local mentors or tutors for gifted children
- volunteer to start a club (such as Destination Imagination, Odyssey of the Mind, robotics, math club, writing club, newspaper)
- start an artist-in-residence program for your classroom or school

Conclusion

Parent involvement in any child's schooling can be a significant positive force. To effectively contribute to their child's education, parents need the cooperation and support of school personnel.

We're all pioneers in developing awareness and support for young gifted children. If you can spark in your school or community any small interest in developing a child's exceptional strengths, that effort has the potential to multiply. You will have established a precedent for the future, a basis upon which to build adaptations for other children. Reaching parents is essential to this cause. Welcome and promote positive parent involvement. Doing so is a precious investment in all young children.

Can You Help?

Child's name: _____

Dear Parent/Caregiver:

We are interested in ways that you might be able to volunteer. Please answer the following questions and return this form to me by _____

We are also looking for additional items for the classroom. Our wish list includes: _____
_____

Do you have any time to help out in our classroom? We need parents who are willing to help with: _____
_____

Do you have a special skill or talent to share with our class? _____
_____

Please provide days and times when you are willing to help either consistently or on an as-needed basis:

I can help with special projects in the classroom: _____
_____

I can help with take-home projects: _____
_____

I can come into the classroom on (day of the week): _____
_____

I can provide the following items: _____
_____
_____

If you're unable to provide any of the items, can you suggest people or organizations in the community who might do so? Suggested donors: _____
_____
_____

Parent's name: _____
Phone: _____
Email: _____

Thank you for your interest in your child's classroom. If you have any questions, please call, email, or stop by.
Teacher's signature: _____
Phone: _____
Email: _____

Can You Share?

Child's name: _____

Dear Parent/Caregiver:

This term, our class will study: _____
_____

I'm wondering if you have any items related to this unit that you would be willing to donate or loan. We could use items such as: _____
_____
_____

Please provide donations by (date): _____

Please let me know how you can help by completing the brief form at the bottom of this sheet and sending it to school with your child.

Thank you for your interest in your child's classroom and for your support. If you have any questions, be sure to email, call, or stop by the classroom.

Teacher's signature: _____
Phone: _____
Email: _____

- cut here ✂ -

Child's name: _____ **Date:** _____
To: _____ **From:** _____
Phone: _____
Email: _____

I can donate these items: _____
_____

I can loan these items. (Please specify the length of the loan—one day, for term, and so forth. If you would like to share these items in person, please let me know that as well.) _____
_____
_____

Comments: _____
_____
_____

Questions for Your Child's Parent-Teacher Conference

Child's name: _____

Dear Parent/Caregiver:

Our parent-teacher conference is scheduled for _____ (date) at _____ (time). Before the conference, it would be helpful if you could take a few minutes to think about and respond to the following questions. This will help guide the conference time so that we can address strengths, concerns, and weaknesses. Please bring the completed sheet to our conference as a guide.

1. What are your child's strengths? What does she or he do best? _____
   _____
   _____

2. At home, what does your child like to do? What are his or her hobbies or special interests? _____
   _____
   _____

3. How would you describe your child's personality outside of school? _____
   _____
   _____

4. How does your child get along with other children outside of school? With adults? _____
   _____
   _____

5. How does your child feel about school? What are the things that she or he communicates about school? __
   _____

6. What concerns or issues would you like to share about your child (at home and school)? _____
   _____

On the back of this form, please list any questions or concerns you would like to talk about during our conference.

Thank you for taking time to answer these questions. I look forward to seeing you at the conference.

Teacher's signature: _____

Phone: _____

Email: _____

For Parents

Books for Parents of Young Gifted Children

Delisle, James R. *Parenting Gifted Kids: Tips for Raising Happy and Successful Children*. Waco, TX: Prufrock Press, 2006. This book provides specific tips and practical advice for raising gifted children. Stories and vignettes are used throughout the book to illustrate real-world situations.

Fertig, Carol. *Raising a Gifted Child: A Parenting Success Handbook*. Waco, TX: Prufrock Press, 2008. This book provides information about finding optimal learning opportunities in a variety of academic and talent areas.

Galbraith, Judy. *The Survival Guide for Gifted Kids: For Ages 10 and Under*. Minneapolis: Free Spirit Publishing, 2013. Galbraith helps young gifted children understand and cope with the stresses, benefits, and demands of being gifted. For many elementary-age children, this book is their first exposure to the fact that they're not alone and they're not "weird." It includes advice from gifted kids.

Galbraith, Judy. *You Know Your Child Is Gifted When . . . : A Beginner's Guide to Life on the Bright Side*. Minneapolis: Free Spirit Publishing, 2000. Parenting a gifted child can be a mixed blessing. It helps to know what to look for, what to expect, and what other parents have experienced. This lighthearted introduction to life with a gifted child is a great place to start.

Galbraith, Judy, and Jim Delisle. *When Gifted Kids Don't Have All the Answers: How to Meet Their Social and Emotional Needs*. Minneapolis: Free Spirit Publishing, 2015. This book addresses the social-emotional needs of giftedness both inside and outside the classroom. It provides practical strategies with vignettes that show a variety of perspectives and personalities.

George, David. *Young Gifted and Bored*. Bethel, CT: Crown House Publishing, 2011. Resources help parents recognize boredom and underachievement and strategies help elicit depth in the curriculum. This book is written for both parents and teachers.

Heilbronner, Nancy N. *10 Things Not to Say to Your Gifted Child: One Family's Perspective*. Tucson, AZ: Great Potential Press, 2011. This is one family's perspective on raising gifted children and the story of its journey.

Hertzog, Nancy B. *Ready for Preschool: Prepare Your Child for Happiness and Success at School*. Waco, TX: Prufrock Press, 2008. Readers will find a chapter that provides strategies for strengthening the relationship between home and school as well as facilitating the transition from home to school.

Jolly, Jennifer L., Donald J. Treffinger, Tracy Ford Inman, and Joan Franklin Smutny (eds.). *Parenting Gifted Children: The Authoritative Guide from the National Association for Gifted Children*. Waco, TX: Prufrock Press, 2011. This publication combines research and practical information about gifted children and focuses on the joys and struggles of parenting a gifted child.

Klein, Barbara. *Raising Gifted Kids: Everything You Need to Know to Help Your Exceptional Child Thrive*. New York: AMACOM, 2007. Offers practical information on the unique challenges of raising gifted children. Chapters start with identifying giftedness, then move on to addressing and working with the various aspects of your gifted child, including selecting a school.

Kurcinka, Mary Sheedy. *Raising Your Spirited Child: A Guide for Parents Whose Child Is More Intense, Sensitive, Perceptive, Persistent, and Energetic*. New York: HarperCollins, 2006. A valuable, practical, and popular resource for teachers and parents, this book includes hundreds of specific suggestions to help children monitor themselves and develop self-control.

National Association for Gifted Children. *Parenting for High Potential*. Designed for parents, this magazine is published eight times per year. It is available to members of NAGC.

Rogers, Karen B. *Re-Forming Gifted Education: Matching the Program to the Child*. Tucson, AZ: Great Potential Press, 2002. With information on programming for gifted education, this book offers advice and suggestions in selecting and matching a program to the various aspects of a gifted child.

Smutny, Joan Franklin. *Stand Up for Your Gifted Child: How to Make the Most of Kids' Strengths at School and at Home*. Minneapolis: Free Spirit Publishing, 2001. This book includes several chapters about advocacy and educational options. It is no longer in print but is still widely available online and at libraries.

Smutny, Joan Franklin, Kathleen Veenker, and Stephen Veenker. *Your Gifted Child: How to Recognize and Develop the Special Talents in Your Child from Birth to Age Seven*. New York: Ballantine Books, 1989. This book includes an extensive chapter on advocacy and intervention to benefit young students. It offers parents specific suggestions and examples for supplementing their child's formal education.

Walker, Sally Yahnke. *The Survival Guide for Parents of Gifted Kids: How to Understand, Live with, and Stick Up for Your Gifted Child*. Minneapolis: Free Spirit Publishing, 2002. The chapter titled "Advocacy: Working for Improvement" provides sensible suggestions for influencing schools to be more "user-friendly" toward gifted children. Topics range from consulting with the classroom teacher to effecting change at the state level. This book is no longer in print but is still widely available online and at libraries.

Webb, James T., Janet L. Gore, Edward R. Amend, and Arlene R. DeVries. *A Parent's Guide to Gifted Children*. Tucson, AZ: Great Potential Press, 2007. A true guide to all aspects of giftedness, including characteristics, school advice, home relationships, and social-emotional characteristics. The book also offers advice to address working with gifted students. It includes real stories and guidance from psychologists and educators.

Webb, James T., Elizabeth A. Meckstroth, and Stephanie S. Tolan. *Guiding the Gifted Child: A Practical Source for Parents and Teachers*. Tucson, AZ: Great Potential Press, 1989. This is a primer on understanding and nurturing gifted children. It includes chapters on motivation, discipline, peer and sibling relations, stress management, and depression. This book won the American Psychological Association's Best Book Award.

Organizations and Online Resources for Parents of Young Gifted Children

If you have access to the Internet, you can find all kinds of information about giftedness online—as well as support from other parents. Please note that website urls often change. If you have difficulty reaching one of the sites listed here, try searching for the organization's name or contacting another organization. Many sites offer links to other gifted resources. Some of the organizations offer members-only access in addition to public information.

Council for Exceptional Children (CEC)
www.cec.sped.org • 888-232-7733
CEC is the largest international professional organization dedicated to improving the educational success of individuals with disabilities and gifts and talents. CEC advocates for governmental policies, sets professional standards, provides professional development, and helps professionals obtain conditions and resources necessary for effective professional practice.

Davidson Institute for Talent Development
davidsongifted.org • 775-852-3483, ext. 435
The mission of this organization is to recognize, nurture, and support profoundly intelligent young people and to provide opportunities for them to develop their talents to make a positive difference. The organization offers various programs for families, individuals, and educators, as well as information for advocacy of gifted education.

Gifted Child Society
www.giftedchildsociety.com • 201-444-6530
Founded by parents, this organization sponsors many activities designed to assist gifted children and their parents, including programs and seminars related to learning difficulties (LD), attention deficit hyperactivity disorder (ADHD), behavior and social skills, school issues, and advocacy.

GT LD Network
www.gtldnet.org
This organization provides support and information regarding gifted children and children with learning differences. It also has a free listserve.

Hoagies' Gifted Education Page
hoagiesgifted.org
This website contains lots of information on giftedness and has links to many gifted organizations. Find material for parents, educators, and kids.

National Association for Gifted Children (NAGC)
nagc.org • 202-785-4268
Join NAGC and receive its *Parenting for High Potential* magazine. NAGC's "Resources for Parents" and "Gifted by State" pages might be of special interest to you.

National Society for the Gifted & Talented
nsgt.org • 800-572-6748
The society is committed to acknowledging and supporting the needs of gifted and talented children. It offers resources for educators, students, and families.

Neag Center for Gifted Education and Talent Development
nrcgt.org • 860-486-4826
Located at the University of Connecticut, this organization plans and conducts research on giftedness.

Supporting Emotional Needs of the Gifted (SENG)
sengifted.org • 844-488-SENG (844-488-7364)
SENG is an international organization that helps parents, educators, children, and teens better understand the high points and hassles of growing up gifted. Each annual SENG conference includes a program for children eight to fourteen years old, staffed by local teachers of gifted children, graduate students, and certified counselors.

CHAPTER 10
Understanding and Meeting Children's Social and Emotional Needs

Usually Aparna eagerly joined group activities and wanted to lead whatever was going on. Lately, though, she seemed to be going through the motions. Her focus was somewhere else. She gazed out the window, picked at her cuticles, or traced wood-grain patterns with her finger.

When the aide took the class out for recess, the teacher, Ms. Lambert, invited Aparna to stay in and help water the plants. She talked to her student with gentle concern and learned that Aparna's family had recently given away their dog, Scoot, because her mom was going to have extensive surgery and needed a long period of bed rest for her recovery. Aparna had myriad worries: Why hadn't her parents told her they were going to give Scoot away? Was Scoot as confused and afraid as she was? Would the surgery hurt? Could her mom die? If her mom had to stay in bed, who would fix supper and help Aparna with her homework? Would her parents ever give her away?

In workshop presentations, we ask parents and teachers, "Who made a difference in your life? How did that person help you? Share this with someone seated near you." Then we watch respondents' faces light up and listen as the room becomes animated, filled with a noisy exuberance. More often than not, the people being described in these conversations are loved and long-remembered teachers.

When adults reflect on people who positively influenced their lives, it's often teachers who believed in them, encouraged their attempts, listened to them, and expressed interest in them as people—not just in their achievements. This passing on of courage and hope is one of teaching's greatest rewards.

Meeting Children's Many Needs

As a teacher, your own professional fulfillment likely comes in part from having the opportunity and the ability to affirm and motivate your students—not only in their intellectual growth, but also in their affective development. The gifted children in your classroom have unique social and emotional needs. Exceptional abilities have little value if children can't use them to feel happy and successful in their own lives. Perhaps only a small fraction of the ability to thrive in life is determined by intellectual intelligence. Other factors are more crucial in determining children's personal destinies. How children feel about themselves is far more important than what they know. In other words, "I can" is more significant than IQ. Carol Dweck's research on mindset demonstrates that successful individuals have a growth mindset. They believe everyone can change and grow through effort, and they are continually developing their abilities. Those with a fixed mindset, by contrast, believe that ability is carved in stone and that they need to prove themselves and their abilities.[1]

What qualities lead children to personal fulfillment? Children need to be able to:

- be aware of themselves and of how they affect others
- understand and manage their emotions
- comfort themselves
- motivate themselves
- communicate and get along with others
- be willing to work and stretch their learning
- make thoughtful, constructive decisions

Gifted Children Are Different

While all children need to develop these qualities, the social and emotional characteristics of gifted children are often unique. Chapter 1 touches on several general qualities of highly intelligent and able children, including asynchronous development, enigmatic behavior, and a passionate and imaginative nature (see "What Are You Looking For?" on pages 7–9). For adults, and even for other children, the apparent contradictions between gifted children's rare abilities and their social and emotional behavior can be confusing.

Asynchrony across domains combined with developmentally appropriate behavior and characteristics cause discomfort for many adults working with gifted children. The adults wonder: How can a child who is so intelligent be so out of step when it comes to fitting in with classmates? How is it that I can be having an adult-level conversation with a four-year-old one minute, and then the next minute the child is pushing a classmate to be first in line? Asynchrony adds complexity to the task of addressing the social and emotional needs of young gifted children.

Gifted children *are* different. Modern mental health professionals and gifted educators focus attention on the whole gifted child by identifying and investigating the social and emotional aspects of giftedness along with characteristics of academic performance.

Giftedness is not a clearly defined construct; as a result, gifted education can be an emotional, controversial topic. An enormous range of ideas exists about what types of instruction are appropriate for young, highly able children. This complexity extends to gifted children's social and emotional needs—what these needs are, how they are demonstrated, and how teachers and parents can best respond to them.

COMMON MISCONCEPTIONS ABOUT YOUNG GIFTED CHILDREN

Here are a few common, inaccurate assumptions about young gifted children:

1. Gifted children don't need help; they can succeed on their own.
2. They are self-motivated and therefore "teach themselves."
3. They love to teach other children.
4. Gifted children are proud to be held up as examples of model work and behavior.
5. They are natural loners and tend not to have many friends.
6. They get good grades and are successful in everything they do.
7. Gifted identification cannot occur until third or fourth grade.
8. Acceleration of content or grade skipping is socially and emotionally detrimental to gifted children.
9. Every child is gifted in some way.[2]

These are common myths within gifted education, and they ring especially true for young gifted children. While one of these ideas may be true for a specific child, none pertains to all or even most gifted children.

[1] Carol S. Dweck. *Mindset: The New Psychology of Success: How We Can Learn to Fulfill Our Potential* (New York: Ballantine Books, 2006): 6–7.

[2] This list is adapted from "Myths About Gifted Students" by the National Association for Gifted Children (www.nagc.org/myths.aspx).

A MORE COMPREHENSIVE VIEW OF CHILDREN'S NEEDS

We can't simply apply a linear, cause-and-effect analysis about who young gifted children are and what they need. These children's intellectual and emotional lives are complex, created by an intricate interweaving of ideas, feelings, and situations.

Being gifted usually amplifies a child's emotional life in depth and intensity. For most young gifted children, high intelligence is an asset in their social and emotional adjustment. As a group, gifted children's overall self-concept and self-control levels are more highly developed than those of their age peers. Yet enormous diversity exists among individual children. Gifted children have a vast range of social and emotional characteristics.

High intelligence has both positive and negative aspects. With gifted children, it's often the *degree* of difference from the norm that creates vulnerability. As intelligence increases, so does the possibility for misunderstanding. To develop and enjoy their abilities, young gifted children need understanding and support. It is important to focus on the positive aspects of giftedness in order to help gifted children develop in healthy ways.

Research on gifted children's psychosocial adjustment is often contradictory. These contradictions remind us that we can't broadly apply one approach, method, or philosophy to all gifted children. Instead, we can be fascinated and curious. We can wonder how each child sees and feels in a given situation. We can explore how each student needs to be engaged to make a project worthwhile. We can discover what works for a particular child.

How Does It Feel to Be Gifted?

What does it feel like to be gifted? Many of us will never really know. But if we listen to our students, we can get at least a glimpse. One of our older students gave this explanation: "People expect me to be abnormally brilliant and brilliantly normal." For gifted children, it's normal to be abnormal. There's nothing we can tweak to change them into "normal" children. Just as a plant can't help turning toward light, these children can't deny their heightened awareness, sensitivity, curiosity, and intensity.

Judy Galbraith identifies "Eight Great Gripes of Gifted Kids." These gripes have been gathered through years of surveying thousands of gifted kids ages ten and under. The following are the eight main gripes:[3]

1. We miss out on activities other kids get to do while we're in GT [gifted and talented] class.
2. We have to do extra work in school.
3. Other kids ask us for too much help.
4. The stuff we do in school is too easy and it's boring.
5. When we finish our schoolwork early, we often aren't allowed to work ahead.
6. Our friends and classmates don't always understand us, and they don't see all our different sides.
7. Parents, teachers, and even our friends expect too much of us. We're supposed to get A's and do our best all the time.
8. Tests, tests, and more tests!

Maybe the greatest challenge for young gifted students is that they're like square pegs trying to fit into round holes. Nothing is wrong with these children, but they may be out of sync with many of their age-mates in terms of personal identity and adult expectations. As we look at the social and emotional characteristics of young gifted children, it is easy to spot and focus on the challenging aspects. In order to work effectively with these children, it is critical to focus instead on the positive aspects of giftedness.

Social and Emotional Issues in Young Gifted Children's Lives

Let's look at some qualities that make young gifted students different, what drives these children, and how we can understand, support, and nurture them.

Intensity

Gifted students may demonstrate their high level of intensity in many areas. This intensity can be seen in the children's emotions, behavior, attitudes, and interests, and may manifest in a variety of ways. Emotional intensity, for example, can be positive—exuberance, excitement, giddiness, or energy. Emotional intensity may also include crying, anxiety, explosive outbursts, paralyzing fear, or anger. Intensity can also manifest as a physical reaction such as heart palpitations, sweating, headaches, or nausea.

---

[3] Judy Galbraith. *The Survival Guide for Gifted Kids: For Ages 10 & Under* (Minneapolis: Free Spirit Publishing, Inc., 2013): 24.

Gifted children exhibit intense characteristics in all environments. The following are factors that may affect the level of intensity:

- Highly able children tend to feel and respond with intensity. Young gifted children tend to respond to a situation by *experiencing* the situation and the emotions within the situation more intensely than most other children do.

- Although in some ways gifted students are more developmentally advanced than their age-mates, they are at times required to tolerate restrictions on their exploration and learning that feel stifling. This can lead to extreme frustration and less tolerance for a situation.

- Gifted children tend to be highly sensitive and to have deep emotional responses. Gifted children may wonder why others feel that they are overreacting, which may lead them to view themselves as less able to cope, thus lowering their self-esteem.

- Extremely bright young children are usually more conscious of a situation as a *whole* with many related components. They may experience more intensity because they comprehend the complexities and multiple layers of an issue and are trying to explain their view.

- Since gifted children are usually curious and have *more* questions than other children have, gifted children may assume that they are less intelligent and knowledgeable than others—or they may feel that they know more than others.

- Highly able youngsters process more information, which may lead them to work faster or slower than their classmates, causing them to focus on that learning difference.

- With their vivid imaginations, young gifted children may be frustrated because they want to pursue more creative opportunities and cannot understand the constraints that they are required to work within.

- Perceiving that adults and other children believe they should succeed without help, gifted children may hesitate to ask for help when they need it.

- Bright, creative children feel frustrated when resources and time limit the work these children want to do. They often feel that they are compromising their goals and abandoning more than they are producing. This level of conformity often leads to misbehavior, boredom, and underachievement.

Many activities in this chapter can help your students identify situations that trigger their intensity and can help reduce their stress level and change their attitude or situation. Consider especially the ideas discussed in "Coping Strategies" beginning on page 161.

Sensitivity

Quesha came home from first grade, slammed the door, and declared, "I hate math!" "Honey, you're doing very well in math," her dad exclaimed. "Yeah," Quesha replied, "but some of the other kids are having a lot of trouble. It bothers me when they get frustrated."

Like Quesha, many young gifted children are highly sensitive. This sensitivity can be emotional as well as physical.

Emotional sensitivity may take many forms. For example:

- Arriving in his second-grade classroom, Troy clings to his mother, hides his face, and says nothing.
- Seeing that she's made a tiny mistake, Yona is distraught.
- Phoenix seems to worry about everyone and everything: his family, his classmates, a child he saw crying in the supermarket, floods on the other side of the world.
- With Jeriah, *everything* matters—a lost pencil, an accidentally dropped volleyball, a seemingly terse comment from the teacher.

Physical sensitivity may include intense reaction to sound, lighting, clothing, materials in the classroom, or smells. For example, Anthony covers his ears when the classroom gets too loud. Kavya refuses to participate in activities with certain art materials because of the feeling on her hands. Ivana is the first to ask what the smell is when someone uses hand lotion across the room.

Often, gifted children become angry or upset because they think that other people just don't care. What other children may not notice can have an immense impact on gifted children. These students may take other people's lack of sensitivity as a personal attack. We need to help these students understand that it's not that other people don't care, but that others simply don't always see and feel things in the same way.

We can help gifted students understand how and why other people's ideas and behavior might be different from their own. Analogies are one way to approach this. For example: "If we were TV sets, some of us would get five channels. Some would be wired for basic cable and would pick up a lot more. Some people, like you, Haley, would have a satellite dish and could pick up more information and ideas and feelings than many others."

Hearing these kinds of reassuring reminders regularly, over time, can help children understand and manage their sensitivity and respond to situations and events in a more socially acceptable way. Class activities focused on appreciating differences can also be of help. (See "Helping All Children Appreciate Differences" beginning on page 166.)

Structure and Control

Studies show that intellectually gifted individuals at all ages exhibit the following characteristics:[4]

- good self-concept
- high self-confidence
- independence
- internal control
- high level of values and ethics
- empathy

Add up these characteristics, and you have structure and control. Here's a brief example overheard by one preschool teacher: Four-year-old Lena announced, "I know everything!" "Okay," challenged Duncan, age five, "how much is three plus three?" Lena countered, "I'm not telling." This scenario demonstrates that Lena wants to control the structure of the environment and have a sense of where she stands in relation to her peers.

Often knowledge and skills come easily to gifted children. They are unaware that learning is not as easy for others. Young gifted students may make negative comments toward others because they do not understand the differences in ability among children. It is important for teachers to help gifted children understand these differences because of the children's high level of intensity, sensitivity, and empathy. When young gifted children feel that they have some control over how they think and behave, this has a tremendous effect on their academic achievement and self-concept.

The crux of self-control lies in children's understanding of the environment and its expectations. They must not only have options but also have the ability to *make choices* that help them do what they want to do. Because gifted children usually have astute awareness, vivid imagination, and excellent memory, you can help them learn to use their self-control to make wise choices.

From preschool on, many gifted children tend to exert more focused time, energy, willpower, and perseverance in achieving their constructive goals than other children do. In facing challenges and seeking goals, children need to become aware that they always have some choice over their behaviors and attitudes. They need to become conscious that their choices can work *for* them or *against* them.

How can you facilitate this awareness? Appeal to gifted children's sense of structure and control:

- Tell the children what to expect. Allow lead time and give a transition warning before an activity will end. For example: "Rhea, you'll have ten more minutes with the microscope. Then it will be time for all of us to write in our journals."
- Give explanations and reasons for processes and jobs. Make sure the explanations are clear and do not elicit debate.
- Rather than automatically intervening to assist children, ask, "How can I help?" Keep this in mind even with very young students.
- Separate parts of a situation and help children distinguish between those which they have control over and those which they don't. For example: "You may write a story, a poem, or a skit—that's for you to decide. It must be about one of the four questions we just finished discussing."
- Teach and depend on shared control—both within small groups and with the class as a whole. Help students negotiate and reach a consensus on how they will cooperate.
- Define limits and help the children understand the consequences of possible choices. (Chapter 8 discusses ways to help groups of children cooperate and make choices. See "Guidelines for Grouping Young Children" beginning on page 137.)
- Teach creative decision making. (See page 162 for a complete description of a creative decision-making process.)

---

[4] Gary A. Davis, Sylvia B. Rimm, and Del Siegle. *Education of the Gifted and Talented* (Upper Saddle River, NJ: Pearson, 2011). This is a textbook focusing on the history of gifted education, definitions, characteristics, and programming.

Perfectionism

Many adults are concerned about perfectionism in gifted children. Meanwhile, ironically, adults often facilitate perfectionism as we constantly remind children to do their best. For perfectionists, reminders like this are troubling. They worry, "If it is not my best, will the teacher take the assignment? I don't like the assignment, so how can I do my best? I can always do better, so how can I turn in my best?" Although seeking perfection can be motivating and gratifying, certain behaviors associated with doing so—frustration, anger, avoidance, and disruptiveness—are troublesome. For example, Tyrone may trace the letter *b* carefully across his page until he turns a loop the wrong way. Then, seeing his mistake, he responds with rage, breaking his pencil and hurling it across the room.

A myriad of factors contribute to such perfectionism. Adults and children tend to impose high expectations on a student who has a particular ability or talent. It isn't unusual for gifted children to hear remarks such as "For someone who already knows how to subtract, you sure ought to be able to remember to hang up your jacket!" Typically, too, gifted children experience a heavy emphasis on performance, both at home and at school. For instance, when neighbors visit four-year-old Leon's family, he's brought out to recite his alphabet monologue ("*A* is for artichoke, *b* is for banana . . ."). Many parents and children are conditioned to see the value of intelligence reflected on paper, in the official terms of test scores and grades. If young children are put on display and praised only for their achievements, they may feel valued not for themselves but for what they can produce—for being "smart" and "right." These young children may conclude that they have to be perfect to be fully accepted. Some move through the elementary years and into their teens thinking, "I am my parents' report card," or "I'm valued for what I can accomplish."

Perfectionism can be an adaptive behavior, an attempt by children to control their lives and their world. It can also be situational: a conflict might arise over a project that's more important to the child than to the teacher, or that interferes with the teacher's lesson plans. Situational perfectionism is sometimes mislabeled as "overachievement" when a child does more than we think is healthy—when we think the child should be satisfied with less.

Easy skill mastery may condition gifted children to a relatively effortless existence. If students are developmentally advanced for their age, most of what they're expected to learn comes easily. They aren't accustomed to struggling. When they eventually face tasks that are difficult to master, they may quickly reject the activities as impossible. Gradually, these students internalize the expectation that they should "know better." Even very young children may deny themselves permission to make mistakes and may avoid activities that might show their weaknesses.

Perfectionism is rooted in caring about how something ought to be. But, especially in the early years, gifted children's experiences and fine motor skills can't accommodate the intricacies of their mental capacities. These children's asynchronous development impedes their accomplishing what they envision in their elaborate imaginations. For example, children may know the story and the details they want to convey; however, their fine motor skills do not enable them to write the story to their expectations. This breach between performance and ideals can lead to frustration and sometimes disruptive behavior.

The following suggestions may help you guide each child to try new things and to accept and learn from less-than-perfect attempts:

Teach courage. Transformation comes through trials. Tell the child, "I know you can try it."

Reward trying. Sometimes we're tempted to say, "It's okay how it turned out, as long as you did your best." With a bright child who might have complicated goals, this can imply that a project represents—or should represent—the child's very best attempt. Not everything is worth a child's greatest effort and time investment. Encourage the student to try doing something new for the fun of it, or simply to give it a try. This helps the child stay motivated and persist in the face of frustrations.

Expect progress, not perfection. Remind the student and yourself that completion is sometimes a better goal than perfection.

Prioritize tasks. Help students recognize tasks that are worthy of a strong effort and others that are not as important but just need to be completed. For example, telling children that you are expecting them to work for only fifteen minutes instead of thirty minutes on a task can be helpful.

Applaud persistence. You might say, "Heroes keep on working at something, even when they're not sure how things will turn out. And look at you. You kept on trying, even when you weren't sure how it would turn out!"

Break down the task. At one time or another, we've all felt overwhelmed by a huge goal. Help a child accomplish a larger project by defining and working through a series of small, attainable goals. In this way, you'll set the stage for a sense of "I can"—and for success. We tell our students, "Inch by inch, it's a cinch. Yard by yard, it's hard."

Acknowledge learning. Let a child know that you expect progress, not perfection. Ask, "What did you learn while you were doing this? What part did you enjoy most? What might you try next time? How might you do it differently next time?"

Ask, "What's good about it?" To turn children's attention away from flaws and toward what they have learned and accomplished, you might say, "You've told me you're disappointed with some parts of your project. Now tell me what's right about it."

Help the child discover meaning. Notice choices the child makes and ask questions such as: "What were you thinking about when you were choosing which colors to use? Why do you think you enjoyed that so much?"

Honor the time invested. Tell the student, "You gave a lot of your time to this. It must have been important to you."

Focus on processes as well as products. You might ask, "How did you decide to change the experiment in the way you did? What are you most proud of?"

Make mistakes okay. Everyone makes mistakes. Help your students see that mistakes are inevitable and are part of the learning process. You can call work "practice." You might comment on your own mistakes when they occur. For example: "Oops—I cut all these shapes for our math project too small. Next time I'll know to measure more carefully. Who has an idea for how we can use shapes this size?"

Underachievement and Lack of Motivation

Children are always motivated. It's just that what we want and what they want are not always the same. Again, causes for an apparent lack of motivation among young gifted children are interwoven with self-concept, social adjustment, and environmental issues. A bright student who's an underachiever may be motivated by personal needs and rewards. Following is a list of some traits of underachievers from the work of Dr. Sylvia Rimm[5] and Diane Montgomery:[6]

- perfectionism
- too many ideas and an inability to narrow down the ideas
- lack of motivation
- withdrawal from classroom activities
- resistance to attending school, chronic stomachaches, headaches, and so forth
- teasing, taunting, or bullying, leading to a hopeless attitude
- sadness, depression, or sleeplessness leading to powerlessness and a belief that achievement is something that they can control
- challenges in the child's personal life, such as a change in a parent's job, a new schedule, a parent in jail, custody issues, living with a relative, and so on
- more interest in social aspects of school than in academics
- opinion that assignments are not challenging or interesting
- disorganization and inability to find previous work for a long-term project
- inability to see the value or importance of turning assignments in to the teacher
- lack of understanding or skills necessary to complete a project and inability to ask for help
- belief that the rewards of achievement are not worth the effort
- inability or unwillingness to accept the purpose of an assignment

---

[5] Sylvia Rimm. *Why Bright Kids Get Poor Grades and What You Can Do About It: A Six-Step Program for Parents and Teachers* (Scottsdale, AZ: Great Potential Press, 2008). This book offers a look at the types of underachievement, with descriptions and strategies to help reverse the underachievement.

[6] Diane Montgomery. "Why Do the Gifted and Talented Underachieve? How Can Masked and Hidden Talents Be Revealed?" *Able, Gifted and Talented Underachievers* edited by Diane Montgomery (West Sussex, UK: John Wiley and Sons, 2009).

- desire to be independent
- wielding power by refusing to comply
- desire to punish a parent or teacher
- desire to lower adult expectations—especially if the child has always received attention for model work
- fear of success leading to higher expectations and pressures
- refusal to try in order to mask a fear of failure and to protect the child's ego
- desire to gain peer acceptance by not standing out as a high performer
- use of underachievement to get focused concern and help from parents and teachers

To get at the root of a child's apparent lack of motivation, ask yourself, "What might be involved? Why? And what might help?" Sometimes your questions will lead you straight to an answer. It may be a good idea to consult with the child's parent as well. The child is likely to be the most valuable source of information. Ask the student to identify favorite and least favorite activities and give reasons. Probe the child's interests. Learn about what's going on at home. You may gain valuable information that can help you guide the child to more productive, worthwhile school time.

Coping Strategies

Children need to have some way to regulate their moods and keep distress from burdening their ability to think. But most young children simply haven't lived long enough to have acquired such coping skills. Their usual response to frustration is to withdraw or to lash out. Childhood is a crucial time for shaping lifelong coping behaviors. When emotional habits become established, they're harder to change later in life.

COPING IDEAS TO SHARE WITH STUDENTS

As a teacher, you can guide and reinforce children in their efforts to find positive ways to soothe their own feelings and sustain self-confidence. Here are some suggestions to offer your students:[7]

Learn to tolerate stress and anxiety. Tell children that stress and anxiety are normal aspects of life.

Teach children relaxation techniques and how to focus on moving through a stressful situation. Deep breathing and counting activities are techniques that can be helpful. You can find a wide variety of information online by searching for "relaxation techniques for children." You will need to try out the techniques you find, as the effectiveness depends on the individual.

Try it out in your mind. Tell children that their mind is a place to try out new experiences. Mentally walk them through what has happened, what might happen, or how else they might act or have acted. Review other possible choices and anticipate consequences.

Set SMART goals. SMART goals are *specific, measurable, attainable, realistic,* and *timely.* For example, the goal of the first week of ice skating is not to reach the Olympics; it is to be able to skate across the ice without falling down. Academics need SMART goals, too. If a child doesn't know how to do addition, solving a multistep math problem is not the goal; the goal is to learn addition. Small, attainable goals are the key to moving forward.

Use positive self-talk, optimism, and a growth mindset. Teach children the value of positive self-talk in instilling optimism: "I can manage. I can do this. Look how much I've done." Using a growth mindset is saying, "I am unable to do this now but will be able to do this with practice or over time." It is believing that skills and ideas can change, grow, and develop.

Change the channel. Help children recognize that their minds and behavior are instruments they can regulate. Introduce them to the idea that their thinking is like a TV set—it has pictures and words. Tell students to "watch" their thinking and see whether their thoughts are working for or against them. If they see that their thinking isn't helping them, they can "switch channels."

Read about it. Bibliotherapy is the use of books to understand and cope with life events, such as winning, losing, teasing, moving, having difficulty in schoolwork, asking for help, or experiencing divorce. Through reading, children can find reassurance that they are not alone in their problems and can gain useful information about how others have developed courage and found solutions. *Some of My Best Friends Are Books* by Judith Wynn Halsted is an

---

[7] Maureen Neihart. *Peak Performance for Smart Kids: Strategies and Tips for Ensuring School Success* (Waco, TX: Prufrock Press, 2008). This is an amazing resource that offers seven strategies for working with all students, but specifically gifted students.

excellent resource you can use to track down books for children (or you) that will offer insights on how to cope with a wide range of life situations.

Use creative decision making. Because most gifted children reason at high levels, they're quite insightful. Help children follow a process to consider choices and experience control over situations. If you wish, give students a copy of "My Problem-Solving Plan" (pages 171–172) and go over the steps with them.

USING "MY PROBLEM-SOLVING PLAN" WITH YOUNG CHILDREN

Explain the steps in this way:

1. **Define the problem.** Have children ask themselves, "What would I like to be different? Is this my problem or someone else's? Is it a problem I can solve? Can I solve it by myself, or will I need help?" Guide children to think of all aspects of the problem: what's happening, why it is a problem, for whom it is a problem, who's involved, and what consequences are occurring or could happen.
2. **Find the facts.** Help children learn what each person involved needs and wants and what led to the troublesome situation. Guide children to identify and recognize various viewpoints and perceptions of the situation.
3. **Brainstorm ideas.** Explain that *brainstorming* means considering all the possible ways to solve the problem. Tell children to list all their ideas—even silly ones or those that seem impossible. Suggest that they think of all their ideas first without judging any of them.
4. **Consider the best ideas.** Once students have run out of ideas, help them evaluate each idea. Have them ask, "What might happen if I do that? How could I make this idea work? How might this idea help me? How might it help others? Could it hurt anyone?" Remind children to be solution finders rather than faultfinders. Help them see how they can move from *thinking* about the problem to *doing* something about it. Have them list a few of the ideas in the order in which they want to try the ideas. Remind children that even great ideas sometimes don't work.
5. **Make a plan.** Encourage students to choose the idea that seems best. They should then decide to try it for a specific length of time based on the situation. It may be a one-time try, or the idea may need to be tried two times a day for a week,

or perhaps it's an idea that should be tried only during recess.
6. **Review how the plan has worked.** Once children have given their idea a reasonable trial, help them evaluate the results. If the problem is solved, point out how the children have taken charge and made a positive change. For example: "Good for you, Carla. You solved your problem! Now you know how to think things through." Be sure to have children think about what they've learned and what they might do in the future to avoid or solve a similar problem.
7. **Try again.** If the problem isn't solved yet, help children change the plan slightly or greatly and try again. Reassure students that some problems are tricky and take more work to solve than others. Express confidence in the students' ability to persevere and solve the problem. Support children in trying other ideas and, if necessary, in looking at the problem from different points of view.

BUILDING CHILDREN'S SELF-ESTEEM

Another important way to help children learn coping skills is to support and nurture their sense of personal worth. Take some time for activities that build self-confidence and self-esteem. *Just Because I Am* by Lauren Murphy Payne is loaded with easy ideas and activities you can use to foster children's self-esteem and confidence.

Introversion[8]

It's the fifth day of school, and five-year-old Gus is eager to get outside and play. Once outdoors, though, Gus lingers at the edge of the playground. He shifts his focus from the shrieking commotion of his classmates and gazes around in a wandering, random fashion. After Gus's impatience for recess, his teacher is perplexed. This isn't the behavior she'd expected.

Understanding the social and emotional qualities and needs of young gifted children means being aware of introversion as one basic personality trait. Everyone's personality fits somewhere along a continuum from extroverted to introverted, and we all need both qualities to some degree. Extroverts are essentially energized by being with other people, while introverts generally regain energy and "process

[8] Chapter 1 includes additional information about introversion in gifted children. See page 14.

information and experiences internally."[9] Gifted people are not necessarily introverted or extroverted; however, introversion is another way in which gifted children can often seem out of step and difficult to understand. "Common Traits of Extroverts and Introverts" below compares some of the social preferences (not abilities) of children who are more outgoing and those who tend to look more inward.

For any introverted child—whether gifted or not—team sports, recess, or other group activities can be especially difficult and even painful. These activities may feel too invasive. Inner-directed children often prefer individualized activities such as track, karate, or gymnastics.

There's nothing inherently antisocial about a child who prefers quiet reflection or one-to-one interaction. You can cultivate trust, sharing, and enthusiasm in this child by forging your relationship a little differently than you do with more outgoing children. To make your classroom more "user-friendly" for young introverts, you might do the following:

- Wait at least three and up to ten seconds after asking a question and before repeating or rephrasing the question or asking a different one. This allows needed time for gifted children (who usually sort through a greater number of possibilities than others in the class) and for introverts (who often prefer to think through their answers before responding).
- Provide private, quiet places such as a cozy corner, library, or small seating area.
- Correct children privately to avoid humiliating them, hurting their feelings, and harming your relationship.
- Provide a variety of grouping options so that children have the opportunity to work alone as well as in groups of varying sizes.

Peer Relationships

With eyes sparkling and words punctuated with flailing arms, Kyle eagerly approached a small group of children in the dramatic play area. "Hey!" he announced. "Let's pretend we're dolphins and talk to each other in signals. I've got the code all figured out! Four beeps mean there's danger approaching, and three short hums mean 'I see something to eat.' And dolphins change colors like chameleons—we can use these different clothes to camouflage—"

Josie interrupted. "We don't want to play dolphins. We're having a pretend birthday party."

Deflated, Kyle moved to a corner and began to play dolphins by himself.

It's widely accepted that by the age of five or six, gifted children are quite aware of being different. Sometimes they—and the other children—think these differences mean that something is wrong with the gifted children. Young gifted children recognize

---

[9] Carol Strip Whitney and Gretchen Hirsch. *A Love for Learning: Motivation and the Gifted Child* (Scottsdale, AZ: Great Potential Press, 2007): 164.

Common Traits of Extroverts and Introverts	
In general, extroverts:	*In general, introverts:*
Learn and think by talking	Process ideas by thinking
Have intense needs to share ideas	May not want to say what they think
Like activities	Have intense needs for privacy
Like variety	Stay with one project for a long time
Crave company	Crave time alone
Are quick to answer	Think reflectively before answering
Welcome interruptions	Resent interruptions
Show feelings	Mask feelings; hide what is important
Want many friends	Want one or few best friends; may feel lonely with others
Are spontaneous; learn by trial and error	Want to understand concepts and situations before experiencing them

the differences but are often unable to communicate the feelings. A child might wonder, "Why do things that don't bother other children bother me? Why do I have so many questions? Why do others not want to play the same things as I do?" Parents may see this as a lack of ability to make friends and become concerned that the child does not have peers the same age.

Regardless of age, the more intelligent people are, the more challenges they often have in finding truly congenial companions. Many gifted children manage quite well socially, but as intelligence increases, so does the potential for peer difficulty. These bright young children may have more trouble finding friends who can fully relate to them and thus may have fewer opportunities to experience understanding and empathy.

Who is a peer and in what setting? Young gifted children tend to select older playmates. Because gifted children are developmentally more advanced, their personalities may be more similar to those of older children than to those of children their age. Although a young gifted child may have older friends outside of school, we may be concerned that the student doesn't seem to have any real friends in class.

Feeling estranged in the classroom is a source of stress for many young gifted children. Here are some factors that can complicate peer relationships:

- Gifted children make up intricate rules for games and create complex play. They gravitate toward children who also crave complicated play, and they sometimes alienate other children.
- Gifted children often come across as bossy because they can be extremely creative and want to organize the play to suit their many ideas. This perception of bossiness is exacerbated when age-mates do not understand the level of play or the story and the gifted child appears to micromanage the situation or story.
- Gifted children realize that they can sometimes see, feel, know, and do things others can't. This can be confusing and alienating.

What can you do to help a gifted child make friends in your classroom? Here are some suggestions:

Reduce competition. Like all kids, most gifted children desperately want to fit in. Refrain from suggesting that bright children are better at something than their classmates. Avoid routinely using gifted children's work or skill mastery as a model. When

you do give recognition, praise other children's work at the same time.

Help the child form relationships based on activities. This might mean that you team the child with one child for computer sharing, another for an art project, and another for math games. Help the child identify peers who have similar interests.

Ask questions. Ask the gifted student, "What do you look for in a friend? What are some ways you might try to make friends? Who has interests like yours?"

Use a variety of grouping techniques. Use various grouping strategies to help gifted children work with a variety of personalities and abilities. It is important to have a purpose behind the grouping. It is easy to group a child who has lower ability and a child with higher ability together so the gifted child can help the other child. This may be important for some groups, but it is critical to make sure this is not the dominant type of grouping. The gifted child should be challenged by the activity as much as others in the classroom. (See Chapter 8 for more information and advice on grouping.)

Use role playing. Role-play social situations with children. Doing this lets them experience the impact of their own behaviors and express their feelings about other children's behavior. Children can act out all the roles in a specific misbehavior situation and create other ways to respond. Role playing is very helpful for the whole class to do to model various communication skills, play situations, and group dynamics.

Focus on nonverbal communication. Play charades by dramatizing various situations without speaking. For example, you might have children mime greeting someone in a friendly way, snubbing someone, taking care of someone who is hurt, or making fun of someone, and then discuss how they feel about each behavior. Using videos of interactions without sound can be a fun way to help children become aware of body language. Ask children to interpret what they see. For example: "What's happening here? What is each character feeling?"

Model friendship and respect for the child. Model the best qualities of friendship, teaching respect and understanding as a basis for a healthy relationship.

The Need for Empathy

Four-year-old Renee wailed that she had lost Brown Bear. Wanting to soothe Renee, her teacher told her, "Just go play with something else, and Brown Bear will show up when you least expect it." Renee replied, "Then I least expect it right now!"

This example illustrates an important point: platitudes don't help. In this situation, Renee's response told the teacher that she didn't want to have her feelings brushed aside. She wanted empathy.

Research shows that when students feel that their teachers have high empathy for them, significant benefits result: academic achievement, positive self-concept, and attendance improve. So do positive peer relationships in the classroom. In addition, children also commit less vandalism and have fewer discipline problems.[10] This evidence has powerful implications in working with gifted children.

Empathy isn't just a nice idea; it's constructive energy. You can convey empathy in many ways, but perhaps the most important way is by *listening*. To do this, you must offer the child your full attention. As you listen, focus on what the child is saying as if nothing else at that moment matters as much as the child's thoughts and feelings.

Instead of trying to fix the problem for the child, work to understand what the situation means to the child. Show your interest by nodding and offering short words of understanding: "I see. Uh-huh." Repeat and paraphrase what you hear without adding your own ideas; this tells the child whether you really understand. If possible, use the child's own words. If you need to paraphrase, use a tentative tone of voice: "It sounds like you're pretty confused. Are you?" Or: "It sounds like that really hurt you. Am I right?" Ask for clarification and amplification: "I'd like to know how you felt about that. What were some of the ways you were feeling when he said that? What are you feeling now?"

You want to help children recognize their feelings, understand them, and know that they're acceptable: Refrain from offering advice or making comparisons to other children. Focus your attention on gathering information and identifying feelings and understanding what these feelings signify to a particular child. A student who can identify personal feelings can do something about them. "I'm

mad" might mean that the child feels left out or embarrassed. Later, you can guide the student to try constructive solutions to this lonely situation. But you must first earn the child's trust through your sincere interest and understanding.

Your goal is to help students understand themselves and gain confidence to look for ways to solve their problems. Ask questions that encourage students to try new behaviors. For example: "What would you like Nadia to do? What could you say to her about that?" Be careful not to let the child feel that you're taking sides or assigning blame for anything. When problems arise, it is important to share feelings in private first. Then, when the child is calm, move into problem solving.

You may want to arrange some private time with a child in need of empathy. A few intimate minutes each day can send a powerful message and allow you to offer the student real support.

Self-Understanding and Self-Acceptance

After a father attended a talk on characteristics of giftedness, he approached the speaker and divulged, "Thank you for curing me. I always thought I was crazy. I felt that no one else saw and felt the way I did. Now I know there was nothing wrong with me."

This man's frank remarks remind us of what it can be like for some bright, creative children. So often, no one explains what being gifted is all about. As a teacher, you can help children recognize, accept, and value their differences. Self-understanding is a basis for self-esteem, for wise decision making, and for wholesome social and emotional relationships.

Gifted children know and feel they're different. But, as with all children, their only frame of reference is themselves. It can be difficult for them to understand how or why other students don't see things the way they do. One five-year-old put this poignantly by saying, "I understand others better than they understand me."

Many of the strategies we've suggested for addressing intensity, sensitivity, control issues, perfectionism, underachievement, coping skills, introversion, peer relationships, and empathy will help you guide your students toward self-understanding and self-acceptance. You'll find many additional suggestions in Judy Galbraith's *The Survival Guide for Gifted Kids: For Ages 10 & Under.* This sensitive

---

[10] Jason J. Barr. "The Relationship Between Teachers' Empathy and Perceptions of School Culture." *Educational Studies* 37, no. 3 (July 2011): 365–369.

book reflects gifted children's thoughts, feelings, and eccentricities and offers models that balance the need to fit in and belong with self-esteem and integrity. The book offers reflections from students' own perspectives across various ages.

Recognition of gender differences and stereotypes is important when focusing on self-understanding and self-acceptance. For example, young boys who are interested in dramatic play and are more creative with art materials are often considered to be more feminine. In general, this trait is not widely accepted for boys. Girls who are drawn to blocks and building materials are generally considered more masculine, which has an impact on their interactions with other girls in the class. It is important for everyone to recognize it is okay for children to explore activities outside traditional gender roles. Working toward acceptance of a variety of roles for all children in all learning areas is crucial. Providing feedback and interaction with these children about what it is they are playing will help provide strengthened self-concept and encouragement to try new things.

Helping All Children Appreciate Differences

Sharing differences in an affirming atmosphere can enable *all* of your students to get to know themselves and their classmates. Use a variety of means to guide children in doing this: small-group and large-group activities; writing, drawing, and reading experiences; and role plays with puppets, dolls, stuffed animals, or toy figures. Following are some suggestions to get you started.

Points of Pride: On long sections of butcher paper (sliced in half lengthwise), ask students to draw or cut and paste pictures from magazines, catalogs, and newspapers to illustrate "points of pride." Encourage children to choose any activity or event in which they demonstrated pride. These might include personal, social, or academic accomplishments; ways they've helped a friend, the classroom, or the planet; or something new they've attempted to do. Ask the children to explain the meanings of their own pictures.

All I Want to Be: This activity helps infuse meaning and purpose into classroom tasks. Ask children to brainstorm "all they want to be"—basketball player, geologist, gardener, teacher, parent, firefighter, or astronaut. Invite children to draw, write, or

role-play the possibilities that they foresee in their own lives. To extend this activity, have a discussion about why children like their chosen careers, specifically focusing on the characteristics of the job. For example, does a student want to be a basketball player for love of the sport, because it's fun to play with friends, for the money, for the fame, to be on TV, or to help others?

Temperature Reading: When children are in small groups, "take their temperature." On a scale from one ("as sad as I can be") to ten ("so happy I could burst"), ask students how they'd measure their present temperature. They can explain why if they choose. You can start. This activity helps children accept the range of feelings in themselves and others. This is a good way to start and end the day, so children can also understand that feelings can change often.

I Like Myself When: Ask children to explain what behaviors they use when they like themselves. Then discuss with them what they can do to like themselves more of the time. Ask what they can do to help others feel good about themselves, too.

My Pictures: Ask each child to bring to school in an envelope several photographs or pictures cut from magazines. These can picture anything the children choose. If you want to focus on feelings, then you can provide them with specific directions, such as: "Find three images that make you happy, proud, or excited, and find two images that make you sad, unhappy, or mad." Group children in pairs, and have partners share and tell each other about their pictures. This is a productive way to have students connect things that make them feel certain ways and recognize that friends may or may not have similar reactions to the same pictures and images.

Tell Me About You: Again working in pairs, have students interview each other and then describe their partner to the class, sharing several facts they have learned. Questions may include: "What is your favorite activity?" "How do you describe yourself?" "What is your best memory?" "What is your favorite item?"

Lots 'n' Lots: Give sentence starters and have the entire class come up with as many ideas as they can. You may want to write each sentence starter on the board, along with the various endings children provide. This is a good activity to do at various times of the year, so that you could compare the lists or focus on concerns or important reminders. Here are some sentence starters you might want to use:

- The things I like best about my class are . . .
- I like it when friends do this . . .
- I don't like it when friends do this . . .
- The best thing I could do for myself is . . .
- I am very happy that . . .

How It Feels to Be Happy: Ask children how it feels to be happy. How do they know they are happy? Where do they feel happiness? How can they explain happiness to someone who doesn't know what the word *happy* means? What can they do to help other children feel happier? You can use both verbal and nonverbal communication in this exercise.

Building Social Skills: Many times, self-esteem is based on knowing what to do. Get a book on manners or other social skills for young children and go over one situation a week. Let children role-play these in little scenes. The lessons in *Taking Part*, a program developed by Gwendolyn Cartledge and James Kleefield, offer an excellent means for teaching and reinforcing social skills in young children. The Center on the Social and Emotional Foundations for Early Learning (CSEFEL) website (csefel.vanderbilt.edu) provides a multitude of resources and book lists for a variety of social-emotional situations, relationship building, and specific social-emotional skills.

Compliment Jar or Superhero Cape: Having a compliment jar in the classroom is an interactive way for students to recognize behavior of peers. The idea is that classmates place notes in the jar during the day or week, and these are shared with the class at the end of the day or week. This provides a way for children to recognize good behavior among classmates. (For example: "I liked how Shannon helped me pick up the stuff from my backpack when it spilled.") If your class is too young for writing, use a superhero cape instead. Tell your students that superheroes are friends and help others. When a child is spotted being a good friend, the child gets to wear the superhero cape.

There are many more ways you can help children get to know each other, appreciate the ways in which they are different, and grow in self-esteem and respect for others. For example, you can invite children to read, tell, or act out stories that let them experience different points of view. A simpler—and

very effective—strategy is to use students' first and last names as spelling words. Every day, try to give each child ten seconds of personal attention. Welcome or leave each child with a greeting, a smile, a pat on the back, and eye contact. You'll find many additional simple but wonderful ideas in *100 Ways to Enhance Self-Concept in the Classroom* by Jack Canfield and Harold C. Wells.

Considering Early Entrance and Acceleration

The school principal was at a loss for a simple answer to a problem. Marisa, a highly gifted child, had entered kindergarten a year early. Now, after finishing first grade at age five, she was languishing in a grade-level curriculum that held no challenge for her. Marisa tested three to five grade levels above the norm in reading, math, and reasoning skills. She was small, however, and during class she was shy, withdrawn, and reluctant to contribute. Her advanced intellectual abilities found no company in the classroom, and on the playground she was at a disadvantage in size and coordination.

"Marisa's much happier in first grade than she was in kindergarten, but I'm reluctant to advance her another grade," the principal explained to the child's father. "In first grade, she has the advantage of being among children near her age. Although she's far ahead of them academically, she'll relate to them more comfortably socially and emotionally than she would relate to older children. If we put her ahead one more grade, the curriculum still won't be significantly more challenging—and she'll have all the developmental disadvantages of being several years younger than her classmates. If we advanced your daughter to a grade based on her test scores, she'd be in fifth grade at age six!"

Early entrance into kindergarten and grade acceleration in elementary school are considered standard tools for responding to the needs of young high-ability children. Those options are clearly appropriate in many instances, and the children find a comfortable niche for intellectual, social, and emotional growth.

However, the complexities of giftedness and myths surrounding gifted education and acceleration defy simplistic options. For example, the idea of putting a six-year-old in a fifth-grade classroom because that's where her test scores place her can be disturbing to teachers. Equally troubling may be the notion that we might force a young gifted child to wait an extra year before starting kindergarten simply because his birthday misses an arbitrary deadline by a few weeks or months. Regardless of when a child starts kindergarten or what grade the child skips, every gifted student continues to have special needs that require accommodation in the classroom.

In 2004, Nicholas Colangelo, Susan Assouline, and Miraca Gross published *A Nation Deceived: How Schools Hold Back America's Brightest Students*. It provided the most in-depth research report on acceleration to date. The authors researched and identified the types of acceleration used and the various myths surrounding acceleration. They also provided resources and case studies. In 2015, *A Nation Empowered: Evidence Trumps the Excuses Holding Back America's Brightest Students* was published as a follow up, reinforcing the success of acceleration. "The research is robust and unanimous in support of acceleration. You have to really search to find any qualified negatives."[11]

As we try to meet the needs of gifted students, it is important to understand the various types of acceleration options. *A Nation Deceived* identified eighteen types of acceleration.[12] We will focus only on the three types that frequently affect early childhood and primary classrooms. These include:

- early admission to kindergarten
- early admission to first grade
- grade skipping

When looking at these types of acceleration, questions arise. What about the social and emotional effects? How might children suffer from acceleration or grade skipping? If we accelerate them now, what is the long-term effect on the student? How will transitions between grades or schools be affected? Often we have more questions than answers. The reality is that because of their asynchronous development, young gifted children won't fit perfectly into any

grade. The classroom teacher needs to understand their skills and differentiate the curriculum to meet the needs of individual students. Sometimes, this is better accomplished in the next grade up.

Acceleration is not about pushing the child; rather, it is meeting the educational needs of the child. We need to focus on the overall educational needs of the student and consider the social and emotional effects of the current situation as well as the accelerated situation. Research shows that when acceleration is thoughtful, most gifted children thrive—academically, socially, and emotionally.

Conversely, children who are held back tend to lose ground in all three areas. For children who are required to receive instruction at a level significantly below their ability level, many problems can ensue. Children often develop poor study habits, grow apathetic, lose motivation, or become maladjusted. They may resent "putting in their time." Even in the best situations, these children may retreat into their internal world of imagination or devise some negative external means of intellectual stimulation and challenge. Consequently, they may be mislabeled as children who can't focus or pay attention.

Early Entrance

Early entrance to kindergarten or first grade may be the best acceleration option for young gifted children. Early entrance allows for the child's intelligence to be better accommodated and for a peer group to be established. It saves the student from later disruption of skipping a grade. By being more academically challenged in the earliest grade, a bright child is likely to have fewer of the emotional problems that typically result from facing academic challenges after years of coasting along. Early entrance can set the stage for many young gifted children to continue to thrive and excel throughout their school experience, to participate in more activities, to feel secure within a peer group when they express their ideas, and to experience more interdependence and cooperation.

Acceleration

When you recognize an extremely bright child in your classroom, you might wonder whether the child would benefit from acceleration. Your role in making this recommendation is extremely important. As you begin to work with any young gifted student, keep in mind that you're in a unique

---

[11] Susan G. Assouline, Nicholas Colangelo, Joyce VanTassel-Baska, and Ann Lupkowski-Shoplik. *A Nation Empowered: Evidence Trumps the Excuses Holding Back America's Brightest Students* (Iowa City, IA: University of Iowa, 2015): 14. This follow-up focuses on information from *A Nation Deceived* and shares updates and additional research completed during the years spanning the study.

[12] Nicholas Colangelo, Susan G. Assouline, and Miraca U. M. Gross. *A Nation Deceived: How Schools Hold Back America's Brightest Students, Volumes One and Two* (Iowa City, IA: University of Iowa, 2004). This is an amazing resource that discusses acceleration as a programming option for gifted children. It explains myths, reflections, and the research backing the positive and negative aspects of acceleration.

position to see the child in action in the classroom setting. No test can evaluate the social or emotional status of your student as well as your firsthand experience and observations. With this insight, you may decide to suggest that a child would be a strong candidate for acceleration, or that the current grade-level assignment is the most appropriate.

The *Iowa Acceleration Scale, Third Edition* is a tool to help schools make effective decisions regarding grade skipping.[13] This tool uses recommendations and input from parents, teachers, and other educators to evaluate the academic and social-emotional characteristics and needs of the gifted student.

Regardless of whether a tool or system is in place, you as the teacher can be an essential advocate for gifted children in your classroom. Use your knowledge and observations to suggest an accurate assessment of the child's abilities to determine the child's intellectual and academic levels. Tests used must include tasks several grades above the current class level. If you are looking to make an acceleration recommendation, the child's development should be above the average for the grade he will move into. (For additional information on testing and assessment, see Chapter 7.)

Discover whether the child prefers older playmates. Since there are more opportunities outside the classroom for the child to be with older children, ask the child's parent about this. Socially and emotionally, many young gifted children are far more appropriately matched with older children.

Ask parents for samples of the child's drawings, writings, and other projects done at home or outside of school. Discuss with the parents how these reflect the child's feelings or attitudes toward learning and working with other children.

Determine if the child's fine and gross motor skills are reasonably adequate for the grade the child will enter. Although you don't want the child to be unduly frustrated, the lack of a specific skill (such as using a scissors or coloring within the lines) isn't a sufficient reason to deny acceleration or early entrance. Gifted children can usually learn creative ways to compensate for temporary motor deficits. It is also possible that deficient motor skills can be taught with extra support.

If you feel that acceleration might be an option for the child, explore the idea with your school system and the parents to add their perspective to your own.[14] It is important to work within the system while advocating for the child.

When grade skipping is chosen, it is important to place the child with a teacher who understands giftedness. The child will be missing specific skills taught during the skipped grade. Often, the child will need a short lesson or explanation of the skill and then will pick up on the task. For example, if the child skipped first grade and missed instruction on the use of capital letters and punctuation in writing, the child's writing will probably not demonstrate these skills. This skill can be explained to the student, who will start to use it.

For early entrance or acceleration to succeed, everyone involved must be invested in the process and optimistic about the outcome. Specifically:

- The *child* must be consulted and must welcome the idea.
- The receiving *teacher* must be carefully selected for qualities of flexibility and enthusiasm; must have positive attitudes toward the acceleration; must be willing to help the child adjust to the new situation; and must demonstrate a welcoming attitude. (Other students in the class will reflect the teacher's attitude.)
- The *parent* must want this placement adjustment; must be willing and able to cooperate with the teacher to arrange tutoring or support for the child in academic areas where there might be a learning gap; and must communicate closely with the teacher about the child's reactions at home.
- The *administration* must coordinate the process and support the child, the teacher, and the parents.

Beyond these considerations, everyone involved must build an ongoing system of evaluation. Expect to make changes and adapt your plan. Acceleration is an initial step, not a panacea. You'll need to keep making adjustments in the pace, depth, and complexity of the child's classroom experience.

---

[14] For additional information on working with parents, see "Enlisting Parents as Colleagues" in Chapter 1, page 14, and "Building Partnerships with Parents" in Chapter 9, page 142.

---

[13] Institute for Research and Policy on Acceleration. *Iowa Acceleration Scale* (Scottsdale, AZ: Great Potential Press, 2009).

Questions and Answers

"Won't children be frustrated if we push them ahead?"

For young gifted children, frustration is more likely to result from already knowing the information and/or having to endure waiting for classmates to grasp new material. Under this circumstance, the classroom becomes an obstacle to bright children's learning. When acceleration is used thoughtfully and carefully, taking into consideration all aspects of a child's needs and characteristics, it's a valuable programming option.

"Isn't it good for a gifted child's self-esteem to be the best in the class?"

The top of the class can be a very vulnerable place. The child may begin to feel pressured to always be "the best." The child may assume the role of always helping classmates and believe that it's futile to ask others for advice. A child at the very top likely has fewer opportunities to learn. The class may limit the child's opportunities to make a real effort and experience pride and success. Many gifted children already feel they do not fit in. Always pointing to them as models is not beneficial to the gifted children. Meanwhile, the other children learn to resent the gifted children.

Conclusion

So often, the "measure" of a gifted student—even one who is very young—comes down to test scores or demonstrated achievement. When you become an advocate for your gifted student's social and emotional growth, you help the student develop the skills needed to succeed in school and life. In focusing on children's social and emotional needs, you also establish a broader, healthier perspective from which caring adults can chart a more sensitive and successful individualized educational experience for each child.

My Problem-Solving Plan

My name: _____

Start by doing steps 1–5.

1. This is the problem:

2. This is what happened and how each person (including me) feels:

3. These are all the ideas I can think of for solving the problem:

4. These are my best ideas and what might happen if I try them:

IDEAS	WHAT MIGHT HAPPEN
_____	_____
_____	_____
_____	_____
_____	_____

➡

5. I'll try this idea:

I'll try my idea at least _____ times a day until _____ (date).
Then I'll see how it's going.

Try your idea until the date you chose in step 5. Then do step 6.

6. My idea worked (circle one): **GREAT   NOT SO GREAT**

Here's what happened:

Here's what I learned:

Here's what I'll do next time:

If your problem still isn't solved, look back at your ideas in step 4. Is there something else you can try? Ask your teacher for another copy of this handout. Keep working on your problem!

7. Here's what I'll do next:

CHAPTER 11
Meeting the Needs of Children from Diverse Populations

Ariela had grown quiet and despondent in her new school. A third grader who spent her earlier years in a predominantly Latino neighborhood, she felt strange in this school where most of the other kids were so different. She missed Mariel, Angelica, Allyce—her best friends from her old school who spoke Spanish, ate familiar food, and played games in the park where everyone came out to barbecue on the weekends. To Ariela, it was a bustling world filled with games, music, spicy cooking, and people of all ages enjoying lively conversations. In the past she had brought this world to life through her writings and artwork, nourishing her talents. But the move to a new home and school was a shock to Ariela's system. She felt rudderless, alone, and lost. A gifted student with interests in many areas, she now tried to be as invisible as possible.

Martin loved learning but became frustrated because he couldn't organize his ideas. Unable to prioritize tasks or pace himself well, he would turn in work that looked like a garbled last-minute job. The harder he tried, the worse things got and the more his self-worth plummeted. There was some discussion that Martin might have ADHD, and his parents focused a lot on getting him to settle down and pay attention. Regardless, Martin was highly creative in how he approached school projects. Trying to respond to a homework question, he told his father that the answer would be different depending on the meaning. "You're overthinking it," his father said. Martin wondered how he could stop "overthinking."

Daniel and Laura lived in a farming community where the nearest town had little more than a few stores and a post office. Laura got to know Daniel in town because he and his father would come in to the feed store her family owned. She saw that Daniel had a funny T-shirt with the picture of a book that had a hole in the front and a worm in the back. "Oh . . . book worm! That's funny," Laura said, and they became friends. They talked about books they read, animals they noticed near the creek, and the new library being built in town. At their small rural school, Laura often put on a cheerful face, but secretly she felt alone and wished there were more kids like her and *like Daniel there. Daniel dreamed of traveling to big cities where he would have many more opportunities to follow his real interests—science and art.*

In the primary grades, discrepancies in children's development, skill, knowledge, and ability are more observable than in the higher grades. As a general rule, teachers of young children often have to juggle considerable differences in learning readiness. Add to this the influence of culture, language, special needs, socioeconomics, and environment, and you have a classroom where the range of knowledge and understanding in any given subject can be significant. Primary teachers often wonder how they can meet the needs of gifted learners whose abilities are likely to be invisible in their classroom, especially given all the other demands requiring their attention from other students.

This chapter focuses on the need for greater perceptivity in assessing the talents of young gifted children in order to adjust instruction and guide children's growth and development.

A Variety of Needs Considered

Young gifted learners come from more varied backgrounds than we could possibly discuss in a single chapter. We will explore *some* of the issues related to identifying and nurturing giftedness in underrepresented populations—those, for example, who come from ethnic minorities, are economically disadvantaged, attend school in rural areas, are girls or boys who don't fit in with peers, are "twice-exceptional" (both gifted and having a learning challenge), do not speak English as their first language, or are highly gifted or creative.

For decades energy and research have gone into identifying and serving these children; still they continue to fall through the cracks. One reason for this is that children identified as gifted have overwhelmingly come from white, middle- and upper-middle-class populations. Many of the "clues" to giftedness we typically look for are rooted in the expressions and behaviors of children from this group. Another reason is that funds for gifted services have declined dramatically across the board, making it even harder for a child from a minority within a minority to receive needed support.

Cultural, Linguistic, and Economic Diversity

Researchers have long recognized and studied children from culturally, linguistically, and economically diverse (CLED) backgrounds and their lack of inclusion in gifted programs. The descriptions in this chapter indicate some of the challenges students from the nondominant society experience, but they are not comprehensive by any means. In general, the wisest course of action is to explore the unique values, beliefs, and systems of communication that need to be understood and honored when meeting the educational and social-emotional needs of young children.[1]

Many cultural groups are underrepresented in gifted programs. We can begin addressing this discrepancy by expanding our understanding of cultural differences and similarities. As you consider the ideas in this chapter, you'll want to keep these facts in mind:

- Giftedness exists in all human groups in roughly the same proportions.
- Culture and environment strongly influence development of certain skills and familiarity and comfort with certain activities.
- Standardized tests are not the only—or even the most—useful means to identify gifted children; in some cases, they are not useful at all.
- The *expression* of giftedness varies among cultures. High-level abilities may be demonstrated through behaviors and accomplishments that are characteristic of a particular group and therefore may not be recognized in the society at large.

Socioeconomic status as well as primary language may provide additional challenges in identification of young students. Families may live in substandard housing or may not have means to support themselves with basic necessities, including regular meals. English may not be the primary language; in some cases, adults in the family may not speak any English at all. Even in communities whose primary language is English, cultural issues can present obstacles to identification. Outside of school, the children may have little or no opportunity to interact with mainstream learning activities that would be helpful in a traditional school-based setting. The more these conditions overlap, the less likely it is that the gifted

---

[1] James J. Gallagher, and Shelagh A. Gallagher. *Teaching the Gifted Child* (Boston: Allyn and Bacon, 1994).

child in these circumstances will be served. The situation is made more complex by the following issues:

- confusing, vague definitions of giftedness
- gifted programs that emphasize measurable academic achievement
- biased identification procedures, especially tests
- a deficit-oriented rather than strength-oriented approach to children whose gifts may present themselves in unexpected ways
- little contact with families to establish the level of acculturation, language acquisition, or any other factors affecting children's learning
- little recognition of the gifts and talents valued by different communities
- differences between immigrant and native born children from the same ethnic background
- limited, competing funds and resources

Added to this challenge is the range of acculturation into North American life, of fluency in English, and of preparedness in school subjects. Whatever a child's background may be, the young gifted student requires appropriate educational intervention to prevent his skills and abilities from being lost. Culture and language do not just orient how children learn, but are fundamental as vehicles for thinking and communication. They *mediate* thinking and learning.

Cultural and Linguistic Diversity

One of the greatest challenges for schools and for the field of gifted education is how to best serve the growing populations of diverse ethnic and linguistic groups. The range of languages, especially in urban areas, is striking. For example, at the time of this writing, Nicholas Senn High School in Chicago has fifty-five nationalities and thirty-five spoken languages represented. A 2014 Pew study projected that young children from minority groups could constitute 51 percent of public school students in kindergarten through eighth grade.[2]

Distinct languages, customs, and values influence how communities in each cultural group interact with schools and how their children thrive in the classroom, even in cases where they were born and raised in the United States or Canada. The following examples show how the identification and

support of young gifted children and, indeed, many children's school experiences can be influenced by ethnic and cultural background.

Gifted children from Native American and Native Alaskan and Hawaiian cultures face continual hardships in the public, often rural schools they attend. Peers and teachers may hold negative ideas about their abilities, motivation, and diligence.[3] In the classroom, some Native children may be perceived as too quiet, reluctant to express their opinions in any form, and therefore inattentive or indifferent. A gifted child may be sitting in a classroom, silently burning with questions, curious about natural phenomena or how electricity works, relishing the sound of poetry, hungry to make friends. Gifted students from this background may benefit from programs that are built solidly on Native values, traditions, and language and that provide challenge and enrichment by weaving community, family, and culture with student interests and talents.

Many traditional Hispanic cultures emphasize respect for elders and others in authority, cooperation, and modesty. Those who immigrate to the United States often hold education in high esteem and see it as the means for their children to have a better life. At the same time, education does not necessarily take precedence over other valued dimensions of life such as family ties and responsibilities. Hispanic and Latino people in America comprise a highly diverse and closely researched group. They come from different nations and include both immigrant and native-born populations. The majority of young Hispanic children in the United States today were born in the country. Depending on their family, their socioeconomic background, and their community, they may have grown up speaking primarily Spanish, Spanish and English, or English.[4]

In some cases, a strong value placed on individual competition, independence, and self-direction may feel foreign or intimidating, and many young gifted Hispanic children do not feel comfortable being singled out for exceptional performance or achievement. They need sensitive mentoring to assist them

[2] Jens Manuel Krogstad, and Richard Fry. "Dept. of Ed. Projects Public Schools Will Be 'Majority-Minority' This Fall." August 18, 2014, in Pew Research Center *Fact-Tank* (www.pewresearch.org/fact-tank).

[3] Stuart Tonemah. "Tess Questions." *Underserved Gifted Populations: Responding to Their Needs and Abilities* edited by Joan Franklin Smutny (Cresskill, NJ: Hampton Press, 2003): 266.

[4] Information on Hispanic cultures comes from *Discovering and Developing Talents in Spanish-Speaking Students* by Joan Franklin Smutny, Kathryn P. Haydon, Olivia Bolanos, and Gina Estrada Danley (Thousand Oaks, CA: Corwin Publishing, 2012).

in using their talents freely. They can begin, for example, by taking on a role that interests them in a group project, or by participating in a science experiment that gives them the challenge they need without feeling exposed.

African-American children who arrive to school in prekindergarten through third grade represent a diversity of communities. Young, sensitive gifted children learn about racial prejudice and notice subtle behaviors that make them feel like outsiders in school; at the same time, their curiosity and keen interest in many things can make them feel at odds with peers. This is true for other groups of children as well, but gifted African-American children feel it particularly acutely. Some of these children get in trouble for not waiting to be called on, for not controlling their creative energy, or for humorous verbal play mistaken for intentional interruption. Young students show their giftedness in different ways, depending on their family's background and circumstances. Care must be taken that young high-ability children do not go unrecognized because their language usage does not conform to traditional standard English.

Young gifted African Americans are highly versatile in how they use and express their talents. Some may read poetry and fiction in advance of their years; others may have little exposure to the written word but spin tales they've learned from their family or neighbors. These children may be exceptionally keen observers of behavior—noting subtle changes in facial expression, intonation, and body language that guide their actions. They need classrooms where they can feel accepted and learn and explore through different media, activities, and resources.

Asian children also represent a range of cultural and ethnic backgrounds. In many instances, children from Asian populations are stereotyped as highly studious and are expected to be so. They are more likely to be included in programs for gifted students than children from other minorities. Though their abilities may sometimes be more obvious, many young gifted Asian children hunger for more creative experiences—more art, more literature, more imaginative activities. Even at a young age, many feel a sense of failure if they do not make top grades in school. It would be a mistake to think, "Oh, bright Asian kids don't need help; they're ahead."

It would also be a mistake to expect all gifted Asian kids to stand out and be readily identified. Asian populations have just as many gifted students who do not fit into the mold as any other group. In some cases, for example, children may have parents with less formal education and belong to communities with strongly held cultural traditions. And many Asian children are taught to respect elders and authority. They may appear quiet, complacent, and polite, yet have a desire to explore and expand their learning which they are hesitant to express. The primary years offer the ideal time for talented Asian students (high achieving or not) to expand their horizons—to worlds and talents they did not know existed.

African immigrants. Young students who emigrated from African countries (or those born in North America but whose parents immigrated) represent a huge range of political, social, religious, linguistic, and cultural backgrounds. Some may know little English, while others may come to school speaking fluent English and performing ahead of American children. In a former English colony such as Kenya or Uganda, for example, children are in a school system like the British one and it tends to be quite rigorous. On the other hand, children whose families emigrated as refugees, such as many from Somalia, may have had minimal schooling and may live in homes where little or no English is spoken. Children's parents may be highly invested in their children's success and want them to do well in school, or they may feel intimidated or distrustful about what and how children are being taught.

Teachers may find some young African students quiet and withdrawn. In part, this is due to the fact that in a number of cultures, children learn to respect elders, particularly teachers, and rarely initiate conversation or ask questions of them. Being encouraged to do something in school that is open ended or creative may be a new and jarring experience for some of these students. Extending learning experiences for the gifted students in this population may be intimidating to them at first. Communication with their parents and learning more about the country and culture of origin are key to supporting them. Building relationships and rapport is essential to understanding their strengths and interests and creating educational programs for their learning.

Young gifted students from the Middle East face unique challenges. At a time when many Westerners associate the Middle East with terrorism, religious fanaticism, and cruelty, children from that part of the world feel the prejudice in their schools and the general society—gifted students particularly so. Parents value their traditions, their customs, and their religion, but they want their children to become educated and to do well in American society. Contrary to stereotype, many immigrants and new citizens from the Middle East value the freedom they have to practice their religion and customs as they wish. Young gifted children from the Middle East, like those from Africa, need creative experiences and a classroom atmosphere of acceptance and understanding. As with other cultures, parents appreciate teachers who take the time to learn about their children's cultural background and who have some basic interest in learning about them. They share more freely about their children and cultures when they feel accepted. Reaching out to parents and community members can go far in helping you support the talents and interests of young gifted learners in the population.

LOOK AND LISTEN

Like our society, our conception of giftedness is growing increasingly diverse. We now understand it to include abilities far beyond academic performance. Some may ask why we need to bother with gifted education at all since everyone is "gifted" in some areas and less so in others. It is true that most children have talent in some area of their lives. When we teach to our students' strengths and interests and use those to address deficiencies as well as enhance learning, *all children* in the class benefit, including those who are gifted. Despite this, a number of factors (including culture, language, ethnicity, and socioeconomic factors) can still mask the exceptional ability of gifted children, and the time to address this problem is in the primary grades.

In order to reach students of high potential in diverse groups, particularly those with less access to resources, we need to understand what giftedness means to the people involved. When looking at children from diverse populations, your basic guidelines should be these:

1. **Use the broadest definition of giftedness to include diverse abilities.** The idea is to recognize exceptional needs and abilities however they

occur. Draw on different sources to assess ability (see the list that follows), remembering that conventional tests and assignments may reveal little of a student's actual potential.

2. **Find and serve as many young children with high potential as possible.** For example, by focusing on multiple intelligences and different learning modalities, you can better serve a diverse group of children. Our classrooms often draw on linguistic and logical-mathematical intelligences. Bodily-kinesthetic, naturalist, interpersonal, musical, and spatial intelligences can open up the lives of these promising students. Teaching to children's preferred learning modality (style)— auditory, visual, or kinesthetic—increases the opportunity to serve and enrich learning for gifted children who might not otherwise realize their potential.

3. **Provide *all* students with high level, engaging, open-ended, hands-on curriculum opportunities.** Doing so will foster development of skills and abilities and showcase them in often overlooked ways.

You can also identify giftedness among a diverse group of young children through some of the following strategies:

- **Use checklists.** We provide several in this book: the "Checklist of My Child's Strengths" (for parents—pages 22–23) and the "Student Observation Forms" (for teachers—pages 124–130). Consider every possibility of exceptional skill when seeking to discover a child's outstanding abilities. Other research-based checklists (*Kingore Observation Inventory, U-STARS~PLUS* program—see pages 204 and 216) can help identify giftedness.

- **Find a child's "best performance."** Look for any sign of exceptional, even isolated, performance that could represent unidentified abilities. If you find one outstanding ability, such as memory for music, you can build on a child's confidence by creating opportunities for her to use that talent. A single encouraging experience can often produce a ripple effect on the child's self-assurance and on the competence she begins to show in other directions.

- **Consider "processing" behaviors,** such as risk taking and the ability to hypothesize and improvise.

- **Ask other teachers** what they have observed or experienced concerning the child.
- **Trust your hunches.** If you suspect that a child has exceptional abilities, your hunch is probably based on something.
- **Make classroom observations,** being aware of the student's cultural background.
- **Spend time with the child** to gain insight into his thinking process, aspirations, home activities, and sense of self.
- **Solicit the parent's views** about the child's talents, abilities, and expressions of creative and critical thinking. Chapters 1, 2, and 9 discuss ways to communicate with parents and include several letters and forms to facilitate this process.
- **Keep parents informed.** Parent involvement is essential in finding and serving very young gifted children from underserved populations. If you keep parents informed and look for ways they can help, you are likely to empower them with a sense of being able to contribute. They'll be invested and more interested in cooperating with you to reinforce your classroom activities.
- **Visit community events** and frequent the local stores, cultural centers, and restaurants. Make it known to your students and their families that you are interested in all of their public celebrations and traditions.

The last item on the previous list will make your classroom more inviting to parents and families. Language and cultural differences should not keep anyone away from your door, even if they speak little or no English. If your school or district does not have a liaison for families who have a language barrier and you don't feel a student should be placed in that position, try to find one yourself. Local community center workers, librarians, before- and after-school program teachers, and English-speaking parent volunteers are possible candidates. Unless you invite and facilitate parent participation from those who feel the most estranged, you won't be able to fully assimilate their children in your classroom.

FOSTER A MULTICULTURAL AND CULTURALLY RELEVANT ENVIRONMENT

Whatever the makeup of your classroom, it's important to realize that children's expressions can be healthy and appropriate to their culture. Children of diverse cultural groups are often raised with distinctive problem-solving strategies, differing attitudes toward education, ranging degrees of adaptation to the majority culture (whatever it may be), and different languages and language styles. We can't generalize about these children—every child is unique—but we can appreciate the culture from which a child emerges, because this is a factor in how the child exhibits exceptional abilities.

Young gifted learners feel their differences acutely. Living between two cultural worlds is stressful for highly sensitive students, but it can also be a means for them to respond creatively. As they navigate between these worlds, children can combine different elements of their home and school. Cultural celebrations, word explorations, art displays, and story sharing tell the students that they belong. If you open up the classroom to the cultural, ethnic, and linguistic groups represented, you will build a vibrant, global environment from the ground up.

By enhancing multicultural awareness in your classroom, you also provide a place for children of diverse cultures to more comfortably exhibit their exceptional abilities. Following are some ways you can celebrate and include cultural differences:

- Read richly illustrated stories of various cultures. You will find multicultural resources in the "References and Resources" section that starts on page 189 and in Appendix B beginning on page 217. Your school librarian or media specialist can also recommend books to help your students explore various cultures. Select some that you especially like, and you'll convey appreciation and acceptance by your own heartfelt enthusiasm.
- Explore different cultural or ethnic stories related to familiar fairy tales and have the children create new ones.
- Develop your curriculum using culturally responsive pedagogy through inclusive activities and materials for all students.
- Create ethnic or folk crafts and arts; use music, dance, and song in the curriculum. Experiencing the arts and aesthetics of various cultures helps children appreciate differences and expands their creativity.
- Invite students from different cultural backgrounds to share their culture when they feel ready. For example, ask them to tell about a special custom or a favorite food or to teach the class a phrase in their language. If children once lived somewhere else, ask them what they miss most about their old home and what they like best about their new one.

- Use the culture exploration activities suggested in "Originality: Cultural Invention" (page 67), in which children observe their own and other people's cultures and then imagine and create their own original cultures with unique geographies, histories, customs, and artifacts.
- Find websites, blogs, and other means to learn about different American communities and communicate with them.

Economically Disadvantaged Children

Poverty consistently results in children not being identified as gifted. Economic deprivation can impact any child. It affects maternal and child health and social functioning, both of which may relate to school performance.

To function well in their home or community, economically disadvantaged children may develop abilities that are different from other children's. Instead of learning information and skills that require their parents' time and money, these children may show their ability in adapting materials in their lives for different purposes and developing survival skills when dealing, for example, with the need to assume greater responsibility in the home or with the need for parents to work long hours to make ends meet. Young gifted children tend to be deeply attuned to other people's needs and feelings, and are accustomed to finding creative ways to solve problems. While these children have the same potential for academic giftedness as all children do, in many cases the potential may be underdeveloped.

Children from poverty typically have not had the same exposure to blocks, Legos, gears, educational toys, art materials, software, books, mazes, and puzzles as those from higher socioeconomic groupings. The family focus is often on survival, not on school readiness skills. Without exposure to various learning materials, school is often students' first opportunity to experiment with them. Behavior can look younger and delayed for these students since they have not had previous opportunities to use or interact with these items. Some gifted children may seem unmotivated and listless due to hunger, lack of proper nutrition, or lack of sleep.

Teachers of young children can be a decisive force against cumulative deficits in any child—especially in a child from an underserved population. Without appropriate intervention, some children will exhibit

a progressive decline in intellectual growth, achievement scores, or both. It's essential that teachers actively seek additional resources for underprivileged students. Some ways to do this include:

- Provide opportunities for the children to experience and interact with community talent: artists, musicians, engineers, and business owners.
- Improve access to functional technology and find Internet sites related to children's interests. Innovative organizations like Free Geek have found ways to rebuild and recycle used computers for low-income districts.
- Work with parents and community organizations to obtain any material resources that could benefit gifted students and enrich instruction.
- Create a pool of volunteers—parents, community center volunteers, actors—and match them to the children in the classroom based on the child's strength, passion, and personality.

Young Gifted Children in Rural Areas

Gifted children in sparsely populated areas can be difficult to find and serve because doing so requires exceptional effort, often by one teacher who is caring and astute. The scarcity of school personnel relative to the vast geographical distances involved makes identifying children with special talents and abilities a particularly challenging endeavor. Because resources to serve these gifted children are often rare, a teacher plays a vital role in discovering and developing their abilities.

Rural gifted students who come from poor or bilingual areas present additional challenges. Parts of some standardized tests assess knowledge of the traditional mainstream language and culture only. In addition, rural children may have experiences, knowledge, and developed skills that differ from urban or suburban students—for example, with soil types, ecology, weather patterns, animal behavior, animal husbandry, engineering, carpentry, and so on. Researcher and educator Luis Moll called such strengths "funds of knowledge" and showed how understanding these experiences and skills give us a window into students' abilities and how we might serve them in our classrooms.[5]

---

[5] Luis C. Moll. "Funds of Knowledge for Teaching: Using a Qualitative Approach to Connect Homes and Classrooms." *Theory Into Practice*, 31(2): 132–141.

Familiarity with rural communities—their cultures, histories, and socioeconomic life—will reveal potential talent areas:

- Children's adeptness in recognizing and responding to such problems as farm equipment breakdown, weather variability, and dealing with livestock predation
- High ability in hands-on experiences, improvising with materials at hand to invent and rig things
- Strong affinity for animals and knowledge of local ecology, soil science, entomology, and so forth
- Inventive productivity in science and engineering projects (such as those in 4-H)
- Highly developed sight and hearing, enabling children to identify many species of flora and fauna
- Creativity in performing arts, visual arts, crafts, and carpentry

Try to include a range of competencies and talent areas other than test scores to identify student ability and achievement. Nonverbal assessments, one-on-one talks, checklists, analyses of children's work, and anecdotal information from teachers and parents will also help you identify skills and potential.

Collaboration with adjacent districts can be of great help in both finding and serving gifted rural children. Materials, ideas, curricula, and expertise can all be shared. If you teach in a rural area, you might consider some of the following suggestions:

- Use the Internet to create connections between schools and districts and engage in project-centered learning experiences. Various online classroom and curriculum opportunities are available. Distance learning can provide students the opportunity to connect with others in real time or individually at their own pace.
- Share ideas and materials by creating educational videos and games, as well as blogs.
- Transport gifted children to a single location so they can interact with each other and attend workshops in a variety of fields: creative writing, advanced and applied mathematics and science, visual arts, performing arts, and technology.
- Arrange for mentoring opportunities with a teacher who shares a child's passion or interest.

Rural areas, particularly the most sparsely populated and/or disadvantaged, have young gifted children with a fraction of the resources available in urban and suburban areas. However, schools and districts need to avail themselves of the support intended for rural communities. Besides reaching out to community resources (human and material), there are also organizations such as these:

- The Rural School and Community Trust has an initiative, Rural School Innovation Network (RSIN), that fosters a network among the poorest communities to share innovations to improve rural education.
- The Rural Trust Global Teacher Fellowship broadens the learning experiences of educators who desire new teaching approaches through exposure to ideas around the globe. Most recent fellows are exploring energy technologies, art, architecture, environmental issues, and education as applied to culture and language, schooling and curriculum development.
- The Foundation for Rural Education and Development (FRED) has awarded millions of dollars since it began in 2001. In 2014, sixteen rural public schools gained grants for improving or expanding technology for rural children who would otherwise lack access to the quality and diversity of learning experiences they deserve and need.

Gifted Girls

Though challenges remain for gifted girls and women today, significant progress has occurred over the past decade. Young girls today see more men taking care of children, more girls in sports, and more women in science and engineering. At the same time, different expectations for boys and girls vary across populations (cultures, socioeconomic groups, environments), making it difficult to know what happens to promising young girls as they grow older. Even at a young age, gifted girls respond to spoken and unspoken expectations about who and what they can aspire to be. Many are on an obstacle course that leads them into well-documented gender discrepancies in self-esteem, course-taking patterns, test results, and eventual career status and earning power.

At the same time, though, studies also show that girls tend to *start out* ahead of boys. Compared to young boys of the same age, girls are likely to:

- be more robust
- read and count earlier
- score higher on IQ tests during preschool
- be ready for formal schooling at an earlier age
- outperform boys in most studies of early entrants to elementary school

Even into second grade, gifted girls are more like gifted boys than like other girls in their interests, activities, and career aspirations. They appear more socially adjusted than other girls or gifted boys. Throughout elementary school, gifted girls tend to score higher on achievement tests than gifted boys.

YOUNG GIFTED GIRLS NEED EARLY SUPPORT

Despite their abilities and some of the advantages they have over boys, many gifted girls adjust by blending into their environment and not demonstrating their strength to others. Feeling confident with their abilities depends on many variables, such as their socioeconomic background; positive, nurturing relationships with teachers; access to resources; and family support for their talents. Without these, girls may decide that their abilities don't fit in. For many girls, their giftedness goes "underground" as they work to blend in by conforming to what they see other girls being praised for. And, as age goes up, many girls' self-esteem and expectations ebb. While young gifted girls typically have high career aspirations and vivid career fantasies—to be astronauts or paleontologists, for example—by adolescence, the same girls have experienced more than a decade of socialization and have often "adjusted" their aspirations to lesser goals.

Research has shown that, ultimately, the greatest challenge gifted girls will face is not achievement in school but rather achievement in life. Even after years of high performance in school and college, too many women either question their aspirations, yield to the social pressure to settle for lesser goals, or do not focus on themselves as important. To understand the process by which they fail to realize their unique abilities, we have to look at the problem from a life-span perspective. The social and emotional issues that gifted young women experience actually begin when they are in primary and middle school.[6]

It is therefore in the primary grades that teachers can inspire gifted girls to pursue their interests and apply their gifts and talents in situations that engage and motivate them. Without early recognition and support, giftedness in girls is often simply lost. Research clearly shows that by the time they reach high school gifted girls expect less of themselves than gifted boys do—and others expect less of them.

---

[6] Many of the study results discussed in this section are cited in *Smart Girls in the 21st Century: Understanding Talented Girls and Women* by Barbara Kerr and Robyn McKay (Tucson, AZ: Great Potential Press, 2014).

WAYS TO INSPIRE YOUNG GIFTED GIRLS

The good news is that you, as a teacher, can be enormously effective in reversing negative stereotypes and expanding the horizons of gifted girls in the earliest years of schooling. The key to maintaining hope and confidence for gifted girls is nurturing their belief that they can act effectively and make decisions independently. The period of preschool through kindergarten is critical in inspiring gifted girls. Here are several strategies for you to consider:

- Seek to identify gifted girls at a young age, to give them early opportunities to experience their exceptional abilities.
- Use portfolios and observations to assess children's abilities so you know what you are dealing with. School readiness tests alone often don't allow very bright children to demonstrate the extent of their abilities.
- Find peers with similar abilities and interests, so gifted girls will feel safe to progress.
- Give young girls specific, positive feedback about their abilities—especially in math and science.
- Support young girls' effort and persistence in pursuing their passions and goals, despite difficulties encountered.
- Help young girls see mistakes and failures as creative learning experiences.
- Demonstrate considerate, effective, assertive ways for girls to express themselves.
- Reward assertiveness.
- Integrate, rather than separate, girls and boys, but also permit gifted girls to work together at a more advanced level.
- Monitor and compare your classroom interactions with girls and with boys. Make it a point to call on girls as often as you call on boys, to give girls informative responses, and to resist "overhelping" girls by giving them answers.
- Stress goal setting and problem solving at a very young age. Make sure to encourage every girl to think for herself and grow in self-confidence.
- Reward exploration. Girls need external feedback. Recognize them with a nod, a smile, or a word when they explore as well as when they excel.
- Let a gifted girl know that you value her uniqueness. For example, you might tell a girl, privately, "You were the only one to think of that!"
- Encourage gifted girls to learn to struggle and persist.

- Provide role models through books, speakers, and films.
- Be alert to signs of boredom: poor class participation, daydreaming, or sadness. Discrepancies between ability and performance are signs of underachievement.
- If a four- or five-year-old girl shows particularly high intelligence, recommend testing for early admission to kindergarten or for special preschool gifted programs.
- Be aware of gender-role stereotyping in toys, games, computer programs, books, and other learning materials.
- Include biographies and images of great women leaders in the curriculum, providing opportunities for girls to explore their unique accomplishments in a variety of fields.
- Caution parents about areas where they may unwittingly see their boys as more able than their girls and their girls as more competent in social skills. Explain how these expectations can be a detriment to their daughters' growth.
- Stress to parents that all children run, climb, and spill things in school. Suggest that they send their daughters to school in clothes that are suitable for these activities.
- Be aware that some parents hinder their daughters with lower expectations. Due to lack of information, they don't see their daughters as gifted and may not recommend them for gifted programs.

Gifted Boys

Gifted boys also struggle with issues related to gender. The American ideal of masculinity begins its work on boys early—through family expectations, peer relationships, and the media. Gifted boys particularly struggle because they do not always adhere to the standard of what a "real boy" should be or do. These are common challenges:

- Sensitive boys may be vulnerable to bullying or social pressures from family or peers who expect them to be tough.
- Gifted boys may seem out of control and unready for gifted programs because their energy and enthusiasm know no bounds and present a greater challenge for teachers.
- In a context where they are significantly ahead of the class, gifted boys may interrupt, grab things from other children, or challenge authority.

- Those who are not athletic are often ridiculed for poor performance or nonparticipation.
- Artistically inclined boys can be ostracized by peers who see the arts as a "girls' thing."
- Unassertive boys who avoid conflict can be harassed by family members and peers who want them to "stick up for themselves" or "be a leader."

Gifted boys face additional problems during the primary grades. It is well known that girls have greater verbal development and social maturity in the early grades than boys. Even when giftedness is factored in, boys may not appear suitable for gifted programs because their social and emotional development has not kept pace with their intellectual abilities. A greater focus today on literacy and testing could skew assessment in favor of gifted girls over boys who at this early stage tend to have greater strengths in spatial and mathematical thinking through hands-on projects. Many gifted girls at the primary level are more able to study either on their own or in a small group, at least for some of the time, while gifted boys prefer to play and often need more active engagement.

The behavior of young gifted boys can work against their getting into gifted programs or schools. In kindergarten and first grade, for example, some struggle to keep still for short periods of time. Others find it hard to take turns, share, or work together even in a class of other gifted children.

WAYS TO INSPIRE YOUNG GIFTED BOYS

- Provide many hands-on activities that keep their hands and minds engaged.
- Try to place gifted boys with others like them, or with boys who have their interests and enthusiasm.
- Explore ways to provide new challenges to boys who are distracting the class and seem disengaged; talk to them about their interests and experiment with alternative activities that show their strengths.
- Focus on areas where many gifted boys excel—for example, spatial thinking, designing, and constructing.
- Find a classroom assistant familiar with these boys who can support them in finding new topics, products, or interests.
- Communicate with parents to discover their boys' interests and talents, and try to integrate some of these into the curriculum.

- Be an advocate for gifted boys and help teachers, administrators, and parents understand that their social-emotional development is out of sync with their giftedness and they are not necessarily "misbehaving."
- Experiment with ways to set reasonable boundaries for gifted boys while also providing support for them to explore their gifts.
- Assist the shy or withdrawn gifted boys by giving them special assignments for the class (for example, doing research in support of a science experiment, or writing scripts, podcasts, and stories on topics the class is studying).

Twice-Exceptional: Gifted Children with Learning Differences

Some young children have two seemingly contradictory sets of needs: They are gifted *and* have a learning disability.[7] These double-labeled children are often at greater risk of not receiving assistance because their learning difficulty masks their giftedness or their giftedness masks their learning difficulty. Some of these twice-exceptional children can appear to be average students and thus miss services they need. Clinical diagnosis is necessary to detect dual exceptionalities and discrepancies in abilities, such as visual or spatial strengths, auditory processing deficiencies, or problems with executive function and attention.

Often, *deficiencies* in gifted students with learning difficulties are more apparent to teachers than their *abilities*. The pressure to ensure that all children reach minimum proficiency in all content areas by the end of the year certainly plays a role here. Yet teachers can address deficiencies in skill and knowledge while still encouraging talents to blossom. Children need *both* strategies to develop confidence and pride. We recommend that you begin with their strengths (experience, talents, and character)—the foundation of their self-confidence, motivation, and growth.

Teachers need to be especially aware of the risk of mistaking children who have learning differences with those who are underachievers, because

their characteristics can be identical. Similarly, the behaviors often associated with ADHD, can also appear in gifted or creative children who feel frustrated by a restrictive school or home environment. Some may have ADHD and be creative and gifted, but in order for them to realize their potential, they need a teacher who sees their strengths and actively addresses them while they also learn tools to cope with their learning difficulty. Caution is the best approach, since a number of factors could be at work in a twice-exceptional student's school difficulties. If a student seems particularly frustrated with, challenged by, or uninterested in a task, or if you observe unusual discrepancies among particular ability function levels, you will want to consider a referral to your school's special education office for further investigation.

Gifted children with autism spectrum disorders (ASD) can present some difficult, though not unsolvable challenges for teachers. With sensitive support, they can make unique contributions to the world. These students have many of the distinguishing characteristics of other gifted learners, but also some marked challenges. They typically lack the social skills of peers; they need more structure in the classroom and sometimes struggle understanding directions; they require extra support in the area of executive function and academic skills. Many also struggle with language and communication. A child with Asperger's syndrome can flourish and grow in a classroom where her teacher helps her develop her talents while also addressing her problem areas. Often gifted children with Asperger's can amass a tremendous amount of information on a topic that interests them, but have trouble seeing the "big picture." These children can indeed be creative if allowed to do so in a way that's best for them— through focusing on the many parts and details of a thing and reassembling it into a new product. Lacking the assumptions others bring to an assignment enables them to see it differently.

A committed teacher is a keen observer and can detect the behaviors of a uniquely challenged gifted child: one such behavior may be the struggle to conform to learning styles that don't work for him, or it may be a limitation—for instance, in a child's auditory processing—that remains undetected and prevents him from discovering his abilities. Young gifted learners with auditory processing disorders can appear slow in class. Their hearing problem may prevent them from putting sounds and letters

---

[7] Many schools and publications now use the terms *learning differences* or *learning difficulties* instead of *learning disabilities*. The words *disabled* and *disabilities* have negative connotations that can get in the way of students', teachers', and parents' ability to understand and remediate children's learning challenges.

together for longer than usual. If you see a young child asking others to repeat themselves over and over, turning to another child to ask for clarification, reading lips, or struggling to follow verbal directions, you can be the one to direct that child toward his gifts and offer help in getting treatment for his deficit. Knowing and documenting not just signs of trouble but a student's strengths enables the teacher to provide a more accurate picture of a learner who might otherwise be mislabeled. Without the right kind of intervention, the future of these promising children appears uncertain at best. Scenarios such as the following are not uncommon.

Yuri clearly demonstrates high ability in kindergarten through first grade. By the end of second grade, though, something seems off. He struggles to follow through on assigned work, in part because he does not understand what the teacher wants. This makes third grade even more difficult and he starts acting out in class. Meanwhile, at home, Yuri's knowledge of science abounds and he has also started learning about art on YouTube. The adults in his life don't intervene because he is doing well enough in school and he is young. His loss is that the learning difficulty, whatever it is, creates frustration and limits his talents.

Rosalie shows rare ability in activities that include visual or performing arts. But in academics, she has a host of problems that interfere with her learning. She struggles in language arts and appears incapable of following directions, paying attention, and participating in group work. Rosalie's thoughts jump from topic to topic, and she performs poorly on tests. She becomes an immediate candidate for special education services. Her loss is that from her earliest years of school, she will receive a message of lack—of what she cannot do or be.

Francisco exhibits serious deficits in social development, but, like other gifted students, striking talent in a number of subjects. His knowledge of the entire city transit system is nothing short of phenomenal. He can tell anyone who wants to know what train or bus to take to reach a destination and the times when they leave. He recently conducted research on Wallace's flying frog, amassing vast amounts of information on its habits, habitat, and so forth. While Francisco surpasses other students, even gifted students, in collecting and memorizing facts, he has trouble connecting what he has learned to other things or seeing the big picture. Imagining scenarios is difficult. He can't,

for example, think about what might happen to this species if the habitat became compromised because it isn't compromised at present.

Gifted children with physical disabilities can encounter a paradox, too: They are viewed as both inadequate (because of their disability) and competent (because of their giftedness). Teachers need to be aware of this tendency to expect less of students with disabilities and should do all they can to make them feel included and accepted in the classroom. Consulting with parents enables teachers to understand the nature of certain disabilities more fully and to hear stories about the experiences, interests, and talents these children have. Therefore, while we work to understand and accommodate a disability, a student's passion, talent, and competence must be our critical focus.

Highly Gifted Children

We pay great attention to increments of intelligence for children of below-average ability, and we adjust our expectations and programs to match their needs. However, we seem to consolidate highly intelligent children into a single group of "bright" or "gifted" students. If we recognize that some children have IQs in the extremely low range of 25, 40, and 55, we also need to help those who are just as unusual on the higher end. In fact, there's more variation in intelligence among highly gifted students than there is among those who are average or moderately gifted.

Highly gifted children seem to have minds like satellite dishes. These students are extra perceptive about people, issues, and ideas. They can be conscious of many things at once, make connections that are both unique and logical, and integrate and analyze relationships. Because exceedingly gifted children see many layers of meaning for any situation or idea, their responses in the classroom can differ markedly from the teacher's concept of the topic.

Complex thinking can also lead these children to be extremely precise and to require precision from others. For example, to a child who fully knows the difference between a species and a variety, it matters very much which term you use. Highly gifted children can feel outraged if they aren't taken seriously. You might find yourself drawn into arguments over things that seem insignificant to you but are highly significant to your exceptional student.

TRAITS OF HIGHLY GIFTED CHILDREN

Keeping up with highly gifted students can be a tremendous challenge. In order to meet this challenge, it helps to understand some of the characteristics and abilities these students often exhibit:

A voracious appetite for intellectual stimulation and learning. Many highly gifted children learn in leaps. For example, a student may learn all the moves of chess in one game. A child may grasp an entire concept quickly; once the underlying pattern is mastered, it can be almost impossible for her to break it down into steps. Drill and practice can feel like torture to this child, whose natural tendency is to crave novelty and reject repetition and redundancy. If you have explained division and the child understands it, she will find it useless and even painful to be required to "show her work" repeatedly. A child with this level of ability might balk at homework that offers no novel learning value, or refuse to do more than one problem on a worksheet.

Multiple focusing. To meet his "minimal daily requirement" of intellectual stimulation, a highly gifted child may need to find ways to concurrently supplement the regular classroom "dosage"— perhaps by reading a book while you're explaining a concept, or by expanding a math computation while you're still teaching it.

Insatiable curiosity. The highly gifted child is characterized by intense curiosity, often asking questions such as: Why are some batteries rechargeable? How does sound come out from the iPad? How big is the universe?

Exceptional memory. Many extremely gifted children can pinpoint minute details and include them in elaborate explanations. What the child remembers, you may forget. In fact, you may need to explain what "forget" means and how "forgetting" happens. Otherwise the child might think that you're lying or pretending not to know and become angry!

Immersion. Astronomy is a favorite fascination for highly gifted kids; it's a subject that opens up infinite uses of math and physics. Other children are ravenous for information about geography, dinosaurs, or rocks. One child, for example, might be totally involved with the Olympics: She knows all the events, how they are judged, which countries and athletes are favored, and more. She's interested in the games' Greek origins, has moved from that to Greek letters (which she uses as codes), myths, and goddesses—and she wants to share it all. Highly gifted children often live with a series of passions, devouring all the experiments and information and people who are willing to listen about one subject and then, after they are satiated, moving on to rock-and-roll stars, steam trains, or fossils. These children may benefit from being allowed to integrate the class material into their current enchantment.

Empathy. Highly gifted students can be empathetic with just about anything or anyone. There are numerous reports of how these children can be intuitively perceptive. Many parents can't allow their very young highly gifted children to watch the news on TV because of the intensity with which children feel all the inhumanities they see. A gifted child may empathize with a tree being cut down and cry in sympathetic pain. He may worry that the letter he mails will be squashed and hurt in the mailbox or bag. In sports, a child might show something close to shame when his team wins and worry about how the other team feels. With an exceptionally gifted student, you may need to spend extra time dealing with perceived injustices. For example, you might arrange for a child to place her toy horses in a "corral" on the shelf rather than store them in a heap.

Vulnerability. Any potential adjustment for gifted children is amplified for the highly gifted child, who is often more vulnerable to social and emotional problems. Sources of this vulnerability include asynchronous development, alienation, lack of understanding, intense sensitivity, adult expectations, and inappropriate educational services. Children may experience social and intellectual rejection where none was intended. Their vivid imaginations often make it difficult for them to live up to their own expectations.

Social alienation. At school, many highly gifted four- or five-year-olds are seen as withdrawn, socially immature, or emotionally disturbed because they can't find mutual companions in their classroom. A highly gifted child may be chronologically age six, but mentally age ten. Such a child may not relate comfortably to classmates. Insisting that the student stay with her age-mates can exacerbate this alienation. Usually, older children can congenially interact with younger ones about subjects that are of mutual interest.

Poor handwriting. Some extremely bright children seem to have a writing disability. Expressing what they know with a pencil in their hand is a tedious, frustrating chore. As a response to this frustration, these children may reduce the elaborate descriptions in their minds to a few words on paper, thus avoiding a focus on minutiae when they want to move ahead with other ideas and projects. A child might think to himself, "The enormous glacier obstructed the fjord's passage." Yet, faced with the obstacle of a slow-moving pencil, he'll choose to write simply, "The big ice sticks out." Creative teachers can look for alternative ways for these children to demonstrate what they think and know—for example, by using a computer, speaking into a recorder, or creating visual depictions that they can explain orally.

Energy. Highly gifted children may be exceptionally active if they are intellectually "starving."

IDENTIFYING HIGHLY GIFTED CHILDREN

We find highly gifted young students by comparing how their development exceeds what's expected of average children. Often, these exceptional children's abilities to verbalize and imagine—to reason abstractly, to construct meaning, and to understand deeply—are years ahead of their chronological age.

In seeking to recognize extreme giftedness, let the child show you what she can do. Provide ever more complicated problems to solve. Listen to the parents and let them tell you about their child outside the confines of the classroom. Recommend IQ testing and look for the areas or subtests with the highest scores as well as the full scale and composite scores. You can suggest that the *Stanford-Binet Intelligence Scale (Form L-M)* be administered. Though replaced by the updated *Stanford-Binet Fourth Edition* and other useful instruments, the earlier *L-M* raises the ceiling for students with exceptionally high scores. It's the only standardized IQ test we have to measure young children's intelligence in the highest ranges.

WHAT NEXT?

Although only about one in several hundred children might be considered highly gifted, these children, like all children, need appropriate learning experiences. Most of these unique students require an individually differentiated school program to accommodate qualities that are rare for their age peers. Expecting an extremely gifted student to conform to a regular classroom routine is as inappropriate as

placing a moderately gifted child in a special education class for slow learners and asking him to slow down his learning to keep pace with the class. We must allow exceptionally gifted children to excel.

Much literature has demonstrated the possible problems that may ensue from requiring highly gifted students to endure instruction at a level significantly below their ability. These problems include poor study habits, apathy, lack of motivation, and maladjustment. Even in the best situations, children may retreat into their internal world of imagination, or devise some external means of intellectual stimulation and challenge. Consequently, they may be mislabeled as students who can't focus or pay attention. To eliminate potential problems, we need to provide highly gifted children academic challenges that are commensurate with their intellectual ability and academic achievement level.

Usually, there's no accommodation in our schools for highly gifted children. That place needs to be created. When using the ideas presented in this book, you might need to go further and make unprecedented, radical adaptations. For example, it may be worthwhile to place a highly gifted child in a higher grade for a particular subject, such as math, so she can have the support of substantive interaction with intellectual peers. As the child's regular teacher, you might find that this eases your curriculum planning as well. Monitor the situation and expect to make continual adjustments.

Associate with other professionals and families who have experience with highly gifted children and acceleration.[8] One excellent resource is the Hollingworth Center for Highly Gifted Children (www.hollingworth.org). This center publishes a newsletter and offers valuable information about networking, conferences, services, and other organizations of interest to adults working with exceptionally gifted young children.

PRODIGIES

Prodigies need to be mentioned separately, if only to balance what the popular media often presents as "gifted children." Prodigies have a distinct, extreme form of giftedness that is sometimes exploited on television and in other ways. While a gifted child usually has great general ability, a prodigy usually has a more focused, specialized, and dominant

---

[8] For a discussion of acceleration, see "Considering Early Entrance and Acceleration" beginning on page 167.

ability—as well as a powerful drive and confidence to develop it in a nurturing environment. Prodigies are often younger than age ten, yet they perform at the level of highly trained adults. Prodigies can excel in poetry, music, mathematics, chess, physics, gymnastics, or languages, to name a few areas. A child who is a prodigy may or may not have high academic abilities.

You'll need to be extremely flexible in working with a child prodigy. There's a precarious balance between what's appropriately responsible to the development of talent and what's confining or exploitative. Because prodigies sometimes need to leave class for performances or practices, you can cooperate with their unusual requirements by allowing some "give" in certain school demands. In some instances, you may want to excuse the young prodigy from supplemental work on certain subjects or projects and instead allow time for the intense focus required to develop special talents.

Children with High Energy

High energy often accompanies high intelligence. Highly intelligent children may seem to be always busy, distractible, and hungry for activity. In young gifted children, we may hear rapid, excessive, almost compulsive speech accompanied by animated gesturing with the entire body.

Teachers need to integrate gifted children's often intense, highly active physical needs. This is of special concern when a child's intellectual peers are older and more physically developed. In these situations, brighter children may feel physically inadequate and avoid playground games that demonstrate their relatively inferior psychomotor development.

Often, preschool and other early childhood experiences focus on "socializing" beginning students. Circle time can become excruciatingly constricting to small children with the urge to move. Sometimes, with gifted students who have a great deal of energy, circle-time compliance becomes an educational goal. Yet, paradoxically, being encouraged to move about—as long as others are not disrupted—can facilitate learning for active, gifted children.

In our classrooms, we can provide opportunities for appropriate release of high energy. One way to do this is by adapting our behavior expectations in order to harness children's energy in constructive ways. For example:

- We can allow children to read while standing up.
- We can let children quietly manipulate a plaything to release energy while they are listening in a group.
- We can arrange for active preschoolers to have alternatives to naps. In one school we know of, a gifted program for three-, four-, and five-year-old children is scheduled during rest time, with learning station activities that offer many possibilities for children to use physical energy.
- We can teach children relaxation techniques (taking a deep breath, counting to ten, visualizing a peaceful place) that can help them gain self-control.

There's a long social history of expecting boys to be active and girls to be compliant. It's damaging to expect that girls should be more sedate than boys.

As mentioned before, young gifted children are sometimes misdiagnosed as having attention deficit hyperactivity disorder (ADHD). Gifted education consultant Sharon Lind has developed a useful perspective on highly active children.[9] She suggests that, before referring a child for ADHD placement, teachers should gain more information about the child.

Lind's exploratory approach might reward you with more cooperation. She suggests that you look for ways to modify the environment in order to more appropriately meet the learning styles and abilities of the child. This student might need a curriculum that is on a level more commensurate with her abilities. To feel accepted, she may need to be placed with intellectual peers. It may be helpful to simply ask her to explain to you why she needs to move about or doesn't complete the work you assign. You can monitor her behavior and try to determine what activity precedes a bout of disruptiveness. And because gifted children are often capable of multiple focusing, you might observe the student to see if she's capable of following instructions even if she appears not to be listening. Ask yourself, too, if disruptions could be attention-getting devices. If this seems to be the case, make an effort to give the child more attention for positive behavior.

---

[9] Sharon Lind. "Overexcitability and the Gifted." *Supporting the Social and Emotional Needs of the Gifted: 30 Essays on Giftedness, 30 Years of SENG* (Poughquag, NY: SENG, 2012): 31–42.

Questions and Answers

"Some of the children in my class are very different from the students I usually teach. There's so much I don't know about these children! How can I tell if I'm really bringing out the best in a child?"

At times it's almost impossible to know what's really best for a child. This is especially true when working with diverse populations. With so many variations in culture, language, environment, ability level, learning style, and so on, teachers can feel overwhelmed by the prospect of trying to reach these students. It is a tall order and one that requires the joint effort of teachers, parents, and school personnel. As teachers, we are in an ideal position to notice, to bear witness—and to explore the talents and abilities, as well as struggles, of our students. With the insights we've gained, we can try to accommodate different needs and remain open to reevaluating and adjusting our programs. We can continue to learn more about our students and how we can cultivate their enthusiasm for learning. As always, our best guides are the children and what their words, actions, and responses tell us.

"Doing more for gifted kids seems hard enough but I do what I can. Reaching underrepresented populations seems beyond anyone's capacity. Our district has few resources and little interest in gifted education right now. Administrators and teachers are scrambling to raise the competency level for all our kids. What options do I have?"

With funding removed from gifted programs around the United States and high-stakes tests applying unprecedented pressure on schools and districts, many teachers feel cautious. They wonder if incorporating more creative work will put students at risk of being less prepared for a test. They hear stories about good teachers who turned at-risk students around but who lost their jobs because test scores did not immediately reflect the growth and change witnessed by all, including parents. This is a difficult climate in which to reach the students discussed in this chapter. However, helpers are often around if you look for them. Drawing on a pool of parent and community volunteers has worked for some teachers we have known. Other options might include working with like-minded colleagues on creative projects that meet the needs of different kinds of learners and inviting professionals from the community (studios, companies, shops, independent artists) to share what they do. Integrating into your curriculum the ideas, life experiences, and quality resources you can acquire from other people allows you to create an environment where gifted young students of all kinds can discover new interests and talents.

Conclusion

The vast majority of educators today are committed to becoming more aware of and sensitive to children's varying needs, characteristics, and abilities. As we continue to work with gifted children, we must keep in mind that no one suggestion can serve them all; no single idea is universally appropriate. As you encounter diverse populations in your own classroom, your best, most effective approach is to stay open, interested, and flexible. Help your students learn to do this, too. And always remember your goal: to give every child the opportunity to learn, grow, and develop his or her potential.

References and Resources

Chapter 1

Betts, George T., and Maureen Neihart. "Profiles of the Gifted and Talented." *Gifted Child Quarterly* 32, no. 2 (1988): 248–253. Six profiles of gifted children offer a close look at the feelings, behaviors, and needs of these children. Also included are cues for identifying and nurturing gifted children who fit each profile: *successful, divergent, underground, dropout, double-labeled,* and *autonomous*.

Clark, Barbara. *Growing Up Gifted: Developing the Potential of Children at Home and at School.* Upper Saddle River, NJ: Pearson, 2012. A classic text to familiarize educators with information and processes for understanding and teaching gifted children.

Colangelo, Nicholas, and Gary A. Davis. *Handbook of Gifted Education.* Upper Saddle River, NJ: Pearson, 2002. Broad array of information about giftedness including, definitions, theories of intelligence, creativity, curriculum, and diversity.

Colangelo, Nicholas, Susan G. Assouline, and Miraca U. M. Gross. *A Nation Deceived: How Schools Hold Back America's Brightest Students, Vols. 1 and 2.* Iowa City, IA: University of Iowa Press, 2004. An amazing resource that discusses acceleration as a programming option for gifted children. Details myths, reflections, and the research backing the positive and negative aspects of acceleration. The report can be downloaded for free at www.accelerationinstitute.org.

Davidson Institute for Talent Development. "Gifted Education Policies." Last updated December 23, 2014. www.davidsongifted.org/db/statepolicy.aspx. An interactive site that provides information on gifted education programs and policies state by state.

Davis, Gary A., Sylvia B. Rimm, and Del Siegle. *Education of the Gifted and Talented.* Upper Saddle River, NJ: Pearson, 2010. A textbook focusing on the history of gifted education, definitions, characteristics, and programming.

Gardner, Howard. "Are There Additional Intelligences? The Case for Naturalist, Spiritual, and Existential Intelligences." *Education, Information, and Transformation.* J. Kane, ed. Englewood Cliffs, NJ: Prentice-Hall, 1999. Gardner's paper explores the process of identifying an intelligence and examines evidence of three new intelligences not included in his landmark book, *Frames of Mind*.

———. *Frames of Mind: The Theory of Multiple Intelligence.* New York: Basic Books, 1993. A provocative exploration of intelligence that broadens our conceptions of giftedness.

———. *Intelligence Reframed: Multiple Intelligences for the 21st Century.* New York: Basic Books, 1999. Resource pulls on a variety of articles and research about multiple intelligences.

Kingore, Bertie. *Portfolios: Enriching and Assessing All Students, Identifying the Gifted, Grades K–6.* Des Moines, IA: Leadership Publishers, 1993. Elaborates on purposes, practices, and implementations in creating portfolios for young gifted children.

Lind, Sharon. "Are We Mislabeling Over-Excitable Children?" *Understanding Our Gifted* 5, no. 5A (1993): 1–10. An essential perspective to consider in identifying children who might not match the expected behavior profile. Lind offers many alternative ways to respond to a child's giftedness and to aberrant behaviors.

Marland, S. P. Jr. *Education of the Gifted and Talented: Report to the Congress of the United States by the U.S. Commissioner of Education.* Washington, DC: U.S. Government Printing Office, 1972. (Government Documents Y4.L 11/2: G36). The first national report on gifted education, the Marland report details one of the most widely known definitions of giftedness.

Meckstroth, Elizabeth A. "Guiding the Parents of Gifted Children: The Role of Counselors and Teachers." *Counseling Gifted and Talented Children: A Guide for Teachers, Counselors, and Parents.* Roberta M. Milgram, ed. Norwood, NJ: Ablex Publishing, 1991: 95–120. Specific information on teacher-parent conferences, involving parents in identifying gifted children, helping parents acknowledge and understand giftedness, and organizing and facilitating parent discussion groups.

National Association for Gifted Children. "Redefining Giftedness for a New Century: Shifting the Paradigm." March 2010. www.nagc.org. Position paper for NAGC approved in 2010. Includes an updated definition of giftedness.

The 1994 State of the States Gifted and Talented Education Report. Austin, TX: Council of State Directors of Programs for the Gifted, 1994. A concise overview of state-by-state information and charts about support, funding, mandates, policies, practices, program populations, and more. Utilized to provide a snapshot of previous funding.

Olszewski-Kubilius, Paula, Lisa Limburg-Weber, and Steven Pfeiffer. *Early Gifts: Recognizing and Nurturing Children's Talents.* Waco, TX: Prufrock Press, 2003. Focuses specifically on identifying talent and what it may look like across various domains.

Renzulli, Joseph S. *The Enrichment Triad Model: A Guide for Developing Defensible Programs for the Gifted and Talented.* Mansfield Center, CT: Creative Learning Press, 1977. The initial work introducing the enrichment triad model and the three-ring conceptions of giftedness.

Renzulli, Joseph S., ed. *Systems and Models for Developing Programs for the Gifted and Talented.* Mansfield Center, CT: Creative Learning Press, 1986. Includes a variety of programming models of giftedness and includes chapters on the enrichment triad model.

Renzulli, Joseph S., and Sally M. Reis. *The Schoolwide Enrichment Model: A Comprehensive Plan for Educational Excellence.* Mansfield Center, CT: Creative Learning Press, 1985. Focuses on the use of schoolwide enrichment within the three-ring conception of giftedness.

Richert, E. Susanne. "Excellence with Justice in Identification and Programming." *Handbook of Gifted Education.* Nicholas Colangelo and Gary A. Davis, eds. Upper Saddle River, NJ: Pearson, 2002: 146–158. Focuses on various issues with identification and sound ideas for programs and identification practices in your school. Richert's article is one of many reasons to have the *Handbook of Gifted Education*—an extensive collection of the writings of many respected experts in the field of gifted education—on your reference shelf.

Silverman, Linda Kreger. *Giftedness 101.* New York: Springer Publishing, 2013. Provides in-depth information on the history of giftedness and a variety of definitions. Includes detailed information about formal intelligence testing.

———. "The Gifted Individual." *Counseling the Gifted and Talented.* Linda Kreger Silverman, ed. Denver, CO: Love Publishing, 1993: 3–28. One of many sensitively written chapters depicting the intricate, complex characteristics and needs of gifted children.

Smutny, Joan Franklin, Kathleen Veenker, and Stephen Veenker. *Your Gifted Child: How to Recognize and Develop the Special Talents in Your Child from Birth to Age Seven.* New York: Ballantine Books, 1989. Comprehensive explanations help parents and educators understand the characteristics and needs of young gifted children.

Sternberg, Robert J. *Beyond IQ: A Triarchic Theory of Human Intelligence.* New York: Cambridge University Press, 1985. Information for understanding and appreciating intelligence as demonstrated through intelligent behavior.

Sternberg, Robert J., and Janet E. Davidson, eds. *Conceptions of Giftedness.* New York: Cambridge University Press, 2005. Implicit and explicit theoretical approaches within a variety of domains are discussed. Chapters include the triarchic theory, three-ring conception, and Tannenbaum's psychosocial model.

Tannenbaum, Abraham. "Giftedness: A Psychosocial Approach." *Conceptions of Giftedness.* Robert J. Sternberg and Janet E. Davidson, eds. New York: Cambridge University Press, 1986. Tannenbaum details his theoretical psychosocial model.

Webb, James T., Elizabeth A. Meckstroth, and Stephanie S. Tolan. *Guiding the Gifted Child: A Practical Source for Parents and Teachers.* Scottsdale, AZ: Great Potential Press, 1981. Based on information from guided parent discussion groups, this book speaks from people's personal experiences of living with and learning from gifted children. It describes qualities of gifted children in a manner that helps readers become familiar with the ways they can help children develop their best "selves." Includes chapters on motivation, discipline, peer and sibling relations, stress management, and depression. Winner of the American Psychological Association's Best Book Award.

Chapter 2

Armstrong, Thomas. *Multiple Intelligences in the Classroom.* Alexandria, VA: ASCD, 2009. Information on exploring your own intelligences and suggestions for bringing Gardner's theory of multiple intelligences into your classroom.

Carbo, Marie, Rita Dunn, and Kenneth Dunn. *Teaching Students to Read Through Their Individual Learning Styles.* Needham Heights, MA: Allyn & Bacon, 1991. A book to help teachers and parents reduce reading failure through early diagnosis of individual characteristics and by matching methods and materials to individual styles and strengths.

Diamond, Marian, and Janet Hopson. *Magic Trees of the Mind: How to Nurture Your Child's Intelligence, Creativity, and Healthy Emotions from Birth through Adolescence.* New York: Penguin Putnam: 1998. Based on the authors' research and interviews with other brain and behavioral scientists.

Galbraith, Judy. *The Survival Guide for Gifted Kids: For Ages 10 & Under.* Minneapolis: Free Spirit Publishing, 2013. Helps young gifted children understand and cope with the stresses, benefits, and demands of being gifted.

Jensen, Eric. *Brain-Compatible Strategies.* Thousand Oaks, CA: Corwin Press, 2004. Filled with easy-to-use, brain-compatible activities that aid learning.

———. *Teaching with the Brain in Mind.* Alexandria, VA: ASCD, 2005. A comprehensive book about the brain that applies research to classroom teaching.

Pashler, Harold, M. McDaniel, D. Rohrer, and R. Bjork. "Learning Styles: Concepts and Evidence." *Psychological Science in the Public Interest* 9, no. 3 (2008): 103–119. A look at the practices used to determine a student's particular learning style and their effectiveness.

Pentominoes. Games and activities using geometric shapes that support logical thinking and problem solving and explore area, perimeter, symmetry, and congruence. Available for purchase from www.eaieducation.com.

Willis, Judy. *How Your Child Learns Best: Brain-Friendly Strategies You Can Use to Ignite Your Child's Learning and Increase School Success.* Nappersville, IL: Sourcebooks, 2009. Helpful brain compatible strategies are provided for home and school use.

———. *Research Based Strategies to Ignite Student Learning: Insights from a Neurologist and Classroom Teacher.* Alexandria, VA: ASCD, 2006. Learn about the benefits of teaching elementary students how their brains work.

———. *Teaching the Brain to Read: Strategies for Improving Fluency, Vocabulary, and Comprehension.* Alexandria, VA: ASCD, 2009. Provides brain friendly strategies that help with reading.

Winebrenner, Susan, and Dina Brulles. *Teaching Gifted Kids in Today's Classroom: Strategies and Techniques Every Teacher Can Use.* Minneapolis: Free Spirit Publishing, 2012. Teachers learn what to do with the child who already knows what you are going to teach. Specific strategies with step-by-step instructions and reproducible forms are presented.

Winebrenner, Susan, and Lisa M. Kiss. *Teaching Kids with Learning Difficulties in Today's Classroom: How Every Teacher Can Help Struggling Students Succeed.* Minneapolis: Free Spirit Publishing, 2014. Strategies and techniques every teacher can use to motivate struggling students, including those who are gifted.

Chapter 3

ABCya! (www.abcya.com). Search "grade 1 educational games and apps" for a huge list of computer games and activities specifically for children in first grade.

Burns, Monica. "14 Virtual Tools for the Math Classroom." Edutopia. Updated March 2, 2015. www.edutopia.org/blog/11-virtual-tools-math-classroom-monica-burns. This page compiles virtual tools and iPad apps that can be used during math lessons.

DS Examiner. "The Ultimate STEM Guide for Kids: 239 Cool Sites About Science, Technology, Engineering, and Math." Master's in Data Science. Published July 14, 2014. www.mastersindatascience.org/blog/the-ultimate-stem-guide-for-kids-239-cool-sites-about-science-technology-engineering-and-math. An extensive list from Master's in Data Science of STEM sources for educators and students.

Education.com (www.education.com). Search "first grade math games" for online, interactive math games for first graders.

Hands On: Pentominoes. Palo Alto, CA: Creative Publications, 1986. Full of ideas for using Pentominoes (shapes made with different configurations of five squares) that focus on problem-solving skills, logical thinking, testing of hypotheses, identifying alternative solutions, and recording data.

Heacox, Diane. *Making Differentiation a Habit: How to Ensure Success in Academically Diverse Classrooms.* Minneapolis: Free Spirit Publishing, 2009. A book embedded with good, useable teaching strategies.

Kaplan, Susan. "The ABC's of Curriculum for Gifted Five-Year-Olds: Alphabet, Blocks, and Chess?" *Journal for the Illinois Council of the Gifted* 11 (1992): 43–44. Enthusiastically discusses several major components of curricula for the gifted child in terms of the child's and the teacher's creativity and preferred approach.

Kingore, Bertie. *Differentiation: Simplified, Realistic, and Effective: How to Challenge Advanced Potentials in Mixed-Ability Classrooms.* Austin, TX: Professional Associates Publishing, 2004. Differentiation is made practical, and easy to read, understand, and implement.

———. *Reaching All Learners: Making Differentiation Work.* Austin, TX: Professional Associates Publishing, 2007. Provides specific examples and simplified procedures for differentiating instruction.

———. *Rigor and Engagement for Growing Minds: Strategies that Enable High-Ability Learners to Flourish in All Classrooms.* Austin, TX: Professional Associates Publishing, 2014. A practical book that is full of ideas to engage and challenge learners.

Pappas, Christopher. "15 Free Must-Have iPad Apps for Elementary Students." eLearning Industry. Published September 29, 2013. www.elearningindustry.com. This page lists iPad apps helpful for elementary school students to practice and learn everything covered in school.

PBS Kids. "Elementary STEM Resource Roundup." Iowa Public Television. site.iptv.org/education/story/894/pbs-kids-elementary-stem-resource-roundup. A list of STEM-related and inspired television programs and websites with online learning games for elementary students.

Reis, Sally M., Deborah K. Burns, and Joseph S. Renzulli. *Curriculum Compacting: The Complete Guide to Modifying the Regular Curriculum for High-Ability Students.* Mansfield Center, CT: Creative Learning Press, 1992. Designed to help teachers "compact" or streamline the curriculum through a practical, step-by-step approach. Includes suggestions for pretesting, preparing optional assignments, and record-keeping.

———. "Curriculum Compacting: A Process for Modifying Curriculum for High Ability Students." Storrs, CT: The National Research Center on the Gifted and Talented, 1992. A one-hour training tape and accompanying facilitator and teacher guides.

Renzulli, Joseph S., and Sally M. Reis. *The Schoolwide Enrichment Model: A Comprehensive Plan for Educational Excellence.* Mansfield Center, CT: Creative Learning Press, 1985. Focuses on the use of schoolwide enrichment within the three-ring conception of giftedness.

Robinson, Ann, Bruce Shore, and Donna Ennerson. *Best Practices in Gifted Education: An Evidence-Based Guide.* Waco, TX: Prufrock Press, 2007. Concise, research-based advice for educators and parents.

Samara, John, and Jim Curry, eds. *Developing Units for Primary Students: A Guide to Developing Effective Topical, Integrated, and Thematic Units of Study for Primary-Level Students with Sixteen Teacher-Generated Sample Units.* Bowling Green, KY: KAGE Publications, 1994. This book's subtitle says it all.

Smutny, Joan Franklin, Sally Y. Walker, and Elizabeth A. Meckstroth. *Acceleration for Gifted Learners, K–5.* Thousand Oaks, CA: Corwin Press, 2007. Dispels common myths about acceleration, considers social-emotional factors, and provides tools for determining the most appropriate learning options for gifted students.

Viorst, Judith. *Alexander and the Terrible, Horrible, No Good, Very Bad Day.* New York: Aladdin Paperbacks, 1987. Students will empathize with Alexander and the anger he feels on a day in which everything goes wrong. A modern classic.

Chapter 4

Arnosky, Jim. *Crinkleroot's Guide to Giving Back to Nature.* New York: G.P. Putnam's Sons Books for Young Readers, 2012. A marvelous main character "born in a tree and raised by bees" takes young children on a journey to their own backyards and shows them what they can discover there. Includes ideas on the things kids can do in their immediate environment to help the natural world.

Barth, Edna. *Turkeys, Pilgrims, and Indian Corn: The Story of the Thanksgiving Symbols.* New York: Clarion Books, 1975. A thorough treatment of all the legends and symbols of the American harvest celebration, this book is a good reference for studying the early colonial experience and how the first Thanksgiving evolved.

Baylor, Byrd, and Peter Parnall. An award-winning author-artist team has created a series of books about nature in the southwest and its connection to people. Teachers and parents of young children will treasure the simple, elegant prose and breathtaking illustrations. Following are five recommended titles:

- *Everybody Needs a Rock.* New York: Aladdin Paperbacks, 1985. How you go about discovering just the right rock for you is something a young girl explores in this wonderful tale.

- *I'm in Charge of Celebrations.* New York: Aladdin Paperbacks, 1995. Set in the desert, this is the story of a young girl who creates her own celebrations, based on the unique moments and experiences of her daily life in nature.

- *The Desert Is Theirs.* New York: Aladdin Paperbacks, 1975. Who would want to live in the desert? A discovery of the people, animals, and plants living there.

- *The Other Way to Listen.* New York: Aladdin Paperbacks, 1997. An old man shares his wisdom with a young boy who wants to know how the old man can hear things in nature that no one else does.

- *The Way to Start a Day.* New York: Aladdin Paperbacks, 1986. An exploration of people around the world and how they welcome the new day.

BigOrrin (www.bigorrin.org). Young students learning about American Indian nations, past and present, can research the Wampanoag people on this website. Information includes questions young children commonly ask; sections on culture, language, and pictures; as well as links applicable to different ages.

Bowden, Marcia. *Nature for the Very Young: A Handbook of Indoor and Outdoor Activities.* New York: John Wiley & Sons, 1989. A lively collection of activities uses nature exploration as a catalyst to educate and delight young children. Designed for home or school.

Brady, Esther Wood. *Toliver's Secret.* New York: Yearling, 1976. An outstanding classic work of historical fiction that takes place in New York at the time of the American Revolution. Gifted readers will enjoy the tale of suspense and the bravery of a girl hero who outsmarts the British.

Bruchac, Joseph. *Between Earth and Sky: Legends of Native American Sacred Places.* New York: Harcourt Brace & Co., 1996. Bruchac draws on his Abenaki heritage to relay an enchanting lesson between uncle and nephew, emphasizing respect for and protection of our world.

Burningham, John. *Hey! Get Off Our Train.* Dragonfly Books, 1990. This book received a Parents' Choice Award for illustration in 1990. It describes the journey of a young boy who climbs aboard a toy train to go on a trip around the world where he encounters, one by one, endangered animals who want to climb on to escape destruction. A charming, surprising ending!

Capstone Publishers. You Choose: History Series. 31 vols. Mankato, MN: Capstone Press. The thirty-one books in this series cover topics ranging from the dust bowl and westward expansion to the Underground Railroad to the world wars. Each book is structured as a "choose your own adventure" with multiple story paths, dozens of choices, and over ten possible endings. They are geared to a 3 to 4 reading level, but are likely to interest students up through middle school.

Cech, Maureen. *Globalchild: Multicultural Resources for Young Children.* New York: Addison-Wesley Publishing Co., 1991. Using a seasonal format (harvest, new year, spring), this title introduces a wide range of cultural traditions in music, art, games, food, and other areas to emphasize the commonalties all people share.

Cheney, Lynne. *When Washington Crossed the Delaware: A Wintertime Story for Young Patriots.* New York: Simon & Schuster Books for Young Readers, 2004. A beautifully illustrated story about that fateful Christmas night of 1776 after Washington's troops had faced months of defeat. Washington made what ended up being a brilliant decision to stage a surprise attack, but first he and his troops had to get across the frigid Delaware River. This makes a great read-aloud for students studying the American Revolution.

Climo, Shirley. *The Egyptian Cinderella.* New York: Harper Trophy, 1992. Beautifully told and illustrated, this is the story of Cinderella, re-created and set in the world of ancient Egypt.

Craig, Janet. *Wonders of the Rain Forest.* Mahwah, NJ: Troll Communications, 1990. A very helpful introduction to the intricate ecological system of the rain forest. Well written and vividly illustrated.

Cunningham, Kevin, and Peter Benoit. *The Wampanoag.* New York: Scholastic, 2011. An excellent source for young readers about the Wampanoag. It integrates well into the study of the Native Americans who interacted with the Pilgrims and the preservation of their language and culture.

Deutsch, Stacia, and Rhody Cohon. Blast to the Past Series. 8 vols. New York: Aladdin Paperbacks. An engaging historical fiction series that appeals to early to middle elementary readers. Topics include: Betsy Ross, Abraham Lincoln, Walt Disney, Sacagawea, Alexander Graham Bell, Ben Franklin, Martin Luther King Jr., and George Washington.

EDSITEment (www.edsitement.neh.gov). This website, sponsored by the National Endowment for the Humanities, connects visitors to many sites and lesson plans for social studies, language arts, foreign languages, art, and culture—all standards-aligned and providing cross-curriculum connections.

ePals (www.epals.com). Teachers and classrooms in more than 200 countries can collaborate on projects and share information, resources, and ideas. Teachers create profiles, outlining their projects, the country, and age levels. Site administrators ensure that ePals is school safe. All teachers should explore this site.

Field, Nancy, and Corliss Karasov. *Discovering Wolves: A Nature Activity Book.* Middleton, WI: Dog-Eared Publications, 1991. An adventurous journey into the world of wolves and an outstanding contribution to environmental awareness for young children. Offers eighteen fun, thought-provoking activities that encourage critical thinking on the subject of the wolf. Produced in cooperation with the Timber Wolf Alliance.

Fogliano, Julie. *If You Want to See a Whale.* New York: Roaring Brook Press, 2013. A little boy and his basset hound long to see a whale. Extraordinary voyage of the imagination, transporting the child to a place where the humpback, in all its magnificence, finally emerges. Excellent catalyst for a study or project on whales.

Fox, Mem. *Whoever You Are.* New York: First Voyager Books, 2001. An exploration of the world's diverse cultures, races, nationalities, ethnic groups, and languages, focusing on their differences and commonalities. Also available as an English-Spanish bilingual edition.

Fritz, Jean has won numerous awards for her humorous, story-based portrayals of various aspects of American History. Children will delight in the friendly, funny prose and inviting illustrations of the following titles:

- *And Then What Happened, Paul Revere?* New York: Puffin Books, 1996. An exciting read highlighting little-known facts about Paul Revere and his famous midnight ride.

- *Can't You Make Them Behave, King George?* New York: Puffin Books, 1996. A fascinating and accessible history for young readers detailing the life of King George III from childhood through the American Revolution.

- *George Washington's Breakfast.* New York: Puffin Books, 1998. A young boy, who shares a name with the first United States president, goes on a mission to learn about his namesake, including what the president ate for breakfast.

- *Shh! We're Writing the Constitution.* New York: Puffin Books, 1997. A chronicle of the summer of 1787, where delegates from the thirteen states secretly drew up the United States Constitution.

- *What's the Big Idea, Ben Franklin?* New York: Puffin Books, 2000. A book for young readers detailing the life of Benjamin Franklin.

- *Where Do You Think You're Going, Christopher Columbus?* New York: Puffin Books, 1997. A simple, short biography of the Spanish explorer who accidentally discovered the Americas.

- *Where Was Patrick Henry on the 29th of May?* New York: Puffin Books, 1997. A chronicle of the life of lawyer Patrick Henry and the events that led to his famous speech.

- *Who's Saying What in Jamestown, Thomas Savage?* New York: Puffin Books, 2010. A history of the life of the young interpreter and mediator between the Algonquin people and the colonists at Jamestown.

- *Who's That Stepping on Plymouth Rock?* New York: Puffin Books, 1998. A book explaining how Plymouth Rock went from being just a rock to a place of historical significance.

- *Why Don't You Get a Horse, Sam Adams?* New York: Puffin Books, 2000. An accessible biography of the rebel leader Samuel Adams.

- *Will You Sign Here, John Hancock?* New York: Puffin Books, 1997. A fun biography highlighting facts about the first signee of the Declaration of Independence.

Harness, Cheryl. *Three Young Pilgrims.* New York: Aladdin Paperbacks, 1995. Draws young readers into the everyday life of the Allerton family as they cope with the challenges of being among the first settlers at Plymouth. Includes Harness's vivid illustrations and many useful facts.

Hayes, Joe. *Watch Out for Clever Women!/¡Cuidado con las mujeres astutas!* El Paso, TX: Cinco Puntos Press, 1994. An entertaining collection of Latin folk tales in English and Spanish featuring amazingly clever women who repeatedly manage to save the day. Hayes is a recognized raconteur from the American Southwest.

Hoagies' Gifted Education (www.hoagiesgifted.org). One of the most extensive online resources for gifted students of all ages. The website includes reading lists that cover all subjects and topics.

Hoare, Ben. *DK Eyewitness Books: Endangered Animals.* New York: DK Publishing, 2010. Explores biodiversity, endangered species around the world, and the conditions that threaten their survival.

KinderART (www.kinderart.com). Offers many multicultural art projects for grades K–12. Students can explore projects that focus on the wide diversity throughout the world through masks, drums, and papier-mâché in places like Africa, Australia, China, Japan, Mexico, and North America.

Kindersley, Barnabas, and Anabel Kindersley. *Children Just Like Me: A Unique Celebration of Children Around the World.* New York: DK Publishing, 1995. Explores cultural commonalities and differences—as well as the unique challenges and advantages—of children from all over the world. Young students will enjoy the book's perspective of children speaking to other children.

Jenkins, Steve. *Almost Gone: The World's Rarest Species.* New York: HarperCollins, 2006. Through colored, cut-paper collage and text, students discover the unique lives of twenty-one endangered animals and the conditions that threaten their survival. A Caldecott Honor Book illustrator, Jenkins beautifully integrates image and text to engage young readers in the urgent subject of conservation. Each page offers another example of the delicacy of the world's ecologies and the need to protect not only habitats, but the species that live and contribute to them.

Levine, Ellen. *If Your Name Was Changed at Ellis Island.* New York: Scholastic, 2006. A question-and-answer book for young readers full of illustrations and personal accounts about Ellis Island and the immigrants who came through there.

——. *If You Traveled on the Underground Railroad.* New York: Scholastic, 1993. A question-and-answer book about a slave trying to escape on the Underground Railroad.

——. *If You Traveled West in a Covered Wagon.* New York: Scholastic, 2006. A useful and informative question-and-answer book for young readers that traces the life and experiences of a pioneer traveling to Oregon in the 1840s.

Locker, Thomas is an artist who creates exquisite oil paintings for a wide range of books on nature, integrated with geographic and historic subjects. The following titles are ideal for young gifted students who will love the sumptuous paintings that unfold with the text, inviting readers into new worlds:

- *Home: A Journey Through America.* New York: First Voyager Books, 2000. Locker's paintings accompany the words of great American writers, past and present, such as Henry David Thoreau, Willa Cather, and others.

- *John Muir: America's Naturalist.* Golden, CO: Fulcrum Publishing, 2010. A beautifully illustrated book teaching children about the life of John Muir. Includes excerpts from Muir's writing.

- *Walking with Henry: Based on the Life and Works of Henry David Thoreau.* Golden, CO: Fulcrum Publishing, 2002. Using painting, Locker attempts to show children the wonders of the natural world through the eyes of Thoreau.

- *Where the River Begins.* New York: Puffin Books, 1993. Two brothers, Josh and Aaron, set out on a quest to discover the origin of the river that flows past their house.

Locker, Thomas, and Robert Baron. *Hudson: The Story of a River.* Golden, CO: Fulcrum Publishing, 2004. Details the history of the Hudson River.

Manitonquat. *The Children of the Morning Light: Wampanoag Tales as Told by Manitonquat.* New York: Simon & Schuster Children's Publishing, 1994. These lively stories by Wampanoag elder and storyteller Manitonquat take young readers on a journey into the cultural traditions and history of the Wampanoag people. Accompanied by evocative, full-page acrylics, the tales will ignite the imaginations of young students as they learn about Kishtannit, the Big Spirit, whose singing creates the world, ocean, sun, moon, time, and space. Other stories explore the vicissitudes of human life with humor and wisdom.

Martin, Rafe. *The Boy Who Lived with the Seals.* New York: The Putnam & Grosset Group, 1996. Enhanced by luminous paintings, this is a poignant retelling of a classic Chinook Indian legend about a boy who disappears one day while playing by the river.

———. *The Rough-Face Girl.* New York: The Putnam & Grosset Group, 1998. This haunting and richly illustrated version of Cinderella comes from Algonquin Indian sources.

McDermott, Gerald. An award-winning filmmaker and picture book artist and writer, his books on tales and myths from cultures around the world are a rich resource for grades K–3. McDermott's vibrant illustrations reflect the artistic styles of the cultures where the stories originated:

- *Anansi the Spider: A Tale from the Ashanti.* New York: Henry Holt & Co., 2009. An adaptation of the traditional folktale from Africa. Combines traditional designs with authentic Ashanti language rhythms.

- *Arrow to the Sun: A Pueblo Indian Tale.* New York: Puffin Books, 1977. Through very original and colorful illustrations, the author relates an inspiring Pueblo tale of a child's meeting with his father—the sun.

- *Coyote: A Trickster Tale from the American Southwest.* Boston, MA: HMH Books for Young Readers, 1999. Coyote wants to fly like a crow, but his boastful nature prompts Crow to teach him a lesson.

- *Musicians of the Sun.* New York: Simon & Schuster's Children's Publishing, 1997. A tale about how the Lord of Night sent his musicians to fill the world with joy.

- *Papagayo: The Mischief Maker.* Boston, MA: HMH Books for Young Readers, 1992. A mischievous parrot saves the moon and shows that he is a true friend, even if he is noisy.

- *Raven: A Trickster Tale from the Pacific Northwest.* Boston, MA: HMH Books for Young Readers, 2001. A retelling of the classic tale of how Raven tricked the Sky Chief and brought light to the world.

- *Zomo the Rabbit: A Trickster Tale from West Africa.* Boston, MA: HMH Books for Young Readers, 1996. Zomo wants wisdom but must gain it from the Sky God by completing three tasks.

Menzel, Peter. *Material World: A Global Family Portrait.* San Francisco, CA: Sierra Club, 1994. To create this book, sixteen famous photographers traveled to thirty countries to photograph families in their own environments. Factual information about the countries, families, and their histories is included. Most captivating are the photographs. This is a visual way for young students to see how different people all over the world live and what types of things are valuable to them in their lives. Peter Menzel did another book called *What the World Eats* (Tricycle Press, 2008), using the same concept to highlight each family's food.

Milios, Rita. *Imagi-size: Activities to Exercise Your Students' Imagination.* Marion, IL: Pieces of Learning, 1996. A rich collection of activities for first through fourth grades that can be integrated into existing lessons or used as readiness activities for other content. Also a wonderful source for visual learners who enjoy using their imaginations to solve problems.

Miller, Frances A. *Eliza Lucas Pinckney.* Castro Valley, CA: Quercus, 1987. A short biography from American history, this is a good story-time book about the early colonists of South Carolina.

Milord, Susan. *Hands Around the World: 365 Creative Ways to Build Cultural Awareness & Global Respect.* Charlotte, VT: Williamson Publishing, 1992. Designed to expand cultural awareness and global respect, this volume is packed full of activities and information about cultures and races around the world. Includes an appendix listing organizations of interest and suppliers of multicultural materials.

Musgrove, Margaret. *Ashanti to Zulu: African Traditions.* New York: Puffin Books, 1992. This ABC book depicts twenty-six of Africa's ethnic groups and shows Africa's vast, rich cultural heritage. Beautifully written; colorfully and elegantly illustrated.

National Geographic Education (www.nationalgeograpic.com /education). Includes a bounty of resources for K–12 teachers; engaging activities; standards-based units; interactive mapping; GeoStories that offer interactive maps, media, and narrative; teacher programs; audio/video sources; online magazines; and more, making it an ideal resource for gifted students.

Native Languages of the Americas: Preserving and Promoting American Indian Languages (www.native-languages.org). A nonprofit organization dedicated to the survival of Native American languages. Created and maintained by Native American people, the organization's website is an extraordinarily extensive database on Native American languages and cultures across the country. The richness of the information brings many of the continent's First Nations to life in the present day.

Osborne, Mary Pope. Magic Tree House Series. New York: Random House. Early readers as young as preschool or kindergarten up through early elementary enjoy these historical time travel books that take Jack and Annie back in time to important places and events in history. Many of the books come with "Fact Trackers," companion books that provide historical information, context, and drawings.

Penner, Lucille Recht. *The Pilgrims at Plymouth.* New York: Scholastic, 2006. This story is about the Pilgrims on the *Mayflower* and in the early years in America, and about the role that the Indians played in the Pilgrims' survival.

Plimoth Plantation (www.plimoth.org). A nonprofit, historic living museum that provides an engaging, experiential learning environment to teach visitors about the lives of the English and Native people who lived there. The official website features an award-winning activity where kids can assume the role of history detective to find out what happened at the famous celebration at Plimoth in 1621. Also includes other useful activities and sources of information.

Rainforest Alliance Kids (www.rainforest-alliance.org/kids). An international, nonprofit organization dedicated to conservation and sustainable living. The website offers excellent, standards-aligned lesson plans in social studies, language arts, and science for children preK–8 and includes activities, games, projects, and extended learning opportunities through the Adopt-a-Rainforest program.

Sewall, Marcia. *People of the Breaking Day.* New York: Atheneum Books, 1990. Masterfully re-creates the world of the Wampanoag people, who lived in southeastern Massachusetts when the Pilgrims landed. A wonderful companion book to *The Pilgrims of Plimoth.*

———. *The Pilgrims of Plimoth.* New York: Aladdin Books, 1996. Using the Pilgrims' style of speech, the author has vividly re-created the voyage to the New World and the daily life in the early, foundational years of Plymouth Colony.

Sisk, Dorothy. *Creative Teaching of the Gifted.* New York: McGraw-Hill, 1987. A useful resource for teachers and parents that offers a conceptual understanding of how to meet the creative needs of talented children. Includes a range of helpful ideas and examples.

Smutny, Joan Franklin, and S. E. von Fremd. *Differentiating for the Young Child: Teaching Strategies Across the Content Areas, PreK–3.* Thousand Oaks, CA: Corwin Press, 2010. Divided by subject areas, this book addresses the common difficulties teachers have differentiating at the primary level where students present a tremendous diversity of skill, knowledge, and ability. The authors offer strategies to streamline the process and promote creative thinking and intellectual discovery across key discipline areas. Charts with high- and low-preparation

strategies enable teachers to do more for gifted learners and to adopt a more incremental approach to meeting a broader range of student needs.

Smutny, Joan Franklin, and S. E. von Fremd, eds. *Igniting Creativity in Gifted Learners, K–6: Strategies for Every Teacher.* Thousand Oaks, CA: Corwin Press, 2009. This compendium of how-to's *for* teachers *by* teachers presents a tremendous range of creative methods to advance the higher-level thinking and imagination of gifted learners. Different subjects in reading, writing, social studies, mathematics, science, and the arts, the book feature strategies that include but also exceed curriculum standards for young learners who need more challenge and more creative ways to show their true potential. Teachers can easily adapt ideas to different needs and age groups.

Teaching with Primary Sources (www.tpsnva.org). An extraordinary resource designed originally for Northern Virginia schools and funded by the Library of Congress for K–12 classrooms. The website enables teachers to access the library's vast primary source materials for lesson plans, share ideas with other teachers, and teach the process of history-making to young gifted students. The site supports the development of research skills like visual literacy, online research, and library quests.

Terrell, Sandy. *Roberto's Rainforest.* El Cajon, CA: Interaction Publishers, 1995. This innovative and activity-filled book is a scientific "canoe trip" that allows young naturalists to explore a tropical rain forest in South America.

Torrance, E. Paul. *The Search for Satori and Creativity.* Buffalo, NY: Creative Education Foundation, 1979. A groundbreaking work on the creative process, including recognition of the Japanese understanding of satori—a concept Torrance applies to discovery and invention in the classroom.

Torrance, E. Paul, and Dorothy A. Sisk. *Gifted and Talented in the Regular Classroom.* Buffalo, NY: Creative Education Foundation Press, 1997. An excellent guide by two experts in creative education, full of useful concepts and procedures to use in the classroom.

United States Environmental Protection Agency (www.epa.gov/students). The EPA's student website exposes students of all ages to environmental conditions around the globe and enables them to learn about their own communities. Offers educational games, guided research, and many creative ideas for engaging young children in environmental issues. Includes information on service projects that teachers have done with their students.

Waters, Kate. *Sarah Morton's Day: A Day in the Life of a Pilgrim Girl.* Photographs by Russ Kendall. New York: Scholastic, 2008. With detailed photographs from the Plimoth Plantation Living Museum in Massachusetts, this story of the daily life and duties of a young Pilgrim girl makes the historical period far more accessible and interesting to primary-age students.

———. *Tapenum's Day: A Wampanoag Indian Boy in Pilgrim Times.* Photographs by Russ Kendall. New York: Scholastic, 1996. An excellent companion book to *Sarah Morton's Day* that combines photographs from Plimoth Plantation in Massachusetts to explore the village, culture, and customs of the Wampanoag through the eyes of a young boy.

Weller, Frances Ward. *I Wonder If I'll See a Whale*. New York: Philomel Books, 1991. An engaging book about a young girl's seafaring trip to find a whale. Young readers encounter the great but gentle "monster" of the sea and learn about its daily living habits.

Young, Ed. *Lon Po Po: A Red-Riding Hood Story from China*. New York: Puffin Books, 1996. A fairy tale told in exquisite detail, this is a dramatic rendition of the Little Red Riding Hood story set in China.

Chapter 5

Ada, Ama Flor. *A Magical Encounter: Latino Children's Literature in the Classroom*. Upper Saddle River, NJ: Pearson, 2002. Offers books in English and in Spanish—a vast bibliography by Latino and Latina authors, organized by genre, language, and major topics or themes. Teachers can use this source to stimulate creativity, higher-level thinking, and literacy through books young children can relate to.

Adams, Ansel. *Ansel Adams Wall Calendar*. New York: Little, Brown & Co., annually. Representing a variety of natural environments and seasons, this yearly wall calendar provides an exquisite display of the artist's most iconic photographs. These evocative images are useful catalysts for creative activities in the classroom. We suggest laminating them for repeated use.

Arnosky, Jim. *Crinkleroot's Guide to Knowing the Trees*. Belmont, CA: Simon & Schuster, 1992. Crinkleroot is a master at engaging young children in the wonder of the natural world. Along with the illustrations, the text encourages students to be like scientists, charting the growth and changes of trees, and teaches them how to identify different species. Wit and beauty highlight the world of trees and make children feel that Crinkleroot is taking them into the woods with him.

Artful Thinking (www.pzartfulthinking.org). A program developed by Harvard's Project Zero and TCAPS (Traverse City, Michigan Area Public Schools) in order to integrate art into regular classroom instruction. The website is full of ideas on how teachers can use visual art and music in their lessons to develop students' critical thinking skills and promote meaningful learning.

Arts Every Day (www.artseveryday.org). A nonprofit organization dedicated to providing students a strong cultural education through arts education and experiences and by integrating the arts into everyday learning. The website includes many helpful tips and resources for educators.

Bernard, Robin. *Tree for All Seasons*. National Geographic Children's Books, 2001. A large sixteen-page book with exquisite photographs will amaze and inform beginning readers, including English language learners.

Birney, Betty G. *The World According to Humphrey*. New York: Puffin Books, 2005. The first in a series of short novels about the classroom pet hamster, narrated from his point of view. Ideal for gifted, independent readers from young primary to fifth grade, and also very engaging for reading aloud to younger students.

Bledsoe, Lucy Jane. *Amelia Earhart*. Belmont, CA: Simon & Schuster, 1989. Well-told story of Amelia Earhart's life. Includes a great deal of background information for classroom use.

———. *Phillis Wheatley: First in Poetry*. Belmont, CA: Simon & Schuster, 1989. An inspiring odyssey of Phillis Wheatley's rise from slavery to her life as a poet.

Blizzard, Gladys S. *Come Look with Me: Enjoying Art with Children*. Watertown, MA: Charlesbridge Publishing, 1996. A wonderful book for introducing imaginative and critical thinking, the author uses twelve works of art that feature children and poses questions that invite young students to probe the world behind the paintings.

Bryant, Jen. *A River of Words: The Story of William Carlos Williams*. Grand Rapids, MI: Eerdmans Books for Young Readers, 2008. This Caldecott Honor winner is a story of the life of William Carlos Williams and a wonderful introduction to his free verse composition.

Bryant, Margaret A., Marjorie Keiper, and Anne Petit. *Month by Month with Children's Literature: Your K Through 3 Curriculum for Math, Science, Social Studies, and More*. Tucson, AZ: Zephyr Press, 1995. Offers a dynamic curriculum for teaching to all literacy levels and includes a year's worth of literature-based language units effectively integrated into content areas. Specific and comprehensive, this book offers many creative activities for the primary level.

Carter, Polly, May McNeer, Doris Faber, and Harold Faber. *Exploring Biographies of Nellie Bly, Albert Einstein & George Washington Carver*. New York: Scholastic, 1992. Simply told biographies of Nellie Bly, Albert Einstein, and George Washington Carver are informative, useful aids for young students curious about great pioneers.

Christensen, James C., and Renwick St. James. *The Art of James Christensen: A Journey of the Imagination*. Seymour, CT: The Greenwich Workshop Press, 1994. The extraordinary fantasy art of James Christensen mingles with myths, legends, and fables to create a rich source for teachers and parents to use when inspiring creative expression in themselves and their children. The text of the artist's imaginative "journey" lends enchantment and inspiration to this special book.

Clegg, Luther B., Etta Miller, Bill Vanderhoof, Gonzalo Ramirez, and Peggy K. Ford. "How to Choose the Best Multicultural Books." www.scholastic.com/teachers. Includes descriptions of fifty multicultural books favored by top educators, writers, and artists, as well as their advice on how to evaluate literature to ensure its accuracy and freedom from stereotype or cultural bias.

Climo, Shirley. *The Egyptian Cinderella*. New York: Harper Trophy, 1992. Beautifully told and illustrated, this is the Cinderella story re-created and set in the world of ancient Egypt.

Cook, Carole, and Jody Carlisle. *Challenges for Children: Creative Activities for Gifted and Talented Primary Students*. West Nyack, NY: The Center for Applied Research in Education, 1985. Designed for K–3 teachers, this volume offers a unique and vast collection of activities in social studies, language arts, math, and science as well as in specialized areas such as library skills, creative arts, and independent learning. You can select activities to support the curriculum, a specific skill, or a particular content area in meeting the individual needs of talented young children in the classroom.

Coombs, Kate. *Water Sings Blue: Ocean Poems*. San Francisco: Chronicle Books, 2012. An engaging exploration of the sea through the poetry of Kate Coombs and Meilo So's breathtaking watercolors. Young readers or listeners will love discovering the beauty and endless mysteries of the sea.

Culham, Ruth. *The Writing Thief: Using Mentor Texts to Teach the Craft of Writing*. Newark, DE: International Reading Association, 2014. An excellent guide that includes many genres of writing for elementary teachers demonstrating how young writers develop their craft by reading and internalizing the texts of great authors.

Cummings, E.E. *Hist Whist and Other Poems for Children*. New York: Liveright Publishing, 1983. A wonderful collection of poems to stimulate creative responses in young children.

Dorfman, Lynne R., and Rose Cappelli. *Mentor Texts: Teaching Writing Through Children's Literature, K–6*. Portland, ME: Stenhouse Publishers, 2007. A user-friendly guide by two experienced teachers on the use of "mentor texts" in teaching writing to gifted students who can select more challenging literature for their writing.

EDSITEment (www.edsitement.neh.gov). This website, sponsored by the National Endowment for the Humanities, connects visitors to many sites and lesson plans for social studies, language arts, foreign language, art, and culture—all aligned with standards and providing cross-curriculum connections.

Educational Uses of Digital Storytelling (digitalstorytelling.coe.uh.edu). A useful resource for educators for integrating digital storytelling into many educational activities.

Edutopia (www.edutopia.org/arts-integration-resources). The website has tons of articles, lesson plans, ideas, and other resources on how to integrate art into everyday learning, as well as stories of successful arts integration from teachers.

Ernst, Lisa Campbell. *Little Red Riding Hood: A Newfangled Prairie Tale*. New York: Simon & Schuster Books for Young Readers, 1998. A clever retelling of the Red Riding Hood fairy tale with some notable differences from the traditional version with engaging illustrations by the author.

Fantasia. Burbank, CA: The Walt Disney Studios, 1940. A modern classic, this film integrates animation with classical music performed by the Philadelphia Orchestra under the direction of Leopold Stokowski.

Fantasia 2000. Burbank, CA: The Walt Disney Studios, 1999. The sequel to *Fantasia*, this film integrates animation with classical music performed by the Chicago Symphony Orchestra conducted by James Levine.

Farjeon, Eleanor, and Herbert Farjeon. *Heroes and Heroines*. London: British Library, 2011. A delightful collection of poems that cleverly portray the lives of heroes and heroines (beginning with Alexander the Great) through rollicking rhymes and ironic, witty portraits.

Fisher, Leonard Everett. *Marie Curie*. New York: Antheneum Books, 1994. Through spare yet evocative prose and striking black-and-white illustrations, the author-artist re-creates the remarkable life of Marie Curie.

Fleishman, Paul. *Joyful Noise: Poems for Two Voices*. New York: HarperCollins, 2005. A book of energetic poetry where poems are structured for two to read aloud together. Each poem has specific lines for readers to speak aloud at specific times. This is a delightful way to incorporate reader's theater and poetry, and by creating simple voice recordings, it becomes a fun project to share with parents.

Fletcher, Ralph. *Poetry Matters: Writing a Poem from the Inside Out*. New York: HarperCollins, 2002. A lively and engaging approach to all genres of poetry that will make children eager to write their own poems. While this book is geared toward older students, it can be adapted to primary grades and is ideal for young gifted writers.

Fractured Fairytales (www.readwritethink.org). This interactive tool from ReadWriteThink invites students to turn fairy tales on their head while simultaneously learning about character, point of view, story structure, and so forth. The website also includes other lesson ideas related to fairy tales and tons of other free programs for use in reading and language arts instruction.

Fredericks, Anthony. *Creative Activities for Gifted Readers: Dynamic Investigations, Challenging Projects, and Energizing Assignments, Grades 3–6*. Culver City, CA: Good Year Books, 2007. Full of exciting challenges for young gifted language arts students, including word games, puzzles, reader's theater, and long-term projects that develop critical and creative thinking. A volume for students K–2 is also available.

Gaylord, Susan K. (www.makingbooks.com). The website is a treasure for both teachers and children. Gaylord, an experienced teacher and artist, provides step-by-step instructions on how to make books with students of all ages, integrating creativity with curriculum. Children become highly motivated and inspired to write in books they have made with their own hands.

Gibbons, Gail. *Tell Me, Tree: All About Trees for Kids*. New York: Little, Brown Books for Young Readers, 2002. An excellent oversized book containing vivid watercolor pictures of children of different ethnic backgrounds that teaches students about the parts of trees, their uses, and their ecology. Information on making tree identification books is included.

Godwin, Sam. *From Little Acorns: A First Look at the Life Cycle of a Tree*. Mankato, MN: Picture Window Books, 2004. An ideal source for emergent readers, through the questions of a curious squirrel and the forest animals who answer them, this book teaches young students about the growth cycle of an oak tree as well as the effects of seasonal changes.

Gwynne, Fred. *Pondlarker*. New York: Simon & Schuster Books for Young Readers, 1990. A witty alternative to the traditional frog-prince story, this tale offers a surprise ending to Pondlarker's quest for that magical princess he hopes will turn him into a handsome prince.

Heller, Ruth. *Behind the Mask: A Book About Prepositions*. New York: Puffin Books, 1998. Clever rhymes and bold illustrations take young readers on a tour through the world of prepositions and how they function. Also check out these other books by Heller:

- *Color.* New York: Grossett & Dunlap, 1995. Through playful verse and vibrant illustrations, this book introduces young students to the basic and scientific principles of color.

- *Kites Sail High: A Book About Verbs.* New York: Puffin Books, 1998. An introductory grammar book that teaches children about verbs.

- *Merry-Go-Round: A Book About Nouns.* New York: Puffin Books, 1998. Playful rhymes and illustrations are used to teach young children about nouns.

- *Mine, All Mine: A Book About Pronouns.* New York: Puffin Books, 1999. An introductory grammar book using rhyme and illustration to teach children about pronouns.

Hoberman, Mary Ann. *You Read to Me, I'll Read to You Series.* New York: Little, Brown Books for Young Readers. This series for younger elementary students, emerging to early readers, provides opportunities for low-pressure read aloud. Stories and poems are color coded, so each child picks a color to read and the blue words are read in chorus.

Hopkins, Lee Bennett. *My America: A Poetry Atlas of the United States.* New York: Simon & Schuster Books for Young Readers, 2000. A beautifully illustrated compilation that takes children on a journey through American poetry, state by state.

Ingoglia, Gina. *The Tree Book: For Kids and Their Grown-ups.* New York: Brooklyn Botanic Garden, 2013. This guide from the Brooklyn Botanic Garden explores questions young children have about trees, focusing on thirty-three trees from different habitats across the United States. The botanical watercolor artwork beautifully illustrates the trees in different seasons.

Leimbach, Judy, and Sharon Eckert. *Primary Book Reporter: Independent Reading for Young Learners.* Waco, TX: Prufrock Press, 1998. Designed for use in grades K–2, this resource provides useful activity sheets that offer meaningful, imaginative experiences for young students who are already reading.

Levy, Nathan, and Janet Pica. *There Are Those.* Hightstown, NJ: Nathan Levy Associates, 1982. This mind-bending book uses a poetic essay and a series of intriguing visual images to introduce and explore the art of perception. A creative book for parents and teachers alike.

Lewis, J. Patrick, compiler. *National Geographic Book of Animal Poetry: 200 Poems with Photographs That Squeak, Soar, and Roar!* Washington, DC: National Geographic Children's Books, 2012. National Geographic brings its stunning photographs to bear on a wide range of poems about animals. From classic to modern children's poems, this bounty of words, images, rhythms, and verse dance among the pictures of animals squeaking, soaring, and roaring through the natural world.

Livingston, Myra Cohn. *I Never Told and Other Poems.* New York: Margaret K. McElderry Books, 1992. The author helps young readers cherish these poems, recognize many of their own experiences and feelings, and explore new ways of thinking.

Ludwig, Amy. *Forest Has a Song: Poems.* New York: Clarion Books, 2013. A beautiful collection of poems and watercolor illustrations that explore the forest in different seasons through the senses of a young girl. This is an ideal book for engaging young readers in the woodland world.

Marshall, Rita. *I Hate to Read!* Mankato, MN: Creative Editions, 2013. Designed to entice the most reluctant reader, this book offers children a wacky adventure in which a little boy discovers that words in a book can take on lives of their own.

Martin, Rafe. *The Rough-Face Girl.* New York: The Putnam & Grosset Group, 1998. This haunting and richly illustrated version of the Cinderella story comes from Algonquin Indian sources.

Meddaugh, Susan. *Cinderella's Rat.* New York: Walter Lorraine Books, 1997. This humorous retelling features a humble rat and the adventures he encounters when Cinderella's fairy godmother turns him into a coachman. Susan Meddaugh's art and wit will delight primary classrooms.

Milios, Rita. *Imagi-size: Activities to Exercise Your Students' Imagination.* See page 194 for information.

Miller, Debbie S. *Are Trees Alive?* London: Walker Childrens Paperbacks, 2003. A unique approach to the study of trees, this book compares children to trees, where roots function somewhat like feet, bark like skin, and leaves like hair. Through this lens, young students discover various trees from the baobab in Africa to the bristlecone pine of California.

Norton, Donna E. *Multicultural Children's Literature: Through the Eyes of Many Children.* Upper Saddle River, NJ: Pearson, 2012. A popular and extensive volume that will assist teachers in finding the best multicultural literature for children and adolescents.

O'Keeffe, Georgia. *Georgia O'Keeffe.* New York: The Viking Press, 1976. Includes a discussion of the stimulus behind the painting *Music—Pink and Blue No.1* (1918, oil on canvas).

Perry, Sarah. *If . . .* Los Angeles, CA: J. Paul Getty Trust Publications, 1995. The author-artist presents extraordinary wonders (cats that can fly, mountains that appear like sleeping dogs) and helps young children perceive the inconceivable and imagine the unimaginable. This is a useful source for young writers and artists.

Putumayo Kids. CDs from the Putumayo Kids record label introduce children to different cultures through music. The CD collections feature songs with kid-friendly lyrics and rhythms from international artists. To purchase, visit their website at www.putumayo.com/putumayo-kids.

Schenk de Regniers, Beatrice, Eva Moore, Mary Michaels White, Maurice Sendak, and Jan Carr. *Sing a Song of Popcorn: Every Child's Book of Poems.* New York: Scholastic, 1988. Drawn from the work of renowned poets, 128 selections come even more alive with exquisite illustrations by nine Caldecott Medal–winning artists.

Scieszka, Jon. *The True Story of the Three Little Pigs!* New York: Puffin Books, 1989. This whimsical version of the three little pigs story is told from a unique perspective—that of the Big Bad Wolf, who claims he is neither big nor bad but was "framed" by irresponsible reporters.

Shange, Ntozake. *I Live in Music.* New York: Welcome Books, 1994. A poem that embodies the syncopated style of the music she loves, this piece by Shange—evocatively illustrated by Romare Bearden's paintings—is a moving tribute to the power and magic of music.

Silverstein, Shel. *Falling Up.* New York: HarperCollins Childrens Books, 1996. A book of whimsical poems and drawings by one of America's best-loved children's authors.

Smutny, Joan Franklin. "Enhancing Linguistic Gifts of the Young." *Understanding Our Gifted* 8, no. 4 (1996): 1, 12–15. This is a conceptual framework for, and introduction to, language arts and the young gifted child. The author challenges the limited expectations conventionally held about the potential of primary students and demonstrates how to nurture in these young ones a love for reading and writing—even poetry.

Smutny, Joan Franklin, and S. E. von Fremd. *Differentiating for the Young Child: Teaching Strategies Across the Content Areas, PreK–3.* See page 195 for information.

Smutny, Joan Franklin, and S. E. von Fremd, eds. *Igniting Creativity in Gifted Learners, K–6: Strategies for Every Teacher.* See page 195 for information.

Solga, Kim. *Draw!* Danbury, CT: Grolier Publishing, 1993. For parents or teachers, this creative and uncomplicated book offers ten unique drawing projects as well as numerous variations that will stimulate the imagination of children ages 6–11.

———. *Paint!* Cincinnati, OH: North Light Books, 1991. Crystal colors, dots of color, and face painting are some of the many activities offered in this book to help young children uncover their unique creative talents.

Stone, Tanya Lee. *Amelia Earhart: A Photographic Story of a Life.* New York: DK Publishing, 2007. An example of Dorling Kindersley's excellent biography series for young students featuring photographs and art and offering substantive information for primary classrooms. Biographies from DK Publishing range across historic periods, genders, races, and nationalities.

Sullivan, Charles, compiler. *Imaginary Gardens: American Poetry and Art for Young People.* New York: Harry N. Abrams, 1989. This book has no adult-imposed categories and no chapter divisions so it can be opened to any page to begin experiencing poems and art of various styles, tone, and historical periods. Young readers can make their own discoveries and select their favorite poems.

Sweet, Melissa. *Carmine: A Little More Red.* Boston: Houghton Mifflin, 2005. A fresh, brightly illustrated version of Little Red Riding Hood follows the adventure of Carmine the young artist. Each page beautifully integrates a new vocabulary word into the story making this book most appropriate for middle to upper elementary students.

Taleypo the Storyteller (www.marilynkinsella.org). This website is maintained by Marilyn Kinsella, an experienced teacher and storyteller, and is a practical resource on how to integrate stories and storytelling into the classroom. The Teacher/Teller page includes teaching ideas, study guides that integrate multiple subjects and inspire imagination and critical thinking, bibliographies, and links to other storytelling sites.

Thomas, Joyce Carol. *Brown Honey in Broomwheat Tea.* New York: HarperCollins, 1995. Through a series of tender and moving poems, the author evokes the rich heritage, warmth, and love that permeate the world of a young African-American girl and her family.

Torrance, E. Paul. *Creativity: Just Wanting to Know.* Pretoria, South Africa: Benedic Books, 1994. The value of this particular volume is that the author, a well-known pioneer in researching and teaching creativity, has compiled his articles and papers from 1958 through 1994.

A Touch of Greatness. DVD. Directed by Robert Downy Sr. New York: First Run Features, 2005. An inspiring and educational documentary film about extraordinary elementary teacher Albert Cullum, who believed that all students have greatness in them and need imaginative experiences with great literature (for example, Shakespeare, Sophocles, Shaw), poetry, drama, world history, and fine art to realize their potential. A pioneer in the 1960s and 70s, he remains so today. You can read more about the documentary and purchase the DVD at www.pbs.org.

Wilcox, Leah. *Falling for Rapunzel.* New York: Puffin Books, 2005. The hilarious wordplay that leads to a series of miscommunications, which, combined with the whimsical artwork, is a guaranteed source of fun and creative thinking.

Willems, Mo. *Goldilocks and the Three Dinosaurs: As Retold by Mo Willems.* New York: Balzer & Bray, 2012. This is a clever, highly original new version of the story young students know so well. The humor will delight adults as well as children.

Wood, Audrey, and Bruce Wood. Children's literature author and her artist son offer several humorous and unconventional alphabet stories that will delight and inspire gifted children of all ages:

- *Alphabet Adventure.* New York: Blue Sky Press, 2001. The lowercase letters of the alphabet are on their way to their first day of school but are held up when letter i loses her dot.

- *Alphabet Mystery.* New York: Blue Sky Press, 2003. Young children can learn their lowercase letters in this fun mystery.

- *Alphabet Rescue.* New York: Blue Sky Press, 2006. The lowercase letters work together to build a fire truck and save the day.

Young, Ed. *Lon Po Po: A Red-Riding Hood Story from China.* See page 196 for information.

Chapter 6

Abruscato, Joe, and Jack Hassard. *The Whole Cosmos Catalog of Science Activities for Kids of All Ages.* Glenview, IL: Good Year Books, 1997. Complete with illustrations, explanations, and poetry, this book is a giant-sized collection of over 275 science activities for adults and children to explore together.

Anno, Masaichiro, and Mitsumasa Anno. *Anno's Mysterious Multiplying Jar.* New York: Penguin Putnam Books for Young Students, 1999. Simple text and pictures introduce the complex mathematical concept of factorials in a context both beautiful and mysterious.

Anno, Mitsumasa. *Anno's Counting House.* New York: Philomel Books, 1982. Children learn the first ten numbers and the basics of addition and subtraction through a delightful story about ten children who move to a new house.

———. *Anno's Magic Seeds*. New York: Penguin Putnam Books for Young Readers, 1999. This retelling of the classic Jack and the Beanstalk tale teaches children about multiplication and challenges them to keep track of Jack's growing fortune.

———. *Anno's Math Games*. New York: Puffin Books, 1997. Multiplication, sequence and ordinal numbering, measurement, and direction are introduced in this book using puzzles, games, and activities.

Bernard, Robin. *Tree for All Seasons*. See page 196 for information.

Bowden, Marcia. *Nature for the Very Young: A Handbook of Indoor and Outdoor Activities*. See page 192 for information.

Branley, Franklyn M. *Sunshine Makes the Seasons*. New York: HarperCollins, 2005. An introduction to the sun and how it affects our planet, this book includes useful experiments to help children understand seasonal transformations.

Burns, Marilyn. *The Greedy Triangle*. New York: Scholastic, 2008. One of Burns's "Brainy Day Books," this volume ushers the young reader into the wondrous world of mathematical ideas and properties, integrating them into a whimsical and lively story about an ambitious triangle.

———. "How to Make the Most of Math Manipulatives." *Instructor* 105, no. 7 (1996): 45–51. A recognized expert in the field of early childhood mathematics offers helpful advice and suggestions on strategies she uses to avoid common problems and pitfalls with math manipulatives. Her ideas are clearly explained and easy to follow. Today, students can extend their learning through interactive games, puzzles, and problem solving through virtual manipulatives available online.

———. *Spaghetti and Meatballs for All!* New York: Scholastic, 2008. A witty and humorous tale that introduces children to the concept of area and perimeter.

Burns, Marilyn, and Stephanie Sheffield. *Math and Literature, Grades K–1*. Sausalito, CA: Math Solutions Publications, 2004. A resource containing math lessons for grades K–1.

———. *Math and Literature, Grades 2–3*. Sausalito, CA: Math Solutions Publications, 2004. A math and literature resource for students.

Butterfield, Moira. *1,000 Facts About Wild Animals*. New York: Scholastic, 1993. While focusing on animals, the author also examines volcanoes, rivers, deserts, rain forests, weather, and other facets of our planet. A good resource for science units.

Carle, Eric. Check out the following vivid and imaginative picture book resources for teaching mathematics, science, and languages arts from Carle:

- *A House for Hermit Crab*. New York: Simon Spotlight, 2014. Readers follow Hermit Crab on his search to find a new home and accept change.

- *Eric Carle's Animals, Animals*. Compiled by Laura Whipple. New York: Puffin Books, 1999. Carle's illustrations bring to life the works of famous poets such as Lewis Carroll, Emily Dickinson, Shakespeare, and many others.

- *Erick Carle's Opposites*. New York: Grosset & Dunlap, 2007. A book about opposites for young children.

- *The Grouchy Ladybug*. New York: HarperCollins, 1996. Children learn about the importance of good manners and friendship as they travel with this grumpy insect.

- *The Very Hungry Caterpillar*. New York: Philomel Books, 1994. A classic tale of a very hungry caterpillar who grows and grows and eventually becomes a butterfly.

Cherry, Lynne. *The Great Kapok Tree: A Tale of the Amazon Rain Forest*. New York: Voyager Books, 2000. This story about a lush rain forest has captivated children of all ages since its publication.

Chevat, Richard. *The Magic School Bus Science Explorations*. New York: Scholastic, 1994. A gentle introduction to a variety of science topics such as sound, weather, and seeds, this book integrates explanations with short activities to stimulate discussion.

ChildDrama.com (www.childdrama.com). Playwright, director, and educator for more than thirty years, Matt Buchanan has an education section on his website that is extraordinary—drama techniques to use in the curriculum (including science and math), ideas on what has worked with kids from firsthand experience, and more.

Clement, Rod. *Counting on Frank*. New York: Gareth Stevens Publishing, 1999. A story about a nerdy boy who can't help asking questions about the everyday world around him. Gifted young children love it since they ask the same sorts of questions! But Frank has the answers.

Clements, Andrew. *A Million Dots*. New York: Atheneum Books for Young Readers, 2006. Yes, there are actually a million dots in this book. The best-selling author of *Frindle* has created a visual treat for the imagination as you see page after page of dots incorporated into the illustrations. Each page has a "dot count" alongside interesting numbers facts. For example, the fact at dot number 153,000 is "A queen-size bedsheet is woven from more than 153,000 feet of cotton thread."

Cole, Joanna. Magic School Bus Explorations Series. Vols. A, B, and C. New York: Scholastic, 1995. The three, wonderful books in this series for young children focus on a wide range of science topics from outer space to digestion. These books will inspire a sense of wonder in children through their imaginative and whimsical storytelling and hands-on activities.

Contemporary African Art Gallery (contempafricanart.com). The Contemporary African Art Gallery in New York provides images of prominent artists from different countries who are experimenting with shape, light, design, and so forth.

Cook, Carole, and Jody Carlisle. *Challenges for Children: Creative Activities for Gifted and Talented Primary Students*. See page 196 for information.

Demi. *One Grain of Rice*. New York: Scholastic, 1997. Set in India, this tale of the clever young girl Rani delights readers as she outsmarts the unfair provincial raja. As the story unfolds, exponential growth is illustrated on the pages and by the story itself. Many supporting lesson plans can be found on the Internet. Even gifted children as young as four or five will enjoy this book, though older ones will be able to follow along with the math.

Eckert, Sharon, and Judy Leimbach. *Primarily Math: A Problem Solving Approach*. San Luis Obispo, CA: Dandy Lion Publications, 1993. A pioneer work in math education, this book offers teachers strategies that will help students in grades 2–4 reason, develop problem-solving skills, and expand their ability to communicate mathematical concepts.

Ferrier, Jean-Louis. *Picasso*. Jean-Maris Clarke, trans. Paris: Terrail, 1996. This paperback volume is a comprehensive and engaging exploration of Pablo Picasso's genius. It contains a wide range of his styles and reproductions, including both sculptures and paintings.

Fetzner, Mary. *Simple Story of the 3 Pigs and the Scientific Wolf*. Marion, IL: Pieces of Learning, 2000. Combining the well-known fairy tale with the study of simple machines, this book connects imagination and science to engage students in a creative, interdisciplinary manner.

Field, Simon Quellen. *Gonzo Gizmos: Projects & Devices to Channel Your Inner Geek*. Chicago: Chicago Review Press, 2003. This book contains many wonderful projects for young learners—all sorts of devices with easy-to-use illustrations and diagrams.

Fisher, Leonard Everett. *Look Around! A Book About Shapes*. New York: Viking Juvenile, 1987. An imaginative resource for primary teachers and their students that makes the geometric universe accessible and alive for young learners.

Freeman, Christopher. The following two excellent math books target inductive thinking in a structured and creative way. They are directed toward grades 4–6, but younger talented math students will love the challenge.

- *Drawing Stars & Building Polyhedra*. Waco, TX: Prufrock Press, 2005. Students learn to draw stars eight or more points and to assemble 3-D shapes.

- *Hands-On Geometry: Constructions with Straightedge and Compass, Grades 4–6*. Waco, TX: Prufrock Press, 2010. Students learn how to draw accurate constructions of many different shapes using geometry tools.

Friedman, Aileen. *A Cloak for the Dreamer*. New York: Scholastic, 1994. A whimsical tale about a tailor's son trying to make a cloak using circles alone. An imaginative entrée into the world of geometry.

Gates, Phil. *Nature Got There First: Inventions Inspired by Nature*. New York: Kingfisher, 2010. An extraordinary resource for teachers seeking creative applications for science concepts, this book shows how nature (plant and animal life) has inspired the modern world's most ingenious inventions.

Gibbons, Gail. *Tell Me, Tree: All About Trees for Kids*. See page 197 for information.

The Gorilla Foundation (www.koko.org). A nonprofit organization dedicated to the preservation, protection, and well-being of great apes. The website provides information about gorillas—a favorite subject of many children—as well as many teacher resources. Students can explore topics such as interspecies communication, conservation, behaviors, language, and intelligence.

Great Explorations in Math & Science (GEMS) (www.lhsgems .org). A developer and publisher of science and math curriculum and professional development resources, GEMS offers the *Seeds of Science/Roots of Reading* units that integrate research-based and field-tested science and literacy in engaging ways in many classrooms.

Greenaway, Theresa. *Tree Life*. Photographs by Kim Taylor. New York: DK Publishing, 1992. Part of the Look Closer series, this book invites children to explore the wide range of animal species that inhabit trees all around the world. A valuable resource for helping students appreciate what trees contribute to life on our planet. Designed for six- to ten-year-olds, the series includes a wide range of environments, from coral reef to pond life, forests, and swamps.

Grover, Max. *Amazing and Incredible Counting Stories! A Number of Tall Tales*. Boston, MA: HMH Books for Young Readers, 1995. Through a series of sensational (and improbable) newspaper stories, readers can count giant banjos, pickle balloons, and time-saving jelly faucets. A witty introduction to the world of numbers for the very young child.

Hoban, Tana. Hoban's books stand alone in getting students to see the shapes all around them. Her exquisite photographs open up their eyes and invite them on a treasure hunt for a variety of shapes. We recommend the following:

- *Cubes, Cones, Cylinders, and Spheres*. New York: Greenwillow Books, 2000. Hoban teaches children to recognize these shapes in their environment.

- *Shapes, Shapes, Shapes*. New York: Greenwillow Books, 1996. An excellent book for exploring shapes all around the child's immediate environment—both inside and outside.

K3 Teacher Resources (www.k-3teacherresources.com). A must-see website for every primary teacher. Resources are as immense as teaching ideas. Includes a helpful section on technology in the classroom.

Kid Info (www.kidinfo.com/Science/Endangered_animals). One of the best reference websites for students, teachers, and parents on endangered species—what the term means, how species become listed, as well as activities that help students become aware of the challenges these species face and the organizations that seek to address them.

Leimbach, Judy. *Enrichment Units in Math*. Waco, TX: Prufrock Press, 2009. This collection of math materials is ideal for students ready to go beyond practicing computational skills and other basic concepts taught in the regular curriculum.

Locker, Thomas. An extraordinary oil painter who illuminates scientific wonders through art. His artwork is a powerful catalyst for engaging young minds in the science and art of the natural world. We recommend the following:

- *Cloud Dance*. Boston, MA: HMH Books for Young Readers, 2002. In this book, cumulus, cirrus, and stratus clouds dance across the sky in different seasons and times of day.

- *Mountain Dance*. Boston, MA: HMH Books for Young Readers, 2001. An exploration deep into the earth where geological forces affect the formations on the earth's surface.

- *Rachel Carson: Preserving a Sense of Wonder.* With text by Joseph Bruchac. Golden, CO: Fulcrum Publishing, 2009. The story of Rachel Carson's extraordinary life is shown through the museum quality paintings of Thomas Locker.

- *Water Dance.* Boston, MA: HMH Books for Young Readers, 2002. This book shows the vast journey of water through the world.

Locker, Thomas, and Candace Christiansen. *Sky Tree: Seeing Science Through Art.* New York: HarperCollins, 2001. This book shows a tree's transformation through the seasons and the creatures that live around it.

McGregor, Debbie, and Wendy Precious. "Dramatic Science." *Science and Children* 48, no. 2 (October 2010): 56–59. www.read ingrockets.org/content/pdfs/dramatic_science.pdf. A wonderful article for teachers of primary grades who want to teach science to young students through the lively art of drama. Authors from the U.K. share how they used acting techniques and the positive results in terms of increased motivation and learning.

Metropolitan Museum of Art. *Museum Shapes.* New York: Little, Brown Books for Young Readers, 2005. A beautiful book featuring a wide range of artists from the museum's collections that expose children to simple and complex shapes.

Miller, Debbie S. *Are Trees Alive?* London: Walker Childrens Paperbacks, 2003. A unique approach to the study of trees, this book compares children to trees, where roots function somewhat like feet, bark like skin, and leaves like hair. Through this lens, young students discover various trees from the baobab in Africa to the bristlecone pine of California.

National Geographic Kids (kids.nationalgeographic.com). Extensive offering for children of all ages—links to explore many topics, videos, interactive learning opportunities, games, and more. The video section contains videos that can be viewed for free about everything from animals to science experiments to weather. A great resource to supplement lessons in all kinds of subject areas.

NGAkids Art Zone (www.nga.gov). Search "NGAkids Art Zone" to find an extraordinary variety of rich, interactive art activities, many free apps, and images for children to work with. Students can create portraits, landscapes, and collage in the style of different artists and even learn digital photography and digital photo editing.

Oppenheim, Joanne. *Have You Seen Trees?* New York: Scholastic, 1995. Told in the form of a poem accompanied by lush illustrations, this book suits young children just learning about trees and the different ways they support animals and people and is an effective and graceful integration of poetry, artistry, and science.

Pallotta, Jerry. *Icky Bug Shapes.* New York: Scholastic, 2004. Most kids love learning about "icky bugs," but in this picture book they will also explore circles, squares, rectangles, stars, and other shapes in the bugs' bodies.

Pappas, Theoni. *The Adventures of Penrose the Mathematical Cat.* San Francisco: Wide World Publishing, 1997. Learning mathematical topics and doing the activities become far more engaging and accessible with Penrose the cat leading the way.

———. *Fractals, Googols and Other Mathematical Tales.* San Francisco: Wide World Publishing, 1993. Real numbers, exponents, dimensions, and geometry among other topics come alive in Pappas's stories.

PBS Teachers STEM Education Resource Center (pbslearn ingmedia.org). True to its high standards in producing TV programming related to STEM, PBS offers extensive STEM resources for grades preK–12 in the form of sponsored websites, a number of them related to different TV series. PBS also partners with NASA to create teacher resources on climate change.

Pinczes, Elinor. *One Hundred Hungry Ants.* Boston, MA: HMH Books for Young Readers, 1993. An entertaining way to introduce children to the principles of division, this book will entice any child with a love of rhyme, picnics, and bugs (even if he or she doesn't like math).

———. *A Remainder of One.* Boston, MA: HMH Books for Young Readers, 1995. A wonderful way to stimulate mathematical reasoning—all in the service of helping poor Joe from not being the remaining, lone bug after dividing the others into lines.

Pollock, Steve, and Brian Lane. *Ecology.* New York: DK Publishing, 2005. One of the "Eyewitness" books, this volume explores how animals, plants, energy, and matter interconnect in habitats around the world. A rich resource for teachers to integrate with other science curricula.

Pope, Joyce. *Animal Homes.* Mahwah, NJ: Troll Communications, 1994. An imaginative introduction to the habitats of nature's various animals.

Poppe, Carol A., and Nancy A. Van Matre. *K–3 Science Activities Kit.* West Nyack, NY: The Center for Applied Research in Education, 1988. A well-sequenced and comprehensive sourcebook for all ability levels, this volume offers five science units—weather, nutrition, birds, trees, and pets—and a total of forty activities. Includes illustrations, reproducible materials, management suggestions, and charts of critical-thinking skills required for each activity.

Pratt, Kristin Joy. *A Swim Through the Sea.* Nevada City, CA: Dawn Publications, 1994. Written and illustrated by a sixteen-year-old, this alphabet book features wonderful wordplay and presents a lot of information to curious minds with the guidance of an amiable seahorse.

———. *A Walk in the Rainforest.* Nevada City, CA: Dawn Publications, 2007. A rich entrée into the world of a rain forest with its many varied animals, plants, and people. A small ant tells it all.

Rohmann, Eric. *Time Flies.* New York: Dragonfly Books, 1997. Inspired by the theory that birds are modern relatives of dinosaurs, this wordless book involves young students in a thrilling journey through time with a series of oil paintings that will spur creative imagination.

Schmidt, Stanley F. Life of Fred Elementary Series. Reno, NV: Polka Dot Publishing. With humor and illustrations, elementary math unfolds through the story of Fred Gauss, the five-year-old math professor at Kittens University. Young gifted students will delight in the breadth of learning that these math stories—which can be used as full math curriculum up through calculus—

contain. Math concepts are artfully interwoven in an authentic manner that engages children from start to finish.

Schneck, Marcus. *Patterns in Nature: A World of Color, Shape, and Light.* New York: Crescent Books, 1991. A marvelous source for exploring shapes and patterns in nature, this book includes more than 120 full-color photographs that inspire original thinking and insight in children of all ages.

Scholastic Books. *Trees and Forests: From Algae to Sequoias: The History, Life, and Richness of Forests.* New York: Scholastic, 1995. Part of the Voyages of Discovery series, this volume covers a great deal of content on tree life around the world. Through art and text, as well as intriguing graphics and special effects, it provides a powerful catalyst and interactive guide for exploration and discovery.

Schwartz, David M., offers some witty and imaginative math books, beloved by young children. In each, children step into the mathematical world exploring measurement, proportion, and a whole alphabet book's worth of ideas.

- *G Is for Googol.* Berkeley, CA: Tricycle Press, 1998. An alphabet book exploring many math concepts and filled with math trivia.

- *If You Hopped Like a Frog.* New York: Scholastic, 1999. A book explaining ratios and proportions to children through the amazing abilities of animals.

- *Millions to Measure.* New York: HarperCollins, 2006. A book investigating and explaining length, weight, and volume measurements that covers both the standard and metric systems.

Science Buddies on Pinterest (www.pinterest.com/sciencebuddies). Pinterest is a popular resource for educators to share ideas and activities. Check out Science Buddies' Pinterest page for hands-on projects in science, technology, engineering, and math. The K–3 board features activities perfect for primary-age learners.

Scieszka, Jon. *Math Curse.* New York: Viking Books for Young Readers, 1995. Bold illustrations and witty text entice both students and teachers into the wonders of mathematics and its applications in everyday living.

SketchUp. A resource for creating digital 3-D models. Gifted primary students can see their ideas quickly translated into three-dimensional shapes, which frees their imagination. A free download for educators is available at www.sketchup.com/3Dfor/k12-education.

Smutny, Joan Franklin, and S. E. von Fremd. *Differentiating for the Young Child: Teaching Strategies Across the Content Areas, PreK–3.* See page 195 for information.

Smutny, Joan Franklin, and S. E. von Fremd, eds. *Igniting Creativity in Gifted Learners, K–6: Strategies for Every Teacher.* See page 195 for information.

The Space Place (www.spaceplace.nasa.gov). A website maintained by NASA that teaches kids about space and the solar system. The "Parents & Educators" section features extensive resources, including interactive learning activities, science project ideas, writing adventure stories, building spacecraft, games, puzzles, and more.

STEAM (www.stemtosteam.org). An educational initiative from the Rhode Island School of Design, STEAM's website provides useful information on the importance of art in STEM and includes application examples, news, and ideas in their resource section.

Svedberg, Ulf. *Nicky the Nature Detective.* New York: R&S Books, 1988. This charming book is an informative and entertaining guide for the beginning naturalist, describing changes in flora and fauna from season to season while also offering exciting ideas for nature activities.

Taylor, Barbara. *Forest Life.* New York: DK Publishing, 1993. Part of the Look Closer series, this volume gives young children an intimate view of forest life that provides insights into plants and animals in original and creative ways.

Terrell, Sandy. *Roberto's Rainforest.* El Cajon, CA: Interaction Publishers, 1995. This innovative and activity-filled book is a scientific "canoe trip" that allows young naturalists to explore a tropical rain forest in South America.

Torrance, E. Paul, and H. Tammy Safter. *Incubation Model of Teaching: Getting Beyond the Aha!* Buffalo, NY: Bearly, 1990. This trailblazing book offers a conceptual knowledge of creative "incubation" and of how to design more innovative teaching approaches that will tap children's natural curiosity, playfulness, spontaneity, and invention.

Van Der Meer, Ron, and Bob Gardner. *The Math Kit: A Three-Dimensional Tour Through Mathematics.* New York: Macmillan Publishing, 1994. A captivating approach to the study of mathematics, this book includes graphic representations of the properties of simple arithmetic, multiplication tables, and decimal places; three-dimensional models of the Pythagorean theorem, solid polygons, and trigonometric angles; games; and a complete glossary of math terms.

WebMuseum (www.ibiblio.org). An online resource containing information about artists and their works of art, different styles of art, and periods in art history. Search "web museum" to find database pages.

Wells, Robert. *Can You Count to a Googol?* Morton Grove, IL: Albert Whitman & Co., 2000. An exploration of our number system that builds by powers of 10 and a history of the googol, including how it got its name.

———. *How Do You Lift a Lion?* Morton Grove, IL: Albert Whitman & Co., 1996. An engaging introduction to the principles behind pulleys, screws, levers, wheels, and other simple machines.

———. *What's Smaller Than a Pygmy Shrew?* Morton Grove, IL: Albert Whitman & Co., 1995. From a pygmy shrew to an insect to things so tiny you need a microscope, this book explores the miniature universe in intriguing ways.

White, Nancy. *The Magic School Bus Explores the World of Animals.* New York: Scholastic, 2000. Readers take a journey to different habitats to find the right "home" for an animal that inexplicably appeared in Ms. Frizzle's classroom.

Wilkes, Angela. *The Amazing Outdoor Activity Book.* New York: DK Publishing, 1996. An action-packed book, with more than fifty creative outdoor projects for children to build, grow, collect, draw, make, and bake. A good resource for parents or teachers that includes easy-to-follow instructions.

Wood, John Norris. *Woods and Forests: Nature Hide and Seek Book.* Huntsville, AL: Reading's Fun Ltd, 1997. A visually beautiful introduction to the wonderful creatures hiding behind bushes, under rocks, and inside holes in the tree, this book presents many important facts about animals and the habitats—American and European woodlands—they occupy.

Chapter 7

Gellman, E. S. *School Testing: What Parents and Educators Need to Know.* Westport, CT: Praeger, 1995. This excellent resource for anyone involved in making children's educational decisions explains tests and their uses and misuses. Written for those with little or no training in testing.

Hess, Frederick M., and Michael Q. McShane, eds. *Common Core Meets Education Reform: What It All Means for Politics, Policy, and the Future of Schooling.* New York: Teachers College Press, 2014. Essays by academics and policy analysts on integrating Common Core Standards with existing efforts at accountability and other reforms.

Hunsaker, Scott, ed. *Identification: The Theory and Practice of Identifying Students for Gifted and Talented Education Services.* Waco, TX: Prufrock Press, 2012. The book contains four sections: Theoretical Foundations, Professional Foundations, Identification Practices, and Instrumentation. Leading experts in gifted education take an in-depth look at the identification of gifted and talented students.

Johnsen, Susan K., ed. *Identifying Gifted Students: A Practical Guide.* Waco, TX: Prufrock Press, 2011. Susan shares an overview of assessment, definitions, models and characteristics of gifted students, different approaches to assessment, making placement decisions, and evaluating effectiveness.

Kingore, Bertie. *Assessment: Timesaving Procedures for Busy Teachers.* Austin, TX: Professional Associates, 2007. Practical guidelines for organization and management of Assessment.

———. *Developing Portfolios for Authentic Assessment, PreK–3.* Thousand Oaks, CA: Corwin Press, 2008. Includes rubrics, samples, reproducibles, and procedures for developing assessment portfolios and integrating them into classroom instruction.

———. *The Kingore Observation Inventory (KOI): Equitable Practices to Recognize and Differentiate for High Ability.* Austin, TX: Professional Associates Publishing, 2001. Presents a structure of behaviors that young gifted children typically demonstrate.

Pattison, Darcy. *What Is Common Core?* Little Rock, AR: Mims House, 2013. An overview and introduction to the Common Core State Standards.

Roeper Review: A Journal on Gifted Education. Bloomfield Hills, MI: The Roeper School. Most issues of this quarterly journal include a "Testing" section that reviews instruments used for assessing gifted children. A collection of these articles, available from the Roeper School, would be a valuable resource for learning the intricacies of testing gifted children.

Sattler, Jerome M. *Assessment of Children: Cognitive Foundations.* San Diego, CA: Jerome M. Sattler, Publisher, 2008. The most comprehensive reference available on testing children.

Smutny, Joan Franklin, Kathleen Veenker, and Stephen Veenker. *Your Gifted Child: How to Recognize and Develop the Special Talents in Your Child from Birth to Age Seven.* New York: Ballantine Books, 1989. Comprehensive explanations to help parents and educators understand the characteristics and needs of young gifted children.

Webb, James T., and Patricia A. Kleine. "Assessing Gifted and Talented Children." *Testing Young Children: A Reference Guide for Developmental, Psychoeducational, and Psychosocial Assessments.* J. L. Culbertson, and D. J. Willis, eds. Austin, TX: Pro-ed., 1993. This chapter examines the general process and some specific suggestions for testing gifted children.

Chapter 8

Choice, Penny, and Sally Walker. *The New RtI: Response to Intelligence.* Marion, IL: Pieces of Learning, 2011. Shares a different way of looking at RTI, Response to Intervention, in order to consider learning differences at both ends of the learning continuum.

Gentry, Marcia L., and Jamie MacDougall, "Total School Cluster Grouping: Model, Research and Practice." Mansfield Center, CT: Creative Learning Press, 2008. This paper presents a systematic survey of clustering problems from the combinatorial point of view.

Kulik, James, and Chen-Lin Kulik. "Ability Grouping and Gifted Students." *Handbook of Gifted Education.* Nicholas Colangelo and Gary A. Davis, eds. Upper Saddle River, NJ: Pearson, 2002. Research-based information about the effects of ability grouping on gifted students.

Rogers, Karen B. *Re-Forming Gifted Education: How Parents and Teachers Can Match the Program to the Child.* Scottsdale, AZ: Great Potential Press, 2002. This book contains an analysis of research on gifted education.

———. *The Relationship of Grouping Practices to the Education of the Gifted and Talented Learner: Research-Based Decision Making.* Storrs, CT: National Research Center on the Gifted and Talented, 1991. This book does a splendid job of explaining research on grouping practices and relating it to the specific educational needs of gifted students. While remaining sensitive to all populations, the author addresses a range of critical issues and concerns, focusing on the dilemma many bright students face in cooperative learning situations.

Winebrenner, Susan, and Dina Brulles. *The Cluster Grouping Handbook.* Minneapolis: Free Spirit Publishing, 2008. Explains how the Cluster Grouping Model differs from other grouping practices and how to implement, sustain, and evaluate school-wide cluster grouping.

———. *Teaching Gifted Kids in Today's Classroom: Strategies and Techniques Every Teacher Can Use.* Minneapolis: Free Spirit Publishing, 2012. The authors demonstrate how to adapt curriculum for gifted students focusing on compacting and differentiation.

Chapter 9

Alvarado, Nancy. "Adjustment of Adults Who Are Gifted." *Advanced Development* 1 (1989): 77–86. Insightful and helpful for parents of gifted children who may not acknowledge their own exceptional qualities and the effects these have on their lives.

Berger, Sandra L. *Supporting Gifted Education through Advocacy.* Washington, DC: National Association for Gifted Children, 1990, ERIC Digest No. E494. Concise and directly applicable suggestions for parents and educators. This article may be freely reproduced and distributed. files.eric.ed.gov/fulltext/ED321499.pdf.

Colangelo, Nicholas, Susan G. Assouline, and Miraca U. M. Gross. *A Nation Deceived: How Schools Hold Back America's Brightest Students.* Iowa City, IA: University of Iowa Press, 2004. This is an amazing resource that discusses acceleration as a programming option for gifted children. It details myths, reflections, and the research backing the positive and negative aspects of acceleration. This report can be downloaded for free at www.accelerationinstitute.org.

Delisle, Jim. *Parenting Gifted Kids: Tips for Raising Happy and Successful Gifted Children.* Waco, TX: Prufrock Press, 2006. This book provides specific tips and practical advice for raising gifted children. Stories and vignettes are used throughout the book to provide real-world situations.

DeVries, Arlene, and James T. Webb. *Gifted Parent Groups: The SENG Model.* Scottsdale, AZ: Great Potential Press, 2007. Gives a detailed description of both content and process for developing and conducting guided discussion groups for parents of gifted children.

Dinkmeyer, Don, and Gary D. McKay. *Systematic Training for Effective Parenting (STEP).* Fredericksburg, VA: STEP Publishers, 2007. A complete parenting program that includes a handbook for parents, videos, and leader's materials. The *Leader's Resource Guide* includes an excellent short course in facilitating parent groups and group dynamics ("Part One: STEP Group Leadership," pp. 16–30). STEP publications are often available in libraries or through schools. Visit www.steppublishers.com for more information or to purchase.

Fertig, Carol. *Raising a Gifted Child: A Parenting Success Handbook.* Waco, TX: Prufrock Press, 2009. Provides information about finding optimal learning opportunities in a variety of academics and talent areas.

Galbraith, Judy, and Jim Delisle. *When Gifted Kids Don't Have All the Answers: How to Meet Their Social and Emotional Needs.* Minneapolis: Free Spirit Publishing, 2015. Addresses the social-emotional needs of giftedness both inside and outside of the classroom. Provides practical strategies and vignettes with a variety of perspectives and personalities.

George, David. *Young Gifted and Bored.* Bethel, CT: Crown House Publishing, 2011. This book, written for both parents and teachers, provides resources for parents to recognize boredom and underachievement with strategies to help elicit depth in the curriculum.

Harvard Family Research Project. "Parent-Teacher Conference Tip Sheets." October 2010. www.hfrp.org. This document provides information and guidelines for the various stakeholders in parent-teacher conferences and provides some concrete suggestions and strategies.

Hertzog, Nancy B. "Prepare Your Child for Happiness and Success at School." *Ready for Preschool.* Waco, TX: Prufrock Press, 2008. This chapter provides strategies for strengthening the relationship between home and school as well as facilitating the transition from home to school.

Keirouz, Kathryn S. "Concerns of Parents of Gifted Children: A Research Review." *Gifted Child Quarterly* 34, no. 2 (1990): 56–63. An excellent, concise source.

Klein, Barbara. *Raising Gifted Kids: Everything You Need to Know to Help Your Exceptional Child Thrive.* New York: AMACOM, 2007. This book includes practical information on the unique challenges of raising gifted children. Chapters start with "is my child really gifted" to addressing and working with the various aspects of your gifted child, including selecting a school.

Knopper, Dorothy. *Parent Education: Parents as Partners.* Boulder, CO: Open Space Communications, 1994. A monograph in the Professional Development Series, Current Themes in Gifted Education, edited by Elinor Katz, this book presents a concise, useful reference and action guide supported with anecdotes and interpretations. Useful for busy professionals and parents.

Kurcinka, Mary Sheedy. *Raising Your Spirited Child: A Guide for Parents Whose Child Is More Intense, Sensitive, Perceptive, Persistent, Energetic.* New York: HarperCollins, 2006. A valuable, practical, and popular resource for teachers and parents. Includes hundreds of specific suggestions to help children monitor themselves and develop self-control.

Meckstroth, Elizabeth A. "Guiding the Parents of Gifted Children: The Role of Counselors and Teachers." *Counseling Gifted and Talented Children: A Guide for Teachers, Counselors, and Parents.* Roberta M. Milgram, ed. Norwood, NJ: Ablex Publishing, 1991: 95–120. Specific information on teacher-parent conferences, involving parents in identifying gifted children, helping parents acknowledge and understand giftedness, and organizing and facilitating parent discussion groups.

———. "Paradigm Shifts into Giftedness." *Roeper Review* 15, no. 2 (1992): 91–92. The article explores how a gifted child affects the family.

Mitchell, Patty Bruce, ed. *An Advocate's Guide to Building Support for Gifted and Talented Education.* Washington, DC: National Association of State Boards of Education, 1981. A classic handbook for effective advocacy with numerous resources to support gifted education at all levels and stages. Visit NASBE online at www.nasbe.org.

National Association of Gifted Children. *Parenting for High Potential.* This magazine is designed for parents and published eight times a year. It is available to members of NAGC.

Rogers, Karen B. *Re-Forming Gifted Education: How Parents and Teachers Can Match the Program to the Child.* Scottsdale, AZ: Great Potential Press, 2002. This book includes information on programming for gifted education and offers advice and suggestions in selecting and matching a program for the various aspects of a gifted child.

Silverman, Linda Kreger, ed. *Counseling the Gifted and Talented.* Denver, CO: Love Publishing, 1993. A seminal text on the counseling and psychological aspects of giftedness. Check out her chapter "Counseling Families," which discusses the concerns of families of gifted children and offers strategies to address those concerns.

Smutny, Joan Franklin, Kathleen Veenker, and Stephen Veenker. *Your Gifted Child: How to Recognize and Develop the Special Talents in Your Child from Birth to Age Seven.* See page 204 for information.

Treffinger, Donald, Tracy Inman, Jennifer Jolly, and Joan Franklin Smutny. *Parenting Gifted Children: The Authoritative Guide from the National Association for Gifted Children.* Waco, TX: Prufrock Press, 2010. This publication combines research and practical information about gifted children and focuses on the joys and struggles of parenting a gifted child.

Webb, James T., Elizabeth A. Meckstroth, and Stephanie S. Tolan. *Guiding the Gifted Child: A Practical Source for Parents and Teachers.* See page 190 for information.

Webb, James T., Janet L. Gore, Edward R. Amend, and Arlene DeVries. *A Parent's Guide to Gifted Children.* Scottsdale, AZ: Great Potential Press, 2007. This book provides a true guide to all aspects of giftedness including characteristics, school advice, home relationships, social-emotional characteristics, and advice to address how to work with these students. Includes real stories and guidance from psychologists and educators.

Winebrenner, Susan, and Lisa M. Kiss. *Teaching Kids with Learning Difficulties in Today's Classroom: How Every Teacher Can Help Struggling Students Succeed.* Minneapolis: Free Spirit Publishing, 2014. Strategies and techniques every teacher can use to motivate struggling students, including those who are gifted.

Chapter 10

Adelson, Jill, L. and Hope E. Wilson. *Letting Go of Perfect: Overcoming Perfectionism in Kids.* Waco, TX: Prufrock Press, 2009. Provides description of types of perfectionism and strategies to use at home and school to help with negative perfectionism traits.

Canfield, Jack, and Harold C. Wells. *100 Ways to Enhance Self-Concept in the Classroom.* Upper Saddle River, NJ: Pearson, 1994. A classic, friendly guide that will inspire you.

Cartledge, Gwendolyn, and James Kleefield. *Taking Part: Introducing Social Skills to Children, PreK–Grade 3.* Champaign, IL: Research Press, 2009. This program for children in preschool through third grade provides more than thirty lessons with activities to build social skills such as listening, respecting the property of others, resolving conflicts, and communicating nonverbally. Includes stick puppets and a teacher's manual.

Center on the Social and Emotional Foundations for Early Learning (www.csefel.vanderbilt.edu). Dedicated to strengthening the capacity of Head Start and childcare programs, the center offers many free resources for teachers and caregivers on their website.

Clark, Barbara. *Optimizing Learning: The Integrative Education Model in the Classroom.* Columbus, OH: Merrill Publishing, 1986. A great leader in gifted education shows how and why to integrate control (physical, chosen, and perceived), cognitive processes, intuition, and more in a responsive learning environment.

Colangelo, Nicholas, Susan G. Assouline, and Miraca U. M. Gross. *A Nation Deceived: How Schools Hold Back America's Brightest Students.* See page 205 for information.

Cross, Tracy, L. *The Social and Emotional Lives of Gifted Kids: Understanding and Guiding Their Development.* Waco, TX: Prufrock Press, 2005. Provides background information about social and emotional characteristics and the key concepts and ideas to guide students.

———. *On the Social and Emotional Lives of Gifted Children: Issues and Factors in Their Psychological Development.* Waco, TX: Prufrock Press, 2011. The sections titled "About Gifted Children: Who They Are and Why" and "Guiding Gifted Children" provide some background information about social-emotional characteristics in relation to developmental theories as well as practical advice and tips for working with students.

Daniels, Susan, and Michael M. Piechowski, eds. *Living with Intensity: Understanding the Sensitivity, Excitability, and Emotional Development of Gifted Children, Adolescents and Adults.* Scottsdale, AZ: Great Potential Press, 2009. An in-depth look at Dabrowski's overexcitabilities and strategies, and examples to understand and work with individuals who demonstrate them.

Davis, Gary A., Sylvia B. Rimm, and Del Siegle. *Education of the Gifted and Talented.* Upper Saddle River, NJ: Pearson, 2010. A textbook focusing on the history of gifted education, definitions, characteristics, and programming.

Delisle, James R. *Guiding the Social and Emotional Development of Gifted Youth: A Practical Guide for Educators and Counselors.* New York: Longman, 1992. An essential resource that's very useful in the areas of self-concept, school achievement, and invitational education; specific adjustment concerns of gifted students; strategies, activities, materials, and conditions to promote self-control and achievement; and more.

Dreyer, Sharon Spredemann. *The Bookfinder: A Guide to Children's Literature About the Needs and Problems of Youth Aged 2–15.* Vols. 1–5. Circle Pines, MN: American Guidance Service, 1977–1994. A resource tool that includes a subject index to match children with books they'll want to read or have read to them. Includes age interest range and synopsis of every book. Later volumes are also available on CD-ROM.

Dweck, Carol S. *Mindset: The New Psychology of Success: How We Can Learn to Fulfill Our Potential.* New York: Ballantine Books, 2006. Introduces the positive psychology approach and using a growth mindset. Provides research, examples, and strategies to use a growth mindset.

Fonseca, Christine. *Emotional Intensity in Gifted Students: Helping Kids Cope with Explosive Feelings.* Waco, TX: Prufrock Press, 2011. Wonderful resource with vignettes and strategies on how to work with the students and their social-emotional needs, written for both teachers and parents.

Galbraith, Judy. *The Survival Guide for Gifted Kids: For Ages 10 & Under.* See page 190 for information.

Galbraith, Judy, and Jim Delisle. *When Gifted Kids Don't Have All the Answers: How to Meet Their Social and Emotional Needs.* See page 205 for information

George, David. *Young Gifted and Bored.* See page 205 for details.

Goldstein, Arnold P., and Gerald Y. Michaels. *Empathy: Developmental Training and Consequence.* New York: Psychology Press, 1985. How and why to be more empathetic.

Goleman, Daniel. *Emotional Intelligence: Why It Can Matter More than IQ.* New York: Bantam Books, 2005. Goleman argues convincingly that how we use our intelligence is more important than how much intelligence we have. Provocative reading for teachers and parents alike.

Halsted, Judith Wynn. *Some of My Best Friends Are Books: Guiding Gifted Readers.* Scottsdale, AZ: Great Potential Press, 2009. This book provides a comprehensive guide to finding literature related to characteristics of giftedness.

Janos, Paul M., and Nancy M. Robinson. "Psychosocial Development in Intellectually Gifted Children." *The Gifted and Talented: Developmental Perspectives.* F.D. Horowitz and M. O'Brien, eds. Washington, DC: American Psychological Association, 1985: 149–195. One of many useful, insightful, research-based chapters in a superlative anthology on giftedness.

Katz, Elinor. *Affective Education: Self Concept and the Gifted Student.* Boulder, CO: Open Space Communications, 1994. A concise overview of gifted children's self-concept related to models of intelligence, motivation, achievement, and other home and school issues.

Kurcinka, Mary Sheedy. *Raising Your Spirited Child: A Guide for Parents Whose Child Is More Intense, Sensitive, Perceptive, Persistent, Energetic.* New York: HarperCollins, 2006. A valuable, practical, and popular resource for teachers and parents. Includes hundreds of specific suggestions to help children monitor themselves and develop self-control.

Lawrence, Gordon. *People Types and Tiger Stripes: Using Psychological Type to Help Students Discover Their Unique Potential.* Gainesville, FL: Center for Applications of Psychological Type, 2009. A practical, easy-to-understand explanation of personality types. Several chapters relate types to successful teaching and classroom issues such as motivation, curriculum, learning modalities, and teaching styles.

Montgomery, Diane, ed. *Able, Gifted and Talented Underachievers.* West Sussex, UK: John Wiley and Sons, 2009. Explains the origins of underachievement in gifted and talented students. We recommend the chapter "Why Do the Gifted and Talented Underachieve? How Can Masked and Hidden Talents Be Revealed?"

Myers, Isabel Briggs, and Peter B. Myers. *Gifts Differing: Understanding Personality Type.* Mountain View, CA: Davies-Black Publishing, 1995. A look at personality types, with sections focused on teaching and learning.

NAGC. "Myths About Gifted Students." Available at www.nagc.org. NAGC's list of the most prevalent myths in gifted education, with evidence explaining why the myth is untrue. The website includes links to further information.

Neihart, Maureen. *Peak Performance for Smart Kids: Strategies and Tips for Ensuring School Success.* Waco, TX: Prufrock Press, 2008. An amazing resource with seven strategies to work with all students but specifically gifted students.

Neihart, Maureen, Sally M. Reis, Nancy M. Robinson, and Sidney M. Moon, eds. *The Social and Emotional Development of Gifted Children: What Do We Know?* Waco, TX: Prufrock Press, 2002. Provides a variety of chapters with research that focuses on various aspects of social-emotional characteristics including perfectionism, gender differences, peer pressure, acceleration, and underachievement among others.

Payne, Lauren Murphy. *Just Because I Am: A Child's Book of Affirmation.* Minneapolis: Free Spirit Publishing, 2015. A picture book on fostering self-esteem in preschool, early elementary school, childcare settings, and the home.

Rimm, Sylvia. *Why Bright Kids Get Poor Grades and What You Can Do About It: A Six-Step Program for Parents and Teachers.* Scottsdale, AZ: Great Potential Press, 2008. A look at the types of underachievement with descriptions and strategies to help reverse it.

Roeper, Annemarie. *Educating Children for Life: The Modern Learning Community.* Monroe, NY: Trillium Press, 1990. Roeper lovingly inspires us to nurture children in developing responsibility, interdependence, and positive behaviors and attitudes along with their unique qualities.

Silverman, Linda Kreger. "A Developmental Model for Counseling the Gifted." *Counseling the Gifted and Talented.* Linda Kreger Silverman, ed. Denver: Love Publishing, 1993: 51–78. One of many sensitively written chapters in a comprehensive resource depicting the intricate, complex characteristics and needs of gifted children. Essential reading.

Supporting Emotional Needs of the Gifted, eds. *30 Essays on Giftedness: 30 Years of SENG.* Poughquag, NY: SENG, 2012. A selection of articles from the thirty years of SENG written by leading experts in the field of gifted education with topics ranging from parenting information, curricular recommendations, understanding giftedness, and adult reflections of experiences.

Webb, James T., Elizabeth A. Meckstroth, and Stephanie S. Tolan. *Guiding the Gifted Child: A Practical Resource for Parents and Teachers.* See page 190 for information.

Chapter 11

Baldwin, Alexinia Y., ed. *Culturally Diverse and Underserved Populations of Gifted Students.* Thousand Oaks, CA: Corwin Press, 2004. A joint publication by Corwin Press and the National Association for Gifted Children and part of the Essential Readings in Gifted Education series (Sally M. Reis, ed.). A collection of articles, this book is packed full of information and ideas on the obstacles faced by culturally diverse gifted students and strategies for identifying and addressing their learning needs.

Baum, Susan M., and Steven V. Owen. *To Be Gifted and Learning Disabled: Strategies for Helping Bright Students with LD, ADHD, and More.* Mansfield Center, CT: Creative Learning Press, 2004. Twice-exceptional students are one of the most at-risk populations of gifted students, and they need understanding and intervention. This volume provides tremendous insight into the lives of these children and what we can do to develop their talents.

Bernal, Ernesto M. "Delivering Two-Way Bilingual Immersion Programs to the Gifted and Talented: A Classic Yet Progressive Option for the New Millennium." *Underserved Gifted Populations: Responding to Their Needs and Abilities.* Joan Franklin Smutny, ed. Cresskill, NJ: Hampton Press, 2003: 141–156. Innovative examination of giftedness and bilingualism and an exploration of a multicultural curriculum and how it could be implemented.

Birely, Marlene. *Crossover Children: A Sourcebook for Helping Children Who Are Gifted and Learning Disabled.* Reston, VA: The Council for Exceptional Children, 1995. Contains a wealth of information to assist teachers and parents of twice-exceptional children.

Borland, James H., and Lisa Wright. "Identifying Young, Potentially Gifted, Economically Disadvantaged Students." *Gifted Child Quarterly* 38, no. 4 (Fall 1994): 164–171. A concise description and procedure to find gifted kindergarten students in urban schools using site-appropriate methods: observation, dynamic assessment, and the concept of best performance.

Castellano, Jaime, and Andrea Dawn Frazier, eds. *Special Populations in Gifted Education: Understanding Our Most Able Students from Diverse Backgrounds.* Waco, TX: Prufrock Press, 2011. Collection of research and practical guidance by experts in a variety of fields focusing on the needs of gifted girls, boys, English language learners, African Americans, those with special learning needs, those in rural communities, and much more. A helpful reference for teachers looking for a broader understanding of gifted learners.

Daniels, Susan, and Michael M. Piechowski, eds. *Living with Intensity: Understanding the Sensitivity, Excitability, and Emotional Development of Gifted Children, Adolescents and Adults.* See page 206 for information.

ERIC Education Resources Information Center (www.eric.ed.gov). Visit ERIC online for great, free information on many specific topics regarding diverse populations and other aspects of gifted education.

Foundation for Rural Education Development (www.fred.org). A nonprofit organization that sponsors programs and activities that improve the educational, social, and economic conditions of rural areas in the United States and Canada.

Gilligan, Carol. *In a Different Voice: Psychological Theory and Women's Development.* Cambridge, MA: Harvard University Press, 1993. This revolutionary book was the first of its kind in 1982 and has continued to this day to bear witness to the earliest messages girls receive from the world around them.

Gross, Miraca U. M. *Exceptionally Gifted Children.* New York: RoutledgeFalmer, 2004. An extraordinary follow-up from the 1993 edition which profiled fifteen children and followed their lives through school—their emotional and social lives, their achievement and underachievement. This book looks at those early years but takes readers through the next ten years. The students speak for themselves.

The Hollingworth Center for Highly Gifted Children (www.hollingworth.org). This center is a national support network dedicated to meeting the needs of highly gifted children. Find lots of information at their website, as well as links to other gifted resources and networking opportunities.

Kerr, Barbara A. *Smart Boys: Talent, Manhood, and the Search for Meaning.* Scottsdale, AZ: Great Potential Press, 2001. Examination of the social and emotional issues of gifted boys whose sensitivities, enjoyment of things not traditionally "male," and intellectual passions place them at odds with gender norms and often subject them to misunderstanding and ridicule. Practical guide on how to support such promising boys.

———. *Smart Girls: A New Psychology of Girls, Women, and Giftedness.* Scottsdale, AZ: Great Potential Press, 2005. A wealth of information about meeting the needs of gifted girls. Includes many ideas focused on specific topics such as minorities, extraordinary talents, programs, and young gifted children.

Kerr, Barbara A., and Robyn McKay. *Smart Girls in the 21st Century: Understanding Talented Girls and Women.* Tucson, AZ: Great Potential Press, 2014. Examines modern, smart girls' development, types of intelligence, and barriers to their achievement. Includes information on adolescence and college, gifted minority girls and women, twice-exceptional girls, career options, and eminent gifted women.

Martin, Darlene E., David K. Sing, and L. 'Alapa Hunter. "Na Pua No'Eau: The Hawaiian Perspective of Giftedness." *Underserved Gifted Populations: Responding to Their Needs and Abilities.* Joan Franklin Smutny, ed. Cresskill, NJ: Hampton Press, 2003: 179–203. Excellent contribution to the needs of Hawaiian gifted students and their communities, and description of an innovative program to address these needs.

Phillips, Lynn M. *The Girls Report: What We Know and Need to Know About Growing Up Female.* New York: The National Council for Research on Women, 2000. This report explores many dimensions of girls' lives as they move through the millennium. While still exploring major concerns addressed in earlier reports, this latest one looks at the extraordinary resiliency, intelligence, and vision possessed by girls. With the proper support and vigilance, such talents continue to develop as girls become women.

Ramirez, Al. "Gifted and Poor: America's Quiet Crisis." *Underserved Gifted Populations: Responding to Their Needs and Abilities.* Joan Franklin Smutny, ed. Cresskill, NJ: Hampton Press, 2003: 129–138. Clear, incisive report on the negative impact of poverty, especially on the gifted, and the necessary steps to reverse the loss of talent in so many communities. Includes an excellent list of recommendations.

Reis, Susan M. "Toward a Theory of Creativity in Diverse Creative Women." *Creativity Research Journal* 14, nos. 3 and 4 (2002): 305–316. A comprehensive study of how creativity develops in girls and women and the internal and external forces that restrict but also shape the expression of their gifts.

Rural School and Community Trust (www.ruraledu.org). This organization focuses on rural school improvement and innovation. Visit the website for information about the Rural

School Innovation Network (RSIN) and the Rural Trust Global Teacher Network.

Slocumb, Paul D., and Ruby K. Payne. *Removing the Mask: Giftedness in Poverty.* Highlands, TX: aha! Process, 2000. Alternative strategies for discovering high potential among students of poverty. Offers practical guidance on what behaviors and products to look for and includes identification instruments and other processes that illuminate hidden gifts and talents. Demonstrates the importance of support systems for identified gifted students who may not get much encouragement anywhere else.

Smutny, Joan Franklin, ed. *Illinois Association for Gifted Journal 2014: Underrepresented Populations.* Illinois Association for Gifted Children, 2014. Articles by practitioners and researchers in touch with the daily lives and struggles of different target populations—from Native Americans to underachieving to those with auditory problems. Authors present practical solutions that support and nurture their talents.

Smutny, Joan Franklin, Kathryn P. Haydon, Olivia Bolaños, and Gina Estrada Danley. *Discovering and Developing Talents in Spanish-Speaking Students.* Thousand Oaks, CA: Corwin Press, 2012. This book covers a lot of material—from the cultural backgrounds of Spanish-speaking students, to their unique abilities and talents, to the different ways teachers can use these strengths to create learning experiences and build relationships with parents and community members.

Smutny, Joan Franklin, and S. E. von Fremd. *The Lives of Great Women Leaders & You.* Margaretta wa Gacheru, cont. Royal Fireworks Press, 2014. Biographies of pioneer women from different cultures and socioeconomic groups and how they overcame obstacles to realize their gifts and contribute to their world. Spotlight on artists (visual and performing), politicians, social reformers, scientists, mathematicians, astronauts, environmentalists, journalists, and more.

Stambaugh, Tamra. *Serving Gifted Students in Rural Settings.* Waco, TX: Prufrock Press, 2015. Exploration of rural education and how to address the needs of gifted learners in rural environments. Includes practical ideas and strategies for identifying and teaching rural gifted students, and for creating support systems for their ongoing needs.

Supporting Emotional Needs of the Gifted, eds. *30 Essays on Giftedness: 30 Years of SENG.* Poughquag, NY: SENG, 2012. See page 207 for details. We recommend reading "Overexcitability and the Gifted" by Sharon Lind.

Thom, Mary. *Balancing the Equation: Where Are Women and Girls in Science, Engineering and Technology?* New York: The National Council for Research on Women, 2001. This report focuses on the importance of advancing women and girls in the sciences and demonstrates the need for systemic change in the primary and secondary grades up through the professional fields which also include engineering and technology.

Tonemah, Stuart. "Tess Questions." *Underserved Gifted Populations: Responding to Their Needs and Abilities.* Joan Franklin Smutny, ed. Cresskill, NJ: Hampton Press, 2003: 261–268. A sensitive portrait of gifted Native Americans by a Kiowa Comanche researcher, teacher, and counselor with forty years of experience in Native American education. Reveals the common strengths and struggles of these students and the steps that must be taken to create substantive change.

Torrance, E. Paul, Kathy Goff, and Neil B. Satterfield. *Multicultural Mentoring of the Gifted and Talented.* Waco, TX: Prufrock Press, 1998. Useful information and practical guidance on developing mentorships that target the unique needs of ethnically diverse and economically disadvantaged children and young people. Specific ideas on identifying mentors and mentees and putting a mentoring program into practice. Important resource for teachers, parents, and community organizations.

U-STARS~PLUS. Equips teachers with tools for early identification of giftedness in multicultural, low socioeconomic, and disabled populations. Available at the website of the Council for Exceptional Children (www.cec.sped.org). Find it under "Special Ed Topics," then click on "Specialty Areas" and "Gifted."

Bibliography

Alvino, J. *Parents' Guide to Raising a Gifted Child: Recognizing and Developing Your Child's Potential.* New York: Ballantine Books, 1985.

American Association of University Women. *How Schools Shortchange Girls.* Washington, DC: AAUW Educational Foundation, 1995.

Anderson, Lorin W., and David R. Krathwohl, eds. *A Taxonomy for Learning, Teaching, and Assessing: A Revision of Bloom's Taxonomy of Educational Objectives.* New York: Pearson, 2001.

Armstrong, Thomas. *Multiple Intelligences in the Classroom.* Alexandria, VA: ASCD, 2009.

Baldwin, Alexinia Y., ed. *Culturally Diverse and Underserved Populations of Gifted Students.* Thousand Oaks, CA: Corwin Press, 2004.

Barr, Jason J. "The Relationship Between Teachers' Empathy and Perceptions of School Culture." *Educational Studies* 37, no. 3 (July 2011): 365–369.

Baum, Susan M., and Steven V. Owen. *To Be Gifted and Learning Disabled: Strategies for Helping Bright Students with LD, ADHD, and More.* Mansfield Center, CT: Creative Learning Press, 2004.

Beecher, Margaret. *Developing the Gifts and Talents of All Students in the Regular Classroom.* Mansfield Center, CT: Creative Learning Press, 1995.

Bousquet, Sarah. "Arab American Experiences in Education." February 20, 2012. Accessed July 28, 2015. files.eric.ed.gov/full text/ED529839.pdf.

Bransford, J. D., A. L. Brown, and R. R. Cocking, eds. *How People Learn: Brain, Mind, Experience, and School.* Washington, DC: National Academy Press, 2000.

Cadwell, Louise Boyd. *Bringing Reggio Emilia Home: An Innovative Approach to Early Childhood Education.* New York: Teachers College Press, 1997.

Callahan, Carolyn M., Tonya R. Moon, and Sarah Oh. "National Surveys of Gifted Programs: Executive Summary 2014." Accessed July 28, 2015, www.nagc.org/resources-publications /resources/key-reports-gifted-education.

Carson, Rachel. *The Sense of Wonder.* New York: HarperCollins, 1998.

Chapman, Carolyn. *If the Shoe Fits: How to Develop Multiple Intelligences in the Classroom.* Palatine, IL: IRI/Skylight Publishing, 1993.

Choice, Penny, and Sally Walker. *The New RtI: Response to Intelligence.* Marion, IL: Pieces of Learning, 2011.

Christensen, James C., and Renwick St. James. *The Art of James Christensen: A Journey of the Imagination.* Seymour, CT: The Greenwich Workshop Press, 1994.

Clark, Barbara. *Growing Up Gifted: Developing the Potential of Children at Home and at School.* Upper Saddle River, NJ: Pearson, 2012.

Coffield, F., D. Moseley, E. Hall, and K. Ecclestone. *Learning Styles and Pedagogy in Post-16 Learning: A Systematic and Critical Review.* London: Learning and Skills Research Centre, 2004.

Colangelo, Nicholas, and Gary A. Davis. *Handbook of Gifted Education.* Upper Saddle River, NJ: Pearson, 2002.

Colangelo, Nicholas, Susan G. Assouline, and Miraca U. M. Gross. *A Nation Deceived: How Schools Hold Back America's Brightest Students,* Vols. 1 and 2. Iowa City, IA: The University of Iowa Press, 2004.

Copple, Carol, and Sue Bredekamp, eds. *Developmentally Appropriate Practice in Early Childhood Programs Serving Children from Birth Through Age 8.* Washington, DC: National Association for the Education of Young Children, 2009.

Cross, Tracy L. *The Social and Emotional Lives of Gifted Kids: Understanding and Guiding Their Development.* Waco, TX: Prufrock Press, 2005.

Daniel, Neil, and June Cox. *Flexible Pacing for Able Learners.* Reston, VA: Council for Exceptional Children, 1988.

Daniels, Susan, and Michael M. Piechowski, eds. *Living with Intensity: Understanding the Sensitivity, Excitability, and Emotional Development of Gifted Children, Adolescents and Adults.* Scottsdale, AZ: Great Potential Press, 2009.

Davidson Institute for Talent Development. "Gifted Education Policies." Last updated December 23, 2014. www.davidsongifted .org/db/StatePolicy.aspx.

Davidson, Neil, and Toni Worsham, eds. *Enhancing Thinking Through Cooperative Learning.* Columbia, NY: Teachers College Press, 1992.

Davis, Gary A., Sylvia B. Rimm, and Del Siegle. *Education of the Gifted and Talented.* Upper Saddle River, NJ: Pearson, 2010.

Delisle, James R. *Guiding the Social and Emotional Development of Gifted Youth: A Practical Guide for Educators and Counselors.* New York: Longman, 1992.

Diamond, Marian, and Janet Hopson. *Magic Trees of the Mind: How to Nurture Your Child's Intelligence, Creativity, and Healthy Emotions from Birth through Adolescence.* New York: E. P. Dutton, 1998.

Dweck, Carol S. *Mindset: The New Psychology of Success: How We Can Learn to Fulfill Our Potential.* New York: Ballantine Books, 2006.

Edwards, Carolyn, Lella Gandina, and George Forman, eds. *The Hundred Languages of Children: The Reggio Emilia Experience in Transformation.* Santa Barbara, CA: Praeger, 2012.

Elkind, David. *The Power of Play: Learning What Comes Naturally.* Philadelphia, PA: Da Capo Press, 2007.

Feldhusen, John, Joyce VanTassel-Baska, and Ken Seeley, eds. *Excellence in Educating the Gifted.* Denver, CO: Love Publishing, 1989.

Feldman, David Henry, and Lynn T. Goldsmith. *Nature's Gambit: Child Prodigies and the Development of Human Potential.* New York: Teachers College Press, 1991.

Fisher, Maurice. "Early Childhood Education for the Gifted: The Need for Intense Study and Observation." *Illinois Council for the Gifted Journal* 11 (1992): 6–9.

Gadzikowski, Ann. *Challenging Exceptionally Bright Children in Early Childhood Classrooms.* St. Paul, MN: Redleaf Press, 2013.

Galbraith, Judy. *The Survival Guide for Gifted Kids: For Ages 10 & Under.* Minneapolis: Free Spirit Publishing, 2013.

Galbraith, Judy, and Jim Delisle. *When Gifted Kids Don't Have All the Answers: How to Meet Their Social and Emotional Needs.* Minneapolis: Free Spirit Publishing, 2015.

Galinsky, Ellen. *Mind in the Making: The Seven Essential Life Skills Every Child Needs.* New York: HarperCollins, 2010.

Gardner, Howard. *Frames of Mind: The Theory of Multiple Intelligences.* New York: Basic Books, 1993.

———. *Intelligence Reframed: Multiple Intelligences for the 21st Century.* New York: Basic Books, 1999.

Gellman, E. S. *School Testing: What Parents and Educators Need to Know.* Westport, CT: Praeger, 1995.

Gentry, Marcia L., and Jamie MacDougall, "Total School Cluster Grouping: Model, Research and Practice." *Systems and Models for Developing Programs for Gifted and Talented.* J. S. Renzulli and E. J. Gubbins, ed. Mansfield Center, CT: Creative Learning Press, 2009.

George, David. *Young Gifted and Bored.* Bethel, CT: Crown House Publishing, 2011.

Gilligan, Carol. *In a Different Voice: Psychological Theory and Women's Development.* Cambridge, MA: Harvard University Press, 1993.

Goleman, Daniel. *Emotional Intelligence: Why It Can Matter More than IQ.* New York: Bantam Books, 2005.

Graven, Stanley N., and Joy V. Browne. "Visual Development in the Human Fetus, Infant, and Young Child." *Newborn and Infant Nursing Reviews* (December 2008): 200. doi: 10.1053/j.nainr.2008.10.011.

Gross, Miraca U. M. *Exceptionally Gifted Children.* New York: RoutledgeFalmer, 2004.

Halsted, Judith Wynn. *Some of My Best Friends Are Books: Guiding Gifted Readers.* Scottsdale, AZ: Great Potential Press, 2009.

Harvard Family Research Project. "Parent-Teacher Conference Tip Sheets." October 2010. www.hfrp.org/content/download/3295/96777/file/FI-ConferenceTipSheets.pdf.

Hertzog, Nancy. *Ready for Preschool: Prepare Your Child for Happiness and Success at School.* Waco, TX: Prufrock Press, 2008.

Hunsaker, Scott. *Identification: The Theory and Practice of Identifying Students for Gifted and Talented Education Services.* Waco, TX: Prufrock Press, 2012.

Institute for Research and Policy on Acceleration. *Iowa Acceleration Scale.* Scottsdale, AZ: Great Potential Press, 2009.

Jensen, Eric. *Brain-Compatible Strategies.* Thousand Oaks, CA: Corwin Press, 2004.

———. *Teaching with the Brain in Mind.* Alexandria, VA: ASCD, 2005.

Johnsen, Susan K. *Identifying Gifted Students: A Practical Guide.* Waco, TX: Prufrock Press, 2011.

Jolly, Jennifer L., Donald J. Treffinger, Tracy Ford Inman, and Joan Franklin Smutny, eds. *Parenting Gifted Children: The Authoritative Guide from the National Association for Gifted Children.* Waco, TX: Prufrock Press, 2011.

Karnes, Frances A., and Suzanne M. Bean, eds. *Methods and Materials for Teaching the Gifted.* Waco, TX: Prufrock Press, 2009.

Keirouz, Kathryn S. "Concerns of Parents of Gifted Children: A Research Review." *Gifted Child Quarterly* 34, no. 2 (1990): 56–63.

Kerr, Barbara A. *Smart Girls: A New Psychology of Girls, Women, and Giftedness.* Scottsdale, AZ: Great Potential Press, 2005.

———. *Smart Boys: Talent, Manhood, and the Search for Meaning.* Scottsdale, AZ: Great Potential Press, 2001.

Kingore, Bertie. *Assessment: Timesaving Procedures for Busy Teachers.* Austin, TX: Professional Associates, 2007.

———. *Developing Portfolios for Authentic Assessment, PreK–3.* Thousand Oaks, CA: Corwin Press, 2008.

———. *The Kingore Observation Inventory (KOI).* Austin, TX:Professional Associates Publishing, 2001.

———. *Portfolios and Authentic Assessments for Young Children.* Thousand Oaks, CA: Corwin Press, 2008.

———. *Portfolios: Enriching and Assessing All Students, Identifying the Gifted, Grades K–6.* Des Moines, IA: Leadership Publishers, 1993.

———. *Rigor and Engagement for Growing Minds: Strategies that Enable High-Ability Learners to Flourish in All Classrooms.* Austin, TX: Professional Associates Publishing, 2014.

Lewin-Benham, Ann. *Twelve Best Practices for Early Childhood Education: Integrating Reggio and Other Inspired Approaches.* New York: Teachers College Press, 2011

Lovecky, Deirdre V. *Different Minds: Gifted Children with AD/HD, Asperger Syndrome, and Other Learning Deficits.* New York: Jessica Kingsley, 2003.

Maltby, Florence. *Gifted Children and Teachers in the Primary School.* London: Falmer Press, 1984.

Marland, S. P. Jr. *Education of the Gifted and Talented: Report to the Congress of the United States by the U.S. Commissioner of Education.* Washington, DC: U.S. Government Printing Office, 1972.

Meckstroth, Elizabeth A. "Guiding the Parents of Gifted Children: The Role of Counselors and Teachers." *Counseling Gifted and Talented Children: A Guide for Teachers, Counselors, and Parents.* Roberta M. Milgram, ed. Norwood, NJ: Ablex Publishing, 1991: 95–120.

Milgram, Roberta M., ed. *Counseling Gifted and Talented Children: A Guide for Teachers, Counselors, and Parents.* Norwood, NJ: Ablex Publishing, 1991.

Moll, Luis C., et al. "Funds of Knowledge for Teaching: Using a Qualitative Approach to Connect Homes and Classrooms." *Theory Into Practice* 31, no. 2 (1992): 132–141.

Montgomery, Diane. "Why Do the Gifted and Talented Underachieve? How Can Masked and Hidden Talents Be Revealed?" *Able, Gifted and Talented Underachievers.* Diane Montgomery, ed. West Sussex, UK: John Wiley and Sons, 2009.

National Association for Gifted Children. "Myths About Gifted Children." Accessed July 28, 2015. www.nagc.org/resources-publications/resources/myths-about-gifted-students.

———. "Redefining Giftedness for a New Century: Shifting the Paradigm." March 2010. www.nagc.org/about-nagc/who-we-are/nagc-position-statements-white-papers.

Neihart, Maureen. *Peak Performance for Smart Kids: Strategies and Tips for Ensuring School Success.* Waco, TX: Prufrock Press, 2008.

Neihart, Maureen, Sally M. Reis, Nancy M. Robinson, and Sidney M. Moon, eds. *The Social and Emotional Development of Gifted Children: What Do We Know?* Waco, TX: Prufrock Press, 2002.

The 1994 State of the States Gifted and Talented Education Report. Austin, TX: Council of State Directors of Programs for the Gifted, 1994.

O'Keeffe, Georgia. *Georgia O'Keeffe.* New York: The Viking Press, 1976.

Olszewski-Kubilius, Paula, Lisa Limburg-Weber, and Steven Pfeiffer. *Early Gifts: Recognizing and Nurturing Children's Talents.* Waco, TX: Prufrock Press, 2003.

Pashler, Harold, M. McDaniel, D. Rohrer, and R. Bjork. "Learning Styles: Concepts and Evidence." *Psychological Science in the Public Interest* 9, no. 3 (2008): 103–119.

Payne, Lauren Murphy. *Just Because I Am: A Child's Book of Affirmation.* Minneapolis: Free Spirit Publishing, 2015.

Phillips, Lynn M. *The Girls Report: What We Know and Need to Know About Growing Up Female.* New York: The National Council for Research on Women, 2000.

Piirto, Jane. *Creativity for 21st Century Skills: How to Embed Creativity into the Curriculum.* Rotterdam, Netherlands: Sense Publishers, 2011.

———. *Talented Children and Adults: Their Development and Education.* Waco, TX: Prufrock Press, 2007.

———. *Understanding Those Who Create.* Scottsdale, AZ: Great Potential Press, 1998.

Porter, Louise. *Gifted Young Children: A Guide for Teachers and Parents.* St. Leonards, NSW, Australia: Allen and Unwin, 1999.

Reis, Susan M. "Toward a Theory of Creativity in Diverse Creative Women." *Creativity Research Journal* 14, nos. 3 and 4 (2002): 305–316.

Renzulli, Joseph S. *The Enrichment Triad Model: A Guide for Developing Defensible Programs for the Gifted and Talented.* Mansfield Center, CT: Creative Learning Press, 1977.

Rimm, Sylvia. *Keys to Parenting the Gifted Child.* Scottsdale, AZ: Great Potential Press, 2006.

———. *Why Bright Kids Get Poor Grades and What You Can Do About It: A Six-Step Program for Parents and Teachers.* Scottsdale, AZ: Great Potential Press, 2008.

Robinson, Ann. "Cooperation or Exploitation: The Arguments Against Cooperative Learning for Talented Students." *Journal for the Education of the Gifted* 14, no. 3 (1990): 9–27, 31–36.

Robinson, Ann, Bruce Shore, and Donna Ennerson. *Best Practices in Gifted Education: An Evidence-Based Guide.* Waco, TX: Prufrock Press, 2007.

Roedell, Wendy C., Nancy Jackson, and Halbert B. Robinson. *Gifted Young Children.* New York: Teachers College Press, 1980.

Roeper, Annemarie. *Educating Children for Life: The Modern Learning Community.* Monroe, NY: Trillium Press, 1990.

Rogers, Karen B. *Re-Forming Gifted Education: How Parents and Teachers Can Match the Program to the Child.* Scottsdale, AZ: Great Potential Press, 2002.

———. *The Relationship of Grouping Practices to the Education of the Gifted and Talented Learner: Research-Based Decision Making.* Storrs, CT: National Research Center on the Gifted and Talented, 1991.

Schwartz, Lita Linzer. *Why Give "Gifts" to the Gifted? Investing in a National Resource.* Thousand Oaks, CA: Corwin Press, 1994.

Silverman, Linda Kreger. "Counseling Families." *Counseling the Gifted and Talented.* Linda Kreger Silverman, ed. Denver, CO: Love Publishing, 1993.

———. "The Gifted Individual." *Counseling the Gifted and Talented.* Linda Kreger Silverman, ed. Denver, CO: Love Publishing, 1993: 3–28.

Sisk, Dorothy. *Creative Teaching of the Gifted.* New York: McGraw-Hill, 1987.

———. *Making Great Kids Greater: Easing the Burden of Being Gifted.* Thousand Oaks, CA: Corwin Press, 2009.

Smutny, Joan Franklin, ed. *Underserved Gifted Populations: Responding to Their Needs and Abilities.* Cresskill, NJ: Hampton Press, 2003.

———. *The Young Gifted Child: Potential and Promise, an Anthology.* Cresskill, NJ: Hampton Press, 1997.

Smutny, Joan Franklin, Kathryn P. Haydon, Olivia Bolaños, and Gina Estrada Danley. *Discovering and Developing Talents in Spanish-Speaking Students.* Thousand Oaks, CA: Corwin Press, 2012.

Smutny, Joan Franklin, Kathleen Veenker, and Stephen Veenker. *Your Gifted Child: How to Recognize and Develop the Special Talents in Your Child from Birth to Age Seven.* New York: Ballantine Books, 1989.

Smutny, Joan Franklin, and S. E. von Fremd. *Differentiating for the Young Child: Teaching Strategies Across the Content Areas, PreK–3.* Thousand Oaks, CA: Crowin Press, 2010.

Smutny, Joan Franklin, and S. E. von Fremd, eds. *Igniting Creativity in Gifted Learners, K–6: Strategies for Every Teacher.* Thousand Oaks, CA: Corwin Press, 2009.

Smutny, Joan Franklin, and S. E. von Fremd. *Teaching Advanced Learners in the General Education Classroom: Doing More with Less!* Thousand Oaks, CA: Corwin Press, 2011.

Smutny, Joan Franklin, Sally Y. Walker, and Elizabeth A. Meckstroth. *Acceleration for Gifted Learners, K–5.* Thousand Oaks, CA: Corwin Press, 2007.

Snowden, Peggy L. "Education of Young Gifted Children." *Illinois Council for the Gifted Journal* 11 (1992): 51–60.

Starko, Alane J. *Creativity in the Classroom: Schools of Curious Delight.* White Plains, NY: Creative Education Foundation Press, 1995.

Sternberg, Robert J. *Beyond IQ: A Triarchic Theory of Human Intelligence.* New York: Cambridge University Press, 1985.

Supporting Emotional Needs of the Gifted, eds. *30 Essays on Giftedness: 30 Years of SENG.* Poughquag, NY: SENG, 2012.

Tannenbaum, Abraham. "Giftedness: A Psychosocial Approach" *Conceptions of Giftedness.* Robert J. Sternberg and Janet E. Davidson, eds. New York: Cambridge University Press, 1986.

Thom, Mary. *Balancing the Equation: Where Are Women and Girls in Science, Engineering and Technology?* New York: The National Council for Research on Women, 2001.

Tomlinson, Carol A. *How to Differentiate Instruction in Mixed-Ability Classrooms.* Alexandria, VA: ASCD, 2004.

Torrance, E. Paul. *Creativity: Just Wanting to Know.* Pretoria, South Africa: Benedic Books, 1994.

———. "Growing Up Creatively Gifted: A 22-Year Longitudinal Study." *The Creative Child and Adult Quarterly* 5, no. 3 (1980): 148–158, 170.

———. *The Search for Satori and Creativity.* Buffalo, NY: Creative Education Foundation, 1979.

———. "Testing the Creativity of Preschool Children." *The Faces and Forms of Creativity.* Ventura, CA: Ventura County Superintendent of Schools Office, 1981: 65–80.

———. *Why Fly? A Philosophy of Creativity.* Norwood, NJ: Ablex, 1995.

Torrance, E. Paul, Kathy Goff, and Neil B. Satterfield. *Multicultural Mentoring of the Gifted and Talented.* Waco, TX: Prufrock Press, 1998.

Torrance, E. Paul, and Dorothy A. Sisk. *Gifted and Talented in the Regular Classroom.* Buffalo, NY: Creative Education Foundation Press, 1997.

Treffinger, Donald J. *Encouraging Creative Learning for the Gifted and Talented: A Handbook of Methods and Techniques.* Los Angeles: National/State Leadership Training Institute on the Gifted and Talented, 1980.

Treffinger, Donald, Tracy Inman, Jennifer Jolly, and Joan Franklin Smutny. *Parenting Gifted Children: The Authoritative Guide from the National Association for Gifted Children.* Waco, TX: Prufrock Press, 2010.

Vygotsky, Lev S. *Thought and Language.* E. Hanfmann, and G. Vakar, trans. Cambridge, MA: MIT Press, 1986.

Webb, James T., Edward R. Amend, Nadia E. Webb, Jean Goerss, Paul Beljan, and F. Richard Olenchak. *Misdiagnosis and Dual Diagnoses of Gifted Children and Adults: ADHD, Bipolar, OCD, Asperger's, Depression, and Other Disorders.* Scottsdale, AZ: Great Potential Press, 2005.

Webb, James T., Janet L. Gore, Edward R. Amend, and Arlene DeVries. *A Parent's Guide to Gifted Children.* Scottsdale, AZ: Great Potential Press, 2007.

Webb, James T., and Patricia A. Kleine. "Assessing Gifted and Talented Children." *Testing Young Children.* J. L. Culbertson and D. J. Willis, eds. Austin, TX: Pro-ed., 1993.

Webb, James T., Elizabeth A. Meckstroth, and Stephanie S. Tolan. *Guiding the Gifted Child: A Practical Source for Parents and Teachers.* Scottsdale, AZ: Great Potential Press, 1994.

West, Thomas G. *In the Mind's Eye: Visual Thinkers, Gifted People with Dyslexia and Other Learning Difficulties, Computer Images, and the Ironies of Creativity.* Buffalo, NY: Prometheus Books, 1997.

Whitney, Carol Strip, and Gretchen Hirsch. *A Love for Learning: Motivation and the Gifted Child.* Scottsdale, AZ: Great Potential Press, 2007.

Wiggins, Grant, and Jay McTighe. *Understanding by Design.* Alexandria, VA: ASCD, 2005.

Willis, Judy. *How Your Child Learns Best: Brain-Friendly Strategies You Can Use to Ignite Your Child's Learning and Increase School Success.* Naperville, IL: Sourcebooks, 2009.

———. *Research Based Strategies to Ignite Student Learning: Insights from a Neurologist and Classroom Teacher.* Alexandria, VA: ASCD, 2006.

———. *Teaching the Brain to Read: Strategies for Improving Fluency, Vocabulary, and Comprehension.* Alexandria, VA: ASCD, 2009.

Willis, Scott. "Teaching Young Children: Educators Seek 'Developmental Appropriateness.'" *Curriculum Update* (November 1993): 1–8.

Winebrenner, Susan, and Dina Brulles. *The Cluster Grouping Handbook.* Minneapolis: Free Spirit Publishing, 2008.

———. *Teaching Gifted Kids in Today's Classroom: Strategies and Techniques Every Teacher Can Use.* Minneapolis: Free Spirit Publishing, 2012.

Winebrenner, Susan, and Lisa M. Kiss. *Teaching Kids with Learning Difficulties in Today's Classroom: How Every Teacher Can Help Struggling Students Succeed.* Minneapolis: Free Spirit Publishing, 2014.

Wurm, Julianne. *Working in the Reggio Way: A Beginner's Guide for American Teachers.* St. Paul, MN: Redleaf Press, 2005.

Yoon Yoon, So, and Marcia Gentry. "Racial and Ethnic Representation in Gifted Programs: Current Status of and Implications for Gifted Asian American Students." *Gifted Child Quarterly* 53 (February 2009): 121–136.

Zhao, Yong. *World Class Learners: Educating Creative and Entrepreneurial Students.* Thousand Oaks, CA: Corwin Press, 2012.

Zong, Jie, and Jeanne Batalova. "Sub-Saharan African Immigrants in the United States." *Migration Information Source.* October 30, 2014.

Appendix A
Tests for Identifying Young Gifted Children

Following are descriptions of some tests that can be useful in identifying young gifted children. To acquire or use any of these tests, please consult with your school or district psychologist. Certain training qualifications may be required to order, administer, and interpret the tests.

Note: Nearly all tests have some bias toward the majority culture. When a description is preceded by an asterisk (*), this indicates that the test is relatively less dependent on acculturation and English language acquisition, and is likely to be more appropriate for children from minority cultures.

Cognitive Abilities Test Form 6 (CogAT 6). Grades K–12. Group administered test designed to assess students' abilities in reasoning and problem solving using verbal, quantitative, and nonverbal (spatial) symbols. Takes 30–60 minutes per section to administer.

Differential Ability Scales–Second Edition (DAS–II). Ages 2.6–17.11. Individually administered test that measures overall cognitive ability as well as specific abilities and achievement levels. Includes seventeen subtests and offers out-of-level testing for younger children. Core battery is 45–60 minutes, with diagnostic subtests 30 minutes each.

Fischer Comprehensive Assessment of Giftedness Scale. Grades preK–12. Examines observable classroom and out-of-school behaviors in response to environment. Ranks children's applied motivation, interest, behavior, and creative output as compared with classmates, not national norms. Assesses forty-four characteristics, including areas of precocious development, applied motivation, creative output, and aesthetic perceptions. The view this test provides broadens and deepens the scope for finding gifted children.

Gifted Rating Scales (GRS). Designed to help identify children for placement in gifted and talented educational programs. GRS–Primary: Ages 4.0–6.11 and GRS–Secondary: Ages 6:0–13:11. Validity studies have been conducted linking it to the *Wechsler Preschool and Primary Scale of Intelligence–Third Edition (WPPSI–III)* and measures of potential in other domains.

Goodenough-Harris Drawing Test. Ages 3–15.11. Brief, nonverbal test of intellectual ability. Can be administered individually or in a group. Involves perception, abstraction, and generalization. Evaluation measures the complexity of the child's concept formation. Administration and scoring take little training; testing time required is usually less than 10 minutes.

Kaufman Assessment Battery for Children–Second Edition (KABC–II). Ages 3–18. Culturally fair ability test for all the children you serve. An individually administered measure of cognitive ability. Assesses mental-processing and problem-solving abilities with minimized use of language and academic experiences. Includes sixteen subtests grouped in three scales: Sequential Processing, Simultaneous Processing, and Achievement. Administration time is 25–70 minutes.

McCarthy Scales of Children's Abilities. Ages 2.6–8.6. Measures verbal, perceptual-performance, quantitative, general cognitive, memory, and motor abilities. Best used for initial screening; not recommended for assessing gifted children. Individually administered by a trained examiner in 45–60 minutes.

Naglieri Nonverbal Ability Test–Second Edition (NNAT-2). Ages 4–18. The NNAT-2 provides a nonverbal, culturally neutral assessment of general ability that is ideal for use with a diverse student population. With the use of progressive matrices for seven grade-based levels, this versatile test is well-suited for identifying gifted and talented students. Administration time is 30 minutes.

Otis-Lennon School Ability Test–Eighth Edition (OLSAT 8). Grades K–12. Group test appropriate for initial screening, though may show lower scores than individual IQ tests. Assesses cognitive abilities related to success in school learning. Eleven verbal and ten nonverbal abilities tested include categories of Verbal Comprehension, Verbal Reasoning, Pictorial Reasoning, Figural Reasoning, and Quantitative Reasoning. Administration time is 75 minutes.

Peabody Picture Vocabulary Test–Fourth Edition (PPVT–4). Ages 2.6–90+ years. Measures receptive vocabulary for Standard English. Useful for assessing the English vocabulary in non-English-speaking children, but not for general gifted identification. Takes 10–15 minutes to complete.

Raven's Coloured Progressive Matrices. Ages 5–11. Measures nonverbal or abstract reasoning and general ability to perceive and think clearly. A good measure of general intellectual functioning, though scores have a low correlation with academic performance. Easily individually administered in 15–30 minutes by an examiner with no special training.

Scales for Identifying Gifted Students (SIGS). Ages 5–18. Comprehensive, observational instrument available for identifying gifted students. This standardized, norm-referenced instrument is completed by teachers or parents and provides an effective method for identifying gifted children.

Scales for Rating the Behavioral Characteristics of Superior Students–Third Edition (Renzulli Scales). Grades K–12. A tool for teachers to identify students for general and specific gifted and talented programs by rating student strengths in the areas of learning, creativity, motivation, leadership, art, music, drama, precision and expressive communication, planning, mathematics, reading, technology, and science.

Screening Assessment for Gifted Elementary and Middle School Students–Second Edition (SAGES-2). Ages 7–12. Individual or group administered instrument to identify students for gifted programs that emphasize aptitude and achievement at either the screening level or the final selection stage. Subtests are Reasoning and General Information. Administration time is 30–45 minutes.

Slosson Intelligence Test–Revised Third Edition (SIT–R3–1). Ages 4–65. Brief, individually administered intelligence test that is highly dependent on language. Best used as an initial screening device. Assesses mathematical reasoning, vocabulary, auditory memory, and information. Scores are correlated with the *Stanford-Binet Intelligence Scale, Form L–M.* Can be administered by a briefly-trained examiner in 10–20 minutes.

*Stanford-Binet Intelligence Scale–Fifth Edition (SBI5). Ages 2–65+ years. Individually administered IQ test useful for identifying gifted children. Has sufficient ceiling to accommodate quantifying abilities in most young gifted children. Twelve subtests identify specific strengths and weaknesses.

*System of Multicultural Pluralistic Assessment (SOMPA). Ages 5–12. Measures cognitive, perceptual-motor, and adaptive behavior of black, white, and Hispanic-American children. Aims to be racially and culturally nondiscriminatory, but needs to be interpreted with caution. Administration is individual and requires 2½–3 hours by a trained examiner.

*Test of Early Mathematics Ability–Third Edition (TEMA–3). Ages 3.0–8.11. Measures formal and informal concepts and skills through progressive probes or questions that allow exploration of the child's mathematical thinking skills. Testing time is 40 minutes.

Test of Early Reading Ability–Third Edition (TERA–3). Ages 3.6–8.6. Measures early reading abilities. Individual administration takes 30 minutes.

Test of Nonverbal Intelligence–Fourth Edition (TONI–4). Ages 6.0–89.11. Offers an assessment of intelligences, aptitude, abstract reasoning and problem solving. Completion time is 15–20 minutes.

*Torrance Test of Creative Thinking (TTCT). Grades K–12. Measures creative, productive thinking in verbal and figural dimensions. Also scores for fluency, flexibility, originality, and some elaboration. Useful with minority or culturally disadvantaged young children; for other children, informal observation assessment might be adequate instead. Takes 30 minutes.

*Universal Nonverbal Intelligence Test–Second Edition (UNIT–2). Grades K–12. Entirely stimulus and response administration format incorporating eight hand and body gestures. Three testing options include: Abbreviated, Standard, and Full Scale batteries. Administration time is 10–60 minutes.

U-STARS~PLUS. Equips teachers with tools for early identification of giftedness in multicultural, low socioeconomic, and disabled populations. Available at the website of the Council for Exceptional Children (www.cec.sped.org). Find it under "Special Ed Topics" then click on "Specialty Areas" and "Gifted."

*Wechsler Intelligence Scale for Children–Fifth Edition (WISC–V). Ages 6.0–6.11. Widely used to assess gifted children. Provides twelve subtests, three IQ scores, and four index scores for identification of relative strengths. The Performance Scales of all the Wechsler tests can be used with less language and cultural bias. Individually administered in about 60 minutes.

*Wechsler Preschool and Primary Scale of Intelligence–Third Edition (WPPSI–III). Ages 2.6–7.3. Widely accepted to assess young gifted children. Particularly useful because it assesses 12 different abilities to identify specific strengths and relative weaknesses. Individually administered by a highly trained examiner; takes approximately 30–60 minutes.

Appendix B
More Resources for Teachers

Additional books and materials for use with gifted primary-age children, divided into six major subject areas. Children's resources are so extensive that here we only offer what we ourselves have used and found helpful in the classroom.

Art, Music, Dance, and Theater

Arts Education Partnership (www.aep-arts.org). A national coalition of organizations dedicated to providing children with quality arts education in and out of school. The website contains research and information on arts education in each state.

The Arts in Every Classroom (www.learner.org). A video library about arts programs and arts applications that play an essential role in classroom learning. Search "the Arts in Every Classroom" for information on developing arts-based units.

Bany-Winters, Lisa. *On Stage: Theater Games and Activities for Kids.* Chicago: Chicago Review Press, 2012. Drama education through games, puppetry, pantomime, and more.

Chris Van Allsburg (hmhbooks.com/chrisvanallsburg). A whimsical site enticing visitors into the world of the fictional character Harris Burdick

Corsi, Jerome R. *Leonardo Da Vinci: A Three-Dimensional Study.* Rohnert Park, CA: Pomegranate Artbooks, 1995. Presented in three dimensions along with an informative text, Da Vinci's most magnificent conceptualizations take on new life for children.

Daywalt, Drew. *The Day the Crayons Quit.* New York: Philomel Books, 2013. Duncan wants to color, but when he opens his crayon box, he finds letters from the crayons stating that they want to quit. This imaginative story sparks creativity.

Delafosse, Claude, and Gallimard Jeunesse. *Landscapes.* New York: Scholastic, 1993. A First Discovery Art Book, this intriguing volume enables young readers to notice painters' unique styles in a series of famous landscapes.

——. *Musical Instruments.* New York: Scholastic, 1994. One of the Scholastic Voyages of Discovery books, this volume focuses on the performing arts.

——. *Paintings.* New York: Scholastic, 1993. A First Discovery Art Book with brightly painted, transparent pages introduces great works of art to the youngest readers in a playful, accessible way.

——. *Portraits.* New York: Scholastic, 1993. A First Discovery Art Book that focuses on famous portraits and draws the young child into the world of artistic representation.

Frith, Margaret. *Frida Kahlo: The Artist Who Painted Herself.* New York: Grosset & Dunlap, 2003. Accompanied by the illustrations of award-winning artist Tommie dePaola, this creative text engages young readers by telling its story through the words of a young girl, also named Frieda, who has chosen to write a report on the famous artist.

George, Richard. *Roald Dahl's James and the Giant Peach: A Play.* New York: Puffin Books, 1982. Adapted from Roald Dahl's novel *James and the Giant Peach,* in this play, a giant peach takes an orphaned boy to the land of his dreams. We suggest using this play for reader's (chamber) theater. Also check out the play adaptations of *Charlie and the Chocolate Factory* (2007), *The BFG* (1993), and *The Twits* (2003).

Hayes, Ann. *Meet the Marching Smithereens.* New York: Harcourt Brace & Co., 1995. A rhythmic text offers facts about marching band instruments, while endearing animal musicians keep the parade moving in sparkling style.

——. *Meet the Orchestra.* New York: Voyager Books, 1991. An unusual introduction to the orchestra describes the instruments—strings, brass, woodwinds, and percussion— and offers interesting information about them while animal musicians prepare for a performance.

Herbert, Susan. *The Cat's History of Western Art.* Boston, MA: Little, Brown & Co., 1994. Thirty-one delightful color illustrations depict a "catty" twist to well-known surveys of Western art. Includes masterful images with annotated notes by an eminent art historian.

Hort, Lenny. *The Boy Who Held Back the Sea.* New York: Dial Books, 1987. The retelling of this old Dutch tale is masterfully illustrated by Thomas Locker. A wonderful way to integrate literature and the art of the Dutch Masters.

International Torrance Legacy Creativity Awards (www .centerforgifted.org). Sponsored by the Center for Gifted and the Midwest Torrance Center for Creativity, students between the ages of 8 and 18 are invited to submit their finest work in creative writing, visual art, musical composition, and invention for this yearly competition. Submissions are accepted January through August.

Jeunesse, Gallimard. *Paint and Painting: The Colors, the Techniques, the Surfaces: A History of Artists' Tools.* New York: Scholastic, 1994. A Voyages of Discovery book that deals with visual arts.

KidsArt (kidsart.com). A huge selection of resources, tools, and ideas for teaching art to children.

King-Smith, Dick. *Pigs Might Fly.* New York: Puffin Books, 1990. From the author of popular book *Babe* comes this story about a piglet runt who learns to swim and becomes a hero. We suggest using this book for reader's (chamber) theater.

Kohl, MaryAnn F., and Kim Solga. *Discovering Great Artists: Hands-On Art for Children in the Styles of the Great Masters.* Bellingham, WA: Bright Ring Publishing, 1996. Children learn about great artists by experimenting with different media—sculpture, paint, pencil, cartoon, folk art, and more.

———. *Great American Artists for Kids: Hands-On Art Experiences in the Styles of Great American Masters.* Bellingham, WA: Bright Ring Publishing, 2008. Seventy-five great artists—some well-known, others new—present a rich collection of techniques and styles for children to explore in art activities of their own.

Les Chats, Peles. *Long Live Music!* New York: Harcourt Brace & Co., 1995. A magical, lighthearted story about a boy and his dog fleeing a monster who's stolen the boy's instruments in order to stop all music.

Locker, Thomas. *Miranda's Smile.* New York: Dial Books, 1994. A charming story, illustrated by the author, about an artist-father who wants to capture his daughter's smile in a portrait. When she loses a tooth, he has to find another way to continue his work.

———. *The Young Artist.* New York: Dial Books, 1989. An exquisite book about the life of a young painter. The story is accompanied by many luminous paintings.

Marin, Guadalupe Rivera. *My Papa Diego and Me: Memories of My Father and His Art/Mi papa Diego y yo: recuerdos de mi padre y su arte.* San Francisco: Children's Book Press, 2013. An intimate portrait of Diego Rivera through the eyes and storytelling of his daughter.

Martin, Mary, and Steven Zorn. *Masterpieces.* Philadelphia: Running Press, 1990. One of the most original coloring books on the market features sixty famous paintings and many facts about the artists, their styles, and all the ways they broke the rules of their day to create their art.

Micklethwait, Lucy. *I Spy Two Eyes: Numbers in Art.* New York: Mulberry Books, 1998. No ordinary counting book, this volume contains magnificent works of art featuring a variety of artists dating from the fifteenth century to the present. A great deal to explore and discuss.

Namioka, Lensey. *Yang the Youngest and His Terrible Ear.* New York: Yearling, 1992. The youngest member of a family of new immigrants faces giving a violin performance to attract students for his father.

Rolling Jr., James Haywood. *Come Look with Me: Discovering African American Art for Children.* New York: Lickle Publishing, 2005. An inspired book full of stunning African-American art. An important addition to any classroom, especially since few of these great artists are well-known.

Spolin, Viola. *Theater Games for the Classroom: A Teacher's Handbook.* Evanston, IL: Northwestern University Press, 1986. A classic in theater education that is still valuable for today's classrooms.

Stanley, Diane. *The Gentleman and the Kitchen Maid.* New York: Dial Books, 1994. This truly original art book tells the story of a young art student who notices in two museum paintings a growing love between a gentleman and kitchen maid. Sadly, the lovers are frozen and immobile—until the students find a solution to their problem.

Tessellations.org (www.tessellations.org). Inspired by M.C. Escher, this resource is designed for elementary, middle, and high school geometry. A wonderful integration of art and mathematics.

Tonatiuh, Duncah. *Diego Rivera: His World and Ours.* New York: Abrams Books for Young Readers, 2011. Winner of the Pura Belpre Award, this beautifully illustrated book engages young students in the story of Diego Rivera as an artist and poses this question: If Diego Rivera were alive today, what would he paint?

Venezia, Mike. *Claude Monet.* New York: Scholastic, 2014. A beautifully written and illustrated book in the Getting to Know the World's Greatest Artists series—individual books that focus on different famous artists.

———. *Pierre Auguste Renoir.* New York: Children's Press, 1996. Another lovely book in the Getting to Know the World's Greatest Artists series. See others at www.mikevenezia.com.

Welton, Jude. *Impressionism.* New York: DK Publishing, 2000. Re-creates and explores the world of impressionism as it evolved through a group of pioneering artists. Examines the social changes that inspired this art form, the lives the artists led, and the kinds of materials they used. Published in association with the Art Institute of Chicago.

Environment and Ecology

BirdWatching. Braintree, MA: Madavor Media. A great aid to any study on birds, this bimonthly magazine provides invaluable information and hundreds of beautiful photographs on the fine art of birding, as well as regular reports on endangered species and rare bird sightings. Visit their website for more resources at www.birdwatchingdaily.com.

Cherry, Lynne. *The Armadillo from Amarillo.* New York: Voyager Books, 1999. Gives children a lesson in geography and ecology through the unique lens of a curious armadillo and a helpful eagle who agrees to fly him around.

Defenders of Wildlife (www.defenders.org). The website offers many resources, including *Defenders Magazine,* and covers a range of current issues relating to endangered species and environmental conditions.

George, Jean Craighead. *The Missing 'Gator of Gumbo Limbo.* New York: HarperCollins, 2000. The author leads young children through an ecological mystery in a Florida rain forest.

The Jane Goodall Institute (www.janegoodall.org). The website includes videos, articles, blogs, and background information about the programs the institute supports in various countries.

Kessler, Cristina. *All the King's Animals: The Return of Endangered Wildlife to Swaziland.* Honesdale, PA: Boyds Mills Press, 2001. Jam-packed with color photographs. The author-photographer does a masterful job of relating a true story about conservation efforts little known in the United States.

Kind News. The Humane Society of the United States. This magazine encourages kids to coexist humanely with animals and become active in efforts to protect them. Includes profiles of some extraordinary kids and has three reading levels: grades K–2, 3–4, and 5–6. Visit their website at www.humanesociety .org and search for "Kind News."

Locker, Thomas. *In Blue Mountains: An Artist's Return to America's First Wilderness.* Hudson, NY: Bell Pond Books, 2000. An inspiring exploration of wilderness through the breathtaking paintings of Thomas Locker.

Luenn, Nancy. *Mother Earth.* New York: Aladdin Paperbacks, 1995. A sensitive exploration of nature's many gifts and of the importance of conservation—presented beautifully in word and watercolor—for young readers.

Mattson, Mark, and Robert J. Mason. *Environmental Atlas of the United States.* New York: Scholastic, 1993. A very useful resource for designing activities on the environment, the book is easy to use and divides its sections according to main themes such as forests, garbage, and water.

National Audubon Society (www.audubon.com). A rich resource for teachers that investigates a wide range of ecological and environmental topics around the globe.

National Geographic (www.nationalgeographic.com). The website has some amazing content for teachers to utilize in the classroom and as background information.

National Wildlife Federation (www.nwf.org). The website is an excellent resource for teachers designed to increase global awareness of the need for proper use and management of Earth's resources—soil, air, water, forests, minerals, and plant and animal life. Includes many links, short videos, examples of classroom projects, and opportunities to learn about vulnerable species and what can be done to support them.

The Nature Conservancy (www.nature.org). An educational website focusing on the preservation, expansion, and protection of habitats. Includes information from its magazine, short videos, success stories, and an emphasis on the science of conservation.

Nivola, Claire A. *Planting the Trees of Kenya: The Story of Wangari Maathai.* New York: Farrar, Straus, and Giroux, 2008. A sumptuous and vivid telling of the extraordinary life of Wangari Maathai, founder of the Greenbelt Movement in Kenya and winner of the 2004 Nobel Peace Prize.

Project Learning Tree (www.plt.org). An award-winning environmental education program for kids. The initial materials need to be received through a training session; however, there are many student activities available on their website related to environmental education.

Project Wild (www.projectwild.org). A wildlife conservation education program. The initial materials need to be received through a training session; however, there are many student activities available on their website related to sustaining wildlife and aquatic environments.

Robinson, Sandra Chisholm. *The Wonder of Wolves: A Story and Activities.* Lanham, MD: Roberts Rinehart Publishing, 1997. A moving tale about the special bond between wolves

and the Nuu-chah-nulth people of Vancouver's west coast. This beautifully conceived and presented book is filled with activities designed to inform young children and adults about one of the most misunderstood animals.

Schimmel, Schim. *Dear Children of the Earth: A Letter from Home.* Minocqua, WI: Cooper Square Publishing, 1994. Schimmel combines beautiful acrylic paintings, lyrics, and stories to write a love letter to humans from Mother Earth, calling for conservation and protection.

Schlank, Carol Hilgartner, and Barbara Metzger. *A Clean Sea: The Rachel Carson Story.* Culver City, CA: Cascade Pass, 2002. Tells the story of Carson's life as a marine biologist and the world's first environmentalist.

Temple, Lannis, ed. *Dear World: How Children Around the World Feel About Our Environment.* New York: Bodley Head Children's Books, 1994. A wonderful and moving collection of quotes and drawings by kids around the world on the subject of our environment and the threats it currently faces.

Winter, Jeanette. *The Watcher: Jane Goodall's Life with the Chimps.* New York: Schwartz & Wade, 2011. Engaging and imaginative approach to the Jane Goodall story, inspiring young children to become "watchers" of wildlife in their own right.

Language Arts
BIOGRAPHY AND AUTOBIOGRAPHY

Academy of Achievement (www.achievement.org). The website provides video clips and interviews with notable individuals. Students can search for people via their interest area, challenges they overcame, or personality traits. Includes helpful information for teachers as well as recommended books about these individuals.

Ajmera, Maya, Aloteju Omolodun, and Sarah Strunk. *Extraordinary Girls.* Watertown, MA: Charlesbridge Publishing, 2000. Examples of girls throughout the world who live extraordinary lives.

Bedard, Michael. *Emily.* New York: Delacorte Press, 1992. A sensitively written tale about a young girl who manages to meet Emily Dickinson and enter the poet's extraordinary world.

Christensen, Bonnie. *The Daring Nellie Bly: America's Star Reporter.* New York: Dragon Fly Books, 2009. The captivating, true story of the intrepid woman reporter who defied the restrictive world of the mid-nineteenth century to achieve her goals and make a difference in society and who has inspired legions of girls and young women.

Cohn, Diana. *Dream Carver.* San Francisco: Chronicle Books, 2002. Evocative story based on the life of Oaxacan woodcarver, Manuel Jimenez.

Davies, Jacqueline. *The Boy Who Drew Birds: A Story of John James Audubon.* New York: Houghton Mifflin, 2004. Engaging story for young readers that explores the mystery of yearly migration and how Audubon devised a way to track what really happens to the birds.

Greenfield, Eloise. *Mary McLeod Bethune.* New York: HarperCollins, 1977. An inspiring account, this volume relates the monumental achievements of a black educator. Jerry Pinkney's illustrations are outstanding.

Kovacs, Deborah, and James Preller. *Meet the Authors and Illustrators, Vols. 1 and 2.* New York: Scholastic, 1991. A useful reference for learning about the world of authors and illustrators, this source contains biographical information that will intrigue and inspire both you and your class.

Locker, Thomas, and Madeleine Comora. *Rembrandt and Titus: Artist and Son.* Golden, CO: Fulcrum Publishing, 2005. A creative approach to the life of Rembrandt through historical fiction and the evocative paintings of Thomas Locker.

Meltzer, Brad. *I Am Amelia Earhart.* New York: Dial Books, 2014. An imaginative telling of a young Amelia Earhart determined to take to the skies. This book will appeal to young readers and inspire them to follow their passions.

Nelson, Kadir. *Nelson Mandela.* New York: Katherine Tegen Books, 2013. A Coretta Scott King Honor book by award-winning author and artist Kadir Nelson, tells in verse and illustrations the life story of this great South African leader.

Nelson, S.D. *Black Elk's Vision: A Lakota Story.* New York: Abrams Books for Young Readers, 2015. The story of Black Elk told from a Native American perspective. Includes Black Elk's visions as a little boy, his experiences in the battles at Little Big Horn and Wounded Knee, and his journeys to New York and Europe with Buffalo Bill's Wild West show.

Pinkney, Andrea Davis. *Dear Benjamin Banneker.* Boston, MA: HMH Books for Young Readers, 1994. This inspiring story about Benjamin Banneker, a free black man during the time of slavery, tells of his accomplishments as an astronomer, a mathematician, and the author of the first published almanac by an African-American man. Also describes Banneker's extraordinary correspondence with Secretary of State Thomas Jefferson, pleading on behalf of his people.

Smutny, Joan Franklin. *Manifesto of the Gifted Girl.* Unionville, NY: Royal Fireworks Press, 2010. A simple guide for the gifted girl questioning what she can aspire to. It weaves together the voices of girls with profiles of accomplished women from different ages and time periods.

FICTION AND NONFICTION

Ada, Ama Flor. *Dear Peter Rabbit.* New York: Aladdin Paperbacks, 1997. In this delightful, behind-the-scenes adventure, Ada interconnects famous characters from some of the best-loved nursery stories.

Anno, Mitsumasa. *Anno's Journey.* New York: Putnam & Grosset, 1977. A beautifully illustrated, wordless book that invites young children into the villages and countryside of an earlier, horse-and-buggy time and encourages them to create their own stories.

Barber, Antonia. *The Monkey and the Panda.* New York: Macmillan Books for Young Readers, 1996. Who is better, the monkey or the panda? Here's a fable that cleverly addresses the issue of jealousy in a way that will enchant young people.

BookHive: Your Guide to Children's Literature (www.cmlibrary.org/bookhive). Sponsored by the Charlotte Mecklenburg Library, this website includes excellent listings and reviews of books for young children from all genres and many cultures.

Cannon, Janell. *Stellaluna.* New York: Harcourt Brace & Co., 1993. A touching story with exquisite illustrations about a baby fruit bat that falls headfirst into a bird's nest and is raised like a bird.

Clark, Ann Nolan. *In My Mother's House.* New York: Puffin Books, 1992. First published in 1941, this Caldecott Honor book still appeals to young readers. Nolan's poems about animals, fields, rivers, lakes, and more are from the child's point of view. Velino Herrera conjures up this world with color and black-and-white illustrations.

Cooney, Barbara. *Island Boy.* New York: Puffin Books, 1991. The story of a young pioneer boy's life on an island with his family.

English Companion (englishcompanion.ning.com). A website for English teachers to ask questions and get help. Two-year-winner of the Edublog Award for Best Educational Use of Social Networking.

Flack, Jerry D. *Mystery and Detection: Thinking and Problem Solving with the Sleuths.* Englewood, CO: Teacher Ideas Press, 1990. Part of the Gifted Treasury series, this volume is an imaginative approach to the study and teaching of critical thinking and problem solving.

Gantschev, Ivan. *The Volcano.* London: Neugebauer Press, 1981. Beautifully illustrated by the author, this book tells of a troublemaking crab named Brok who tries to destroy a volcano.

Giovanni, Nikki. *The Girls in the Circle.* New York: Scholastic, 2004. A spirited, rhyming story ideal for early primary-age children.

Graham, Bob. *Rose Meets Mr. Wintergarten.* London: Walker Books, 2003. Bright illustrations and humorous text convey the language and emotions of childhood as readers watch Rose overcome neighborhood gossip and offer friendship to the mysterious man next door.

Gwynne, Fred. *A Chocolate Moose for Dinner.* New York: Aladdin Paperbacks, 1976. A very literal young lady tries to understand the phrases of the adult world.

Hamilton, Virginia. *When Birds Could Talk & Bats Could Sing.* New York: Scholastic, 1999. Based on African-American folk tales told in the South during the plantation era, this book, by an author whose own grandfather escaped slavery, is lively and entertaining—a testament to the survival of the human spirit.

Henkes, Kevin. *Kitten's First Full Moon.* New York: Greenwillow Books, 2007. A charming story for preK and early elementary students about a kitten encountering her first full moon.

Herriot, James. *Oscar, Cat-About-Town.* New York: St. Martin's Press, 1993. A warm story about a good-natured stray cat left at the veterinarian's to be nursed back to health and his adventures after moving in with a family.

Hobbie, Holly. *Toot & Puddle: Top of the World*. Boston, MA: Little, Brown Books for Young Readers, 2008. One of the many charming stories about the adventurous Toot who, in this tale, doesn't return to Woodcock Pocket, leaving his homebody friend Puddle worried. A *New York Times* best-selling series, in addition to the first Toot & Puddle book, there is *Let It Snow* (2007), *You Are My Sunshine* (1999), *A Present for Toot* (1998), *Wish You Were Here* (2005), *Charming Opal* (2011), and many more.

Howe, James. *I Wish I Were a Butterfly*. New York: Voyager Books, 1987. Rich and colorful illustrations enhance a story about a cricket who wishes to be a butterfly until he discovers that crickets make beautiful music.

International Torrance Legacy Creativity Awards (www.center forgifted.org). See page 217 for more information.

Johnson, Angela. *Down the Winding Road*. New York: DK Publishing, 2000. Two-time winner of the Coretta Scott King Award for fiction, Angela Johnson brings a moving story of young children visiting the old ones in their family.

Jonas, Ann. *Reflections*. New York: Greenwillow Books, 1987. This black-and-white picture book chronicles a child's busy day using backward and upside-down visualizations.

———. *Round Trip*. New York: Greenwillow Books, 1983. Another delightful upside-down and backward book that depicts a journey from the country to New York City and back again.

Kesselman, Wendy. *Sand in My Shoes*. New York: Hyperion Books for Children, 1995. Through a series of evocative coastline images and lyrical text, this book leads children to the final moments of summer and treasured memories of the sea.

Lai, Thanhha. *Inside Out and Back Again*. New York: HarperCollins, 2013. A *New York Times* best seller and a Newbery Honor Book, this extraordinary story comes from the author's early life as a child refugee who escaped Vietnam and moved to the United States with her family, and then had to struggle with the pain of alienation in a school that saw her as an outsider.

Lawhead, Stephen R. *The Tale of Jeremy Vole*. New York: Avon Books, 1990. Narrates the amusing adventures of several animals that live along the river.

Legge, David. *Bamboozled*. New York: Scholastic, 1995. A heartwarming tale of the tender relationship between a grandfather and granddaughter.

Literature Circles Resources Center (www.litcircles.org). An interactive website with guidelines, book lists, resources, and information for teachers and students in elementary and middle school.

Locker, Thomas, and Ashley Foehner. *Washington Irving's Rip Van Winkle*. Golden, CO: Fulcrum Press, 2008. Artist Thomas Locker and teacher Ashley Foehner adapt this popular tale, evoking the spirit and beauty of the Catskill Mountains.

MacLachlan, Patricia. *Sarah, Plain and Tall*. New York: HarperCollins, 2004. When their father invites a mail-order bride to come to their prairie home, Caleb and Anna are captivated by this new mother and hope that she will stay. A touching tale of early pioneer America.

Martin, Bill Jr., and John Archambault. *Knots on a Counting Rope*. New York: Square Fish, 1997. This beautifully illustrated story of love, hope, and courage uses the counting rope as a metaphor for the passage of time and for a boy's emerging confidence in facing his greatest challenge—his blindness.

Monsell, Mary Elise. *Underwear!* Chicago: Albert Whitman & Company, 1988. A humorous tale filled with charming illustrations of a zebra and orangutan who love to wear underwear—all colors, prints, and styles—and who bring a little humor to a grumpy buffalo.

Pinkney, Jerry. *Little Red Riding Hood*. Boston, MA: Little, Brown and Co., 2007. This five-time Caldecott Honor winner lures readers into the popular Red Riding Hood story through richly detailed paintings.

Potok, Chaim. *The Tree of Here*. New York: Alfred A. Knopf, 1993. In an imaginative conversation between a boy and a tree, the author tells an unforgettable story about saying good-bye and starting over.

ReadWriteThink (www.readwritethink.org). An excellent website with strategies and resources in reading and writing instruction for teachers and parents.

Roberts, Lynn. *Little Red: A Fizzingly Good Yarn*. London: Pavilion Books, 2007. Humorous retelling of the classic story.

Scieszka, John. *The Stinky Cheese Man and Other Fairly Stupid Tales*. New York: Scholastic, 1992. A Caldecott Honor classic in fractured fairy tales and nonsense stories that young children love.

Selznick, Brian. *The Invention of Hugo Cabret*. New York: Scholastic, 2007. One of the most extraordinary books for children and adults! The exquisite illustrations combine beautifully with the text to create something that cannot be classified—graphic novel/story/picture book/movie. Gifted children will see themselves in the talented boy main character.

Seuss, Dr., and Jack Prelutsky. *Dr. Seuss: Hooray for Diffendoofer Day!* New York: Alfred A. Knopf, 1998. Young children will adore Miss Bonkers and delight in the clever language and illustrations of this creative collaboration.

Shannon, George. *Tomorrow's Alphabet*. New York: Greenwillow Books, 1996. This book encourages you to play with the alphabet and think ahead. What will each letter become in the future?

Smith, Lane. *Pinocchio, The Boy*. New York: Penguin Putnam Books for Young Readers, 2002. From the much-loved illustrator of over twenty children's books comes this fractured tale of the familiar Pinocchio story.

Tales of Beatrix Potter. Produced by EMI Films Productions Ltd., 1994. The delightful Beatrix Potter characters come to life in this video, an imaginative, musical interpretation of Potter's tales choreographed by Sir Frederick Ashton, composed and scored by John Lanchbery, and danced by members of London's Royal Ballet. 87 minutes.

Teague, Mark. *Pigsty*. New York: Scholastic, 2004. A young boy resists cleaning his room until a number of unkempt pigs move in and wreak havoc. A delightfully humorous story.

Thompson, Julee Dickerson. *Dance of the Rain Gods.* Trenton, NJ: Africa World Press, 1994. With rich and vibrant illustrations, an African-American folk tale brings to life the magic of a rainstorm.

Tichnor, Richard, and Jenny Smith. *A Spark in the Dark.* Nevada City, CA: Dawn Publications, 1994. Colorful illustrations by the authors enrich this transcendent story of how the world was created and will inspire creative responses in young readers.

Udry, Janice May. *What Mary Jo Shared.* New York: Scholastic, 1991. Soft, poetic illustrations reinforce this tender tale about a young girl who looks for something special to share with her class.

Van Allsburg, Chris. *The Polar Express.* Boston, MA: HMH Books for Young Readers, 2000. The journey of a young boy to the North Pole comes to life through Van Allsburg's masterful storytelling and vivid illustrations in this Caldecott Medal winner.

Warren, Sandra. *The Great Bridge Lowering.* Monroe, NY: Trillium Press, 1987. Packed with activities to stimulate original thought in young children, this storybook is a catalyst for creative thinking.

———. *If I Were a Road.* Monroe, NY: Trillium Press, 1987. Like *The Great Bridge Lowering,* this book entices young children into creative work in a unique and appealing way.

Willems, Mo. *Leonardo the Terrible Monster.* New York: Hyperion Books for Children, 2005. A humorous and touching story about a monster who can't scare anyone and who makes a big decision when he finds a boy worth scaring.

Winthrop, Elizabeth. *The Castle in the Attic.* New York: Yearling, 1994. A magical adventure beautifully told.

Yolen, Jane. *Piggins and the Royal Wedding.* San Diego, CA: Harcourt Brace Jovanovich, 1989. A charming story, vividly told and illustrated, of Piggins the pig—a proper butler and a gracious puzzle-solver.

Zelinsky, Paul O. *Rumpelstiltskin.* New York: Puffin Books, 1986. An extraordinary re-creation of the Grimms. The artist's exquisite paintings infuse new life into the familiar story.

POETRY

Boston Museum of Fine Arts. *Who Has Seen the Wind? An Illustrated Collection of Poetry for Young People.* Kathryn Sky-Peck, ed. New York: Rizzoli International Publications, 1993. Published for the Museum of Fine Arts in Boston, this is a delightful book of poetry classics paired with masterpieces from the museum's collection.

Creative Kids Magazine. Excellent magazine for and by kids featuring poetry, stories, games, and more. Visit their website at www.ckmagazine.org.

Dakos, Kalli. *If You're Not Here Please Raise Your Hand: Poems About School.* New York: Aladdin Paperbacks, 1995. A collection of poems about the elementary school experience.

Frank, Josette, ed. *Snow Toward Evening: A Year in a River Valley.* New York: Dial Books, 1990. Nature poems selected by Josette Frank and illustrated by Thomas Locker focus on the beauty and wonder of nature's seasonal transformations.

Jarrell, Randall. *The Bat Poet.* New York: HarperCollins, 1996. A sensitive portrait of a little furry creature with an artistic temperament. Gifted children will love and understand the dilemma he faces.

Koch, Kenneth. *Rose, Where Did You Get that Red? Teaching Great Poetry to Children.* New York: Vintage Books, 1990. A wonderful source for teaching children to write poetry.

———. *Wishes, Lies, and Dreams: Teaching Children to Write Poetry.* New York: HarperCollins, 1999. Koch and New York's Public School District 61 share their poetry.

Lee, Dennis. *The Ice Cream Store: Poems.* New York: HarperCollins, 2014. A lively collection of poems about colorful people, creatures, and places that young children will love.

Prelutsky, Jack. *The Dragons Are Singing Tonight.* New York: Greenwillow Books, 1998. A whimsical collection of poems about dragons.

———. *Something Big Has Been Here.* New York: Greenwillow Books, 2010. An illustrated collection of humorous poems on a variety of topics. Guaranteed to tickle the fancy of young children.

Schwartz, Alvin. *And the Green Grass Grew All Around: Folk Poetry from Everyone.* New York: HarperCollins, 1999. A rich selection of poems from around the world. Includes a useful index and bibliography.

Silverstein, Shel. *A Light in the Attic.* New York: HarperCollins, 1981. A delightful collection of poems and drawings by one of America's best-loved poets for children.

———. *Where the Sidewalk Ends: The Poems and Drawings of Shel Silverstein.* New York: HarperCollins, 2014. Poems and illustrations by this popular children's poet. The thirtieth anniversary edition includes an index.

Sullivan, Charles, ed. *Imaginary Gardens: American Poetry and Art for Young People.* New York: Harry N. Abrams, 1989. Not a recent book, but an exceptional one. The selection of poems spans a wide range of styles and is historically comprehensive with excellent visuals throughout.

Viorst, Judith. *Sad Underwear and Other Complications: More Poems for Children and Their Parents.* New York: Aladdin Paperbacks, 2000. This collection of poems examines a wide variety of feelings from a child's point of view.

Mathematics

Assouline, Susan, and Ann Lupkowski-Shoplik. *Developing Math Talent: A Guide for Educating Gifted and Advanced Learners in Math.* Waco, TX: Prufrock Press, 2005. An excellent resource for teachers and parents that addresses the needs of high-ability mathematics students.

Burns, Marilyn. *About Teaching Mathematics: A K–8 Resource.* Sausalito, CA: Math Solutions Publications, 2007. Over 240 field-tested lessons designed to develop student understanding and skill through the use of children's literature. A significant figure in math education, Burns knows how to inspire the interest and imagination of children at all ability levels.

Freeman, Christopher. An experienced teacher of gifted math students, Freeman has authored a number of books that focus on integrating inductive thinking into math instruction. Published through Prufrock Press, some favorites include *NIM: Serious Math with a Simple Game* (2005), *Drawing Stars and Building Polyhedra* (2005), and *Compass Constructions: Activities for Using a Compass and Straightedge* (2010).

Instructor. New York: Scholastic. This magazine is a complete teaching resource, covering a wide range of topics from math manipulatives to emotional intelligence. Visit their website at www.scholastic.com/teachers/instructor.

Lasky, Kathryn. *The Librarian Who Measured the Earth.* Boston, MA: Little, Brown & Co., 1994. More than 2,000 years ago, a young man wanted to figure out how he could measure the circumference of the earth without traveling the distance. His answer came within 200 miles of present-day calculations! A true story.

Math Solutions (mathsolutions.com). Designed by pioneer educator and researcher in mathematics Marilyn Burns, this website provides links to most high-quality books and resources in the field.

Schwartz, David. A highly whimsical and prolific math and science writer with a website that provides many resources and a blog, as well as almost fifty books combining math, science, and literature. Examples include *How Much Is a Million?* (1985), *G Is for Googol* (1998), *Q Is for Quark* (2001), *If You Hopped Like a Frog* (1999), and *If Dogs Were Dinosaurs* (2005). Visit his website at www.davidschwartz.com.

Sheffield, Linda Jensen. *Extending the Challenge in Mathematics: Developing Mathematical Promise in K–8 Students.* Thousand Oaks, CA: Corwin Press, 2003. An excellent how-to book for teaching mathematically precocious children. Includes clear, step-by-step instructions and stimulating activities.

Stickels, Terry. *Think-ercises: Math and Word Puzzles to Exercise Your Brain.* Pacific Grove, CA: Critical Thinking Press & Software, 1995. Presents a series of puzzles in order of mathematical difficulty. An unintimidating exploration of critical thinking that emphasizes the joy and fun of learning.

Zaccaro, Edward. So exceptional are Zaccaro's math books that for many teachers, they have become the primary texts, not just supplements. In addition to being imaginative, they accommodate different levels of ability, enabling gifted math students to advance their knowledge and understanding in creative ways. We recommend *Becoming a Problem-Solving Genius: A Handbook of Math Strategies* (2006), *Challenge Math* (2005), *25 Real Life Math Investigations That Will Astound Teachers and Students* (2007), and *The 10 Things All Future Mathematicians and Scientists Must Know (But Are Rarely Taught)* (2003).

Science

Adshead, Paul. *Puzzle Island.* Swindon, UK: Child's Play International, 1990. This delightful alphabet puzzler includes a great many biological and environmental facts for young readers.

Ashby, Ruth. *Jane Goodall's Animal World: Sea Otters.* New York: Aladdin Paperbacks, 1990. Introduces young readers to the wonderful world of the capricious and charming sea otter.

Bass, Joel E., Terry L. Contant, and Arthur A. Carin. *Teaching Science as Inquiry.* Upper Saddle River, NJ: Pearson, 2008. An excellent source for integrating the inquiry method into science instruction to inspire and motivate students. Clear, practical, and manageable for experienced and new teachers alike.

Bender, Lionel. *Inventions.* New York: DK Publishing, 2013. Students can explore such inventions as the wheel, gears, levers, clocks, telephones, and rocket engines. One in a series of Eyewitness Books.

Benson, Laura Lee. *This Is Our Earth.* Watertown, ME: Charlesbridge Publishing, 1994. Simple but grand, lilting verse with short, easy-to-read prose gives the reader an introduction to earth and life sciences.

Branley, Franklyn M. *What the Moon Is Like.* New York: HarperCollins, 1986. An inviting introduction to the wonders of the moon—one that young children will eagerly grasp and that will inspire further interest and inquiry.

Campbell, Brian, and Lori Fulton. *Science Notebooks: Writing About Inquiry.* Portsmouth, NH: Heinemann, 2003. Students act as scientists, using notebooks to record observations and investigate ideas, while also developing literacy skills.

Carle, Eric. *The Tiny Seed.* New York: Little Simon: 2009. Charmingly narrates a flowering plant's life cycle through the seasons.

Cornell, Joseph. *Sharing the Joy of Nature: Nature Activities for All Ages.* Nevada City, CA: Dawn Publications, 1989. This sequel to the author's *Sharing Nature with Children* (1998) is a rich collection of new games and activities for both adults and children. Organized in thematic sequences that inspire awe in nature's many wonders.

The Cousteau Society. *Otters.* New York: Simon & Schuster, 1993. Simple, factual, and exquisitely photographed, this little book unravels the daily living habits of that personable population of sea otters who bob about in the waves of the Northwestern American coast.

———. *Whales.* New York: Simon & Schuster, 1993. A little book with breathtaking photographs of the great whales and their majestic movements underwater. Offers the young reader basic facts and vivid visual impressions.

Donahue, Mike. *The Grandpa Tree.* Niwot, CO: Roberts Rinehart, 2001. This tale of a life cycle takes young readers from a tree's beginning as a sapling to its demise on the forest floor.

Fromer, Julie. *Jane Goodall Living with the Chimps.* Frederick, MD: Twenty-First Century Books, 1992. Describes how Goodall's discoveries about chimpanzees changed how we think about animals, ourselves, and our place in nature. Part of the Earth Keepers series.

Gibbons, Gail. *Caves and Caverns.* New York: First Voyage Books, 1996. An engaging and fascinating journey into the scientific mysteries of caves and caverns—the unusual formations and unusual creatures that lurk inside them. Designed specifically for young children.

Grambling, Lois G. *Can I Have a Stegosaurus, Mom? Can I? Please?* Mahwah, NJ: BridgeWater Books, 1995. Enlivened by dynamic illustrations, this unusual tale for dinosaur fans has a surprise ending.

Herbert, Don. *Mr. Wizard's Supermarket Science.* New York: Random House, 1980. Useful as a general science source, this volume gives directions for 100 simple experiments. Includes pertinent information on scientific principles involved.

International Torrance Legacy Creativity Awards (www.center forgifted.org). See page 217 for more information.

Jenkins, Steve. *Biggest, Strongest, Fastest.* New York: Houghton Mifflin, 1995. Illustrated with striking cut-paper collages, this book offers a vivid tour of the world of animal life.

Julivert, Maria Angels. *The Fascinating World of Butterflies and Moths.* New York: Barron's Publishers, 1991. Introduces readers to the physical characteristics, habits, and natural environments of various kinds of butterflies.

Keeley, Page, Francis Eberle, Chad Dorsey, Joyce Tugel, and Lynn Farrin. *Uncovering Student Ideas in Science: 25 Formative Assessment Probes, Vols. 1–4.* Arlington, VA: National Science Teachers Association Press. Award-winning series that targets students' ideas on science concepts and provides assessment probes for a wide range of knowledge areas.

Laden, Nina. *Roberto The Insect Architect.* San Francisco: Chronicle Books, 2000. Young children will love the word play, the entomological architecture, the humorous and expressive illustrations, and Roberto himself.

Learningscience.org (www.learningscience.org). Newer science education tools such as real-time data collection, simulations, inquiry-based lessons, interactive Web lessons, micro worlds, imaging, and more.

Leon, Vicki. *Seals and Sea Lions: An Affectionate Portrait.* San Luis Obispo, CA: Blake Publishing, 1988. Describes conditions, activities, and daily living habits of *pinnipeds*—seals, sea lions, and elephant seals. Superbly photographed by several different artists.

Mad Sci Network (www.madsci.org). Maintained by scientists and engineers, this site is an interactive science-teaching tool for students around the world. Free ask-an-expert service and Web-based resources covering a wide range of topics.

Manning, Mick. *A Ruined House.* Cambridge, MA: Candlewick Press, 1996. Rich illustrations and simple language make a dilapidated house from the sixteenth century an enchanting discovery of creatures and growing things.

Plaster, Liz, and Rick Krustchinsky. *Incredible Edible Science: Recipes for Developing Science and Literacy Skills.* St. Paul, MN: Redleaf Press, 2010. This collection of fun and creative science activities for children uses ordinary food products. Kids can eat their projects once they've finished.

The Quirkles: Exploring Phonics Through Science. Springfield, MO: Creative3. A twenty-six-book series in which twenty-six imaginary scientists from another realm enable young students to learn substantive science lessons while also developing skill in language arts. The stories are fun, the characters appealing, and the experiments strengthen an inquiry approach to science and offer extended learning opportunities for gifted children. Visit the Quirkles website at www.quirkles.com.

Resnick, Jane Parker. *Wolves and Coyotes.* Chicago: Kidsbooks, 1995. Part of the Eye On Nature series, this volume has much to teach young children about the lives and daily survival habits of wolves and coyotes.

Robinson, Sandra Chisholm. *Sea Otter River Otter.* Niwot, CO: Roberts Rinehart, 1993. Offers stories and projects that are well structured and beautifully illustrated. Delightful, instructive, and easy to read.

Rothstein, Barry, and Betsy Rothstein. *Eye-Popping 3-D Bugs: Phantogram Creepy-Crawlies You Can Practically Touch!* San Francisco: Chronicle Books, 2011. Rich selection of insect phantograms, which young children will see as unfocused shapes until they put on their 3-D glasses.

Seeds of Science/Roots of Reading. A curriculum integrating science and literacy instruction for second- through fifth-grade teachers. Students assume role of scientists—exploring concepts while researching topics, writing about them, and communicating their discoveries. For more information, visit their website at www.scienceandliteracy.org.

Simon, Seymour. *Volcanoes.* New York: HarperCollins, 2006. A leading science writer for children, Simon invites the young reader on an impressive tour of some of the most fascinating volcanic activity around the world.

Smithsonian Science Education Center (www.ssec.si.edu). Sponsored by the Smithsonian Institute and the National Academies, the SSEC strives to transform the way science is taught. Their website includes high-quality content for teachers and students.

Stokes, Donald, Lillian Stokes, and Ernest Williams. *The Butterfly Book: An Easy Guide to Butterfly Gardening, Identification, and Behavior.* Boston, MA: Little, Brown & Co., 1991. This engaging and accessible guide includes over 140 stunning color photographs of butterflies in all of their life stages. Brings fun, adventure, and learning to the intriguing process of starting a butterfly garden.

Taylor, Barbara. *Rain Forest.* New York: DK Children, 1998. Designed for young readers, this book gives children a closer look at the exotic creatures of the rain forest and their daily living habits.

VanCleave, Janice. Janice VanCleave's Science for Every Kid series has science experiments related to different science topics such as engineering, earth science, biomes, chemistry, physics, and many more.

Willis, Jeanne. *Dr. Xargle's Book of Earthlets.* London: Andersen Press, 2012. Professor Xargle's class of extraterrestrials learns about physical characteristics and behavior of the human body.

Technology
BOOKS
Ashburn, Elizabeth A., and Robert E. Floden, eds. *Meaningful Learning Using Technology: What Educators Need to Know and Do.* New York: Teachers College Press, 2006. This book focuses on the role of technology in creating meaningful learning experiences and in-depth understanding of complex content.

Morrison, Gary R., and Deborah L. Lowther. *Integrating Computer Technology into the Classroom.* Upper Saddle River, NJ: Pearson, 2009. These authors explore the vital importance of integrating computer technology into the classroom curriculum *as a tool* rather than simply a medium for transmitting subject content.

Smaldino, Sharon E. Deborah L. Lowther, and James D. Russell. *Instructional Technology and Media for Learning.* Boston, MA: Allyn & Bacon, 2012. A helpful guide for teachers beginning to explore the practical uses of computer technology and other media in the curriculum and classroom.

ONLINE TECH JOURNALS
The Journal: Transforming Education Through Technology. Chatsworth, CA: 1105 Media. Most current source on educational technology developments; includes many resources, features on schools and classrooms, ideas, and links. Visit their website at thejournal.com.

Media & Methods Magazine. An online guide to technology applications for teachers, administrators, and schools—committed to best practices in grades K–12. Visit their website at www.media-methods.com.

Tech & Learning. New York: NewBay Media. An excellent magazine to help guide teachers in making tech decisions for their students. Visit their website at www.techlearning.com for more information and resources.

TECH WEBSITES
Edutopia (www.edutopia.org). Resources, tools, and articles for teachers.

Electronic Portfolios (www.electronicportfolios.org). An online resource with information on electronic portfolios and how to create one.

4Teachers (www.4teachers.org). Information on the integration of innovative technologies into the classroom.

From Now On (www.fno.org). An excellent online educational technology journal.

The Futures Channel (thefutureschannel.com). Information on new media technologies that connect students with scientists, engineers, and explorers.

International Torrance Legacy Creativity Awards (www.center forgifted.org). See page 217 for more information.

Internet4Classrooms (www.internet4classrooms.com). A free Web portal for high-quality Internet resources.

Teacher Tap (www.eduscapes.com/tap). A free resource for teachers and librarians needing guidance in the use of different technologies.

Social Studies
DocsTeach: The National Archives Experience (docsteach.org). An excellent website to assist educators in teaching with primary source documents. Offers thousands of documents in a variety of media as well as online tools.

iEARN (International Education and Resource Network) (www.iearn.org). A nonprofit organization with thousands of schools in thirty countries. Students can do collaborative work in projects teachers can adapt to their curriculum.

Smithsonian Education (www.smithsonianeducation.org). The website has amazing quests that students can be part of as well as access to lesson plans and resources in Art and Design, Science and Technology, History and Culture, and Language Arts.

GLOBAL AND MULTICULTURAL
Aardema, Verna. *Bringing the Rain to Kapiti Plain: A Nandi Tale.* New York: Puffin Books, 1992. A lovely African tale, originating in Kenya, about a young man who devises a way to beckon the rains to his dry land.

Altman, Linda Jacobs. *Amelia's Road.* New York: Lee & Low Books, 2000. A poignant look at a migrant farm family through the eyes of a little girl. An excellent catalyst for discussion.

Ballard, Robert D. *The Lost Wreck of the* Isis. New York: Scholastic, 1990. Dr. Ballard visits the Mediterranean to explore a Roman shipwreck site and investigate an active underwater volcano. Includes a bibliography.

Coles, Robert. *The Story of Ruby Bridges.* New York: Scholastic, 2010. As the first black child to attend an elementary school, Ruby is escorted to and from first grade by federal marshals. This anniversary edition captures her courage and faith.

Durrell, Ann, and Marilyn Sachs, eds. *The Big Book for Peace.* New York: Dutton Children's Books, 1990. Seventeen stories sensitively depict the wisdom of peace and the foolishness of war.

Goble, Paul. *The Girl Who Loved Wild Horses.* New York: Atheneum Books for Young Readers, 2001. Though a young girl loves her family, she prefers running wild and free with the horses and finally becomes one of them. A retelling of a Native American story.

Joosse, Barbara M. *Mama, Do You Love Me?* San Francisco: Chronicle Books, 2014. An Alaskan child tests the limits of her own independence and of her mother's love—which proves to be unconditional and everlasting. A tenderly told and richly illustrated tale.

Miles, Miska. *Annie and the Old One.* Boston, MA: Little, Brown Books for Young Readers, 1985. A simple but poetically told story of a young Navajo girl and her special relationship with her ancient grandmother, who taught her how to weave.

Munsch, Robert, and Saoussan Askar. *From Far Away.* Toronto: Annick Press, 1995. Developed from a series of actual letters between a young Lebanese girl and the authors, this book chronicles the personal journey every foreign child must make when adjusting to a new world.

Scullar, Sue. *The Great Round-the-World Balloon Race.* New York: Macmillan Children's Books, 1993. Tells the story of Harriet Shaw and her niece and nephew as they set out on an around-the-world balloon race.

Sheldon, Dyan. *Under the Moon.* New York: Dial Books for Young Readers, 1994. After finding an arrowhead, a young girl takes an imaginary journey into the past, where Native Americans lived in a land as yet untouched by others.

Snyder, Dianne. *The Boy of the Three-Year Nap.* Boston, MA: HMH Books for Young Readers, 1993. This Japanese tale is rich and evocative, transporting the young reader into a world of suspense and adventure. A Caldecott Honor book.

Steiner, Barbara. *Whale Brother.* New York: Walker Children's, 1995. Omu is a young boy who wants to learn how to carve like Padloq, a great artist in his community. Omu must learn how to give his carvings life, and an experience with a whale shows him how to do this.

Stevens, Carla. *Lily and Miss Liberty.* New York: Scholastic, 1992. A fictional story of a young girl who makes and sells crowns to raise money for mounting the Statue of Liberty, France's gift to the United States.

West, Caryn. *The Trouble with the Alphabet: Through the Eyes of Innocence.* Lancaster, PA: Colophon House, 2008. An amazing book with poetry and paintings of children from all over the world. There is also a page highlighting a service organization related to the country the child is representing.

HISTORY AND GEOGRAPHY

Blos, Joan W. *A Gathering of Days: A New England Girl's Journal, 1830–32.* New York: Aladdin Paperbacks, 1990. A young girl in the 1800s is forced to face life with a new stepmother. A provocative story told in the form of vivid journal entries.

Bunting, Eve. *Dandelions.* New York: Voyager Books, 2001. Rich, atmospheric pictures enhance this beautifully told story of the trials and accomplishments of a pioneer family who leaves home to settle in Nebraska.

Christiansen, Candace. *Calico and Tin Horns.* New York: Dial Books, 1992. In this fascinating tale of early America, set in the Hudson River Valley, a young girl helps fight to save her family's farm and their right to own it. Based on a true story.

Clifford, Mary Louise. *When the Great Canoes Came.* Gretna, LA: Pelican Publishing, 1993. A fictionalized re-creation of events between 1560 and 1686 in what became the state of Virginia, told from the perspective of the Powhatan Indians. A good historical source.

Discover America State by State series. Ann Arbor, MI: Sleeping Bear Press. A series of alphabet books written by various authors. Their contents highlight states, national landmarks, and sports. Students read a small passage and nonfiction information about the topic.

Doherty, Gillian, Anna Claybourne, and Susanna Davidson. *The Usborne Geography Encyclopedia with Complete World Atlas.* London: Usborne Publishing, 2010. This vividly illustrated and fact-filled guide to the world we live in explores all the major topics of geography, including rocks and minerals, weather and climate, population, industry, and the environment.

Dorris, Michael. *Morning Girl.* New York: Hyperion Paperbacks, 1999. Describes life on an island before the first Europeans arrived.

Geography and Geology for Kids, The Study of Our Earth (www.kidsgeo.com). An online textbook for kids of all ages, enabling them to explore the earth around them. Includes interactive learning games.

Hertzog, Nancy, Ellen Honeck, and Barbara Dullaghan. Smart Start series. Waco, TX: Prufrock Press, 2015. This series teaches adults to foster engaging conversations with children using creative thinking, critical thinking, and mathematical thinking questions. Check out *Around My House!* (2015), *Let's Play!* (2015), and *Let's Go to the Market* (2015).

Kid World Citizen (kidworldcitizen.org). An extraordinary site for teachers and students, encompassing cultures, geographies, animals, arts, and more in projects (for instance, the geography project, diversity calendar) everyone will want to do! Very engaging activities and resources to inspire children and stimulate their curiosity in life around the globe.

Knight, James E. *Jamestown: New World Adventure.* Mahwah, NJ: Troll Communications, 1998. Through black-and-white sketches and three years of diary entries, two English children learn the story of their grandfather's experiences as one of the original Jamestown colonists in 1607.

Penner, Lucille Recht. *Eating the Plates: A Pilgrim Book of Food and Manners.* New York: Aladdin Paperbacks, 1997. Highlights Pilgrim eating habits, customs, and manners in the first colony at New Plymouth; includes biographical references.

Ritchie, Scot. *Follow That Map! A First Book of Mapping Skills.* Toronto: Kids Can Press, 2009. An imaginative, interactive introductory book on mapping concepts and skills that leads readers on a quest to find Sally's dog and cat who escaped the yard—from neighborhood to city to country to the larger world.

Smith, Lane. *John, Paul, George & Ben.* New York: Hyperion Books for Children, 2006. A whimsical telling of the early lives of John Hancock, Paul Revere, George Washington, and Ben Franklin as boys.

Starkey, Dinah. *Atlas of Exploration.* New York: Scholastic, 1993. A colorful and helpful quick reference through the ages of exploration, from ancient Egypt to space explorations today. Includes well-illustrated maps of explorers' routes.

Appendix C
Sources for Gifted Education Materials

The resources listed here provide useful information and materials to support young gifted children's learning, growth, and development, including magazines on gifted education, teaching materials (reproducibles, manipulatives, games, activities, units, etc.), multicultural resources, posters, books, recordings, and videos. We've provided phone numbers and websites so you can request catalogs.

Amazing Kids! Online Magazine
206-331-3807
www.amazing-kids.org

Art Image Publications Inc.
1-800-361-2598
www.artimagepublications.com

A.W. Peller and Associates
Bright Ideas for the Gifted and Talented Catalog
1-800-451-7450
www.awpeller.com

Belin-Blank Center
The University of Iowa
College of Education
319-335-6148
www.education.uiowa.edu

California Association for the Gifted
916-209-3242
www.cagifted.org

The Center for Gifted and
Midwest Torrance Center for Creativity
847-901-0173
www.centerforgifted.org

Center for Gifted Education
The College of William and Mary
School of Education
757-221-2362
education.wm.edu

Corwin Press
800-233-9936
www.corwin.com

Council for Exceptional Children (CEC)
1-888-232-7733
www.cec.sped.org

Creative Education Foundation
508-960-0000
www.creativeeducationfoundation.org

Cricket Magazine
Cricket Media
1-800-821-0115
shop.cricketmedia.com

The Critical Thinking Co.
1-800-458-4849
www.criticalthinking.com

Curriculum Associates, Inc.
1-800-225-0248
www.curriculumassociates.com

Davidson Institute for Talent Development
775-852-3483 ext. 435
www.davidsongifted.org

Educational Assessment Service, Inc.
1-800-795-7466
www.sylviarimm.com

Engine-Uity, Ltd.
1-800-877-8718
www.engine-uity.com

Enslow Publishers
1-800-398-2504
www.enslow.com

ETA hand2mind
1-800-288-9920
www.hand2mind.com

Free Spirit Publishing Inc.
1-800-735-7323
www.freespirit.com

The Gifted Child Society, Inc.
201-444-6530
www.giftedchildsociety.com

Gifted Education Press Quarterly Magazine
703-369-5017
www.giftededpress.com

Great Ideas in Education
1-800-639-4122
www.great-ideas.org

Great Potential Press
520-777-6161
www.greatpotentialpress.com

Greenhaven Press
1-800-877-4253
solutions.cengage.com/greenhaven

GTLD Network
Gifted and Talented with Learning Disabilities
www.gtldnet.org

Hickory Grove Press
563-583-4767
www.hickorygrovepress.com

Hoagies' Gifted Education Page
www.hoagiesgifted.org

Illinois Association for Gifted Children
847-963-1892
www.iagcgifted.org

Institute for the Development of Gifted Education
University of Denver
Ricks Center for Gifted Children
303-871-2607
www.du.edu

Interact
1-800-421-4246
www.interact-simulations.com

Kendall Hunt Publishing Company
1-800-770-3544
www.kendallhunt.com

Magination Press
1-800-374-2721
www.apa.org/pubs/magination

Marbles the Brain Store
877-527-2460
www.marblesthebrainstore.com

McGraw-Hill Education
1-800-334-7344
www.mheonline.com

MENTOR: The National Mentoring Partnership
617-303-4600
www.mentoring.org

MindWare
1-800-999-0398
www.mindware.com

Nathan Levy's StoriesWithHoles.com
732-605-1643
www.storieswithholes.com

**National Association for the Education
of Young Children (NAEYC)**
1-800-424-2460
www.naeyc.org

National Association for Gifted Children (NAGC)
202-785-4268
www.nagc.org

National Council of Teachers of Mathematics (NCTM)
1-800-235-7566
www.nctm.org

National Women's History Project
707-636-2888
www.nwhp.org

Neag Center for Gifted Education and Talent Development
University of Connecticut
860-486-2900
www.gifted.uconn.edu

New Moon
The Magazine for Girls and Their Dreams
1-800-381-4743
newmoon.com

Pearson
1-800-848-9500
www.pearsonschool.com

Peytral Publications
952-949-8707
www.peytral.com

Phi Delta Kappa International
1-800-766-1156
pdkintl.org

Pieces of Learning
1-800-729-5137
www.piecesoflearning.com

Professional Associates Publishing
1-866-335-1460
www.kingore.com

Prufrock Press
1-800-998-2208
www.prufrock.com

The Roeper School
248-203-7300
www.roeper.org

Royal Fireworks Press
845-726-4444
www.rfwp.com

Scholastic Testing Service, Inc.
1-800-642-6787
www.ststesting.com

Skipping Stones **Magazine**
541-342-4956
www.skippingstones.org

Teacher Created Resources
1-888-343-4335
www.teachercreated.com

Teachers.Net
www.teachers.net

Tin Man Press
1-800-676-0459
www.tinmanpress.com

Zephyr Press
Chicago Review Press
1-800-888-4741
www.chicagoreviewpress.com

Index

Reproducible pages are marked in **bold.**

A

ABCya!, 191
Able, Gifted and Talented Underachievers (Montgomery), 207
About My Child form, 14, **20–21,** 121, 145
Abruscato, Joe, 199
Abstract reasoning, 10
    portfolio assessment on, 12
    tiered groups formed based on, 43
Acceleration for Gifted Learners, K–5 (Smutny, Walker, and Meckstroth), 191
Acceleration, grade, 167–169
Accountability, 114
Activity (learning) centers, 34
    bodily-kinesthetic, 36–37
    in child-friendly classroom, 32–33
    helping children use, 37–38
    intrapersonal (quiet center), 37
    linguistic, 35
    logical-mathematical, 35–36
    music, 35
    nature, 37
    observing students in, 42
    rotating through different, 34
    using multiple intelligences, 34–37
    visual-spatial (art), 36
Ada, Ama Flor, 196
Adams, Ansel, 83, 196
Addition fairy tale, 111
Adelson, Jill L., 206
ADHD (attention deficit hyperactivity disorder), 183, 187
Adopted children, 68
Advanced Development, 205
Advanced readers, 31–32
The Adventures of Penrose the Mathematical Cat (Pappas), 202
An Advocate's Guide to Building Support for Gifted and Talented Education (Mitchell), 205
Affective Education: Self Concept and the Gifted Student (Katz), 207
African-American children, 176
African immigrants, 176
Age-appropriate assessment, 115
Alexander and the Terrible, Horrible, No Good, Very Bad Day (Viorst), 46, 191
All I Want to Be activity, 166
Almost Gone: The World's Rarest Animals (Jenkins), 61, 193
Alphabet Adventure (Wood and Wood), 199
Alphabet Mystery (Wood and Wood), 199
Alphabet Rescue (Wood and Wood), 199
Alternative histories activity, 63–67
Altertness, of gifted child, 10
Alvarado, Nancy, 205
Amazing and Incredible Counting Stories! A Number of Tall Tales (Grover), 201
Amazing Kids! Online Magazine, 227
The Amazing Outdoor Activity Book (Wilkes), 203
Amelia Earhart (Bledsoe), 196
Amelia Earhart: A Photographic Story of a Life (Stone), 199
Amend, Edward R., **152,** 206
Anansi the Spider (McDermott), 194
And Then What Happened, Paul Revere? (Fritz), 193
Animal Homes (Pope), 202
Animal interviews, 61
Animal rally, 62
Animals
    animal study activity (science), 98–102
    endangered species activity, 60–63
    gifted children in rural areas and, 179, 180
    tree study and, 107, 108
Anno, Masaichiro, 199
Anno, Mitsumasa, 199
Anno's Counting House (Anno), 199
Anno's Magic Seeds (Anno), 200
Anno's Math Games (Anno), 200
Anno's Mysterious Multiplying Jar (Anno and Anno), 199
Ansel Adams Wall Calendar, 196
Anxiety, coping with, 161
Are Trees Alive? (Miller), 84, 107, 198, 202
Armstrong, Thomas, 190
Arnosky, Jim, 85, 191, 196
Arrow to the Sun: A Pueblo Indian Tale (McDermott), 194
Art(s). *See also* Language arts
    creative response to visual images, 83–85
    geometric shapes activity, 104–105
    multisensory experiences using, 81
    philosophy for teaching, 83
    study of natural world using, 106
    teacher experience and, 94
Art activity center, 36
Artful Thinking program, 95, 196
Artifacts from other cultures, 69
Art Image Publication, Inc., 227
Artistic responses, 84–85
The Art of James Christensen: A Journey of the Imagination (Christensen and St. James), 196
Arts Every Day (website), 196
Ashanti to Zulu: African Traditions (Musgrove), 194
Asian children, 176
Asperger's syndrome, 183
Assessment, 1
    difficulties and questions related to, 113
    dynamic, 13–14
    formative, 115
    IQ testing, 116–120
    NAEYC DAP on, 3
    open-ended *vs.* rigid evaluation, 115
    planning activities for broad-based, 114–116
    portfolio, 11–13, 120–122
    standardized testing, 114, 115–116
    summative, 115
    through observation, 122–123
    time issues with, 123
Assessment of Children: Cognitive Foundations (Sattler), 204
Assessment: Timesaving Procedures for Busy Teachers (Kingore), 204
Assouline, Susan G., 17*n*16, 168, 168*n*11, 205, 206
Asynchronous development, 9, 16, 155, 159
Attendance-taking, whole-group activity for, 33
Attention deficit hyperactivity disorder (ADHD), 183, 187
Attention span, 10
Auditory learning modality, 30–31, 38
Auditory processing disorders, 183–184
Authentic assessment, 11, 115, 116, 120. *See also* Assessment
Autism spectrum disorder (ASD), 183
A.W. Peller and Associates, 227

B

Balancing the Equation: Where Are Women and Girls in Science, Engineering and Technology? (Thom), 209
Baldwin, Alexinia Y., 207
Baron, Robert, 194
Barr, Jason J., 165*n*10
Barth, Edna, 192
Baum, Susan M., 208
Baylor, Byrd, 192
Behavior
    challenging, 9, 10
    enigmatic, 9
    observing misbehavior, 42
Behind the Mask: A Book About Prepositions (Heller), 197
Belin-Blank Center, 227
Benoit, Peter, 64, 192
Berger, Sandra L., 205
Bernal, Ernesto M., 208
Bernard, Robin, 84, 106, 196, 200
Best Practices in Gifted Education (Robinson, Shore, and Ennerson), 191
Betts, George T., 189
Between the Earth and Sky: Legends of Native American Sacred Places (Bruchac), 192
Beyond IQ: A Triarchic Theory of Human Intelligence (Sternberg), 190
Bibliotherapy, 161–162
BigOrrin (website), 192
Billington Jr., John, 65
Biographies
    creating Pilgrim, 66–67
    on great women leaders, 182
    readers' theater and, 88, 90, 91
    resources, 219–220
Birely, Marlene, 208
Birney, Betty G., 88, 196
Bjork, R., 190
Blast to the Past Series (Deutsch and Cohon), 192
Bledsoe, Lucy Jane, 196
Blizzard, Gladys S., 196

Blueberries for Sal (McCloskey), 44, 45
Blue Dog painting series (Rodrigue), 45
Blues songs, 91
Bodily-kinesthetic activity center, 36–37
Bodily-kinesthetic learning. *See* Tactile-kinesthetic learning modality
Bolanos, Olivia, 175*n*4, 209
The Bookfinder: A Guide to Children's Literature About the Needs and Problems of Youth Aged 2–15 (Dreyer), 206
Book-making activities, 85
Books, as coping strategy, 161–162
Borland, James H., 208
Bowden, Marcia, 192, 200
Boys, gifted, 182–183
The Boy Who Lived with the Seals (Martin), 194
Brain-Compatible Strategies (Jensen), 190
Brain research, implications for learning environment, 27–28
Brainstorming, 33, 37, 162, 166
Branching, 45
Branley, Franklyn M., 200
Bransford, J.D., 30*n*5
Bredekamp, Sue, 3*n*3
Brown, A. L., 30*n*5
Browne, Joy V., 28*n*1
Brown Honey in Broomwheat Tea (Thomas), 199
Bruchac, Joseph, 192
Brulles, Dina, 29*n*3, 46*n*1, 137*n*3, 190, 204
Bryant, Jen, 196
Bryant, Margaret A., 196
Budgets, learning/classroom environment and, 38
Building/drama activity center, 36–37
Burningham, John, 192
Burns, Deborah K., 191
Burns, Marilyn, 103, 200
Burns, Monica, 191
Bush, George W., 114
Butterfield, Moira, 200

C

Calendar, whole-group activity for, 33
California Association for the Gifted, 227
Callahan, Carolyn M., 16*n*15
Canfield, Jack, 206
Can't You Make Them Behave, King George? (Fritz), 193
Can You Count to a Googol? (Wells), 203
Can You Help? letter, 145, **148**
Can You Share? letter, 145, **149**
Cappelli, Rose, 197
Carbo, Marie, 190
Carle, Eric, 200
Carlisle, Jody, 196, 200
Carmine: A Little More Red (Sweet), 85, 86, 199
Carr, Jan, 198
Carson, Rachel, 1*n*1, 2*n*2
Carter, Polly, 196
Cartledge, Gwendolyn, 167, 206
Castellano, Jaime, 208
Catalysts
    for alternative fairy tale activity, 86
    for creative composition activity, 91–92
    for creative response to visual images, 83–84
    for creative work, 81, 82
    for readers' theater activity, 88
    for tree study activity, 107
Cech, Maureen, 72, 192
The Center for Gifted and Midwest Torrance Center Creativity, 227
Center for Gifted Education, College of William and Mary School of Education, 227
Center on the Social and Emotional Foundations for Early Learning (CSEFEL), 167, 206
Challenges for Children: Creative Activities for Gifted and Talented Primary Students (Cook and Carlisle), 196
Challenges, importance of having, 38–39
Chameleons, 101
Chapman, Carolyn, 37
Characters, readers' theater, 89–90
Checklist of My Child's Strengths form, 14, **22–23**, 121, 145
Checklists
    identifying giftedness in diverse populations with, 177
    observation, 122, 123, **124–130**
Cheney, Lynne, 192
Cherry, Lynne, 200
Chevat, Richard, 200
Child-created portfolios, 13
ChildDrama (website), 200
Child prodigies, 186–187
Children Just Like Me: A Unique Celebration of Children Around the World (Kindersley and Kindersley), 193
The Children of the Morning Light: Wampanoag Tales as Told by Manitonquat (Manitonquat), 64, 194
Choice, Penny, 204
Christensen, James, 196
Christiansen, Candace, 107, 202
Cinderella's Rat (Meddaugh), 86, 198

Clark, Barbara, 9*n*9, 189, 206
Classroom
    designing, 25–26
    features of child-friendly, 32–33
Class structure/schedule, 33–34
Clegg, Luther B., 196
Clement, Rod, 200
Clements, Andrew, 200
Climo, Shirley, 72, 87, 192, 196
Clinton, Bill, 114
A Cloak for the Dreamer (Friedman), 201
Cloud Dance (Locker), 201
Cluster grouping, 135–136, 140
The Cluster Grouping Handbook (Winebrenner and Brulles), 204
Cocking, R. R., 30*n*5
Coffield, F., 30*n*5
Cognitive Abilities Test Form 6 (CogAT 6), 215
Cognitive Abilities Test, Form 7 (CogAT), 119
Cohon, Rhody, 192
Colangelo, Nicholas, 17*n*16, 168, 168*n*11, 189, 205, 206
Cole, Joanna, 200
Color (Heller), 198
Color, branching activities for teaching, 45
The Color of Distance (Thomson), 101
Color patterns, 34
Come Look with Me: Enjoying Art with Children (Blizzard), 196
Common Core Meets Education Reform (Hess and McShane), 204
Common Core State Standards (CCSS), 2, 43, 58, 59–60, 114
Communication, learning environment and, 29. *See also* Parent-teacher communication/relationship
Compacting the curriculum, 43, 48
Compassion, 29
Competition, reducing, 164
Compliment jar, 167
Computers, 27, 31, 104
Conceptions of Giftedness (Sternberg and Davidson), 8*n*3, 190
Conceptual thinking, creative learning as a link to higher-level, 97–98
Conferences, parent-teacher, 145–147
Contemporary African Art Gallery, New York, 104, 200
Control, gifted child's sense of, 158
Cook, Carole, 196, 200
Coombs, Kate, 197
Cooperative learning, 133–134
Coping strategies, 161–162
Copple, Carol, 3*n*3
Corwin Press, 227
Council for Exceptional Children (CEC), **153**, 227
Counseling Gifted and Talented Children: A Guide for Teachers, Counselors, and Parents, 14*n*11, 189, 205
Counseling the Gifted and Talented (Silverman), 9*n*8, 143*n*1, 190, 206, 207
Counting on Frank (Clement), 200
Coyote: A Trickster Tale from the American Southwest (McDermott), 194
Craig, Janet, 192
Creative activities
    alternative fairy tales, 85–88
    catalysts for, 82
    free verse, 91–94
    guidance for, 82–83
    imagining environmental solutions, 60–63
    interpretive expression, 83–85
    readers' theater/playwriting, 88–91
    sharing work from, 94
Creative Activities for Gifted Readers: Dynamic Investigations, Challenging Projects, and Energizing Assignments, Grade 3–6 (Fredericks), 197
Creative composition, 82, 91–94
Creative divergence, 82, 85–88
Creative Education Foundation, 227
Creative exploration, 82, 88–91
Creative learning
    as link to higher-level conceptual thinking, 97–98
    as link to imaginative thinking, 80–81
Creative response, 82, 83–85
Creative Teaching of the Gifted (Sisk), 195
Creativity/creative thinking
    about spatial relationships and geometric shapes, 103
    alternative histories activity, 64–67
    basic components of, 58–59
    critical thinking and, 58, 63
    cultural invention activity, 67–73
    evaluation/elaboration process, 73–75
    goals for using, 57–58
    importance of, 1–2
    learning environment and, 29
    personal contributions of, 58
    portfolio assessment on, 12
    in the social studies curriculum, 60–74
    standardized testing and, 115–116
    standards and, 58, 59–60
    taxonomy of, 59
Creativity: Just Wanting to Know (Torrance), 199
Creativity Research Journal, 208
Cricket Magazine, 227
Crinkleroot's Guide to Knowing the Trees (Arnosky), 85, 191, 196

Critical thinking
  about spatial relationships, 103
  alternative histories activity, 66–67
  creative activities and, 57, 58, 111–112
  cultural invention activity, 69–73
  endangered/threatened species activity, 62–63
  study of shapes and, 102
The Critical Thinking Co., 227
Crossover Children: A Sourcebook for Helping Children Who Are Gifted and Learning Disabled (Birely), 208
Crying, by gifted child, 16
Cubes, Cones, Cylinders, and Spheres (Hoban), 201
Culham, Ruth, 197
Cultural diversity
  cultural invention activity, 67–73, 179
  IQ testing and, 118–119
Cultural invention activity, 67–73, 179
Culturally Diverse and Underserved Populations of Gifted Students (Baldwin), 207
Culturally, linguistically, and economically diverse (CLED) backgrounds, 174.
    See also Diverse populations, children from
Cultures
  comparing, 69–70
  creating a fictional, 71–73
  creating an animal, 101
  observing commonalties between, 70–71
Cummings, E.E., 197
Cunningham, Kevin, 64, 192
Curiosity
  of gifted child, 10
  in highly gifted children, 185
  portfolio assessment on, 11
Curriculum
  compacting, 43, 48
  extending. *See* Extending the curriculum
  language arts. *See* Language arts
  math. *See* Mathematics
  science. *See* Science
  social studies. *See* Social studies
Curriculum Associates, Inc., 227
Curriculum Compacting: The Complete Guide to Modifying the Regular Curriculum for High-Ability Students (Reis, Burns, and Renzulli), 191
Curriculum narrowing, 58
Curriculum planning
  communication with parents and, 48, **56**
  compacting the curriculum, 43
  documentation and, 47, **55**
  extension activities for groups, 43–45
  extension activities for individuals, 45–47
  NAEYC DAP on, 3
  organization of the curriculum, 42–43
  questions and answers on, 48
  use of time and, 41–42
Curriculum standards
  Common Core State Standards (CCSS), 114
  creativity challenge and, 58
  curriculum planning and, 43
  legislation, 114
  problems with, 114
Curry, Jim, 191
Custom Observation form, 70, **79**
Customs, sharing child's cultural, 69

D
Daniels, Susan, 206, 208
Danley, Gina Estrada, 175n4, 209
Davidson Institute for Talent Development, 16, **153**, 189, 227
Davidson, Janet E., 190
Davidson, Neil, 29n3
Davis, Gary, 9n9, 189, 206
Delisle, James R., 206
Delisle, Jim, 205
Demi, 192
The Desert Is Theirs (Baylor and Parnall), 192
Deutsch, Stacia, 192
Developing Portfolios for Authentic Assessment (Kingore), 204
Developing Units for Primary Students: A Guide to Developing Effective Topical, Integrated, and Thematic Units of Study for Primary-Level Students with Sixteen Teacher-Generated Sample Units (Samara and Curry), 191
Developmentally appropriate practice (DAP)
  NAEYC position statement, 2–3
Developmentally Appropriate Practice in Early Childhood Programs Serving Children from Birth through Age 8 (Copple and Bredekamp), 3n3
DeVries, Arlene R., **152**, 205, 206
Diamond, Marian, 190
Differential Ability Scales–Second Edition (DAS–II), 215
Differentiated instruction
  compacting the curriculum and, 43
  NAEYC principles and, 3
  Response to Intervention (RTI) and, 134–135
  tiered groups and, 43
Differentiating for the Young Child (Smutny and von Fremd), 195, 199, 203
Differentiation: Simplified, Realistic, and Effective (Kingore), 191
Dinkmeyer, Don, 205
Dinosaur activity, 81

Discovering and Developing Talents in Spanish-Speaking Students (Smutny, Haydon, Bolanos, and Danly), 175n4, 209
Discovering Wolves: A Nature Activity Book (Field and Karasov), 192
Distance learning, 180
Diverse populations, children from, 173–188
  cultural and linguistic diversity, 175–179
  economically disadvantaged children, 179
  fostering a multicultural/culturally relevant environment for, 178–179
  growing population of, 175
  high-energy children, 187
  highly gifted children, 184–186
  Hispanic cultures, 175–176
  identifying giftedness in, 177–178
  Native American/Native Alaskan/Hawaiian cultures, 175
  obstacles faced by, 174–175
  prodigies, 186–187
  questions and answers about, 188
  rural areas, children from, 179–180
  twice-exceptional gifted children, 183–184
Division fairy tale, 110
DK Eyewitness Books: Endangered Animals (Hoare), 193
Documentation
  at the beginning of each year, 114
  for compacting and extending the curriculum, 47, **55**
  importance of, 113
  portfolios used for, 120–122
Dorfman, Lynne R., 197
Downy, Robert Sr., 199
Drama/building activity center, 36–37
Dramatizations, 66, 69, 72, 81, 88–91, 112, 164
Draw! (Solga), 199
Drawing Stars & Building Polyhedra (Freeman), 201
Dreyer, Sharon Spredemann, 206
Dual exceptionalities, 183–184
Dunn, Kenneth, 190
Dunn, Rita, 190
Dweck, Carol, 58, 155, 206
Dynamic assessment, 13–14

E
Earhart, Amelia, 92
Early entrance, 167–168
Early Gifts: Recognizing and Nurturing Children's Talents (Olszewski-Kublius, Limburg-Weber, and Pfeiffer), 189
Early identification, 6–17
  advanced/early reading, 31–32
  asynchronous development and, 9
  barriers to, 8
  of children from diverse populations, 177–178
  definitions of giftedness and, 7–9
  dynamic assessment and, 13–14
  enlisting parent's help for, 14–15
  of highly gifted children, 186
  importance of, 7
  interviewing students and, 10–11
  pioneer teachers and, 6–7
  portfolios and, 11–13
  questions and answers on, 16–17
  testing and, 15
Early readers, 31–32
Eccleston, K., 30n5
Eckert, Sharon, 198, 201
Ecology (Pollock and Lane), 202
Economically disadvantaged children, 179
Editing, for alternative histories project, 67
EDSITEment (website), 192, 197
Educating Children for Life: The Modern Learning Community (Roeper), 207
Educational Assessment Service, Inc., 227
Education.com, 191
Education, Information, and Transformation, 189
Education of the Gifted and Talented (Davis, Rimm, and Siegle), 9n9, 189, 206
Education of the Gifted and Talented: Report to the Congress of the United States by the U.S. Commissioner of Education (Marland), 7n1, 189
Edutopia (website), 44, 197
The Egyptian Cinderella (Climo), 72, 87, 192, 196
Elaboration, 59, 73–75
Elementary and Secondary Education Act (ESEA) (1994), 114
Eliza Lucas Pinckney (Miller), 194
Emotional and social needs, 154–170
  coping strategies and, 161–162
  early entrance/acceleration and, 167–169
  empathy, 165
  getting to know oneself and each other exercises for, 166–167
  gifted student perspective, 156
  intensity issues and, 156–157
  introversion and, 162–163
  peer relationships, 163–164
  perfectionism and, 159–160
  questions and answers about, 170
  self-understanding and self-acceptance, 165–166
  sensitivity issues and, 157–158
  structure/control issues and, 158
  teacher's role and, 154–155
  underachievement and, 160–161

Emotional Intelligence: Why It Can Matter More than IQ (Goleman), 207
Emotional intensity, 156–157
Emotional Intensity in Gifted Students: Helping Kids Cope with Explosive Feelings (Fonseca), 206
Emotional sensitivity, 157
Emotion, long-term memory and, 28
Empathy, 165, 185
Empathy: Developmental Training and Consequence (Goldstein and Michaels), 207
Engine-Uity, Ltd., 227
Enigmatic behavior, 9
Ennerson, Donna, 191
The Enrichment Triad Model: A Guide for Developing Defensible Programs for the Gifted and Talented (Renzulli), 8n2, 189
Enrichment Units in Math (Leimbach), 201
Enslow Publishers, 227
Environment. *See* Learning environment
Environmental Protection Agency (website), 195
EPals (website), 192
Eric Carle's Animals, Animals (Carle), 200
Eric Carle's Opposites (Carle), 200
Ernst, Lisa, 197
ETA hand2mind, 227
Evaluation (by student)
    creative thinking and, 59
    portfolio assessment and, 12
    questions used to guide, 74–75
    setting the stage for, 73–74
    What I Learned form, 123, **131–132**
Evaluation (by teacher). *See also* Assessment
    for child-friendly classroom, 33
    of individual students working in groups, 139
    open-ended, 115
    rigid, 115
Eva Moore, Beatrice, 198
Everybody Needs a Rock (Baylor and Parnall), 192
Examiner, role of test, 117–118
Exceptionally Gifted Children (Gross), 208
Exploring Biographies of Nellie Bly, Albert Einstein & George Washington Carver (Carter, McNeeer, Faber, and Faber), 196
Extending the curriculum
    group activities, 43–45
    individual instruction, 45–47
Extroverts, 163

F
Faber, Doris, 196
Faber, Harold, 196
Fairy tales
    created with numbers, 109–111
    creating alternative, 85–88
    interest groups and, 44
    from other cultures, 72
Falling for Rapunzel (Wilcox), 86, 199
Falling Up (Silverstein), 199
Families. *See* Parents/parents of gifted children; Parent-teacher communication/relationship
Fantasia (film), 81, 197
Fantasia 2000 (film), 197
Farjeon, Eleanor, 197
Farjeon, Herbert, 197
Ferrier, Jean-Louis, 201
Fertig, Carol, **151,** 205
Fetzner, Mary, 201
Fictional culture, 71–73
Field, Nancy, 192
Field, Simon Quellen, 201
Fischer Comprehensive Assessment of Giftedness Scales, 215
Fisher, Leonard Everett, 197, 201
Fleischman, Paul, 197
Fletcher, Ralph, 197
Flexibility
    alternative histories activity, 63–67
    creative thinking and, 58–59
    elaboration/evaluation and, 73
    fluency process *vs.,* 65
Flexible grouping, 136–141
Fluency
    creative thinking and, 58, 59
    elaboration/evaluation and, 73
    flexibility process *vs.,* 65
    imagining environmental solutions, 60–63
Fogliano, Julie, 193
Fonseca, Christine, 206
Food theme, 34
Ford, Peggy K., 196
Forest Has a Song: Poems (Ludwig), 198
Forest Life (Taylor), 203
Formal assessment instruments, 15
Formative assessments, 115
Fostered children, 68
Foundation for Rural Education and Development (FRED), 180, 208
Fox, Mem, 72, 193
Fractals, Googols and Other Mathematical Tales (Pappas), 202

Fraction fairy tales, 109–110
Fractions, 105
Fractured fairy tales, 85–88
Fractured Fairytales (website), 197
Frames of Mind: The Theory of Multiple Intelligences (Gardner), 8, 189
Frazier, Andrea Dawn, 208
Fredericks, Anthony, 197
Freeman, Christopher, 201
Free Spirit Publishing Inc., 227
Free verse, 91–94, 100
Friedman, Aileen, 201
Friendships (peer relationships), 28–29, 163–164
Fritz, Jean, 193
From Little Acorns: A First Look at the Life Cycle of a Tree (Godwin), 85, 197
Fry, Richard, 175n2
"Funds of knowledge," 179
Furniture, classroom, 26

G
Galbraith, Judy, 28n2, **151,** 156, 165–166, 190, 205, 206–207
Gardner, Bob, 203
Gardner, Howard, 8, 189
Gates, Marji Purcell, 83
Gates, Phil, 101, 201
Gaylord, Susan, 85, 197
Gellman, E. S., 204
Gender issues
    gender differences/stereotypes, 166
    gifted boys, 182–183
    gifted girls, 180–182
Gentry, Marcia L., 204
Geometry, 98, 102–105
George, David, **151,** 205, 207
George Washington's Breakfast (Fritz), 193
Gibbons, Gail, 83, 107, 197, 201
The Gifted and Talented: Developmental Perspectives, 207
Gifted and Talented in the Regular Classroom (Torrance and Sisk), 195
Gifted Child Quarterly, 189, 205, 208
Gifted Child Society, **153,** 227
Gifted Education Press Quarterly Magazine, 227
Giftedness. *See also* Gifted students
    definitions of, 7–8
    recognizing. *See* Early identification
Giftedness 101 (Silverman), 190
Gifted Parent Groups: The SENG Model (DeVries and Webb), 205
Gifted Rating Scales (GRS), 215
Gifted students. *See also* Diverse populations, children from
    asynchronous development of, 9
    behavioral characteristics of, 9, 10
    boys, 182–183
    in cluster grouping, 136
    common misconceptions about, 155
    coping strategies for, 161–162
    eight "great gripes" of, 156
    emotional and social needs of, 155–165
    girls, 180–182
    grouped with students of similar ability, 136–137
    increased awareness of, 16
    intellectual and emotional needs of, 2
    intensity in, 156–157
    introversion in, 162–163
    parents of. *See* Parents/parents of gifted children
    percent of identified, 16
    perfectionism in, 159–160
    recognizing unique needs of, 6–7
    sense of control and structure in, 158
    sensitivity of, 157–158
    shifting passions of, 9
    teachers examining their feelings about, 144
    traditional cooperative learning groups not benefiting, 133–134
    underachievement and lack of motivation in, 160–161
Gifts Differing: Understanding Personality Types (Myers and Myers), 207
Girls, gifted, 180–182
The Girls Report: What We Know and Need to Know About Growing Up Female (Phillips), 208
G Is for Googol (Schwartz), 203
Globalchild: Multicultural Resources for Young Children (Cech), 72, 192
Goals
    group activities, 139–140
    language arts curriculum, 94–95
    for using creative thinking, 57–58
Godwin, Sam, 85, 197
Goff, Kathy, 209
Goldilocks and the Three Bears, 44
Goldilocks and the Three Dinosaurs (Willems), 85, 86, 199
Goldstein, Arnold P., 207
Goleman, Daniel, 207
Gonzo Gizmos: Projects & Devices to Channel Your Inner Geek (Field), 201
Goodall, Jane, 88
Goodenough-Harris Drawing Test, 215
Good-quality education, meaning of, 2
Gore, Janet L., **152,** 206
The Gorilla Foundation (website), 201

Grade acceleration, 167–169
Grade skipping, 17
Graven, Stanley N., 28*n*1
Great Explorations in Math and Science (GEMS), 201
Great Ideas in Education, 227
The Great Kapok Tree: A Tale of the Amazon Rain Forest (Cherry), 200
Great Potential Press, 227
The Greedy Triangle (Burns), 103, 200
Greenaway, Theresa, 201
Greenhaven Press, 227
Gross, Miraca U. M., 17*n*16, 168, 205, 206, 208
The Grouchy Ladybug (Carle), 200
Group activities
    balanced with independent activities, 31–32
    extending curriculum for, 43–45
    grouping children for, 95
    interest groups, 43–44
    Tic-Tac-Toe Menu for, 44–45
    tiered groups, 43
Group activity center, 38
Grouping. *See also* Group activities
    avoiding group homework for, 139
    cluster, 136
    conflict within group and, 138–139
    disadvantages of traditional cooperative learning, 133–134, 135–136
    goals and group size for, 139–140
    ground rules for, 138
    guidelines for, 137–140
    individual evaluations and, 139
    peer relationships and, 164
    providing variety with, 137
    questions and answers about, 140
    Response to Intervention (RTI), 134–135
    setting clear parameters for, 137–138
    student choice and, 137
Group testing, 116–117
Grover, Max, 201
Growing Up Gifted: Developing the Potential of Children at Home and at School (Clark), 9*n*9, 189
GTLD Network, **153**, 228
Guidance, for creative work, 82–83
Guiding the Gifted Child: A Practical Source for Parents and Teachers (Webb, Meckstroth, and Tolan), **152**, 190, 206, 207
Guiding the Social and Emotional Development of Gifted Youth (Delisle), 206
Gwynne, Fred, 87, 197

H
Half-day kindergartens, 39
Hall, E., 30*n*5
Halsted, Judith Wynn, 161–162, 207
Handbook of Gifted Education (Colangelo and Davis), 189, 190, 204
Hands Around the World: 365 Creative Ways to Build Cultural Awareness & Global Respect (Milford), 194
Hands-On Geometry: Constructions with Straightedge and Compass, Grades 4–6 (Freeman), 201
Hands On: Pentominoes, 191
Handwriting, 17, 27, 186
Harness, Cheryl, 193
Harvard Family Research Project, 145, 146*n*3, 205
Hassard, Jack, 199
Have You Seen Trees? (Oppenheim), 202
Hawaiian cultures, 175
Haydon, Kathryn P., 175*n*4, 209
Hayes, Joe, 193
Heacox, Diane, 191
Heilbronner, Nancy N., **151**
Heller, Ruth, 197
Help Me Help You letter, **40,** 145
Heroes and Heroines (Farjeon and Farjeon), 197
Hertzog, Nancy B., **151,** 205
Hess, Frederick M., 204
Hey! Get Off Our Train (Burningham), 192
Hickory Grove Press, 228
High energy, children with, 187
Highly gifted children, 184–186
High-stakes testing, 58, 188
Hispanic cultures, 175–176
History
    alternative histories activity, 63–67
    fictional culture and, 72
Hist Whist and Other Poems for Children (Cummings), 197
Hoagies' Gifted Education (website), **153,** 193, 228
Hoare, Ben, 193
Hoban, Tana, 201
Hoberman, Mary Ann, 198
Hollingworth Center for Highly Gifted Children, 186, 208
Home: A Journey Through America (Locker), 194
Homework, 14, 139
Hopkins, Lee Bennett, 198
Hopson, Janet, 190
A House for Hermit Crab (Carle), 200
How Do You Lift a Lion? (Wells), 203
How It Feels to Be Happy exercise, 167

How People Learn: Brain, Mind, Experience, and School (Bransford, Brown, and Cocking), 30*n*5
How Your Child Learns Best: Brain-Friendly Strategies You Can Use to Ignite Your Child's Learning and Increase School Success (Willis), 190
Hudson: The Story of a River (Locker and Baron), 194
Hunsaker, Scott, 204

I
Icky Bug Shapes (Pallotta), 202
Identification: The Theory and Practice of Identifying Students for Gifted and Talented Education Services (Hunsaker), 204
Identifying gifted students. *See* Early identification
Identifying Gifted Students: A Practical Guide (Johnsen), 204
If . . . (Perry), 198
If You Hopped Like a Frog (Schwartz), 203
If Your Name Was Changed at Ellis Island (Levine), 193
If You Traveled on the Underground Railroad (Levine), 193
If You Traveled West in a Covered Wagon (Levine), 193
If You Want to See a Whale (Fogliano), 193
Igniting Creativity in Gifted Learners, K–6 (Smutny and von Fremd), 195
I Hate to Read! (Marshall), 198
I Live in Music (Shange), 198
Illinois Association for Gifted Children, 228
Illinois Association for Gifted Journal 2014: Underrepresented Populations, 209
Imaginary Gardens: American Poetry and Art for Young People (Sullivan), 199
Imagination exercises, 62
Imaginative thinking/imaginative activities
    alternative fairy tales, 85–88
    alternative histories activity, 64, 65–66
    animal study, 100–101
    creative learning as a link to, 80–81
    creative response to visual images, 83–85
    free verse, 91–94
    integrating creative processes to stimulate, 82–83
    readers' theater/playwriting, 88–91
    recommendations for, 83
    for study of trees, 107
    taxonomy of, 82
Imagi-size: Activities to Exercise Your Students' Imagination (Milios), 194, 198
I'm in Charge of Celebrations (Baylor and Parnall), 192
Immigrants
    African, 176
    from the Middle East, 177
Incubation Model of Teaching: Getting Beyond the Aha! (Torrance and Safter), 203
Independent activities
    balance of group activities and, 31–32
    importance of, 140
    point of view activity, 45–46
    resident expert activity, 46
    Tic-Tac-Toe Menu, 46–47
    trusting the student and, 47
Individual center time, 34
I Never Told and Other Poems (Livingston), 198
"Information Please" (family letter), 14, **19,** 121, 145
Ingoglia, Gina, 84, 198
Inman, Tracy Ford, **151,** 206
Institute for the Development of Gifted Education, 228
Instructor, 200
Intake interview, 145
Intellectual risk taking, 31
Intelligence Reframed: Multiple Intelligences for the 21st Century (Gardner), 8*n*6, 189
Intelligence (IQ) testing, 114, 116–120
    culturally diverse children, 118–119
    examiner's role in, 117–118
    of highly gifted children, 186
    misinterpretation of test directions, 116
    outside consultants used for, 119–120
    problems with group testing, 116–117
    questions to ask about discrepancies in, 120
    scores for individually administered, 117
    underestimating a child's abilities, 117
    varying scores from different, 116–117
Intensity, in gifted children, 156–157
Interact (resource), 228
Interest groups, 43–45
Interpersonal activity center, 37
Interpretive expression, 83–85
Interviews
    animal, 61
    getting to know your students through, 10–11
    intake, 145
    student, of each other, 166
Intrapersonal activity center, 37
Introversion, 162–163
I Thought You'd Like to Know letter, 47, **56**
I Wonder If I'll See a Whale (Weller), 196

J/K
Janos, Paul M., 207
Jenkins, Steve, 61, 193
Jensen, Eric, 190

The Job of a Traveling Teacher (Gates), 83
John Muir: America's Naturalist (Locker), 194
Johnsen, Susan K., 204
Joint poem, 92
Jolly, Jennifer L., **151,** 206
Journal for the Illinois Council of the Gifted, 191
Joyful Noise: Poems for Two Voices (Fleishman), 197
Just Because I Am: A Child's Book of Affirmation (Payne), 207
K–3 Science Activities Kit (Poppe and Van Matre), 202
K3 Teacher Resources (website), 201
Kandinsky, Wassily, 45
Kaplan, Susan, 191
Karasov, Corlisse, 192
Katz, Elinor, 207
Kaufman Assessment Battery for Children–Second Edition (KABC–II), 119, 215
Keiper, Marjories, 196
Keirouz, Kathryn S., 143n2, 205
Kendall Hunt Publishing Company, 228
Kerr, Barbara, 181n6, 208
Kid Info (website), 201
KinderArt (website), 193
Kindergarten
    cultural invention activity adapted to, 72
    early entrance into, 167–168
    intake interview in, 145
    planning activities within, 39
    in standards-driven era, 2
Kindersley, Anabel, 193
Kindersley, Barnabas, 193
Kinesthetic learners. *See* Tactile-kinesthetic learning modality
Kinesthetic responses, 85
Kingore, Bertie, 120, 121n3, 189, 191, 204
The Kingore Observation Inventory (KOI) (Kingore), 204
Kinsella, Marilyn, 199
Kiss, Lisa M., 191, 206
Kites Sail High (Heller), 197
Kleefield, James, 167, 206
Klein, Barbara, **152,** 205
Kleine, Patricia A., 204
Knopper, Dorothy, 205
Knowledge base, 31
Krogstad, Jens Manuel, 175n2
Kulik, Chen-Lin, 204
Kulik, James, 204
Kurcinka, Mary Sheedy, **152,** 205, 207

L

Lamorisse, Albert, 45
Lane, Brian, 202
Language arts, 80–95
    alternative fairy tales, 85–88
    catalysts for, 82
    creative processes for, 82
    free verse, 91–94
    interpretive expression, 83–85
    map of imaginative activities for, 83
    multimedia activities, 81
    questions and answers about, 94–95
    readers' theater/playwriting, 88–91
    teacher guidance and, 82–83
Language (primary) other than English, 174
Languages of other cultures, 69
Lawrence, Gordon, 207
Learning ability
    benefits and challenges of rapid, 10
    experience and, 27–28
    portfolio assessment on, 12
Learning centers. *See* Activity (learning) centers
Learning differences/learning difficulties, 183
Learning environment. *See also* Activity (learning) centers
    activities covering knowledge base in, 31
    child-friendly classroom for, 32–33
    classroom design, 25–26
    early/advanced readers, 31–32
    implications of brain research on, 27–28
    importance of, 25
    intellectual risk taking in, 31
    learning modalities and, 29–31
    multicultural and culturally relevant, 178–179
    for peer relationships, 28–29
    questions and answers about, 38–39
    real-life situations and manipulatives in, 26–27
    responding with compassion, communication, and creativity in, 29
    small-group or individual activities, 34
    structure in, 29
    whole-group activities in, 33–34
    working with parents for, 32
Learning modalities
    assessment reflecting all, 115
    diverse populations and, 177
    gaining insight into a student's, 38
    identifying a student's, 29–30
    observation of child's misbehavior and, 42

planning lessons using, 38
    teaching to, 30–31, 177
    types of, 30
Learning Styles and Pedagogy in Post-16 Learning (Coffield, Moseley, Hall, and Ecclestone), 30n5
Leimbach, Judy, 198, 201
Lesson planning, multiple intelligences/learning modalities used for, 38
Letting Go of Perfect: Overcoming Perfectionism in Kids (Adelson and Wilson), 206
Levine, Ellen, 193
Levy, Nathan, 198
Lewis, J. Patrick, 198
Life of Fred Elementary Series (Schmidt), 202–203
Limburg-Weber, Lisa, 189
Lind, Sharon, 187n9, 189
Linguistic activity center, 35
Literature, point of view activity, 45–46. *See also* Fairy tales
Little Red Riding Hood: A Newfangled Prairie Tale (Ernst), 197
The Lives of Great Women Leaders & You (Smutny and von Fremd), 209
Livingston, Myra Cohn, 198
Living with Intensity: Understanding the Sensitivity, Excitability, and Emotional Development of Gifted Children (Daniels), 206
Locker, Thomas, 194, 201–202
Logical-mathematical activity center, 35–36
Lon Po Po: A Red-Riding Hood Story from China (Young), 72, 87, 196, 199
Look Around! A Book About Shapes (Fisher), 201
Ludwig, Amy, 198
Lupkowski-Shoplik, Ann, 168n11
Lyman, Frank T. Jr., 28, 29n3

M

MacDougall, Jamie, 204
A Magical Encounter: Latino Children's Literature in the Classroom (Ada), 196
Magic School Bus Exploration Series (Cole), 200
The Magic School Bus Explores the World of Animals (White), 203
The Magic School Bus Science Explorations (Chevat), 200
Magic Tree House Series (Osborne), 195
Magic Trees of the Mind: How to Nurture Your Child's Imagination (Diamond and Hopson), 190
Magination Press, 228
Making connections, portfolio assessment and, 12
Making Differentiation a Habit: How to Ensure Success in Academically Diverse Classrooms (Heacox), 191
Manitonquat, 194
Maps, 64, 66, 68–69
Marbles the Brain Store, 228
Marie Curie (Fisher), 197
Marland Report (U.S. Commissioner of Education), 7
Marland, S. P. Jr., 189
Marshall, Rita, 198
Martin, Darlene E., 208
Martin, Rafe, 72, 194, 198
Materials
    for building/drama activity center, 36–37
    in child-friendly classroom, 32–33
    for linguistic activity center, 35
    for logical-mathematical activity center, 35–36
    for music activity center, 35
    for nature activity center, 37
Material World: A Global Family Portrait (Menzel), 194
Math activity center, 35–36
Math and Literature, Grades K–1 (Burns and Sheffield), 200
Math Curse (Scieszka), 111, 203
Mathematics
    creative arts/strategies for teaching, 111–112
    creative strategies used for teaching, 97–98
    fractions, 105
    pattern theme for discussing, 34
    questions and answers on teaching, 111–112
    real-life situations and manipulatives for, 26–27
    storytelling used for, 96–97
    study of geometric shapes, 102–105
    tiered group activities for, 43
The Math Kit: A Three-Dimensional Tour Through Mathematics (Van Der Meer and Gardner), 203
Math symbols, 27
Mayflower, 65
McCarthy Scales of Children's Abilities, 215
McCloskey, Robert, 44
McDaniel, M., 190
McDermott, Gerald, 194
McGraw-Hill Education, 228
McGregor, Debbie, 202
McKay, Gary D., 205
McKay, Robyn, 181n6, 208
McNeer, Mary, 196
McShane, Michael Q., 204
Meckstroth, Elizabeth, 14n11, **152,** 189, 190, 191, 205, 206, 207
Meddaugh, Susan, 86, 198
Me in a Different Culture form, 69, **78**
Memory
    of gifted child, 10
    of highly gifted children, 185
    learning and, 28
    portfolio assessment on, 12

MENTOR: The National Mentoring Partnership, 228
Menzel, Peter, 194
Merry-Go-Round: A Book About Nouns (Heller), 198
Metropolitan Museum of Art, 202
Michaels, Gerald Y., 207
Middle East, gifted students from, 177
Milford, Susan, 194
Milios, Rita, 194, 198
Miller, Debbie S., 84, 107, 198, 202
Miller, Etta, 196
Miller, Frances, 194
A Million Dots (Clements), 200
Millions to Measure (Schwartz), 203
"Mind benders," 98
Mindset: The New Psychology of Success (Dweck), 58*n*1, 206
MindWare, 228
Mine, All Mine: A Book About Pronouns (Heller), 198
Misbehavior, curriculum planning and observing, 42
Mitchell, Patty Bruce, 205
Moll, Luis C., 179
Monet, Claude, 104, 105
Montgomery, Diane, 160, 207
Month by Month with Children's Literature: Your K Through 3 Curriculum for Math, Science, Social Studies, and More (Bryant), 196
Moon, Sidney M., 207
Moon, Tonya R., 16*n*15
Moral development, portfolio assessment on, 12
Moseley, D., 30*n*5
Motivation, lack of, 160–161
Mountain Dance (Locker), 201
Movement, 28
Multicultural Children's Literature: Through the Eyes of Many Children (Norton), 198
Multicultural Mentoring of the Gifted and Talented (Torrance), 209
Multidimensional/multisensory learning experiences, 81
Multimedia activities, 81
Multiple intelligences, 8
    activity centers using, 34–37
    assessment reflecting all, 115
    planning lessons using, 38
    resentment toward gifted classmates and, 39
Multiple Intelligences in the Classroom (Armstrong), 190
Multiplication fairy tale, 110–111
Multisensory learning experiences, 81
Murals, 62, 73
Museum Shapes (Metropolitan Museum of Art), 202
Musgrove, Margaret, 194
Music
    blues, 81
    expanding experience of visual images with, 85
    listening for patterns in, 34
    multidimensional learning experiences with, 81
    translated into visual art, 81
    whole-group activity for, 33
Music activity center, 35
Musicians of the Sun (McDermott), 194
Music—Pink and Blue No. 1 (O'Keefe), 81, 198
My America: A Poetry Atlas of the United States (Hopkins), 198
Myers, Isabel Briggs, 207
Myers, Peter B., 207
My Plan to Become an Expert form, 46, **52**
My Problem-Solving Plan form, 162, **171–172**

N

Naglieri Nonverbal Test–Second Edition (NNAT–2), 119, 215
Name card method, 28–29
Nathan Levy's StoriesWithHoles.com, 228
National Association for Gifted Children (NAGC), 8, **152, 153**, 155*n*2, 189, 228
National Association for the Education of Young Children (NAEYC), 2–3, 228
National Council of Teachers of Mathematics (NCTM), 228
National Gallery of Art, 104
National Geographic Book of Animal Poetry, 198
National Geographic Education (website), 194
National Geographic Kids (website), 202
National Society for the Gifted & Talented, **153**
National Women's History Project, 228
A Nation Deceived: How Schools Hold Back America's Brightest Students (Colangelo, Assouline, and Gross), 17, 168, 205
A Nation Empowered: Evidence Trumps the Excuses Holding Back America's Brightest Students (Assouline, Colangelo, VanTassel-Baska and Lupkowski-Shoplik), 17, 168
Native Alaskan cultures, 175
Native American cultures, 175
Native Americans, 64–65
Native Languages of the Americas: Preserving and Promoting American Indian Languages (website), 195
Naturalistic (nature) activity center, 37
Nature for the Very Young: A Handbook of Indoor and Outdoor Activities (Bowden), 192, 200
Nature Got There First: Inventions Inspired by Nature (Gates), 101, 201
Neag Center for Gifted Education and Talent Development, **153**, 228
Neihart, Maureen, 189, 207
New Moon Magazine, 228

The New Psychology of Success: How We Can Learning to Fulfill Our Potential (Dweck), 155*n*1
The New RtI: Response to Intelligence (Choice and Walker), 204
NGAkids Art Zone, 104, 202
Nicky the Nature Detective (Svedberg), 203
The 1994 State of the States Gifted and Talented Education Report, 16*n*13, 189
No Child Left Behind (NCLB) Act (2001), 114
Nonverbal communication, 164
Norton, Donna E., 198
Numbers, creating fairy tales with, 109–111

O

Observation (teacher). *See also* Documentation
    curriculum planning and, 42
    documenting development through, 122–123
    forms, **124–130**
Observation, gifted child's keen sense of, 10
Oh, Sarah, 16*n*15
O'Keefe, Georgia, 81, 198
Olszewski-Kublius, Paula, 189
One Grain of Rice (Demi), 200
One Hundred Hungry Ants (Pinczes), 202
1,000 Facts About Wild Animals (Butterfield), 200
On the Social and Emotional Lives of Gifted Children (Cross), 206
Open-ended assessment, 114–115
Open-ended evaluation, 115
Oppenheim, Joanne, 202
Optimizing Learning: The Integrative Education Model in the Classroom (Clark), 206
Originality
    creative thinking and, 58, 59
    cultural invention activity, 67–73, 179
    elaboration/evaluation and, 73
Osborne, Mary Pope, 195
The Other Way to Listen (Baylor and Parnall), 192
Otis-Lennon Mental Abilities Test–Eighth Edition (OLSAT 8), 116
Otis-Lennon School Ability Test–Eighth Edition (OLSAT 8), 215
Owen, Steven V., 208

P

Paint! (Solga), 199
Pallotta, Jerry, 202
Papagayo: The Mischief Maker (McDermott), 194
Pappas, Christopher, 191
Pappas, Theoni, 202
Parent Education: Parents as Partners (Knopper), 205
Parenting for High Potential (National Association for Gifted Children), **152**, 205
Parenting Gifted Children: The Authoritative Guide from the National Association for Gifted Children, **151**, 206
Parenting Gifted Kids: Tips for Raising Happy and Successful Children (Delisle), **151**, 205
A Parent's Guide to Gifted Children (Webb, Gore, Amend, and DeVries), **152**, 206
Parents/parents of gifted children
    books for, **151–152**
    conferences with, 146–147
    from diverse populations, 178
    early identification with help from, 14–15
    involved in portfolios, 121
    involvement by, 147
    organizations and online resources for, **153**
    perspective of, 142–144
    use of term, 14*n*10
Parent-teacher communication/relationship, 142–147
    about the curriculum, 48, **56**
    benefits of, 144–145
    conferences, 145–147
    importance of, 42
    learning environment and, 32
    NAEYC DAP on, 3
    opening a dialogue for, 145
Parent-teacher conferences, 145–147
Parnall, Peter, 191
Pashler, Harold, 190
Passions, shifting, 9
Patterns theme, 34
Payne, Lauren Murphy, 207
Payne, Ruby K., 209
PBS Teachers STEM Education Resource Center, 202
Peabody Picture Vocabulary Test–Fourth Edition (PPVT-4), 119, 215
Pearson, 228
Peer acceptance, 17
Peer relationships, 28–29, 163–164
Penner, Lucille Recht, 64, 195
Pentominoes, 190
People of the Breaking Day (Sewall), 195
People Types and Tiger Stripes: Using Psychological Type to Help Students Discover Their Unique Potential (Lawrence), 207
Perceptual Reasoning Index (PRI), 118–119
Perfectionism, 12, 31, 159–160
Perry, Sarah, 198
Persistence, 12, 160
Personal exhibit, 14–15

Petit, Anne, 196
Peytral Publications, 228
Pfeiffer, Steven, 189
Phi Delta Kappa International, 228
Phillips, Lynn M., 208
Phillis Wheatley: First in Poetry (Bledsoe), 196
Photographs, of students, 10, 14, 166
Photosynthesis, 84, 106
Physical disabilities, 184
Physical sensitivity, 157
Pica, Janet, 198
Picasso (Ferrier), 201
Picasso, Pablo, 104
Pictures, of students, 10, 14, 166
Pieces of Learning, 228
Piechowski, Michael M., 206, 208
The Pilgrims at Plymouth (Penner), 64, 195
Pilgrim study, 64–67
Pinczes, Elinor, 202
Pinterest, 203
Plan for Compacting and Extending the Curriculum form, **55**
Planning curriculum. *See* Curriculum planning
Playmates, preference for older, 10
Playwriting, 88–91
Plimoth Plantation (website), 195
Poetry
    animal study activity using, 100–101
    creating a joint, 92
    creative composition activity, 92–94
    examples of student, 93
    exposing children to, 92
Poetry Matters: Writing a Poem from the Inside Out (Fletcher), 197
Point of view activity, 45–46
"Points of pride" activity, 166
Pollock, Steve, 202
Pondlarker (Gwynne), 87, 197
Pope, Joyce, 202
Poppe, Carol A., 202
Portfolios
    advantages of, 11
    child-created, 13
    for child-friendly classroom, 33
    child involvement in, 121
    defined, 120
    effective use of, 122
    maintaining, 121
    many examples of same thing in, 123
    parental involvement in, 121
    sending work home and, 123
    sensibility and, 12
    strengths noted in, 11–12
    talking to child about, 121–122
    used for documenting and evaluating progress, 120–121
Portfolios: Enriching and Assessing All Students, Identifying the Gifted, Grades K–6 (Kingore), 121n3, 189
Positive self-talk, 161
Posters, creating, 62
Poverty, children in, 179
Pratt, Kristin Joy, 202
Precious, Wendy, 202
Pretending, 76
Primarily Math: A Problem Solving Approach (Eckert), 201
Primary Book Reporter (Leimbach and Eckert), 198
Primary sources, 90, 91
Problem-solving plan, as coping strategy, 162
Problem-solving strategies, portfolio assessment on, 12
Processes, 105–111
    growth/change in the natural world study, 105–108
    overlapping with properties, 98
    symbols turned into stories, 108–111
Prodigies, 186–187
Professional Associates Publishing, 228
Properties, 98–105
    animal study, 98–102
    discovering mathematical and scientific, 98
    overlapping with processes, 98
    study of shapes, 102–105
Prufrock Press, 228
Psychological Science in the Public Interest, 190
Public installations, 62
Putumayo Kids, 81, 198

Q/R

Questions for Your Child's Parent-Teacher Conference form, 145, **150**
Quiet center, 37
Rachel Carson: Preserving a Sense of Wonder (Locker), 202
Rainforest Alliance Kids, 195
Raising a Gifted Child (Fertig), **151**, 205
Raising Gifted Kids: Everything You Need to Know to Help Your Exceptional Child Thrive (Klein), **152**, 205
Raising Your Spirited Child: A Guide for Parents Whose Child Is More Intense, Sensitive, Perceptive, Persistent, and Energetic (Kurcinka), **152**, 205, 207
Ramirez, Al, 208

Ramirez, Gonzalo, 196
Raven: A Trickster Tale from the Pacific Northwest (McDermott), 194
Raven's Coloured Progressive Matrices, 215
Reaching All Learners: Making Differentiation Work (Kingore), 191
Readers' theater, 88–91
Reading
    bibliotherapy and, 161–162
    flexible grouping and, 136
    identifying early/advanced readers, 31–32
    interest groups in, 44
    storytime, 33–34
    tiered group activities for, 43
Reading and writing activity center, 35
Ready for Preschool (Hertzog), **151**, 205
The Red Balloon (Kandinsky), 45
Re-Forming Gifted Education: Matching the Program to the Child (Rogers), **152**, 204, 205
Reis, Sally M., 190, 191, 207, 208
The Relationship of Grouping Practices to the Education of the Gifted and Talented Learner (Rogers), 204
Relevance, classroom design and, 26
A Remainder of One (Pinczes), 202
Removing the Mask: Giftedness in Poverty (Slocumb and Payne), 209
Renzulli-Hartman Scales, 119
Renzulli, Joseph, 7–8, 8n2, 41, 189, 190, 191
Renzulli Scales, 119
Research Based Strategies to Ignite Student Learning: Insights from a Neurologist and Classroom Teacher (Willis), 190
Resident Expert Contract forms, 46, 47, **53–54**
Resident experts, 46
Response to Intervention (RTI), 134–135
Richert, E. Susanne, 190
Rigid evaluation, 115
Rigor and Engagement for Growing Minds: Strategies that Enable High-Ability Learners to Flourish in All Classrooms (Kingore), 191
Rigor, classroom design and, 26
Rimm, Sylvia, 9n9, 160, 189, 206, 207
Risk taking
    classroom design and, 26
    intellectual, 31
The Rite of Spring (Stravinsky), 81
A River of Words: The Story of William Carlos Williams (Bryant), 196
Roberto's Rainforest (Terrell), 195, 203
Robinson, Ann, 191
Robinson, Nancy M., 207
Rodrigue, George, 45
Roeper, Annemarie, 207
Roeper Review: A Journal on Gifted Education, 204, 205
Roeper School, 228
Rogers, Karen B., **152**, 204, 205
Rohmann, Eric, 202
Rohrer, D., 190
Role playing, 102, 164
The Rough-Face Girl (Martin), 72, 87, 194, 198
Royal Fireworks Press, 228
Rules, for grouping, 138
Rural areas, gifted children from, 179–180
Rural School and Community Trust, 208–209

S

Safter, H. Tammy, 203
Samara, John, 191
Sarah Morton's Day: A Day in the Life of a Pilgrim Girl (Waters), 195
Satterfield, Neil B., 209
Sattler, Jerome M., 204
Scales for Identifying Gifted Students (SIGS), 119, 215
Scales for Rating the Behavioral Characteristics of Superior Students–Third Edition (Renzulli Scales), 216
Schedule, class, 33–34
Schmidt, Stanley F., 202
Schneck, Marcus, 203
Schneck de Regniers, Beatrice, 198
Scholastic Testing Service, Inc., 228
School Testing: What Parents and Educators Need to Know (Gellman), 204
The Schoolwide Enrichment Model: A Comprehensive Plan for Educational Excellence (Renzulli and Reis), 190, 191
Schwartz, David M., 203
Schwartz, Jon, 81
Science
    animal study activity, 98–102
    creative arts/strategies for teaching, 111–112
    creative strategies used for teaching, 97–98
    growth/change in the natural world study, 105–108
    questions and answers on teaching, 111–112
Science and Children, 202
Science Buddies on Pinterest, 203
Scientific responses, 85
Scieszka, Jon, 86, 111, 198, 203
Screening Assessment for Gifted Elementary and Middle School Students–Second Edition (SAGES–2), 216
The Search for Satori and Creativity (Torrance), 58n2, 195
Seasons, discussing patterns of, 34
Seating arrangements, 33

Secondary sources, 90, 91
Self-acceptance, 1650166
Self-esteem, building, 162
Self-evaluation. *See* Evaluation (by student)
Self-understanding, 165–166
Sendak, Maurice, 198
Sense of humor, of gifted child, 10
Sense of wonder, 1
Sensibility, portfolio assessment on child's, 12
Sensitivity, in gifted children, 10, 157–158
Sentence starters, 166–167
Serving Gifted Students in Rural Settings (Stambaugh), 209
Seuss Geisel, Theodor (Dr. Seuss), 88
Sewall, Marcia, 195
Shange, Ntozake, 198
Shapes, Shapes, Shapes (Hoban), 201
Sharing (of student work)
    alternative histories projects, 66–67
    benefits of, 75
    methods of, 94
    working alone *vs.*, 75–76
Sharing time, group, 33
Sheffield, Stephanie, 200
Shh! We're Writing the Constitution (Fritz), 193
Shore, Bruce, 191
Siegle, Del, 9*n*9, 189, 206
Silverman, Linda Kreger, 9*n*8, 143*n*1, 190, 206, 207
Silverstein, Shel, 199
Simple Story of the 3 Pigs and the Scientific Wolf (Fetzner), 201
Sing a Song of Popcorn: Every Child's Book of Poems (Schneck de Regniers, Moore, White, Sendak, and Carr), 198
Sing, David K., 208
Singing songs, 33, 34, 35
Sisk, Dorothy, 195
Situational perfectionism, 159
SketchUp, 103, 203
Skipping Stones Magazine, 228
Sky Tree: Seeing Science Through Art (Christiansen), 107, 202
Slocumb, Paul D., 209
Slosson Intelligence Test–Revised Third Edition (SIT–R3–1), 216
Small-group activities, 34
Smart Boys: Talent, Manhood, and the Search for Meaning (Kerr), 208
Smart Girls: A New Psychology of Girls, Women, and Giftedness (Kerr), 208
Smart Girls in the 21st Century: Understanding Talented Girls and Women (Kerr and McKay), 181*n*6, 208
SMART goals, 161
Smutny, Joan Franklin, **151, 152,** 175*n*4, 190, 191, 195, 199, 203, 204, 206, 209
Social alienation, of highly gifted children, 185
The Social and Emotional Development of Gifted Children (Neihart, Reis, Robinson, and Moon), 207
The Social and Emotional Lives of Gifted Kids (Cross), 206
Social needs of gifted children. *See* Emotional and social needs
Social skills, building, 167
Social studies, 57–**79**
    alternative histories activity, 64–67
    creative activities map for, 59–60
    cultural invention activity, 67–73
    imagining environmental solutions, 60–63
    questions and answers, 75–76
    student evaluation and elaboration of projects, 73–75
Socioeconomic status, 174, 175, 179
Solga, Kim, 199
Some of My Best Friends Are Books (Halsted), 161–162, 207
Songs, 33, 34, 35, 74. *See also* Music
The Space Place (website), 203
Spaghetti and Meatballs for All! (Burns), 200
Spanish speakers, 175
Special Populations in Gifted Education: Understanding Our Most Able Students from Diverse Backgrounds (Castellano and Frazier), 208
Spelling, tiered group activities for, 43
Squanto (Tisquantum), 65
Stambaugh, Tamra, 209
Standardized testing, 2
    creativity and, 115–116
    culturally diverse children and, 118
    IQ tests and, 116
    problems with, 114, 115–116, 117
Standards. *See* Curriculum standards
Standards-driven era, 1–3
Standish, Myles, 65
Stanford-Binet Fourth Edition, 186
Stanford-Binet Intelligence Scale (Form L-M), 186
Stanford-Binet Intelligence Scale-Fifth Edition (SB5), 116, 119, 216
Stanford-Binet Intelligence Scales, 15
STEAM, 203
Stereotypes
    about Asian children, 176
    gender, 166
    of gifted children, 75
Sternberg, Robert J., 8, 8*n*4, 190
St. James, Renwick, 196
Stone, Tanya Lee, 199
Stories/storytelling, 28
    exploring child's cultural heritage with, 69

finding patterns in, 34
mathematical concepts explained with, 96–97, 108–109
mathematical symbols turned into, 109–111
tree, 107–108
Storytime, as a whole-group activity, 33–34
Stravinsky, Igor, 81
Stress, coping with, 161
Structure
    gifted child's sense of, 158
    in learning environment, 29
Student Observation Form I: Learning and Cognitive Development, **124–126**
Student Observation Form II: Writing and Language Development, **127**
Student Observation Form III: Social and Emotional Development, **128–129**
Student Observation Form IV: Fine Motor Development, **130**
Student Observation Forms, 123
Subtraction fairy tale, 111
Sullivan, Charles, 199
Summative assessment, 115. *See also* Evaluation (by student)
Sunshine Makes the Seasons (Branley), 200
Superhero cape, 167
Supporting Emotional Needs of the Gifted (SENG), **153,** 207, 209
Supporting Gifted Education through Advocacy (Berger), 205
The Survival Guide for Gifted Kids: For Ages 10 & Under (Galbraith), 28*n*2, 165–166, 190, 206
The Survival Guide for Parents of Gifted Kids: How to Understand, Live with, and Stick Up for Your Gifted Child (Walker), **152**
Svedberg, Ulf, 203
Sweet, Melissa, 85, 199
A Swim Through the Sea (Pratt), 202
Symbols, math, 27, 108–111
Systematic Training for Effective Parenting (Dinkmeyer and McKay), 205
System of Multicultural Pluralistic Assessment (SOMPA), 216
Systems and Models for Developing Programs for the Gifted and Talented (Renzulli), 189

T

Tactile activity, 105
Tactile-kinesthetic learning modality, 3, 30, 31, 38
Taking Part: Introducing Social Skills to Children, PreK–Grade 3 (Cartledge and Kleefield), 206
Taking Part program, 167
Tannenbaum, Abraham, 8*n*3, 190
Tannenbaum's psychosocial model of giftedness, 8
Tapenum's Day: A Wampanoag Indian Boy in Pilgrim Times (Waters), 195
Task persistence, portfolio assessment on, 12
Taxonomy
of creative thinking, 59
of imaginative thinking, 82
Taxonomy of Teaching, 83
Taylor, Barbara, 203
Teacher Created Resources, 228
Teachers
    early identification and, 6–7
    examining feelings about gifted children, 144
    guidance by, for creative and imaginative activities, 82–83
    relationship with parents, 3, 32, 142–147
    role in child's emotional and social needs, 154–155
Teachers.Net, 228
Teaching Gifted Kids in Today's Classroom (Winebrenner and Brulles), 29*n*3, 46*n*1, 137*n*3, 190, 204
Teaching Kids with Learning Difficulties in Today's Classroom (Winebrenner), 30*n*4, 191, 206
Teaching Students to Read Through Their Individual Learning Styles (Carbo, Dunn, and Dunn), 190
Teaching the Brain to Read: Strategies for Improving Fluency, Vocabulary, and Comprehension (Willis), 190
Teaching with Primary Sources (website), 195
Teaching with the Brain in Mind (Jensen), 190
Teasing, helping children cope with, 28
Tell Me, Tree: All About Trees for Kids (Gibbons), 83, 107, 197, 201
Temperature reading activity, 166
10 Things Not to Say to Your Gifted Child: One Family's Perspective (Heilbronne), **151**
Terrell, Sandy, 195, 203
Testing Young Children: A Reference Guide for Developmental, Psychoeducational, and Psychosocial Assessments, 204
Test of Early Mathematical Ability–Third Edition (TEMA–3), 216
Test of Early Reading Ability–Third Edition (TERA–3), 216
Test of Nonverbal Intelligence–Fourth Edition (TONI–4), 216
Tests/testing, 1. *See also* Intelligence (IQ) testing; Standardized testing
    description of, 215–216
    early identification of gifted students using, 15
Textbooks, 48
Thanksgiving, the first, 65
Thematic instruction, 32, 34
There Are Those (Levy and Pica), 198
Thinking Through Cooperative Learning (Davidson and Worsham), 29*n*3
Think-pair-share strategy, 29
30 Essays on Giftedness: 30 Years of SENG (Supporting Emotional Needs of the Gifted), 207, 209
Thomas, Joyce Carol, 199
Thom, Mary, 209
Thomson, Amy, 101

Three-ring conception of giftedness, 7–8
Three Young Pilgrims (Harness), 193
Tic-Tac-Toe Menu, 44, 46–47, **51**
Tiered groups, 43, 134–135
Time bank, 41–42
Time Flies (Rohmann), 202
Tin Man Press, 228
Tisquantum (Squanto), 65
To Be Gifted and Learning Disabled: Strategies for Helping Bright Students with LD, ADHD, and More (Baum and Owen), 208
Tolan, Stephanie S., **152,** 190, 206, 207
Tonemah, Stuart, 175n3, 209
Torrance, E. Paul, 58, 195, 199, 203, 209
Torrance Test of Creative Thinking (TTCT), 216
A Touch of Greatness (DVD), 199
The Tree Book: For Kids and Their Grownups (Ingoglia), 84, 198
A Tree for All Seasons (Bernard), 84, 106, 196, 200
Tree Life (Greenaway), 201
Trees and Forests: From Algae to Sequoias: The History, Life, and Richness of Forests (Scholastic Books), 203
Trees, study of, 83–85, 106–107
Treffinger, Donald J., **151,** 206
Triangles, 103, 104–105
A Triarchic Theory of Human Intelligence (Sternberg), 8n4
The True Story of the Three Little Pigs! (Scieszka), 86, 198
Turkeys, Pilgrims, and Indian Corn: The Story of the Thanksgiving Symbols (Barth), 192
Twice-exceptional students, 174, 183–184

U/V

Underachievement, 160–161
Underrepresented populations. *See* Diverse populations, children from
Underserved Gifted Populations: Responding to Their Needs and Abilities, 208, 209
Understanding Our Gifted, 189, 199
Universal Nonverbal Intelligence Test–Second Edition (UNIT–2), 216
Unstructured time, 48
U-STARS~PLUS, 119, 209, 216
Vanderhoof, Bill, 196
Van Der Meer, Ron, 203
Van Gogh, Vincent, 83
Van Matre, Nancy A., 202
VanTassel-Baska, Joyce, 168n11
Veenker, Kathleen, **152,** 190, 204, 206
Veenker, Stephen, **152,** 190, 204, 206
Verbal Comprehension Index (VCI), 118–119
The Very Hungry Caterpillar (Carle), 200
Viorst, Judith, 46, 191
Visual images/art
    alternative fairy tales and, 87
    creative response to, 81, 83–85
    cultural invention activity and, 69
    music translated into, 81
    Pilgrim and Wampanoag life, 66–67
Visual learning modality, 30, 31, 38
Visual-spatial learning center, 36
Visual-Spatial Processing subtest, Stanford-Binet Intelligence Scale–Fifth Edition (SB5), 119
Vocabulary
    early and extensive, 10
    intelligence test measuring, 119
    portfolio assessment on, 11
Volunteers/volunteering, 123, 147, 179, 188
von Fremd, S. E., 195, 199, 209
Vulnerability, of highly gifted children, 185

W

Walker, Sally Yahnke, **152,** 191, 204
Walking with Henry: Based on the Life and Works of Henry David Thoreau (Locker), 194
A Walk in the Rainforest (Pratt), 202
The Wampanoag (Cunningham and Benoit), 64, 192
Wampanoag life, 64–65
Watch Out for Clever Women! (Hayes), 193
Water Dance (Locker), 202
Water Sings Blue: Ocean Poems (Coombs), 197
Waters, Kate, 195
The Way to Start a Day (Baylor and Parnall), 192
Weather, discussing patterns in, 34
Weather theme, 34
Webb, James T., **152,** 190, 204, 205, 206, 207
WebMuseum, 104, 203
Wechsler Intelligence Scale for Children, 15
Wechsler Intelligence Scale for Children–Fifth Edition (WISC–V), 116, 118, 216
Wechsler Preschool and Primary Scale of Intelligence, 15
Wechsler Preschool and Primary Scale of Intelligence–Fourth Edition (WPPSI–IV), 116
Wechsler Preschool and Primary Scale of Intelligence–Third Edition (WPPSI–III), 118, 216
Wechsler Verbal Comprehension Index (VCI), 118
Weller, Frances Ward, 196
Wells, Harold C., 206
Wells, Robert, 203

What I Learned form, 123, **131–132**
What I Like form, 46, **49–50**
What's Smaller Than a Pygmy Shrew? (Wells), 203
What's the Big Idea, Ben Franklin? (Fritz), 193
When Gifted Kids Don't Have All the Answers: How to Meet Their Social and Emotional Needs (Galbraith and Delisle), **151,** 205, 207
When Washington Crossed the Delaware: A Wintertime Story for Young Patriots (Cheney), 192
Where Do You Think You're Going, Christopher Columbus? (Fritz), 193
Where the River Begins (Locker), 194
Where Was Patrick Henry on the 29th of May? (Fritz), 193
White, Mary Michaels, 198
White, Nancy, 203
White, Susannah (Winslow), 65
Whoever You Are (Fox), 72, 193
Whole child, the, 81, 155
The Whole Cosmos Catalog of Science Activities for Kids of All Ages (Abruscato and Hassard), 199
Whole-group activities, 33–34, 37
Who's Saying What in Jamestown, Thomas Savage? (Fritz), 193
Who's That Stepping on Plymouth Rock? (Fritz), 193
Why Bright Kids Get Poor Grades and What You Can Do About It: A Six-Step Program for Parents and Teachers (Rimm), 160n3, 207
Why Don't You Get a Horse, Sam Adams? (Fritz), 193
Wilcox, Leah, 86, 199
Wilkes, Angela, 203
Willems, Mo, 85, 199
Willis, Judy, 190
Will You Sign Here, John Hancock? (Fritz), 193
Wilson, Hope E., 206
Winebrenner, Susan, 29n3, 30n4, 46n1, 137n3, 190, 191, 204, 206
Wombats, 60–63
Wonders of the Rain Forest (Craig), 192
Wood, Audrey, 199
Wood, Bruce, 199
Wood, John Norris, 204
Woods and Forests: Nature Hide and Seek Book (Wood), 204
The World According to Humphrey (Birney), 88, 89, 196
A World of Color, Shape, and Light (Schneck), 203
Worsham, Toni, 29n3
Wright, Lisa, 208
Writing activities
    alternative fairy tales, 85–88
    creative response to visual images, 83–84
    creative response to visual images activity, 83–84
    endangered/threatened species activity, 62
    free verse, 91–94
    readers' theater and playwriting, 88–91
Writing and reading activity center, 35
Writing, observation of, 122, **127**
The Writing Thief: Using Mentor Texts to Teach the Craft of Writing (Culham), 197

Y/Z

You Choose: History Series, 192
You Know Your Child Is Gifted When . . . A Beginner's Guide to Life on the Bright Side (Galbraith), **151**
Young, Ed, 72, 87, 196, 199
Young Gifted and Bored (George), **151,** 205, 207
Your Child's Cultural Heritage letter, 68, **77**
Your Child's Personal Exhibit letter, 15, **24,** 121
Your Child's Pictures letter, 10, 14, **18,** 121, 145
You Read to Me, I'll Read to You Series (Hoberman), 198
Your Gifted Child: How to Recognize and Develop the Special Talents in Your Child from Birth to Age Seven (Smutny, Veenker, and Veenker), **152,** 190, 204, 206
Zephyr Press, 228
Zomo the Rabbit: A Trickster Tale from West Africa (McDermott), 194

About the Authors

Joan Franklin Smutny, M.A., is founder and director of the Center for Gifted and Midwest Torrance Center for Creativity. She directs programs for gifted children, teaches graduate courses, serves as editor of the Illinois Association for Gifted Children Journal, and is a regular contributor to the Gifted Education Press Quarterly. The author of many books for teachers and parents, Joan has been honored with the National Association for Gifted Children's (NAGC) Distinguished Service Award and was the 2011 recipient of the NAGC E. Paul Torrance Award for contributions in creativity. She lives in Illinois.

Consultant, author, and educator **Sally Yahnke Walker, Ph.D.,** is an influential advocate for gifted children who has piloted programs, coordinated efforts to support gifted students in schools, and worked for federal and state legislation for gifted education. A former Illinois Education Administrator of the Year, she is the executive director of the Illinois Association for Gifted Children (IAGC) and serves on the Illinois Gifted Advisory Council for the Illinois State Board of Education. Sally lives in Illinois.

Ellen I. Honeck, Ph.D., has been involved in gifted education as a classroom teacher, administrator, gifted specialist, curriculum developer, consultant, adjunct professor, and associate director of the Institute for the Development of Gifted Education at the University of Denver. She is actively involved with NAGC's Early Childhood and Special Schools and Programs Networks and presents at national and international conferences. Ellen is the dean of the Gifted and Talented Academy at Laurel Springs School. She lives in Colorado.

Other Great Resources from Free Spirit

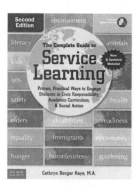

The Complete Guide to Service Learning
Proven, Practical Ways to Engage Students in Civic Responsibility, Academic Curriculum, & Social Action
by Cathryn Berger Kaye, M.A.
Teachers, grades K–12.
288 pp.; paperback; 8½" x 11"; includes digital content

Building Everyday Leadership in All Kids
An Elementary Curriculum to Promote Attitudes and Actions for Respect and Success
by Mariam G. MacGregor, M.S.
Grades K–6.
208 pp.; paperback; 8½" x 11"; includes digital content

The Survival Guide for Gifted Kids
For Ages 10 & Under
by Judy Galbraith, M.A.
Ages 10 & under.
128 pp.; paperback; 2-color; illust.; 6" x 9"

What Do You Stand For? For Teens
A Guide to Building Character
by Barbara A. Lewis
Ages 11 & up.
288 pp.; paperback; B&W photos and illust.; 8½" x 11"

Building Character with True Stories from Nature
by Barbara A. Lewis
Grades 2–5.
176 pp.; paperback; illust.; 8½" x 11"; includes digital content

The Kids' Guide to Working Out Conflicts
How to Keep Cool, Stay Safe, and Get Along
by Naomi Drew, M.A.
Ages 10–15. *160 pp.; paperback; 2-color; illust.; 7" x 9"*

Leader's Guide
Includes 36 reproducible handout masters. For teachers, grades 5–9.
128 pp.; paperback; 8½" x 11"

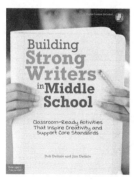

Building Strong Writers in Middle School
Classroom-Ready Activities That Inspire Creativity and Support Core Standards
by Deb Delisle and Jim Delisle
Grades 4–8.
176 pp.; paperback; 8½" x 11"; includes digital content

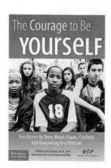

The Courage to Be Yourself
True Stories by Teens About Cliques, Conflicts, and Overcoming Peer Pressure
Edited by Al Desetta, M.A., with Educators for Social Responsibility
Ages 13 & up. *160 pp.; paperback; 6" x 9"*

Leader's Guide
Teachers, social workers, and other adults who work with youth in grades 7–12.
168 pp.; paperback; 8½" x 11"

Interested in purchasing multiple quantities and receiving volume disounts?
Contact edsales@freespirit.com or call 1.800.735.7323 and ask for Education Sales.

Many Free Spirit authors are available for speaking engagements, workshops, and keynotes.
Contact speakers@freespirit.com or call 1.800.735.7323.

For pricing information, to place an order, or to request a free catalog, contact:

Free Spirit Publishing Inc. • 6325 Sandburg Road, Suite 100 • Golden Valley, MN 55427-3629
toll-free 800.735.7323 • local 612.338.2068 • fax 612.337.5050
help4kids@freespirit.com • www.freespirit.com